Monteverdi

AND THE END
OF THE
RENAISSANCE

Monteverdi

AND THE END
OF THE
RENAISSANCE

GARY TOMLINSON

UNIVERSITY
OF CALIFORNIA
PRESS
Berkeley • Los Angeles

*This publication has been supported
by a subvention from the
American Musicological Society*

University of California Press
Berkeley and Los Angeles, California

© 1987 by
The Regents of the University of California

First Paperback Printing 1990

LIBRARY OF CONGRESS CATALOGING IN PUBLICATION DATA

Tomlinson, Gary.
Monteverdi and the end of the Renaissance

Bibliography: p.
Includes index
1. Monteverdi, Claudio, 1567–1643. Vocal music.
2. Music—16th century—History and criticism.
3. Music—17th century—History and criticism.   I. Title.
ML410.M77T7   1987   784′.092′4   84-24104

ISBN 0-520-06980-3

Printed in the United States of America

1 2 3 4 5 6 7 8 9

To my mother and father

Contents

Preface   PAGE ix

Introduction

1

Oppositions in Late-Renaissance Thought:
Three Case Studies   PAGE 3

The Perfection of Musical Rhetoric

2

Youthful *Imitatio* and the First Discovery
of Tasso (Books I and II)   PAGE 33

3

Wert, Tasso, and the Heroic Style (Book III)   PAGE 58

4

Guarini and the Epigrammatic Style (Books III and IV)   PAGE 73

EXCURSUS 1

A Speculative Chronology
of the Madrigals of Books IV and V   PAGE 98

5

Guarini, Rinuccini, and the Ideal of Musical Speech   PAGE 114

EXCURSUS 2

The Reconciliation of Dramatic and Epigrammatic
Rhetoric in the *Sestina* of Book VI   PAGE 141

The Emergence of New Ideals

6
Marino and the Musical Eclogue (Book VI)   PAGE 151

7
Marinism and the Madrigal, I (Book VII)   PAGE 165

8
Marinism and the Madrigal, II
(Developments after Book VII)   PAGE 197

9
The Meeting of Petrarchan and Marinist Ideals
(The Last Operas)   PAGE 215

The End of the Renaissance

10
Monteverdi and Italian Culture, 1550–1700   PAGE 243

Works Cited   PAGE 261

Index of Monteverdi's Works
and Their Texts   PAGE 271

General Index   PAGE 277

Preface

THE MUSIC HISTORIAN focuses first on works of music, whatever else he might survey. These are his primary texts. They are ordered systems of symbols, linguistic webs that conveyed meanings to those who created, performed, and listened to them. The historian's task is to describe what he takes to be those meanings.

In this book I attempt to describe the meanings of the secular works of Claudio Monteverdi, the foremost Italian composer at the end of the Renaissance. My narrative revolves around the works themselves—nine books of madrigals, three complete operas and a fragment of a fourth, and numerous canzonette, *scherzi,* and *arie,* all produced between 1584 and 1642. But it is not restricted to these works. For, as anthropologists, general historians, and others frequently remind us, meaning does not reside in isolated expressive acts but arises from the relations of these acts to their contexts. In seeking to understand the significance of an individual artwork, we seek to describe as fully or, in the fashionable parlance, as "thickly" as possible its connections to the context from which it arose.

These connections take various forms because the context of any work is manifold and complex. The linguist A. L. Becker has enumerated four general categories of relation between a text and its context; they conform rather neatly to the conceptions underlying my book and may serve as the starting point for a synopsis of it. The contextual relations of a text and its constituent units, Becker writes, include "1. The relations of textual units to each other within the text. . . . 2. The relations of textual units to other texts. . . . 3. The relations of units in the text to the intention of the creators of the text. . . . 4. The relation of textual units to non-literary events with which units in the text establish relations of the sort usually called *reference.*"[1] In *Monteverdi and the End of the Renaissance* my narrative shifts among four varieties of interaction between Monteverdi's works and their contexts, each similar to one of Becker's categories: from analysis of individual works (Becker's relations within texts), to the placing of these works in traditions of similar works (relations among texts), to description of Monteverdi's expressive ideals manifested in his works (the creator's intentions), to elucidation of the relations of

1. A. L. Becker, "Text-Building, Epistemology, and Aesthetics in Javanese Shadow Theatre," p. 212. I was introduced to Becker's work by the cultural anthropologist Clifford Geertz, who discusses it in *Local Knowledge,* pp. 30–33.

the works to the broader ideologies of the culture that produced them (extratextual reference).

The organization of the book reflects these more-or-less distinct perspectives. Chapter 1 begins with a sketch of Italian culture in the sixteenth century—a composite portrait, I should say, pieced together from the writings of many historians of the Renaissance. This culture was marked above all by a tense confrontation of many opposed ideologies; two of them, late humanist currents and revivified scholasticism, bear particular relevance to my subject. After this introduction the bulk of chapter 1 reconsiders, in the light of the standoff of humanist and scholastic values, the famous polemics of three important cultural leaders around 1600: Galileo Galilei, the poet Giambattista Guarini, and Monteverdi himself. The chapter as a whole provides a conceptual frame within which to view Monteverdi's achievement.

Chapters 2–9 narrate the story of Monteverdi's secular composition in roughly chronological order (with attention also to his sacred works where necessary to fill out the plot). These chapters are concerned especially with the first three relations of text and context listed above: the structure and coherence of individual works, the place of these works in traditions of like works, and Monteverdi's intent in shaping his works as he did. But of course these relations interact in fundamental ways with the broader perspectives described in chapter 1. So chapters 2–9 extend and elaborate these perspectives, presenting a moving picture of subjects that in chapter 1 had more the quality of a snapshot. Monteverdi's individual development provides an eloquent, sixty-year commentary on the development of his culture.

And, conversely, general changes in his culture illuminate the course of his career. In chapter 10, finally, I plot the trajectory of Monteverdi's career against the background of late- and post-Renaissance values in the half century from 1590 to 1640. As in chapters 2–9, the image is dynamic rather than static, but now the hierarchy of terms is reversed: now Monteverdi's culture elucidates his work. As Italian culture evolved, so also, gradually and not without the strain attendant on so much personal growth, did Monteverdi's world of meanings.

All three sections of this book, it is worth emphasizing, are bound in an essential reciprocal relation. Chapter 1 does not merely provide definitions for the following chapters, nor do chapters 2–9 merely provide evidence for the general conclusions of chapter 10. Instead all the chapters are meant to interact in a manner reminiscent of Dilthey's hermeneutic circle, and each of the four relations of text and context is meant to be deepened by the other three. Clifford Geertz has characterized the interaction I want in this way: "Hopping back and forth between the whole conceived through the parts that actualize it and the parts conceived through the whole that motivates them, we seek to turn them, by a sort of intellectual perpetual motion, into explications of one another."[2] Monteverdi's culture, viewed in

2. *Local Knowledge*, p. 69.

the most comprehensive fashion, tells us about his individual works, just as they, all of them and each of them alone, tell us about it.

My narrative is much enriched by the special nature of the texts in question. For Monteverdi's works are vocal works and therefore involve not one text but two: a preexistent poetic text, with its own meanings arising from all of Becker's categories, and a musical text, constructed to reflect in various ways the meaning of the poetry it sets yet not without its own, more-or-less independent levels of meaning. Vocal compositions are texts within texts; they carry meanings within meanings. Or perhaps, since their meaning arises on every level in essential relation to their state of linguistic duality, it is best to add a fifth category cutting across the other four. The contextual relations of Monteverdi's works, their sources of meaning, include the relations of two recognizably distinct languages joined as a single text.

These relations affect all others as well. Consideration of the internal coherence of the work must now involve not only music but also poetry and the interaction of the two. Consideration of the place of the work in traditions of like works must now refer to purely poetic as well as musico-poetic traditions. Our interpretation of Monteverdi's intentions must embrace interpretation of the meaning he found in the poetry he set. And our conception of the reference of the work to nonmusical and nonpoetic realities is conditioned especially by our ideas of Monteverdi's poetic readings. To deemphasize the poetry Monteverdi set in an attempt to concentrate on his music would be to impoverish at the start the context of his works. For this reason I have devoted much attention to poetic meanings—in individual poems, personal styles, and stylistic traditions—throughout my study.

It should not need to be said, finally, that this story of Monteverdi and the end of the Renaissance is only one of many Monteverdi stories that might be told. In keeping with the conception of text outlined above, I have aspired to convey meaning more than to prove conclusions. That is, I hope to have *described* as fully as I am able, to have constructed a richly significant context for my subject. In such an endeavor, claims of certainty, correctness, and truth do not involve positivistic notions of proof. They are rather—to paraphrase Leo Treitler, a penetrating writer on musical historiography—no more than claims that I have provided the most coherent narrative that is consistent with all my data.[3]

I have tried to include musical examples in the text whenever they are essential to understanding my discussion, though the reader should if possible have complete scores of Monteverdi's works at hand while reading chapters 2–9. In most cases I have consulted original or early sources in preparing my examples. In those cases where I have not—the excerpts from Monteverdi's Vespers of 1610, *Scherzi musicali* of 1632, and *Il ritorno d'Ulisse in patria* and most of the excerpts from works

3. See Leo Treitler, "History, Criticism, and Beethoven's Ninth Symphony," pp. 208–9.

by composers other than Monteverdi—my sources are named in the captions. The translations of Italian poetry and prose are my own unless otherwise noted.

Part of chapter 5 appeared previously in my article "Madrigal, Monody, and Monteverdi's *via naturale alla immitatione," Journal of the American Musicological Society* 34 (1981), 60–108 (© 1981 by The American Musicological Society, Inc.); part of chapter 7 appeared in "Music and the Claims of Text: Monteverdi, Rinuccini, and Marino," *Critical Inquiry* 8 (1982), 565–89 (© 1982 by The University of Chicago; 0093-1896/82/0803-0005$01.00; all rights reserved). One more bibliographic acknowledgment is in order here, to a work whose great importance to my study could not be adequately recognized in my notes. This is the so-called New Vogel: the *Bibliografia della musica italiana vocale profana pubblicata dal 1500 al 1700,* compiled over the past century by Emil Vogel, Alfred Einstein, François Lesure, and Claudio Sartori (Pomezia, 1977). Without this bibliography my work would have taken longer and yielded less. As it would have, also, without the generous support of a fellowship from the John Simon Guggenheim Memorial Foundation, and without leave time and two research grants from the University of Pennsylvania.

My other acknowledgments are more personal: to Mary Watson, who willingly helped in the final preparation of the manuscript; to David Hathwell, editor for the University of California Press, who worked hard to rid my manuscript of countless infelicities and inconsistencies, and to others there, especially Doris Kretschmer and Marilyn Schwartz, who saw it through production; to James Chater, who kindly shared with me his transcriptions of unpublished Marenzio madrigals; to Anthony Newcomb, who nurtured my love and understanding of the madrigal through countless singing evenings at his home (and who never spared the *vini prelibati*); to Louise Clubb, who as teacher and friend guided my studies of Italian literature and life; to Elio Frattaroli, who lent special support at difficult moments; and to many other colleagues, friends, and students who lived graciously with Monteverdi while I lived with him.

Ellen Rosand found time, during a period of innumerable pressing obligations, to read through my manuscript and offer invaluable suggestions. My brother Glenn drank cappuccino with me next to the Duomo and listened patiently, while Jonathan Kerman urged me always not to stint broader perspectives. Joseph Kerman has somehow excelled in three roles, each difficult enough in itself, as mentor, father-in-law, and friend. His vision stands behind the book as its direct and its dialectical stimuli, and his insight has allowed him to understand and encourage my need for both. He read the manuscript, clarifying and sharpening the narrative at countless points. My wife, Lucy Kerman, also read it—we have lost track of how many times—and again and again brought her deep conceptual skills to bear on its improvement. She should know that I accepted her suggestions thankfully, if not always amiably. Her love and support reached much beyond the actual writing of the book, of course, to realms not easily expressed. It is enough to say that the book could not have come into being without her.

INTRODUCTION

1

Oppositions in Late-Renaissance Thought: Three Case Studies

TALIAN CULTURE of the late sixteenth century offers a picture of stark philosophical contrasts and intellectual eclecticism. The unprecedented explosion of information during the previous century, set off in particular by an astonishingly active printing industry and new technological and geographical discoveries, presented literate Italians with a bewildering variety of thoughts on almost any subject and fostered ideological conflicts of increasing severity and clarity. Not surprisingly, then, historians have often conceived of this culture as a confrontation of conflicting intellectual, spiritual, and social forces: classical versus Christian tradition, secular versus sacred realm, Aristotelianism versus Platonism, totalitarianism versus republicanism, feudalism versus capitalism, logic versus rhetoric, and traditional varieties of mystical thought versus emerging scientific rationalism. Indeed William Bouwsma, one of the most eloquent of these historians, has viewed late-Renaissance culture as an even more general conflict of antithetical world-views embracing many of the dichotomies named above; he calls these views the medieval and Renaissance "visions." And, finally, Bouwsma's visions reflect one more pair of opposed terms, often invoked in discussions of Renaissance culture: humanism and scholasticism. It is with these last terms that we will be most lengthily concerned, for they bear especially important implications for the intellectual and artistic climate of the late *cinquecento*. To understand their significance at this time, however, we must quickly trace their origins some three centuries before.[1]

1. On humanism and scholasticism I follow in particular John W. Baldwin, *The Scholastic Culture of the Middle Ages*; Hans Baron, *The Crisis of the Early Italian Renaissance*; William J. Bouwsma, *The Culture of Renaissance Humanism*; Bouwsma, "Renaissance and Reformation"; Bouwsma, *Venice and the Defense of Republican Liberty*; Eric Cochrane, "Science and Humanism in the Italian Renaissance"; Eugenio Garin, *Italian Humanism*; Hanna H. Gray, "Renaissance Humanism"; Paul Oskar Kristeller, *Renaissance Thought: The Classic, Scholastic, and Humanist Strains* (hereafter *Renaissance Thought, I*); Kristeller, *Renaissance Thought, II*; Erwin Panofsky, *Gothic Architecture and Scholasticism*; Jerrold E. Seigel, " 'Civic Humanism' or Ciceronian Rhetoric?"; Seigel, *Rhetoric and Philosophy in Renaissance Humanism*; and Henry Osborne Taylor, *The Medieval Mind*.

3

Paul Oskar Kristeller has taught us that scholastic premises and methods came late to Italy, imported from France in the decades before 1300—just prior, that is, to the first stirrings of Italian humanism. Italian scholasticism was therefore not so much a medieval mode of thought superseded by Renaissance humanism as it was, like humanism, "fundamentally a phenomenon of the Renaissance period whose ultimate roots can be traced in a continuous development to the very latest phase of the Middle Ages."[2] Fourteenth-century writers were aware of its recent origins; for Petrarch, writing in 1367, it was "the modern philosophic fashion."[3] We shall see, in fact, that it coexisted with humanism throughout the Italian Renaissance and dominated certain branches of knowledge that resisted humanist intellectual tendencies.

Scholastic thought arose in the universities of the late Middle Ages and was closely associated from the first with the teaching there of theology, philosophy, natural philosophy, medicine, and law. It was marked by two broad, related tendencies: a reliance on authority and a faith in the absolute truth of knowledge gained through rigorous deductive logic. The Schoolmen accepted as authoritative the major ancient texts in the fields that most concerned them—texts like Justinian's *Corpus iuris civilis,* Aristotle's *Physica* and *De historia animalium,* and of course the Scriptures and Patristic writings. And the most common forms of scholastic writing were determined by their dependence on authoritative texts: the commentary on preexistent works (this would dominate the writings of Italian scholastics) and the *quaestio,* an interpretive format for reconciling the views of various authorities most brilliantly developed in the *Summae* of Thomas Aquinas.

But as this description of the *quaestio* suggests, the authorities seemed to disagree on numerous points, large and small. So the acceptance of their views necessitated an immense interpretive effort to rationalize the apparent discrepancies. The means for this effort were sought in Aristotle's *Organon,* a comprehensive group of logical treatises recovered in its entirety only during the twelfth century. Aristotelian logic, in particular the body of syllogistic methods exhaustively analyzed in the *Organon,* thus provided the foundation for scholastic philosophy, the base on which its greatest monuments were built.

The scholastics' deference to past authority suggests a deeper premise of their thought, one that Bouwsma has linked to the medieval vision in general. The authority of the huge and newly recovered Aristotelian corpus sprang in large part from its awesome comprehensiveness: it presented an ordered view, especially of logic, biology, and other natural philosophy. Indeed, to some medieval scholars it seemed to present a systematic exploration of the full potential of human reason itself. The appeal of such a presentation to scholastic thinkers reveals their funda-

2. Kristeller, *Renaissance Thought, I,* p. 36; see also pp. 116–17.

3. Francesco Petrarch, *On His Own Ignorance and That of Many Others,* p. 53.

mentally optimistic view of man's intellectual capabilities. The scholastic vision and the related medieval vision "assumed not only the existence of a universal order but also a substantial capacity in the human mind to grasp this order."[4] Many scholastic writers were confident that complete knowledge was attainable by man and indeed had already been attained by a few ancient and early Christian writers in their fields of expertise.

But if reality was closed, systematically ordered, and completely apprehensible, as the Schoolmen believed, then knowledge itself must be limited. Accepting the authority of the ancients could ultimately entail rejecting the possibility of new ideas in the disciplines they had mastered. In the debased scholastic tradition of the sixteenth century, to look ahead for a moment, this corollary was frequently followed to its logical end. The minor Aristotelian philosopher Lodovico Boccadiferro, for example, chastised a too-venturesome colleague with these words: "Most of these new opinions are false. Were they true, they would already have been adopted by one of many wise men of past ages."[5] In the face of the geographical, cosmological, technological, and other discoveries of the fifteenth and sixteenth centuries the scholastic deference to authority sometimes hardened into dogmatism, a turn from observation and practical experience to the security of ancient thought that Galileo would ridicule mercilessly. In an era of rapidly expanding intellectual horizons, sixteenth-century scholastics emphasized the claims of reason and theory over the imperfect conclusions drawn from observation and practice. The inability of these late scholastic thinkers to assimilate novel ideas stimulated important questions about scientific, scholarly, and artistic innovation in sixteenth-century intellectual circles and ultimately helped to provoke the first *querelles* of the ancients and moderns.[6]

But we have jumped ahead somewhat and must return now to the origins of humanist thought. Unlike scholasticism, humanism was native to Italian soil, a response to imported scholastic trends that seems to have been nurtured by the circumstances of Italian urban life in the late Middle Ages. The complex network of responsibilities and dependencies necessary to rule these communes and organize their commerce encouraged a pragmatic view of the uses and ends of knowledge, one embodied long before the Renaissance in a professional class of *dictatores,* notaries hired to write speeches, documents, and the like. This worldly, ad hoc use of learning sprang from an engagement with everyday concerns and human actions foreign to scholastic thinkers. It tended therefore to espouse the active life over the seclusion of the *vita contemplativa.* Its expedient pragmatism contrasted sharply

4. Bouwsma, *Venice and Republican Liberty,* p. 5.

5. Quoted from Umberto Pirotti, "Aristotelian Philosophy and the Popularization of Learning," p. 175.

6. See Hans Baron, "The *Querelle* of the Ancients and Moderns as a Problem for Renaissance Scholarship."

with the scholastic view of knowledge as a logical, hierarchical structure rising to systematic understanding.

By the fifteenth century the effects of humanist learning were felt in the Italian universities, long dominated by scholastic subjects like law, medicine, and natural philosophy. Certain scholars, soon referred to as *humanisti,* began to stress the value of the *studia humanitatis,* a group of disciplines that scholastics considered inferior to more systematic studies. The *humanisti* valued moral philosophy over Aristotelian natural philosophy and celebrated the moral teachings derived from poetry and history. They condemned what seemed to them the useless excesses of scholastic logic. And they replaced it with a new dialectic, based as much on Cicero and Quintilian as on Aristotle, that blurred the distinction between scientific demonstration and plausible argumentation and challenged the superiority of formal proof to suasive talk.[7] In place of the logical construction of all-embracing ontologies and the systematizing of individual disciplines, they and their nonacademic comrades like Coluccio Salutati, Leonardo Bruni, and Poggio Bracciolini, all chancellors of the Florentine republic and heirs to the *dictatores,* pursued the more modest end of swaying their fellow men to morally and politically right actions in the real world.

The importance of rhetorical persuasion to this vision is obvious. Indeed the revival and revaluation of ancient and particularly Ciceronian rhetorical practice form the cornerstone of the humanist achievement. This high regard for rhetoric grew in conjunction with a new human ontology, in which the will assumed a centrality at odds with its scholastic position as mediator between reason and the base passions. For the purposes of argument, in fact, the traditional ranking of intellect over will could even be reversed, as when Petrarch, one of the first humanists, wrote, "It is safer to strive for a good and pious will than for a capable and clear intellect. The object of the will, as it pleases the wise, is to be good; that of intellect is truth. It is better to will the good than to know the truth."[8] This celebration of the will as the motivator of virtuous action merged in humanists with an abhorrence of philosophy in a vacuum—of knowledge not put to good use. Already shortly after Petrarch's death Pier Paolo Vergerio united philosophy and rhetoric (and history, another source of practical instruction) in a Ciceronian linkage essential to humanist thought: "By philosophy we learn the essential truth of things, which by eloquence we so exhibit in orderly adornment as to bring conviction to differing minds. And history provides the light of experience—a cumulative wisdom fit to supplement the force of reason and the persuasion of eloquence."[9]

7. Lorenzo Valla and Rudolph Agricola are two of the leading figures in this shift from a syllogistic to a topical logic; see Norman Kretzmann et al., eds., *The Cambridge History of Later Medieval Philosophy,* chap. 43, and Walter J. Ong, *Ramus, Method, and the Decay of Dialogue,* chap. 5.

8. *On His Own Ignorance,* p. 105.

9. Quoted from Benjamin G. Kohl and Ronald G. Witt, eds., *The Earthly Republic,* p. 15.

Humanist esteem for man's will, like the pragmatic humanist view of knowledge and dialectic, arose in interaction with the requisites of communal self-governance. Through the will, more than through the intellect, man's passions could be swayed and channeled to result in right action. And only thus could the special needs of the new society—to accommodate quickly changing circumstances and to persuade others to respond effectively to them—be answered. Behind the humanist exaltation of oratorical persuasion lay a recognition of the passions as dynamic forces directing human thought and action, and a felt need to control and exploit these forces.

In all this the humanist world-view resembles Bouwsma's Renaissance vision, in which the medieval excitement at man's vast intellectual capabilities gave way to a dimmer view of his ability to rationalize the world around him. The systematic, hierarchically ordered medieval ontology now seemed instead a disordered, often baffling reality, and attempts to understand it were characterized most typically by an effort to cope with "the incessant flux of things."[10] Humanists had little faith in the encompassing theories of scholastic thinkers. They recognized the validity of practical experience and accepted its fragmentary and unsystematic nature, albeit uneasily, as the inevitable impression of a complex reality on the imperfect human intellect. Hence they were led to make reason dependent on sense and experience, as Paolo Sarpi, a friend of Galileo and with him a late representative of the humanist tradition, explained:

> There are four modes of philosophizing: the first with reason alone, the second with sense alone, the third with reason first and then sense, the fourth beginning with sense and ending with reason. The first is the worst, because from it we know what we would like to be, not what is. The third is bad because we many times distort what is into what we would like, rather than adjusting what we would like to what is. The second is true but crude, permitting us to know little and that rather of things than of their causes. The fourth is the best we can have in this miserable life.[11]

Because the humanists were not confident that man could explore the furthest limits of knowledge, they tended to adopt a more progressive view of human understanding and achievement than the scholastics. The ancient writers were transformed, in Eric Cochrane's words, "from a series of infallible statements or texts into individual, fallible, historically conditioned human beings." What scholastics regarded as authoritative statements humanists saw as working hypotheses that "carried with them the injunction to try them out in practice."[12] Or, as Petrarch expressed it, "I certainly believe that Aristotle was a great man who knew much,

10. Bouwsma, *Venice and Republican Liberty*, pp. 4–5.

11. Quoted from Bouwsma, *Venice and Republican Liberty*, pp. 519–20; Bouwsma's translation.

12. "Science and Humanism," pp. 1053–54.

but he was human and could well be ignorant of some things, even of a great many things."[13] A new cultural relativism allowed at least the considerable independence of modern from ancient culture and by the sixteenth century even argued its superiority in such areas as technology (where inventions like the compass, the printing press, and gunpowder gave eloquent testimony to modern prowess). In this light we should view frequent late-*cinquecento* claims of artistic autonomy from the ancients, like these words from Jacopo Peri's introduction to *L'Euridice* of 1600: "And therefore, just as I shall not venture to affirm that this is the manner of singing used in the fables of the Greeks and Romans, so I have come to believe that this is the only one our music can give us to be adapted to our speech."[14] We shall see that Monteverdi insisted on a similar autonomy even from more recent musical authorities.

It would be wrong, however, to suggest that humanists abandoned the quest for philosophical truth in realizing the power of rhetoric and admitting the baffling diversity of society and the world. They strove instead, along with Pier Paolo Vergerio, to utilize the limited truths available to them to shape their own and others' responses to the vagaries of life. The unity of philosophy and eloquence, not the abandonment of philosophy, was the central message of Renaissance humanism. And this Ciceronian impulse set Petrarch decisively apart from the earlier Italian *dictatores* as the spokesman for a new cultural force. As Jerrold Seigel has written:

> To speak in favor of solitude was, in Petrarch's terms, to speak as a philosopher. To accept the city and the moral values which the give and take of community life required was to speak as an orator. Petrarch's statements moved continually back and forth between these two positions, between the claims of an abstract wisdom, and the moral standards of the everyday world. This alternation . . . grew out of his attempt to combine the two lives of the philosopher and the orator. Petrarch recognized that rhetoric and philosophy both attracted and repelled each other, and humanist culture embodied this dialectic.[15]

The dialectic that Seigel describes persisted in humanist culture through the sixteenth century and beyond. From the fourteenth to the seventeenth century it was not philosophy itself that the humanists disdained but the view that a systematic philosophical knowledge independent from the ethical ambiguities of daily existence was attainable and desirable.

The humanist perception of reality as fragmentary and even incoherent encouraged the reconsideration of the relationships among the intellectual disciplines and the consolidation of their differing methods and goals. This increased attention to

13. *On His Own Ignorance*, p. 74.
14. From the facsimile of the original edition, edited by Rossana Dalmonte.

15. " 'Civic Humanism' or Ciceronian Rhetoric?," p. 37.

questions of disciplinary autonomy was itself an anti-scholastic tendency, and in the late sixteenth century it heightened tensions between thinkers of humanist and scholastic temperament. Natural philosophy, for example, was seen by all to be governed by universal laws. Its scholastic practitioners aimed to construct necessary demonstrations of these laws, working from observed (or reported) phenomena. They distinguished their discipline, characterized by this logical search for universal truths, from lower disciplines like astronomy, which aimed only to "save the appearances" of observed phenomena through hypothetical mathematical models. But in the face of ever more exact and diverse empirical observation humanists tended to admit their meager understanding of the laws of nature. They came to a healthy acknowledgment of the even less profound understanding embodied in the supposedly authoritative ancient and medieval texts on the subject. And they searched for new investigative tools more flexible than Aristotelian logic—most notably the mathematical reasoning of lower disciplines.

History borrowed its empirical method from natural philosophy but was not, in humanists' eyes, governed by similar immutable laws. The unpredictable actions of man, ruled as often by his passions as by his intellect, formed its subject; the teaching of flexible guidelines for shrewd and self-serving political action in present-day situations was its object. One predictable tendency of humanist historiography, then, was toward the pragmatism of Machiavelli. The early Renaissance link of history with ethics was loosened, arousing hostility among Counter-Reformation clerics.[16]

Poetry, so closely related to rhetoric, retained its ancient ethical aim to instruct with delight; and this aim was extended to music and the pictorial and plastic arts as their rhetorical capabilities were gradually recognized and enhanced. But the lessons of the new historiography were not lost on these arts. They were seen with growing clarity to embody the changing premises and aspirations of the cultures that produced them. Therefore they were guided by cultural relativism rather than eternal principles. Their means to realize their ethical ends changed along with their audience.

This working characterization of the humanist view obviously reaches beyond the notion, still sometimes met with in historical (and especially musicological) writing, of humanism as the revival, study, and translation of the Greek and Roman classics.[17] The careful study of ancient texts was, to be sure, the starting point of many Renaissance humanists. But close textual study was not reserved for the

16. See Bouwsma, *Venice and Republican Liberty,* pp. 304–5, and below, chap. 10.
17. In this I follow all the Renaissance historians cited above in n. 1, among others. Even Kristel- ler, while advocating a limited definition of humanism, hints at its much broader cultural implications; see especially *Renaissance Thought, I,* pp. 17–23, 98–99.

pursuit of their goals and interests. The philological techniques that helped humanists to master, for example, Cicero's eloquent Latin style could serve thinkers of scholastic temperament equally well. An obvious case in point is the Florentine Platonist Marsilio Ficino (1433–99). He employed humanist scholarly techniques—so skillfully, indeed, that his Latin translations of Plato and the Neoplatonists remained in use until the nineteenth century. But he employed them in "the construction of abstract systems of thought which, although different in detail from the scholastic systems of earlier generations, reflect much the same vision of reality."[18] By the sixteenth century as many thinkers of scholastic as of humanist temperament, perhaps, were careful students of ancient texts.

And, more generally, humanist and scholastic perceptions merged in complex and often contradictory ways in most thinking individuals of the period. Sixteenth-century Italian culture was, once again, a strikingly eclectic culture. Even Aristotle could be appreciated and exploited from humanist as well as scholastic perspectives, in mixtures of varying proportion with Plato, the Neoplatonists, ancient rhetoricians, and Christian writers.[19] We should resist the temptation to label individuals "humanist" or "scholastic," although we may perceive a leaning to one or the other of these idealized (and necessarily reified) extremes in their words or actions. The union of antithetical impulses even in individuals reflects the potency of the cultural forces by which thinking Italians of the late Renaissance were, in Bouwsma's phrase, "divided against themselves."

Several broad developments joined in the sixteenth century to intensify the rivalry of these forces. As noted above, the stunning expansion of the printing industry, and the concomitant vast proliferation of ancient and modern viewpoints on countless subjects, fostered eclecticism and reinforced both humanist and scholastic views according to individual temperament. A technological revolution, of which the invention of movable type was one aspect, challenged the superiority of the ancients in many fields, encouraged a pragmatic view of the applications of knowledge, and seemed to legitimize a progressive epistemology. Voyages of discovery further exposed the limitations of ancient knowledge, and weakened European man's traditional notions of his central place in the world. At the same time, finally, religious struggles throughout Europe struck at long-held conceptions of man's relation to God.

These developments nurtured the particularistic, fragmented view of reality,

---

18. Bouwsma, *Venice and Republican Liberty*, p. 43, and "Renaissance and Reformation," pp. 141–42. George Holmes persists in characterizing Florentine Platonism as "humanist" even though he perceives its close relationship to scholasticism; see *The Florentine Enlightenment, 1400–1500*, pp. 243, 265–66.

19. See Charles B. Schmitt, *Aristotle and the Renaissance*. An interesting and by no means isolated example of such syncretic thought is the Platonic primer of the Florentine Francesco de' Vieri *detto il Verino secondo*, *Vere conclusioni di Platone conformi alla Dottrina Christiana, et a quella d'Aristotile* (Florence, 1590).

and the pessimistic estimation of man's ability to comprehend it, of the Renaissance vision. But at the same time, perhaps inevitably, they fostered a desire for a fuller comprehension of reality or a reality more fully comprehensible—for the universal order of the medieval vision. In Italy, attempts to regain this order and rationalize the fragmented intellectual, social, and religious structures of sixteenth-century life sometimes relied on authoritarian dogmatism, a coercive intellectual force descended from an earlier, healthier scholastic reliance on authorities. Such coercion is obvious in the actions of the post-Tridentine Catholic church and more subtly evident in the insistent Aristotelianism of much secular thought after midcentury. Thinking Italians in these years must have faced persistent demands for intellectual orthodoxy.

Ultimately these demands combined with other forces to snuff out the last vital flames of humanism in Italy, to break the bond humanists had forged between eloquence and meaningful human thought and action, and to leave behind a post-Renaissance conception of rhetoric as virtuosic word manipulation and empty display. But this is a later development, one I will examine in my final chapter. Around 1600, humanist tendencies lived on in uneasy coexistence with late outgrowths of scholasticism. In the remainder of this chapter I will trace these conflicting views in scientific and artistic polemics involving three Italians of humanist temperament.

Galileo Galilei

"To call Galileo a humanist may be something of an exaggeration," Eric Cochrane has written. "Yet without the background of humanism, Galileo's accomplishment would be incomprehensible. . . . he can truly be called, if not the last of the humanists, at least a faithful heir of the humanist tradition."[20] In the university professors whom he antagonized from the first years of his career, in the church officials who eventually condemned his views, and even in his only-partly-successful efforts to grapple with his own deeply held preconceptions, Galileo Galilei, heir of the humanist tradition, repeatedly faced the challenge of late scholastic thought. His long struggle to affirm what we may call, with Arthur O. Lovejoy, "a change of taste in universes" provides one of the richest examples of the conflict of humanist and scholastic tendencies around 1600. Its richness arises from Galileo's novel approach to natural philosophy, a discipline that for centuries had been a stronghold of scholastic method and Aristotelian authority. It lies in the subject matter itself, which cut to the heart of man's conceptions about the world around him and could easily overstep the boundary between the physical and the metaphysical,

---

20. "Science and Humanism," p. 1057.

treading on the inviolable toes of scriptural assertion and theological doctrine. And it springs not least from the brilliant, polemical eloquence that Galileo brought to his task, an essentially humanist persuasive force that silhouettes with stark clarity the positions involved and their conflicting premises.[21]

His first teacher of mathematics, Ostilio Ricci, imparted to Galileo a utilitarian view of the discipline, in which mathematics was regarded as a tool by which man might deepen his knowledge of nature and exploit its principles to his advantage. Ricci was a professor in the Accademia del Disegno, the most pragmatic of late-sixteenth-century Florentine academies. He saw in mathematics a practical science that could aid human activities as diverse as military engineering, architecture, and painting.[22] Many of Galileo's early studies, following those of his teacher, were technological rather than theoretical. They aimed at the invention of useful mathematical devices such as a balance to measure specific gravity (1586), about which Galileo wrote his first scientific treatise, and a "geometric and military compass" (1597), widely used throughout Europe soon after its invention. Nor did Galileo forsake this close bond of science and technology in his later years. His discovery of the moons of Jupiter in 1610 suggested to him not only basic revisions of the prevailing view of the cosmos but also a technique for the measurement of terrestrial longitude; he continued to perfect this technique as late as 1636. For Galileo mathematics allowed man to conceptualize precisely, and thus control in some small degree, his world.

Galileo soon extended this dominion of mathematics to the heavens, by a process of terrestrial-to-extraterrestrial analogy rarely absent for long from his cosmological writings. Not until 1623, in *Il saggiatore,* would he write the famous characterization of the universe as a book "scritto in lingua matematica." But the analogy of super- and sublunar realms, so scandalous to the Aristotelian natural philosophers of the day, seemed inevitable to the *galileisti* as early as 1610, when Galileo's telescopic observations—of mountains on the moon, spots on the sun, moons around Jupiter, and so on—shattered the already weakened myth of the unalterable perfection of the heavens.

The assertion of mathematics as the only language adequate for the study of natural philosophy is Galileo's signal achievement.[23] In his day it took pride of place

21. My guides to Galileo's thought, aside from his own works, have been Luigi Bulferetti, "Galileo e la società del suo tempo"; Ernst Cassirer, "Galileo's Platonism"; Eric Cochrane, "The Florentine Background of Galileo's Work"; Cochrane, "Science and Humanism"; Stillman Drake, ed. and trans., *Discoveries and Opinions of Galileo*; Maurice A. Finocchiaro, *Galileo and the Art of Reasoning*; Eugenio Garin, *Science and Civic Life in the Italian Renaissance*; Ludovico Geymonat, *Galileo Galilei*; T. F. Girill, "Galileo and Platonistic Methodology"; Alexandre Koyré, "Galileo and Plato"; Erwin Panofsky, *Galileo as a Critic of the Arts*; Giorgio de Santillana, *The Crime of Galileo*; and William R. Shea, *Galileo's Intellectual Revolution.*

22. Geymonat, *Galileo,* p. 7.

23. Shea convincingly argues this point in *Galileo's Intellectual Revolution.*

as his most aggressive challenge to Aristotelian orthodoxy in the sciences. Traditional natural philosophy, as we have seen, used logical rather than mathematical methods of analysis. Aristotle himself had had little patience with mathematics, and his modern supporters were inclined to the same attitude. As Lodovico delle Colombe, an early opponent of Galileo, indignantly wrote, "In Aristotle's time this was considered a schoolboy's science, learned before any other, . . . and yet these modern mathematicians solemnly declare that Aristotle's divine mind failed to understand it, and that as a result he made ridiculous mistakes." Galileo scribbled his own indignation in the margin of Colombe's treatise: "And they are right in saying so, for he committed many serious errors and mathematical blunders, though neither so many nor so silly as does this author every time he opens his mouth on the subject."[24]

Galileo's esteem for mathematics, then, quickly brought him into direct conflict with Aristotle, the foremost authority on natural philosophy since the thirteenth century, and especially with Aristotle's more rigid sixteenth- and seventeenth-century exegetes. But the conflict involved more than the role of mathematics in natural philosophy. It arose also because Aristotle's science was an empirical one, aspiring to the logical analysis of observed phenomena. Ptolemaic astronomy, with its geocentric world order and injunction to "save the appearances," likewise attempted to explain why things looked the way they did. The idea that appearances might mislead—that they might hide a different, less tractable reality, explicable only in part and only through a combination of close observation and mathematical reasoning—was foreign to both systems of thought. It also contradicted the occasional passages that seemed to support the geocentric scheme in an authoritative text of another sort: the Bible. So Galileo's championing of the Copernican heliocentric system did more than place him in opposition to the ancient philosophers. It pitted him against an embattled church that had recently reaffirmed its medieval vision in order to buttress its authority. And, in the eyes of many, it pitted him against the Word of God.

Galileo's response to those who accused him of subverting established authority was presented most explicitly in two of his works, a long letter to the grand duchess of Tuscany of 1615 on the use of biblical quotations in scientific matters, and *Il saggiatore* of 1623, a scathing defense of his views on the nature of comets from the attack of the Jesuit astronomer Horatio Grassi.[25] Galileo was ever scornful of those who revered authorities to the point of belittling their own sense experience. Addressing Grassi under his pseudonym of Lothario Sarsi in *Il saggiatore*, he

24. Quoted from Drake, *Discoveries*, p. 223.
25. See Galileo Galilei, *Lettere*, pp. 123–61, and *Il saggiatore*. The letter and parts of *Il saggiatore* are translated in Drake, *Discoveries*. The letter is a revised and much expanded version of one to Benedetto Castelli of 21 December 1613 on the same subject (see *Lettere*, pp. 102–9); for a generally convincing analysis of its rhetorical strategies and flaws see Jean Dietz Moss, "Galileo's *Letter to Christina*."

wrote, "In Sarsi I seem to discern the firm belief that in philosophizing one must support oneself upon the opinion of some celebrated author, as if our minds ought to remain completely sterile and barren unless wedded to the reasoning of some other person. . . . Well, Sarsi, this is not how matters stand. Philosophy is written in this grand book, the universe, which stands continually open to our gaze."[26] For physical propositions capable of experimental confirmation no recourse to past authority was necessary: "I cannot but be astonished that Sarsi should persist in trying to prove by means of witnesses something that I may see for myself at any time by means of experiment. Witnesses are examined in doubtful matters which are past and transient, not in those which are actual and present. A judge must seek by means of witnesses whether Peter injured John last night, but not whether John was injured, since the judge can see that for himself."[27]

Since modern technology offered subtler means of observation and experiment than were available to the ancients, such as the telescope, Galileo argued that we should not hesitate to contradict authorities when new evidence demands it. In the *History and Demonstrations Concerning Sunspots* of 1613, therefore, Galileo attacked modern Aristotelians, not the philosopher himself: "They go about defending the inalterability of the sky, a view which perhaps Aristotle himself would abandon in our age." He bridled at the poor estimation of modern intellects that seemed to lie behind the Peripatetic position and expressed a clear belief in the progressive growth of human knowledge: "We abase our own status too much and do this not without some offense to Nature (and I might add to divine Providence), when we attempt to learn from Aristotle that which he neither knew nor could find out, rather than consult our own senses and reason. For she, in order to aid our understanding of her great works, has given us two thousand more years of observation, and sight twenty times as acute as that which she gave Aristotle."[28]

But if Galileo's estimation of human intellect was in absolute terms optimistic, his view of it relative to the complexities of the universe was not. Tempering his optimism, that is, was a strong humanist conviction that man at best could only struggle inadequately to understand the workings of a seemingly fragmented and inscrutable reality. He urged philosophers to admit their ignorance in certain matters rather than clutter their treatises with meaningless catchwords like *influence, sympathy,* and *antipathy*.[29] And in frequently admitting his own ignorance he freed himself to speculate on topics that for technical reasons could not be subjected to experimental corroboration until long after his death, devising, for example, an experiment to measure the speed of light. The enchanting Parable of Sounds in *Il saggiatore* has as its lesson the humility of man's intellect and as its subject a man

26. Drake, *Discoveries,* pp. 237–38; see Galileo, *Il saggiatore,* p. 38.

27. Drake, *Discoveries,* p. 271; see Galileo, *Il saggiatore,* p. 247.

28. Drake, *Discoveries,* pp. 141, 143; see Galileo, *Lettere,* pp. 89–90, 93–94.

29. Galileo, *Il saggiatore,* p. 60; Drake, *Discoveries,* p. 241.

whose knowledge, through long experience, "was reduced to diffidence, so that when asked how sounds were created he used to answer tolerantly that although he knew a few ways, he was sure that many more existed which were not only unknown but unimaginable."[30] Because of his recognition of the limits of human knowledge there was, as William R. Shea points out, "a tension in Galileo's mind between the certitude he claimed for geometrical demonstrations and his awareness of the hypothetical nature of his own speculations. . . . Galileo realized that the human mind could not penetrate the secrets of nature unless it abandoned the preposterous philosophical claim to exhaustive knowledge."[31] This philosophical claim, we have noted, was a characteristic aspiration of the scholastic temperament.

The message of the Parable of Sounds is curiously similar to the reasons for treating the Copernican system as no more than hypothetical that Maffeo Barberini, the new Pope Urban VIII, apparently urged on Galileo in the spring of 1624.[32] If God was capable of things beyond human imagination—a proposition any true Catholic must grant—then who could say that He had not placed the earth in the center of the universe, in spite of what seemed convincing physical evidence to the contrary? Here in a nutshell was the dilemma of the scientist in a world ruled by faith. Galileo had attempted to address this problem in his *Letter . . . Concerning the Use of Biblical Quotations,* a response to those who saw his arguments for the motion of the earth around the sun as contrary to Holy Scripture. His argument there had rested on Augustine's distinction between matters of reason and matters of faith and on the time-honored tradition of nonliteral biblical exegesis. "I should judge," wrote Galileo, "that the authority of the Bible was designed principally to persuade men of those articles and propositions which, surpassing all human reasoning, could not be made credible by science, or by any other means than through the very mouth of the Holy Spirit."[33] In matters of reason, observed phenomena should guide us in the interpretation of relevant scriptural passages, not vice versa.

Yet in combatting interpretations of Scripture that opposed manifest reason and sense experience Galileo returned to the limitations of human understanding:

> I should think it would be the part of prudence not to permit anyone to usurp scriptural texts and force them in some way to maintain any physical conclusion to be true, when at some future time the senses and demonstrative or necessary reasons may show the contrary. Who indeed will set bounds to human ingenuity? Who will assert that everything in the universe capable of being perceived is already dis-

30. Drake, *Discoveries,* p. 258. For the Parable of Sounds see pp. 256–58 and Galileo, *Il saggiatore,* pp. 126–28.
31. *Galileo's Intellectual Revolution,* pp. 90–91.
32. See Finocchiaro, *Galileo and Reasoning,* pp. 10–11, and Santillana, *The Crime of Galileo,* pp.

171–78. Barberini seems to have discussed these views with Galileo already in 1616; see Santillana, pp. 135–36n.
33. Drake, *Discoveries,* p. 183; see Galileo, *Lettere,* p. 131.

covered and known? Perhaps those that at another time would confess quite truly that "those truths which we know are very few in comparison with those which we do not know"?[34]

In an ambivalent formulation, Galileo celebrated human ingenuity even as he despaired of its ultimate ability to decipher the book "which stands continually open to our gaze." And in spite of his pessimism Galileo devoted his life to the search for truths he did not know. His yearning for a systematic conceptualization of the world suggests why, in his *Dialogue Concerning the Two Chief World Systems,* he could only bring himself to pay lip service to the pope's arguments against the conclusive reality of the Copernican model—arguments similar to views he had expressed many times before. Galileo's vision was, in Shea's words, "the great vision of a science in which the real is described by the ideal, the physical by the mathematical, matter by mind."[35] He needed, finally, to transcend sense experience and reach a level of pure intellect, of reality framed in elegant mathematical models. So the yearning for systematic simplicity led Galileo to advance a theory of the tides as the linchpin in his confirmation of the Copernican system—a theory riddled with weaknesses that are obvious to any objective observer of tidal phenomena but that Galileo ignored.

In its transcendent intellectualism Galileo's world-view is, not incidentally, Platonic; his science "was not so much an experimental game as a Platonic gamble."[36] But his pragmatic conjunction of mathematics with technology, his view of authorities as purveyors only of working hypotheses, his belief in the progressive enrichment of knowledge, and his ambivalent recognition of the limitations of human intellect—all these mark Galileo as a "faithful heir of the humanist tradition."

Humanist also, finally, are Galileo's view that his findings should be accessible to the literate Italian public and the means he seized on to realize this view. Galileo's mature works are cast as dialogues and letters—humanist forms that allow a rhetorical emphasis and dialectical flexibility not found in the scholastic treatises of the university philosophers.[37] And in fact the quick triumph of *Il saggiatore* owed more to its masterful polemical rhetoric and sharp-tongued wit than to the scientific arguments it advanced. Galileo's rhetorical prowess in live disputation was almost legendary, and the discomfiture it caused his opponents surely contributed no little part to the implacable ill will some of them bore him. We can measure its positive effect in a letter to Galileo from one of his loyal supporters, the Florentine poet and churchman Giovanni Ciampoli: "It seems impossible to me that one should frequent you and not love you. There is no greater magic than the beauty of virtue and

34. Drake, *Discoveries,* p. 187; see Galileo, *Lettere,* p. 135.
35. *Galileo's Intellectual Revolution,* p. 185.
36. Ibid., p. 186.

37. Cochrane, "Science and Humanism," pp. 1055–57. See also Cochrane, "The Florentine Background," pp. 130–31.

the power of eloquence; to hear you is to be convinced by your truth, and whatever I can do will always be at your service."[38]

The language of Galileo's works is as important as their form. Most of them are written not in Latin, the universal language of natural philosophy before Galileo's time, but in Tuscan Italian, accepted since the days of Pietro Bembo as the common literary language of the peninsula. As he explained in a letter of 1612, Galileo wrote in the vernacular so that all literate Italians could read of his discoveries and theories. He wrote in Italian to break down the barrier between the universities, storehouses of knowledge, and the growing class of educated Italians who had few connections with them. Through his works, he hoped, these readers would "see that just as nature has given to them, as well as to philosophers, eyes with which to see her works, so she has also given them brains capable of penetrating and understanding them."[39] Cochrane's "humanist principle that knowledge is sterile unless it is communicated, that demonstration is useless unless it persuades," rarely found such an able and committed champion.[40]

Behind all these characteristics of Galileo's works—their language, style, and form—lies a last, basic humanist impulse. This is a fascination with written language itself, with the meeting of far-flung minds and dialectic of differing views it enables and the undying legacy it conveys to succeeding generations. In Sagredo's homily on the ingenious inventions of man at the close of the First Day of the *Dialogue,* writing takes pride of place. Sagredo's words may serve as a testament to the undimmed cogency with which Galileo himself speaks to us across four centuries:

> But surpassing all stupendous inventions, what sublimity of mind was his who dreamed of finding means to communicate his deepest thoughts to any other person, though distant by mighty intervals of place and time! Of talking with those who are in India; of speaking to those who are not yet born and will not be born for a thousand or ten thousand years; and with what facility, by the different arrangements of twenty little characters upon a page! Let this be the seal of all the admirable inventions of mankind and the close of our discussions for this day.[41]

Giambattista Guarini

If we can trust the account of Giambattista Guarini's great-grandson, it was in 1605 that Cardinal Robert Bellarmine—the same Bellarmine who eleven years later would warn Galileo of the error of his Copernican leanings—complained in public

38. Quoted from Santillana, *The Crime of Galileo,* p. 96.
39. From his letter to Paolo Gualdo of 16 June 1612; quoted from Drake, *Discoveries,* p. 84.
40. "Science and Humanism," p. 1055.

41. Galileo Galilei, *Dialogue Concerning the Two Chief World Systems,* p. 105. For the Italian, see the facsimile of the first edition of 1632, *Dialogo . . . sopra i due massimi sistemi del mondo tolemaico, e copernicano,* p. 98.

that *Il pastor fido* was more harmful to Catholic morals than Protestantism itself.[42] In Guarini's sensual *tragicomedia pastorale* Bellarmine took on a formidable adversary. *Il pastor fido* had attracted a large and enthusiastic following already in the five years between its completion and its first publication in 1590, and by 1601 it had seen some twenty editions. Its popularity, not only in Italy but in translation throughout Europe, would endure well into the eighteenth century. But from the beginning it labored under charges of stylistic and moral impropriety.

The charges were first leveled, while *Il pastor fido* was still circulating in manuscript copies, in two small treatises of 1586 and 1590 by Giason Denores. They elicited a spirited if pseudonymous defense from Guarini, published in *Il verrato* and *Il verato secondo* of 1588 and 1593, and thus initiated the last great literary polemic of the sixteenth century. The strictly literary issues involved in this quarrel have been detailed elsewhere.[43] Here we shall attempt to characterize the counterpoint of humanist and scholastic inclinations that imbues these issues with a broader cultural resonance and links them to the polemics of Galileo and, we shall see, Monteverdi.

Bellarmine's moral judgments are not irrelevant to the polemic, for Denores was a professor of moral philosophy at the University of Padua, and his commitment to the ethical ends of poetry is evident from the full title of his treatise of 1586: *Discorso di Iason Denores intorno à que' principii, cause, et accrescimenti, che la comedia, la tragedia, et il poema heroico ricevono dalla philosophia morale & civile, & da' governatori delle republiche.*[44] We have seen that moral philosophy was a cornerstone of the educational program of the early humanists, a discipline that allowed them to conceptualize human actions in an otherwise bewildering social setting. But Denores's ethics was no such flexible response to a changing world. It offered instead a set of static, unbending moral guidelines (and in this it found expression also in his *Panegirico* of Venice of 1590).[45] Denores combined these moral strictures with a narrowly orthodox reading of Aristotle's *Poetics* to construct a yardstick by which the utility and success of any poem might be judged. Aristotle spoke only of three genres, the three named in the title of Denores's *Discorso*: tragedy, comedy, and epic. So Guarini's new genre of tragicomedy could not help but be a "mostruoso & disproportionato componimento."[46] Worse, since Denores believed that Aristotle spoke of all genres that could provide moral edification, tragicomedy must be a genre "without any useful end."[47] For Denores, poetic theory constituted an appeal to the eternal truths voiced by earlier authorities.

42. Reported in Nicolas J. Perella, *The Critical Fortune of Battista Guarini's "Il pastor fido,"* pp. 28–29. On Bellarmine's warning of Galileo see Santillana, *The Crime of Galileo,* chap. 6.
43. See in particular Bernard Weinberg, *A History of Literary Criticism in the Italian Renaissance,* chaps. 13, 21, and Perella, *The Critical Fortune,* chap. 1.

44. Perella, *The Critical Fortune,* p. 10.
45. See Bouwsma, *Venice and Republican Liberty,* p. 269.
46. Quoted from Weinberg, *A History of Literary Criticism,* p. 1076.
47. Quoted from Weinberg, *A History of Literary Criticism,* p. 1075.

Guarini rejected Denores's conclusions and their underlying premises. He argued that his tragicomedy was not without a useful end, though this was not one Aristotle could have foreseen. It was, in Guarini's words, "to purge the mind from the evil affection of melancholy."[48] Aristotle's tragedy had aimed instead to purge pity and terror in its spectators—a strange formulation from the *Poetics* that Guarini, along with many other literati of his day, worked hard to interpret. Guarini concluded that such purgation was no longer needed, for "just as the age changes, habits change. . . . what need have we today to purge terror and pity with tragic sights, since we have the precepts of our most holy religion, which teaches us with the word of the gospel? Hence these horrible and savage spectacles are superfluous."[49] The appreciation of historical change evident in these words recalls Galileo's progressive views on technology and the growth of knowledge.

Guarini perceived a clear difference between artistic judgments and physical propositions. He saw that in art, unlike natural science, permanent truths are few and of such general scope that there is room for much adaptation and variety within them. So art should develop, often in unpredictable ways, along with the tastes and customs of its audience: "Particular species, depending upon the will of the artists, cannot be regulated in the same way in which natural effects are regulated; these have their necessary and permanent principles, always in the same state. We should be in a bad way if philosophers were obliged to guess in advance all the combinations that the arts can produce."[50] Just as Guarini saw little need for tragic purgation in his time, so he realized that later generations might find the artworks of his day unsuitable or imperfect: "The arts . . . do not have fixed perfection and magnitude, and we esteem some object as excellent which our descendants will perhaps regard as imperfect."[51] In the quarrel between ancients and moderns that lay behind the polemic over *Il pastor fido,* Guarini sided decisively with the moderns. For him, as Bernard Weinberg noted, "it is the taste of the times that explains and legitimizes the birth of modern tragicomedy."[52]

For Denores, however, Guarini's "will of the artists" was not enough to justify a monstrous creation like *Il pastor fido.* In his *Apologia contra l'auttor del verato* of 1590, Denores affirmed the authority of theory and universal precepts over practice and particular artists and works of art: "I distinguish good poems from bad ones with the measure of art, and not art with the measure of poems; those who observe it are the perfect ones and those who do not observe it are the imperfect ones."[53]

---

48. From Guarini's *Compendio della poesia tragicomica* (1601); translated in Allan H. Gilbert, ed., *Literary Criticism,* p. 522. On Guarini's idea of purgation see also Baxter Hathaway, *The Age of Criticism,* pp. 268–73.

49. From the *Compendio*; translated in Gilbert, *Literary Criticism,* p. 523.

50. Quoted from Weinberg, *A History of Literary Criticism,* p. 682.

51. Quoted from Weinberg, *A History of Literary Criticism,* p. 684.

52. Ibid., p. 1086; see also p. 1104.

53. Quoted from Weinberg, *A History of Literary Criticism,* p. 1084.

Guarini's response was that precepts could be violated when necessary to attain a desired effect. He argued this position, in *Il verato secondo,* from an analogy of poetry with oratory: "To speak contrary to the precepts is not always to speak without art, for since the speaker has no other end than to persuade, in whatever way he does it, and since he knows that sometimes he cannot do it in the ordinary way . . ., he is obliged to transgress the ordinary rules that the rhetoricians prescribe to us. But what he does without art is nevertheless a very great art."[54] The practical needs of effective expression, for Guarini, took precedence over theoretical precepts. And the precepts themselves could be deduced only from artworks; the works came first. According to Guarini this was Aristotle's end in the *Poetics*: "to reduce all poems that he found in his time to universal rules, and not to go about wondering about what particular kinds of poems the following centuries might be able to derive from those same rules."[55] Weinberg has expressed Guarini's position thus: "Practice and precepts are in constant interaction, with no fixity or permanence on either part."[56] (Significantly, when Guarini had recourse to the ancients to help legitimize his procedures, it was most often not to theorists and philosophers that he turned but to the playwrights themselves—to Sophocles, Plautus, Terence, and others.) The fluid interplay of practice and theory might result in artworks different from those of the past, but for Guarini these new works did not therefore sacrifice the *ragionevolezza* essential, for Guarini and Denores alike, to respectable human action.

Guarini devoted much energy to the defense of the mixed nature of his tragicomedy—its mingling of comic and tragic actions and characters and of magnificent and elegant styles. Such mixture—*temperamento* is Guarini's preferred term—played an important role in sixteenth-century literary theory from the time of Pietro Bembo's *Prose della volgar lingua* (published in 1525). Bembo had perceived a joining of *piacevolezza* and *gravità* in the verse of Petrarch and prose of Boccaccio and had established the resulting *variazione* as a requisite of good Tuscan style. Guarini's defense of his mixture of styles relied on the allowance of such procedures by the ancient stylists Demetrius and Hermogenes, but he justified his mixture of actions and characters on different grounds. Here verisimilitude was the point:

> With respect to actions that are great and not great, I cannot see for what reason it is unfitting that they should appear in one same plot, not entirely tragic, if they are inserted with judgment. Can it not be that amusing events intervene between serious actions? Are they not many times the cause of bringing perils to a happy con-

54. Quoted from Weinberg, *A History of Literary Criticism,* pp. 1085–86.

55. Quoted from Weinberg, *A History of Literary Criticism,* p. 682.
56. Ibid., p. 1104.

clusion? But then, do princes always act majestically? Do they not at times deal with private affairs? Assuredly they do. Why, then, cannot a character of high importance be presented on the stage at a time when he is not dealing with important matters?[57]

In real life, Guarini wrote, variety and mixture are common. Nature joins the horse and the ass to create a mule, and copper and tin to create bronze. Musicians join various sounds, painters various colors. And in politics two types of government, "the power of the few and the power of the masses," are joined to form the republic. "But in the republic are not the citizens human persons and the acts of government human operations? If these, that work practically, can be mixed, cannot the art of poetry do it in those things that are done for sport? . . . Why cannot poetry make the mixture if politics can do it?"[58]

Thus Guarini saw in *Il pastor fido*—a poetic drama set in a far-off Arcadia where shepherds spoke ornate periods and honor "was not as yet the Tyrant of our mindes"[59]—a mirror of the varied reality he perceived around him. He defended his play using the premises of a world-view different from Denores's, a humanist view that recognized cultural complexity and accepted the vagaries of historical change. Perhaps, indeed, it was just this unsettling humanist vision that bred the melancholy *Il pastor fido* aimed to dispel.

Claudio Monteverdi

In 1600 the Bolognese music theorist Giovanni Maria Artusi published a dialogue entitled *L'Artusi overo delle imperfettioni della moderna musica*. Here, in the midst of lengthy discussions of musical modes, proportions, and tuning systems, the interlocutors Luca and Vario examined and condemned passages from three madrigals in a novel style that Luca had heard the evening before. Nine short excerpts from two of these madrigals were included as examples in the discussion, but they were printed without their texts, and their composer was not named. Not until 1603 did the musical public at large learn his identity: in that year one of the pieces criticized in *L'Artusi* appeared in the *Quarto libro de madrigali* of Claudio Monteverdi.

The polemic that grew out of Artusi's attack lasted until 1608 and eventually involved Monteverdi himself, his brother, Giulio Cesare Monteverdi, and a music lover writing under his academic pseudonym l'Ottuso whose letters in defense of

---

57. From the *Compendio*; translated in Gilbert, *Literary Criticism*, p. 508.
58. From the *Compendio*; translated in Gilbert, *Literary Criticism*, p. 511.

59. From Richard Fanshawe's translation of 1647; see Giambattista Guarini, *Il pastor fido*, p. 323.

Monteverdi Artusi answered in his *Seconda parte dell'Artusi* of 1603.[60] Once again, the conflicting premises behind the quarrel reflect clearly the fundamental differences of humanist and scholastic attitudes in late-*cinquecento* culture. They involve such familiar questions as the effects of historical change, the relation of past authority to present action, and the connection of theory to practice.

These conflicts were exacerbated, however, in a way that we have not seen in the polemics over science and literature discussed above, by the ambivalent place of music in sixteenth-century thought and the resulting division among musical thinkers.[61] On one side stood the theorists, heirs to the medieval (and scholastic) placement of music among the *quadrivium* of mathematical sciences, which included arithmetic, geometry, and astronomy as well. Their position was supported by the large body of ancient music theory that had been edited and published during the sixteenth century. In their view and that of their ancient predecessors extending back to Pythagoras, the rules of musical practice could be deduced from nature itself through a careful mathematical study of harmonic proportions. Such rules, once logically established, would be immutable, and their application would lead to a perfect musical practice, to which no refinements could be added. Many late-sixteenth-century theorists, the Venetian Gioseffo Zarlino most prominent among them, thought that just such a practice had been achieved by the generations of polyphonists following Josquin. For Artusi, who had studied with Zarlino, composers like Adriano Willaert and Cipriano de Rore marked the apex of modern musical practice.

Opposed to the theorists's view was another conception of music, less rigorous and less dependent on traditional academic definitions of the discipline. Its proponents tended to ally music with poetry and, by extension, with rhetoric. They were fascinated by the miracles supposedly wrought by ancient musicians, but since only a few, inscrutable fragments of ancient music had survived, they remained unfettered by the authority of ancient practice and open to notions of stylistic

60. For an admirable summary of the musical issues of the quarrel see Claude V. Palisca, "The Artusi-Monteverdi Controversy." All the surviving documents of the polemic have been reprinted in facsimile. Artusi's *L'Artusi* (1600), *Seconda parte dell'Artusi* and *Considerationi musicali* (1603), and *Discorso secondo musicale*, published in 1608 under the pseudonym Antonio Braccino da Todi, are included in *L'Artusi overo delle imperfettioni della moderna musica*, ed. Giuseppe Vecchi. Artusi's first *Discorso*, probably from 1606 or 1607, has not survived. Monteverdi entered the fray with a short foreword to his *Quinto libro de madrigali* of 1605, on which Giulio Cesare composed a gloss, the *Dichiaratione della lettera stampata nel Quinto libro de suoi madrigali*, that was appended to Claudio's *Scherzi musicali* of 1607. Both are reproduced in Claudio Monteverdi, *Tutte le opere*, vols. 5, 10. For English versions of most of Artusi's attack on Monteverdi in *L'Artusi*, of Monteverdi's foreword, and of Giulio Cesare's *Dichiaratione*, see Oliver Strunk, ed. and trans., *Source Readings in Music History: The Baroque Era*, pp. 33–52.

61. The following paragraphs advance a reified view of these notions. It is meant to serve as a starting point for the discussion of Monteverdi and Artusi, not to provide a conceptual scheme by which all sixteenth-century theorists and musicians might be easily categorized.

change through history. They viewed music above all as an expressive art, reflecting in this the high humanist regard both for the passions themselves, as determinants of human actions, and for the artist's ability to arouse these passions. And they occasionally concluded, as Guarini had concluded about rhetoric and literature, that "to speak contrary to the precepts is not always to speak without art . . . since the speaker has no other end than to persuade."

The tendencies of this musical humanism are especially apparent in the stylistic innovations for purposes of more effective poetic expression of many sixteenth-century madrigalists and early-seventeenth-century monodists. And it was these composers—Giaches de Wert, Luca Marenzio, Luzzasco Luzzaschi, Peri, even Rore, whose extraordinary versatility allowed him to find a place in both the scholastic and humanist camps—that Monteverdi included in his famous Second Practice. In this new practice, the composer's first concern was expressive force, not structural perfection. Therefore, in Giulio Cesare's famous formulation, the words are "the mistress of the harmony and not the servant."[62] Monteverdi never denied the excellence of the mid-sixteenth-century Prima Pratica of Willaert and others, but he insisted that his own music should not be bound by it.

Artusi's reasoning in his publications of 1600 and 1603 reveals the limitations of much late scholastic thought. There were for him only two justifications for human actions, the authority of past masters and logical or mathematical demonstration. Faced with Monteverdi's use of a melodic diminished fourth, Artusi asked, "Does he have the permission of nature and art thus to confound the sciences? To uphold things done in this manner we need one of two things: either the authority of past writers (and this is not to be found) or demonstration—to this task [Monteverdi] must set himself."[63] Since, in Artusi's view, "every artificer is obliged to account for the things he does in his art," Monteverdi had to defend his novel techniques through rational proofs.[64]

Artusi gave many examples in the two parts of L'Artusi of the sort of demonstration he expected from Monteverdi. Most of his discussions, like that on the proper tuning system for modern music, depended on closely argued mathematical reasoning—which underlined his view of music as a science of numbers but left him helpless to address Monteverdi's central concern of expressive forcefulness. When compelled to address this issue by the first of l'Ottuso's letters, he retreated adroitly behind a display of degenerate scholastic logic. L'Ottuso claimed that Monteverdi's novel music (modulatione) had discovered "in its novelty new chords [concenti] and new emotions [affetti], and not unreasonable ones, though they move far, in some ways, from the old traditions of various excellent Musicians." To l'Ottuso's loose usage of the term concento Artusi opposed a rigorous definition: "Con-

62. *Dichiaratione*, p. 1; translated in Strunk, *Source Readings*, p. 46.

63. *Seconda parte dell'Artusi*, p. 10.

64. *L'Artusi*, fol. 33v.

cento, as it is defined by all wise men, is a mixture of low and high sounds combined in such a way that, when struck, it renders infinite sweetness to the ear. In which definition there are two things to ponder: first, that *concento* is composed of low and high sounds combined; and second, that these combined sounds produce a sweet effect." Now Monteverdi's use of consonances was like that of other composers— Artusi here quoted the opening of the madrigal "Era l'anima mia," a "*concento* that has been used thousands of times by every composer who has ever composed"— and so could not be the source of his novelties. His dissonances were certainly not divided in any of the acceptable mathematical proportions; moreover, like all dissonances, "they have by nature no sweetness or softness; rather they cause an effect of unbearable harshness." Since *concenti* were defined as sweet and dissonances were harsh, dissonances were not *concenti* at all. And since Monteverdi's novel usage lay only in his dissonance treatment, he could not possibly have created the *novi concenti* l'Ottuso claimed for him. Moreover, since Monteverdi had created no new *concenti,* how could he hope to create new *affetti*?

To l'Ottuso's just if imprecisely stated observation of new sounds in Monteverdi's style Artusi responded with a sophistic barrage of semantic hairsplitting, which we might reduce to a self-serving and empty syllogism:

> All *concenti* are sweet-sounding.
> All Monteverdi's novelties are harsh-sounding.
> ∴ Monteverdi has created no novel *concenti.*

Artusi sidestepped the simple truth of l'Ottuso's remark by refusing to acknowledge his imprecise usage of the term *concento.* Just as adroitly he ignored the testimony of his ears. There *were,* after all, new sounds in Monteverdi's madrigals— these are what had inspired Artusi's criticism in the first place.[65] Artusi's rejection of manifest sense experience reminds us of skeptics like the Aristotelian philosopher Cesare Cremonini, who refused to look through Galileo's telescope, fully believing that what Galileo claimed to see there could not exist. And the sophistry of Artusi's argument brings to mind some of Galileo's later opponents, who countered his reasoning with syllogistic "demonstrations" of which the first premises were artificially structured to attain the desired result.[66]

Like Giason Denores, Artusi was firm in his belief that modern practice should answer to the precepts of theory.

> If, with the observation of the precepts and good rules left by the Theorists and observed by all practitioners, we can reach our goal, then what point is there in going beyond these limits and searching for oddities? Do you not know that all

---

65. For Artusi's discussion see the *Seconda parte dell'Artusi,* pp. 6–11.

66. For an example of Galileo's ridiculing of this specious logic see Shea, *Galileo's Intellectual Revolution,* pp. 115–16, 119.

the Sciences and Arts have been regulated by wise men, and that in each the first Elements, Rules and Precepts on which it is founded have been set down, so that, not deviating from principles and good rules, one man may be understood by another?[67]

And, though Artusi disingenuously claimed elsewhere that he respected a practicing artist without theoretical knowledge more than a theorist without practical knowledge,[68] his scorn for those rude musical *artefici* who knew little of theory was apparent:

> There is no doubt that the discussion of difficult and very speculative things does not pertain to the practitioner; it is, rather, the office of the Theorist, since the simple practitioner cannot penetrate deep enough to understand such particulars. Thus it is that, their intellect not allowing them to reach this truth, the compositions of these practitioners show many impertinences and imperfections, which arouse nothing but infinite shame.[69]

In the face of this exaltation of rationalism and the intellect, Monteverdi advanced the claims of the passions of the soul. His Second Practice aimed, as we have said, "to make the words the mistress of the harmony and not the servant." It did so to increase the affective power of the composition as a whole. For had not Plato affirmed, in discussing the three components of music, that the rhythm and harmony should follow the words and "the manner of the diction and the words follow and conform to the disposition of the soul"?[70] Monteverdi's implicit view that the foremost goal of his music was to move the passions provided the rational basis for his Second Practice. It claimed for him the same freedom to break the rules for expressive ends that Guarini had demanded before him. And in so doing it asserted the flexible interaction of theory and practice rather than the rigid scholastic hegemony of one over the other.

On the importance of musical practice Giulio Cesare Monteverdi was especially emphatic in his gloss of his brother's letter. He challenged Artusi to match Monteverdi's works not with theoretical tracts but "with a comparable practical performance":

> Then let him allow the world to be the judge, and if he brings forward no deeds, but only words, deeds being what commend the master, my brother will again find himself meriting the praise, and not he. For as the sick man does not pronounce the physician intelligent from hearing him prate of Hippocrates and Galen, but does so when he recovers health by his wisdom, so the world does not pronounce the musician intelligent from hearing him ply his tongue in telling of the honored harmonic theorists. For it was not in this way that Timotheus incited Alexander to

---

67. *L'Artusi*, fol. 42v.
68. Ibid., fols. 33–34.
69. Ibid., fols. 20–21.

70. *Dichiaratione*, p. 1; see Strunk, *Source Readings*, pp. 46–47, quoted here. Giulio Cesare quotes Plato's *Republic* 398d, 400d.

war, but by singing. To such a practical performance my brother invites his opponent.[71]

Even the terms *First Practice* and *Second Practice,* said Giulio Cesare, were devised by Monteverdi to suggest actual composition and not abstract theory.[72]

Monteverdi's distinction of two different practices itself betrayed a humanist view of historical and cultural change. Monteverdi did not wish to condemn the Prima Pratica but, in his brother's words, "honors, reveres, and commends" it. (Monteverdi's later exercises in the style, like the *Missa in illo tempore* of 1610, support this statement.) He recognized the First Practice as the excellent style of another generation and fought only those who, like Artusi, would establish its precepts as eternal truths. Against such a position, indeed, Giulio Cesare tellingly cited Zarlino himself, Artusi's mentor:

> "It was never nor is it my intention to treat of the usage of practice according to the manner of the ancients, either Greeks or Latins, even if at times I touch upon it; my intention is solely to describe the method of those who have discovered our way of causing several parts to sound together with various modulations and various melodies, especially according to the way and manner observed by Messer Adriano [Willaert]." Thus the Reverend Zarlino concedes that the practice taught by him is not the one and only truth. For this reason my brother intends to make use of the principles taught by Plato and practiced by the divine Cipriano [de Rore] and by modern usage, principles different from those taught and established by the Reverend Zarlino and practiced by Messer Adriano.[73]

Undoubtedly Monteverdi would have been quick to admit, with Guarini, that the artworks "we esteem . . . as excellent . . . our descendants will perhaps regard as imperfect."[74]

Surprisingly, Artusi seemed ready to accede to Monteverdi's position of cultural evolution and diversity in the last document of the polemic, the *Discorso secondo musicale* of 1608—to accede, that is, insofar as it enabled him to cast doubt on the propriety of Giulio Cesare's citation of ancient authority. Plato, wrote Artusi, is irrelevant to the discussion because "he doesn't treat, never treated and, I believe,

---

71. *Dichiaratione,* p. 2; translated in Strunk, *Source Readings,* p. 48.
72. *Dichiaratione,* p. 2; see Strunk, *Source Readings,* p. 49.
73. *Dichiaratione,* pp. 2–3; translated in Strunk, *Source Readings,* p. 49.
74. Already in 1592 the literary theorist Agostino Michele had seized on historical changes in musical style to evidence the ubiquity of such changes in all the arts: "There is nothing under the sun that remains stable and firm, and it is instability that establishes laws for everything terrestrial and mortal. . . . Take music, in which many years ago Giusquino [des Prez] and Adriano [Willaert] flourished; in the past age Cyprian [de Rore] and Orlando [di Lasso] were famous; and in these days Marenzio and [Orazio] Vecchi become singular and illustrious; and nevertheless their manners of composing are so different that it seems they are not practitioners of the same art" (from Michele's *Discorso* in defense of prose comedy and tragedy; quoted from Hathaway, *The Age of Criticism,* p. 106).

never thought of treating modern music; rather, I am convinced that he spoke [only] of that music which flourished in his own time." Artusi admitted that the words were of first importance in the music of Plato's era; this was true because they were "recited to the sound of a single instrument." But Monteverdi's polyphonic music was different. Here the words were not intelligible, and it was the sounds (*l'armonia*) alone, if anything, that moved the listener. So the words must serve the sounds, not vice versa—as in Monteverdi's First Practice, for Artusi still the only legitimate modern practice. And this practice, Artusi concluded, "was determined, ordered, and regulated by the most wise Zarlino, and is the same practice [Marc'Antonio] Ingegneri taught to Monteverdi . . ., though he pays it little heed." Now, suddenly, Artusi became the spokesman for cultural and artistic diversity. After basing many of his own arguments in his earlier writings on the precepts of ancient authorities, he denied Monteverdi the same privilege. The Bolognese theorist managed, though not without self-contradiction, to have it both ways.[75]

In doing so, however, he embroiled himself in further contradictions. His argument against Monteverdi's use of Plato—that Plato spoke only of the music of his own time—was precisely Monteverdi's argument against the extension of the precepts of the First Practice to the music of the Second. And Giulio Cesare had quoted Zarlino's own admission of the limited scope of his theoretical system. Artusi ended his *Discorso* with a testy rejoinder to this citation:

> In the middle of his clarification of the letter, to prove that there is another practice, different from that described by Zarlino, he cites Zarlino's words from the first Chapter of the *Sopplimenti [musicali]*. . . . Therefore there is another practice, which we shall call the second. But if we decide to call the practice of the Greeks and Romans another practice (and there is no doubt that our practice is different from theirs . . .), we can then say that theirs was the first practice, and that the modern one followed by Cipriano and by M. Adriano, first described by Zarlino, is the second, and that Monteverdi's method of composition is the third. Or even the fourth, if we want to distinguish Greek from Roman practice. So that I may conclude that all these things are chimeras, said by Monteverdi, as he admits, only to defend himself from his opponent and because he cannot discover demonstrations to prove the things he has done good and true.[76]

But Artusi's argument, of course, allowed him to draw no such conclusion. His renaming of Monteverdi's practices had no bearing on their essence; it was nominalism of the most hollow sort. Indeed eight pages earlier Artusi had ridiculed just such a thought process concerning a terminological quibble in Giulio Cesare's *Dichiaratione*. We may quote him now against himself: "If . . . he had studied Logic,

75. For this discussion see the *Discorso secondo musicale*, p. 9.   76. Ibid., p. 15.

he would have understood that *nomina sunt ad placitum,* and therefore he would have quieted down. But let us leave these bagatelles, which matter little."[77]

The conflict of humanist and scholastic tendencies in Italian culture of the late Renaissance centered ultimately on the extent of man's ability to conceptualize reality. There was no doubt, on either side, of the pressing need for such conceptualization. For Artusi, only reason and hallowed authority could legitimize action, while Monteverdi, countering Artusi's charges of irrationality, asserted in his preface to Book V that he did not compose by chance, that he built on "foundations of truth." But Artusi and Monteverdi, and late-*cinquecento* humanists and scholastics in general, differed in the lengths to which they would go to preserve the rationalized world order handed down to them by earlier generations. Galileo, Guarini, and Monteverdi were each able to relinquish this order, at least in part, in the pursuit of more accessible and rewarding goals. They accepted the burdens of freedom. This allowed both Guarini and Monteverdi to seek novel expressive techniques; it also earned them the enmity of theorists and involved them in difficult processes of stylistic experimentation, redefinition, and defense. And Galileo, in order to accommodate new evidence from observation or reasoned "thought experiments," often forced himself to sacrifice his urgent Platonic desire to recreate reality as mathematical Idea. He taught the important lesson that knowledge could advance even while taking small steps backward through the admission of seeming paradox and apparently inexplicable phenomena. The actions of Galileo, Guarini, and Monteverdi— and those of many other imaginative personalities of their time, from the historian Paolo Sarpi to the poet Ottavio Rinuccini[78]—were courageous as well as creative acts in an era of growing intellectual authoritarianism.

For writers like Grassi, Denores, and Artusi, on the other hand, the need for rational control was too pressing to allow them this intellectual and creative curiosity. Artusi revealed this need most explicitly in the paeon to order that opens his *Considerationi musicali:* "Everyone tries to be orderly, in himself and in the things relating to his science or art; because where there is no order, there is confusion, and where there is confusion, there cannot be anything useful or honorable to man."[79] Fear of the uncontrollable confusion and irrationality around them extinguished the last spark of creative intellect in these writers. It led them to blind dogma and the exaltation of earlier authorities and caused them to sacrifice precisely that dignity of human intellect that they meant to uphold. Returning to the opening of Artusi's *Considerationi,* we read that "the Ancient Philosophers, most acute and subtle observers and reporters of things," studied the rational order of natural events.

77. Ibid., p. 7.
78. On Sarpi see Bouwsma, *Venice and Republican Liberty,* chap. 8 and passim; on Rinuccini, Gary Tomlinson, "Rinuccini, Peri, Monteverdi, and the Humanist Heritage of Opera," esp. chap. 6, and chaps. 5 and 10 below.
79. *Considerationi musicali,* p. 2.

Thus "they knew that the motion of one heaven was neither slowed nor impeded by that of another, but proceeded inviolably; and that the sun ran its course consistently, never stopping."[80] Artusi grounded his optimistic view of the capabilities of human intellect in the comprehension of such unswerving natural order. He, and others like him, could not admit a universe so topsy-turvy that the sun itself had stopped moving and the earth taken its place.

The importance of the polemic with Artusi lies in the insights it offers into Monteverdi's humanist inclinations. It revealed his awareness of historical change and his understanding that artistic authorities of the past were conditioned by their own cultures to express themselves in ways not necessarily relevant to Italian culture of his own age. In the process it loosened the grip of these authorities on him and, in his view, on his colleagues. The polemic manifested as well Monteverdi's rejection of the scholastic placing of theory over practice. He sensed, as Guarini had, that the two needed to develop together in a continuous process of reciprocal influence and cross-fertilization.

Last and most important, the controversy disclosed Monteverdi's abiding concern to join music to poetry in a single moving and persuasive language. It is this concern that most clearly marks Monteverdi as an heir to humanist ideals. It links him to the humanists' high estimation of man's will and their urge to sway man's passions. It associates his work with their pursuit of rhetorical eloquence, the key to those passions. To be sure, Monteverdi was not the first musician to hold such views. He himself knew that they were shared by the earlier representatives of his Second Practice, and today we know that they extend back at least to the *strambottisti* of the late fifteenth century. But he moved far beyond earlier composers in constructing musical styles of powerful eloquence. His achievement signals the climax of Renaissance humanism in music.

For a musician of humanist leanings like Monteverdi, the expressive power of music was a function of its relation to its text. (And it is a serious if common error to underestimate the complexity and diversity of text-music conjunctions that a late-sixteenth-century composer could command.) The highest goal that music could seek, a goal often attained by Monteverdi, especially in works from the years around 1600, was to form a syntactic and semantic union with its text so perfect that the distinction of musical and nonmusical elements seemed to fade before the heightened oratorical power of a single musical speech. To composers like Monteverdi, musical expression without text must have seemed a contradiction in terms, if indeed they ever conceived of the subject in such terms at all. Instrumental music could astonish, like vocal music, in its virtuosity or fulfill its more usual function as courtly *Gebrauchsmusik*. But the formation of a meaningful, connotative syntax that could appeal to a variety of human passions—the goal of Cicero-

80. Ibid., p. 1.

nian oratory that Monteverdi achieved time and again in his vocal music—was implicitly beyond its means. Monteverdi's own instrumental music, the many ballets, *sinfonie,* and ritornelli in his operas and late madrigal books, was always meant to derive its expressive dimension either from the mimetic gesture it accompanied (in the case of dance music) or from its structural resonance in the texted passages around it.

All this casts the humanist composer in the role of poetic exegete. The wonder of Monteverdi's achievement, simply put, is the unceasing imagination he brought to the fundamental act of the musical transfiguration of poetry. The exegete, however, also learns from his text. The extraordinary variety of responses to poetry in Monteverdi's music was induced, more directly than by any other factor, by the wide stylistic diversity of the poems themselves. In the following chapters we will discuss these changing poetic styles and Monteverdi's responses to them, and finally attempt to place both in the volatile dialectic of humanist and scholastic values in Italian culture around 1600.

THE
PERFECTION
OF
MUSICAL
RHETORIC

2

Youthful *Imitatio* and the First Discovery of Tasso (Books I and II)

ONTEVERDI the musical orator did not immediately find his voice. His first two books of madrigals, published while he was still at Cremona, his birthplace and youthful home, preserve the record of his early steps on the way to this discovery—hesitant steps, along paths well trodden before him, that only infrequently point ahead to the musico-rhetorical triumphs of his mature works. Nevertheless these youthful efforts provide us with a lexicon of techniques and gestures that Monteverdi would develop, sometimes almost beyond recognition, in later compositions. And, not less important, they confess more frankly than the mature works their indebtedness to the music of older, established composers, allowing us a glimpse backward at the byways Monteverdi had already passed on his journey.

The First Book

The main guides of Monteverdi's style in his *Madrigali . . . libro primo* of 1587 are Luca Marenzio and Luzzasco Luzzaschi. They offered Monteverdi two distinct if overlapping stylistic options. Since 1580 the Roman composer Marenzio had been the acknowledged master of the canzonetta-madrigal, a hybrid genre, developed in the 1560s and 1570s by composers like Andrea Gabrieli, that incorporated the light-hearted emotions, lively rhythms, reduced textures, and homophony of the canzonetta into the through-composed context of the madrigal, with its emphasis on textural variety and textual expression. Almost all of Monteverdi's early madrigals show some impact of Marenzio's canzonetta-madrigal; indeed this influence is so great in Book I that Alfred Einstein was led to write of his "impression that it is a collection of canzonette."[1]

Einstein exaggerated, as he well knew. But one has only to note the extensive

---

1. Alfred Einstein, *The Italian Madrigal*, p. 719.

similarities between the madrigals of Book I and Monteverdi's own volume of *Canzonette* of 1584 to feel the truth behind his hyperbole. In tonal type both collections show an almost exclusive use of *cantus mollis* (the "soft hexachord," with B♭ key signature) and *chiavette* (high clef systems); G finals predominate.[2] Also, the madrigals of Book I return again and again to the reduced textures and lilting homophony of the *Canzonette*. (The three-part homophony that opens "Se nel partir da voi, vita mia, sento," in fact, is an exact recall of the beginning of "Chi vuol veder d'inverno un dolce aprile" from the 1584 volume.) From his experience in 1584 Monteverdi knew the canzonetta style well. There is little doubt that he looked especially to Marenzio to justify its incorporation into the more serious madrigalian polyphony of Book I (and none whatsoever, we shall see, that he did so at the time of Book II).

The influential Ferrarese composer Luzzasco Luzzaschi, though he assimilated many features of the Marenzian canzonetta-madrigal, practiced a style of generally greater expressive weight in the only volume he published during the 1580s, his Third Book of madrigals of 1582.[3] His works typically set short lyrics, mostly poetic *madrigali,* developing the lover's complaints and the traditional paradoxes of his impassioned state. In other words, they emphasize emotion. Their music shows a less obvious reliance on canzonetta-like homophony than Marenzio's and a more complex contrapuntal texture, built from the free arrangement and rearrangement of brief, plastic declamatory motives. Most prophetic of Monteverdi's works, however, are Luzzaschi's abrupt shifts of musical style for affective purposes, as in "Gratie ad amor, o me beato e lui," the opening work of the 1582 collection (Ex. 1). The lively, consonant homophony of measures 46–48, reminiscent of the canzonetta-madrigal, gives way suddenly to slower, languishing declamation, with harsh suspended dissonance (at m. 53).

This stylistic shift has, of course, a text-expressive rationale: to capture in music the opposed emotions of the enamored poet, embodied in the final two lines of the lyrics: "sempre il mio cor gioisca, / arda, o mora, o languisca" ("my heart is always joyful, / it burns, or dies, or languishes"). The powerful urge to affective text expression revealed in Example 1 sets Luzzaschi apart from Marenzio—at least from the Marenzio of the early and mid-1580s. Not that there are no such gestures in Marenzio's early works; we shall note one example that Monteverdi imitated below. But they usually do not disrupt the musical flow as violently as Luzzaschi's. The Ferrarese composer seems more willing to resort to musical extremes to express his texts. And, as Monteverdi also distinguished himself from Marenzio

---

2. For a recent definition of sixteenth-century tonal types see Harold S. Powers, "Tonal Types and Modal Categories in Renaissance Polyphony," esp. pp. 436–40.

3. The style is discussed by Anthony Newcomb in *The Madrigal at Ferrara, 1579–1597* 1:115–25.

EXAMPLE 1

sem pre il mio cor gio- i- sca, ar- - da, o

mo- - ra, o lan- gui- sca.

Luzzaschi, "Gratie ad amor,
o me beato e lui," mm. 46–58

already in his First Book by his more radical and disruptive expressive means, it is at least likely that he took to heart Luzzaschi's example as well as Marenzio's.

In stressing Marenzio and Luzzaschi I do not wish to deny—as did Einstein—the important influence on Monteverdi's formative development of his teacher, the Cremonese composer Marc'Antonio Ingegneri.[4] Denis Arnold has identified and described this influence, singling out in particular Ingegneri's love of clear, concise structural organization. Ingegneri's impact on Monteverdi, Arnold notes, is most apparent in the cycle of three madrigals that ends Book I, "Ardo sì, ma non t'amo."[5] We shall perceive it as well in certain conservative madrigals of the Second Book (see below, pp. 56–57) and also in less likely contexts. Ingegneri seems to have grounded his student in a traditional, mainly contrapuntal idiom without striking individuality.[6] To this Monteverdi quickly joined techniques from the more progressive styles of Marenzio, Luzzaschi, and others. If Einstein exagger-

4. *The Italian Madrigal*, pp. 718–21.
5. Denis Arnold, "Monteverdi and His Teachers," pp. 92–98.
6. For examples of Ingegneri's late style see

Marc'Antonio Ingegneri, *Sieben Madrigale,* and G. Francesco Malipiero, ed., *Adriano Willaert e i suoi discendenti.*

ated once again in denying any influence of Ingegneri on his student, then, it is at least true that Monteverdi borrowed the most novel and vital musical techniques of his first madrigals from composers other than his teacher. In this important regard, and in spite of Monteverdi's politic bow to his mentor on the title page (*Madrigali . . . di Claudio Monteverde Cremonese discepolo del sig. Marc'Antonio Ingigneri*), Book I is a declaration of independence from the music master of his youth. From the first, it seems, adumbrating an attitude often made explicit in his later correspondence, Monteverdi did not gladly suffer authority.

The twenty-one madrigals of Book I fall into two groups of works distinct in poetic and musical style in spite of many shared characteristics. The first group shows clearer Luzzaschian features than the second; it dominates the opening half of the collection:

I.	"Ch'ami la vita mia nel tuo bel nome"	
II.	"Se per avervi, oimè, donato il core"	
III.	"A che tormi il ben mio"	
IV.	"Amor per tua mercé vattene a quella"	
V.	"Baci soavi e cari"	(Guarini)
VI.	"Se pur non mi consenti"	
VIII.	"Poiché del mio dolore"	
XII.	"Se nel partir da voi, vita mia, sento"	
XVIII.	"Donna, s'io miro voi, ghiaccio divengo"[7]	

These works typically set the sort of brief, amorous madrigals that Luzzaschi made his specialty. Most of Monteverdi's music moves freely between the imitative treatment of short motivic subjects and three-, four-, or five-part homophony reminiscent of the canzonetta. The generally syllabic delivery of text admits few melismas, and the poems, dwelling on the abstract Platonic paradoxes of the lover's state, afford little opportunity for pictorial madrigalisms. But their frequent references to death, martyrdom, afflicted hearts, and so on led Monteverdi to invoke Luzzaschi's affective style, in which the prevailing quarter-note motion gives way to half- and whole-note motion and consonant harmonies to a texture ridden with suspended dissonance. The abrupt shifts of tempo and mood that result from the incorporation of this style in the emotionally neutral context of the canzonetta-madrigal are the most striking feature of the madrigals of group 1. In this fundamental stylistic dualism they look back especially to the disjointed style of Luzzaschi.

Nine more madrigals of the First Book compose a second group:

---

7. Roman numerals indicate the position of each madrigal in the collection; authors of texts, when known, are given in parentheses.

VII.   "Filli cara e amata"   (Alberto Parma)
IX.   "Fumia la pastorella," *prima parte* ⎫
X.   "Almo divino raggio," *seconda parte* ⎬ (Antonio Allegretti)
XI.   "Allora i pastor tutti," *terza parte* ⎭
XIII.   "Tra mille fiamme e tra mille catene"
XIV.   "Usciam, ninfe, omai fuor di questi boschi"
XV.   "Questa ordì il laccio, questa"   (Giovanni Battista Strozzi *il vecchio*)
XVI.   "La vaga pastorella"
XVII.   "Amor, s'il tuo ferire"

The texts of these works are mainly pastoral: they narrate, in a bucolic setting, the innocent loves and games of shepherds and nymphs. Monteverdi set these poems in the style of the canzonetta-madrigal, which had been associated with verse of pastoral ethos since its earliest development in the 1560s and 1570s. The light-hearted texts offered few chances for tormented emotionalism, and therefore the affective style of group 1, with its striking stylistic contrasts, plays little part in these works. They are canzonetta-madrigals pure and simple. This is not to say, however, that Monteverdi made no attempt in them to express the text. On the contrary, as in Marenzio's madrigals, the frequent mention of dancing, running, singing, garlands, and flowers in their poems called out for pictorial treatment. And Monteverdi developed a full battery of Marenzian commonplaces to answer the call: brief outbursts of dancing homophony in triple meter, lengthy melismas, intertwining melodies, and so on. In all, these pastoral canzonetta-madrigals clearly reveal Monteverdi's study of Marenzio's early works. We shall return to trace in detail the ramifications of this study in discussing Monteverdi's Second Book.

The difference between the Luzzaschian and Marenzian strands in Book I may be clarified by closer scrutiny of one of the madrigals of our first group, "A che tormi il ben mio." Its text is just the sort of lyric that Luzzaschi preferred—brief, paradoxical, and providing the opportunity for affective disjunction and exclamation:

A che tormi il ben mio	Why take my love from me
s'io dico di morire?	if I speak of dying?
Questo, madonna, è troppo gran martire.	This, my lady, is too great a trial.
Ahi vita, ahi mio tesoro!	Ah life, ah my treasure!
e perderò il ben mio, con dir ch'io moro?	and will I lose my love for saying I die?

But this madrigal was never set by Luzzaschi. Instead, Monteverdi found it at the end of Marenzio's Fourth Book of 1584. In music as well as text Monteverdi took much from Marenzio.[8] His opening theme for soprano is like Marenzio's in me-

---

8. For a modern edition of Marenzio's setting see Luca Marenzio, *Sämtliche Werke* 6:41–42.

lodic profile, and from Marenzio he borrowed the idea of combining verses 1 and 2 in his opening point. Monteverdi's affective setting of verse 3 and his freely homophonic setting of verses 4–5 mirror those of the older master, though he characteristically obscured Marenzio's even alternation of semichoirs at "e perderò."

Nevertheless, there remain telling differences between these two settings, differences that bear witness to Monteverdi's Luzzaschian leanings in Book I. Monteverdi sought from the first a darker emotional coloring than Marenzio, avoiding the lilting, canzonetta-like declamation of his predecessor and turning Marenzio's bright major harmonies to minor regions. (Monteverdi's complex double point of imitation here is unique in Book I both in its evocation of the long, supple lines of earlier counterpoint and in the awkward dissonances to which it led its inexperienced composer.) In effect, Monteverdi cast the entire opening of his madrigal in Luzzaschi's affective style, turning to lighter Marenzian gestures only in verses 4 and 5. But even here Monteverdi was more extreme than his model. Marenzio had highlighted the exclamation beginning verse 4 with five-part homophony, slowed rhythms, and a pause in all the voices separating it from what follows (Ex. 2a). Monteverdi, after avoiding a full cadence at the end of verse 3, set "Ahi vita" twice, in slow homophony, to sequential $VII^6 \rightarrow I$ cadences moving first to F and then to C (Ex. 2b). Thus, in the affective amorous complaints of his First Book, Mon-

EXAMPLE 2

(a) Marenzio, "A che tormi il ben mio," mm. 30–37
(*Sämtliche Werke,* ed. Einstein, 6:42)

(b) Monteverdi, "A che tormi il ben mio," mm. 29–36

teverdi betrayed some impatience with the canzonetta-madrigal in the generally greater expressive weight of his music and in his use, in the interest of text expression, of disjunctions of texture more radical than Marenzio would admit. While it is true, then, that Monteverdi had not yet found his voice in 1587, the most striking features of the First Book reveal his search, already at the beginning of his career, for musical means to project compellingly the rhetoric of his texts.

The point is underscored, and some specifically Luzzaschian techniques of Monteverdi's early style are apparent, in another madrigal from Book I, "Baci soavi e cari." The text is the opening stanza of a *canzone* by Giambattista Guarini:

Baci soavi e cari,	Sweet and dear kisses,
cibi della mia vita	sustenance of my life,
c'hor m'involate hor mi rendete il core,	which now steal away, now give back my heart,
per voi convien ch'impari	for your sake I must learn
5 come un'alma rapita	how a stolen heart
non sente il duol di mort'e pur si more.	feels no pain of dying and yet dies.
Quant'ha di dolce amore,	All that is sweet in love,
perché sempr'io vi baci,	whenever I kiss you,
O dolcissime rose,	oh sweetest roses,
10 in voi tutto ripose.	resides in you.
Et s'io potessi ai vostri dolci baci	And if I could, with your sweet kisses,
la mia vita finire,	end my life—
o che dolce morire!	oh what a sweet death!

The end of Monteverdi's setting bears a striking resemblance to the end of Luzzaschi's "Gratie ad amor," part of which I have quoted above (Ex. 3; compare Ex. 1). The similarities here are obvious: the reduced texture at the start, with a descending line in the bottom voice and suspensions above, moving to an incomplete cadence typical of Luzzaschi's style (Monteverdi's two suspended voices, unlike Luzzaschi's one, yield a half cadence), and the almost identical chord progressions in the following four-part homophony (Monteverdi's longer text necessitates his extension of this phrase in measures 47–49). Luzzaschi went on to repeat the phrase on "o

EXAMPLE 3

Monteverdi, "Baci soavi e cari," mm. 42–49

mora" once, rescored for four voices, and that on "o languisca" twice, first transposed up an octave with the parts rearranged, then rescored for five voices. Monteverdi emulated these typical Luzzaschian techniques for extending and varying the musical material. He immediately repeated his setting of "o che dolce morire!" transposed from D to G, rescored for five voices, and with the parts freely rearranged. Then, after returning to canzonetta homophony in order to repeat verse 11 (and thereby repeat his final syntactic period in full), he expanded the three-voice polyphony of "la mia vita finire" to five voices and returned to the dual statement of the final verse with the parts once more rearranged.

Even in a passage so clearly indebted to Luzzaschi as this one, however, two distinguishing features of Monteverdi's early style stand out. On the one hand, Monteverdi's control of dissonance is as yet less sure than Luzzaschi's. In the first statement of "la mia vita finire" he substituted a sixth for Luzzaschi's suspended major seventh and compensated for the resulting blandness with a clumsy simultaneous diminished fourth (B♭-F♯; this sonority, frequent in the First Book, is one that Monteverdi banished from his later *a cappella* madrigals). On the other hand, Monteverdi's harmonic progressions already reveal a stronger sense of tonal direction than Luzzaschi's. He converted Luzzaschi's weakly sequential setting of "o languisca" into an explicit sequence, guided from below by a decisive bassline (D → A / B♭ → F) reminiscent of his *Canzonette*. In later works, with the example of the Mantuan composer Giaches de Wert before him, Monteverdi would more fully exploit such clearly directed harmonic motion.

In addition to Monteverdi's dependence on Luzzaschi, "Baci soavi e cari" also points up the limitations of the young composer's text-setting capabilities in the First Book. Guarini's syntax in this strophe is long-winded at best, contorted and obscure at worst. Monteverdi managed only partially to project it in his music. The complex opening period (vv. 1–6) is constructed of two halves, a vocative antecedent addressing the "Baci" of the opening (vv. 1–3) followed by an independent consequent clause (vv. 4–6). The identical metrical structure of these two phrases, each of two *settenari* (heptasyllabic lines) and an *endecasillabo* (a hendecasyllable), seems to have suggested Monteverdi's somewhat schematic musical response. He accommodated verses 4–5 as a partially transposed repetition of verses 1–2 and then managed to convey a sense of syntactic completion by means of a long affective peroration on verse 6 leading to a full cadence. From here on, however, he was not so successful. Indeed, he seems hardly to have understood Guarini's middle period (vv. 7–10), with its unusual adverbial phrase "perché sempr'io vi baci." He split this period down the middle with a full cadence at the end of verse 8 and an overlong exclamation at the beginning of verse 9. The already difficult syntax is reduced to nonsense. One of the clear signs of Monteverdi's maturation in literary and expressive matters in the 1590s would be his avoidance of texts like this one, texts whose rhetorical gestures did not inspire complementary musical structures.

The Second Book

In his *Secondo libro de madrigali* of 1590 Monteverdi broadened and deepened the youthful eclecticism of the First Book. He broadened it by embracing stylistic traits from recent madrigals of Wert (though this connection would not bear its ripest fruit until the Third, Fourth, and Fifth Books). He deepened it in two ways: in his subtler incorporation of the Luzzaschian affective style of Book I in contrasting musical gestures and especially in his development of Marenzio's canzonetta-madrigal to new expressive ends.

Indeed, the style of the canzonetta-madrigal dominates Book II. But it is a more versatile style now, transcending the monochromatic expressive limitations of the *Canzonette* and the pastoral madrigals of Book I. The best madrigals of the Second Book bear an original and distinctive stamp; they are Monteverdi's earliest master-works. Book II, then, begins with more emulation of Marenzio and includes much that looks back to Book I, but it leads to Monteverdi's personal definition of the canzonetta-madrigal.

Marenzio's presence is explicitly acknowledged in the *alba* that opens the collection, "Non si levava ancor l'alba novella." It borrows numerous elements from Marenzio's "Non vidi mai dopo notturna pioggia," a setting of a Petrarchan strophe from the *Madrigali a quattro voci* of 1585. As is often the case when Monteverdi echoes his own music or that of another composer, the borrowings seem to have been suggested by incidental similarities of wording and assonance between the two texts:[9]

Non si levava ancor l'alba novella	*Non vidi mai* dopo notturna pioggia
né spiegavan le piume	gir per l'aere sereno stelle erranti
gl'augelli al novo lume,	*et fiammeggiar* fra la rugiada e'l gielo,
ma fiammegiava l'amorosa stella	ch'i' non avesse i begli occhi davanti
quando i duo vaghi e leggiadretti amanti. . .	. . . .
	qual io gli vidi a l'ombra d'un bel velo. . . .

The musical similarities between the two madrigals point up some of the most distinctive techniques Monteverdi learned from Marenzio. Monteverdi's opening takes its unusual rhythmic stratification, an upper voice moving in whole notes while a lower voice ascends through the scale in quarter notes, from Marenzio (Exx. 4a and 4b). Like Marenzio, Monteverdi immediately inverted this flexible

---

9. Nino Pirrotta, "Scelte poetiche di Monteverdi," pp. 19–20, has rightly stressed the importance of such modeling in future research on Monteverdi. But his suggestion that the opening of "Non si levava" refers to Wert's "Sorgi e rischiara" should be revised in the light of its closer similarities to "Non vidi mai." See Luca Marenzio, *Ten Madrigals for Mixed Voices,* for a modern edition of "Non vidi mai," whose text is the opening of the fifth strophe of Petrarch's *canzone* "In quella parte dove amor mi sprona." Einstein, *The Italian Madrigal,* p. 722, correctly identified the Marenzian tone of "Non si levava" though not its specific source.

EXAMPLE 4

(a) Marenzio, "Non vidi mai dopo notturna pioggia," beginning
(*Ten Madrigals,* ed. Arnold, p. 14;
quoted by permission of Oxford University Press)

(b) Monteverdi, "Non si levava ancor l'alba novella," beginning

counterpoint and added a third voice in parallel thirds with the ascending voice—thus momentarily creating a texture reminiscent of the villanella. Monteverdi's point of imitation at "ma fiammegiava" borrows its motive ♩♩♪♩♩ ma fiam-me-gia-va, reminiscent of the canzonetta in its sharp rhythmic profile, from Marenzio's setting of the same words. Monteverdi's setting of "quand'i duo . . ." follows Marenzio even more literally (Exx. 5a and 5b). Monteverdi would exploit many of the devices of the canzonetta-madrigal found in this example in his later madrigals: the reduced texture, the blocklike contrast of pairs of voices in parallel thirds, the motivic canzonetta rhythm ♩♪♪♩♩, and the conversion of the duet into a villanella texture by the addition of an independent and melodically disjunct bassline. To be sure, Monteverdi had used some of these techniques already in his First Book; but the example of "Non si levava" demonstrates that Marenzio was his guide in their incorporation in madrigalian polyphony.

A final borrowing, from the *seconda parte* of Monteverdi's two-section madrigal, shows him imitating one of the subtlest of Marenzio's text-setting devices (Exx. 6a and 6b). Here Marenzio had exploited the bipolar villanella texture to bind a dependent participial phrase to its independent consequent, stating one clause in the bassline, the other simultaneously in the parallel thirds above: "così bagnati ancora / li veggio sfavillare, ond'io sempre ardo" ("thus still bathed in tears / I see them glisten, whence I ever burn"). Monteverdi put the technique to similar syntactic use, revealing a strikingly perceptive understanding of Marenzio's methods and at the same time foreshadowing his own rhetorical exploitation of villanella

EXAMPLE 5

(a) Marenzio, "Non vidi mai dopo notturna pioggia," mm. 44–49
(*Ten Madrigals,* ed. Arnold, pp. 18–19;
quoted by permission of Oxford University Press)

(b) Monteverdi, "Non si levava ancor l'alba novella," mm. 31–36

EXAMPLE 6

(a) Marenzio, "Non vidi mai dopo notturna pioggia," mm. 65–69
(*Ten Madrigals,* ed. Arnold, p. 21;
quoted by permission of Oxford University Press)

(b) Monteverdi, "Non si levava ancor l'alba novella," mm. 67–71

textures in the Fourth and Fifth Books: "e come d'alma che si part'e svella / fu la partenza loro" ("and like a soul that departs and is torn from its body / was their separation").

In Example 6b Monteverdi even copied Marenzio's undercut cadence moving to VI. Unlike Marenzio, however, and perhaps revealing the organizational teachings of his mentor Ingegneri, Monteverdi exploited this gesture to achieve a structural coherence extending across the whole of his long madrigal. He had already planted this deceptive harmonic move in his opening theme (see Ex. 4b above). He recalled it with the return of this opening passage at the end of the *prima parte*. (The text at this point—"scopria quest'alma innamorata, e quella," "this enamored soul and that discovered"—is unrelated to the opening line, which the music originally set. The musical reprise results from structural, not text-expressive, concerns.) He returned to it a second time, once again with the opening music, midway through the *seconda parte,* at "E innanzi a l'alba che nel ciel sorgea" ("And before the dawn that broke in the heavens"; here the musical refrain has a text-expressive as well as a structural rationale, linking this line to the similar opening verse: "The new dawn was not yet breaking"). When, finally, this deceptive move returns again in Example 6b, it associates this villanella texture unmistakably with the opening gesture of the *prima parte* and its two reprises. The effect is of a third reprise, now varied extensively. This elegant structural logic disappoints only in that it is largely irrelevant to the musical expression of the text. In later madrigals Monteverdi would succeed in integrating more fully the structural and rhetorical dimensions of his settings.

The text of "Non si levava" is a lengthy madrigal by Torquato Tasso. No fewer than nine settings of Tasso's verse in Book II proclaim Monteverdi's first discovery of this poet.[10] But it was not yet the poet of the epic *Gerusalemme liberata* that attracted Monteverdi nor even, for the most part, the purveyor of the amorous trials and sorrowful separations of "Non si levava." Rather, in poems like "Dolcissimi legami," "Non sono in queste rive," and "Mentr'io mirava fiso," Monteverdi sought out witty trifles on the words, lips, and eyes of the poet's beloved.

These choices reflect a literary tendency in the Second Book that sets it apart from the First—a tendency also apparent in the four madrigals here by Girolamo Casone, the two by Filippo Alberti, the one by Ercole Bentivoglio, and the anonymous "Intorno a due vermiglie e vaghe labra." All these poems stand in the tradition of late-*cinquecento* lyrics that anticipates most conspicuously the impersonal, descriptive, and image-oriented verse of Giambattista Marino.[11] Their authors

10. The authors of all but one of the poems set in Book II are given in Claudio Monteverdi, *Madrigali a 5 voci, libro secondo,* pp. 42–46. The identification of Tasso as the author of "Crudel, perché mi fuggi?" is erroneous; it was published in 1599, with the first word changed ("Lasso, perché mi fuggi?"), in *Rime del molto illustre Signor Cavaliere Battista Guarini.*

11. Pirrotta, "Scelte poetiche," p. 20, refers to the "madrigalismo descrittivo" of the Second Book. On Marino see Gary Tomlinson, "Music and the Claims of Text," and chaps. 6–10 below.

turn away from the torments and paradoxes of the lover's state that had inspired the affective style in Monteverdi's First Book. Instead the poets are concerned with external objects and images of love: flowers, stars, gems, and the like. They sacrifice the contemplation of love's emotions to a description of its glittering appurtenances. Thus they offer extravagant celebrations of the physical attributes of the beloved:

Non sono in queste rive	There are not on these shores
fiori così vermigli	flowers so red
come le labra de la donna mia. . . .	as the lips of my lady. . . .

Or, participating in a thematic tradition reaching at least back to Catullus, they extol the happy state of objects closer to the beloved than they:

Quell'ombra esser vorrei	I'd like to be that shadow,
che'l dì vi segue leggiadretta e bella;	graceful and pretty, that follows you all day,
ché, s'or son servo, i' sarei	because, if I'm your servant now, I'd be your
vostr'ancella. . . .	handmaid. . . .

Or, finally, they traffic in the stock similes of all amorous poetic traditions, likening the beloved's lips to roses and her words to stars and jewels:

Intorno a due vermiglie e vaghe labra	Around two pretty, vermilion lips,
di cui rose più belle	more beautiful than
non ha la primavera,	any roses in springtime,
volan soavi baci a schiera a schiera;	flies host upon host of sweet kisses;
e son più che ha le stelle	and there are, more than the stars
in ciel puro e sereno,	in a clear, serene sky,
più che ha le gemme de la terra in seno,	more than the jewels in the earth's bosom,
motti sonori od amorosi o casti. . . .	musical or amorous or chaste words. . . .

It is significant that this sort of proto-Marinist lyric, though it represents only one facet of Tasso's huge and varied *canzoniere,* epitomizes that of the Pavian philosophy professor and sometime rhymster Girolamo Casone.[12] Nino Pirrotta has suggested that Casone may have played a personal role in determining the new literary orientation of Monteverdi's Second Book; perhaps Casone even introduced the young composer to a group of admirers of Tasso that he had gathered around him in Pavia or Milan.[13] This is an attractive suggestion, and one that inspires further speculation. For if Casone introduced Monteverdi to Tasso's lyrics, it is clear from the texts set in Book II that he introduced him specifically to the poems of Tasso most congenial to his own literary bent. And these poems inhabit a poetic world different from that of the passionate epic verse of Tasso that Monteverdi

12. See his *Rime del Signor Girolamo Casone da Oderzo,* published in 1598.
13. "Scelte poetiche," pp. 16–17. Book II is dedicated to Giacomo Ricardi, president of the senate and Catholic council in Milan. In the dedication Monteverdi refers to a visit he made to Milan, during which he played the viol for Ricardi; see Claudio Monteverdi, *Lettere, dediche, e prefazioni,* pp. 383–84.

settled on in his next two books of madrigals and to which he would return, during the 1620s, with the composition of the *Combattimento di Tancredi et Clorinda*. In fact, with only one exception Tasso's lyric verse disappeared completely from Monteverdi's published works after Book II, supplanted by *ottave* from his *Gerusalemme liberata* and *Conquistata*.[14] The import of this shift is clear. Monteverdi's mature valuation of Tasso—"the divine Tasso, . . . a poet who expresses with all propriety and naturalness in his language those passions that he tends to want to describe"[15]— was inspired by the poet's epic, not his lyric, verse and is signaled in Monteverdi's Third Book of 1592. It is not evident, and indeed is hardly foreshadowed, in Book II. If Casone led Monteverdi, then, he led him in a direction that the composer would repudiate already two years later.

On the basis of the many lyrics by Tasso set in Book II, Pirrotta has perceived a link between it and Tasso's dialogue *La Cavaletta* (published in 1587), with its famous plea to Alessandro Striggio, Wert, and Luzzaschi to reestablish a serious and weighty style in Italian secular music.[16] But my distinction of two stages in Monteverdi's reading of Tasso, the first discovering the poet's amorous lyrics in the manner of Casone, the second turning away from these to the impassioned and serious *Gerusalemme liberata,* runs counter to this view. Most of Tasso's lyrics in Book II are not ones the poet himself would have considered worthy of critical notice in *La Cavaletta*. This is clear from his restriction of his discussion there to those lyric genres legitimized by their inclusion in Petrarch's *Canzoniere*: the sonnet, *ballata, canzone,* and fourteenth-century *madrigale* (but not, of course, its free-formed sixteenth-century variety). In the Tasso lyrics of Book II the flickering passions of some of the texts of Book I—their frequent talk of death, afflicted hearts, bitter martyrdoms, and the like—are extinguished. To set Tasso's poems Monteverdi turned to a style even less weighty than that of the Luzzaschian affective madrigals of the First Book. He moved, in other words, away from the reform that Tasso had called for in *La Cavaletta*. The style that he settled on, the limpid and dispassionate canzonetta-madrigal of Marenzio, did not show a conscious effort to answer the plea of *La Cavaletta*. On the contrary, it was the very style that had probably prompted Tasso's complaint in the first place.[17]

Most of the twenty-one works of Book II display stylistic trappings of the canzonetta-madrigal, but nine madrigals found in a nearly unbroken series in the first half of the collection do so particularly clearly. On stylistic grounds, these

14. The exception is "Al lume delle stelle" in Book VII.

15. From the preface to Book VIII (*Madrigali guerrieri, et amorosi,* 1638); reprinted in facsimile in Monteverdi, *Tutte le opere,* vol. 8; translated in Strunk, *Source Readings,* pp. 53–55.

16. "Scelte poetiche," pp. 17–19; for Tasso's plea see Torquato Tasso, *Opere* 5:150.

17. Pirrotta's argument is weakened also by Monteverdi's modeling of "Non si levava" not on a work of Wert but on one of Marenzio, a composer whom Tasso (pointedly?) ignored in *La Cavaletta*.

works can be separated into three groups. Their increasing sureness of technique, maturity of expression, and stylistic originality suggest that the ordering of these groups preserves at least an approximate chronology of their composition:

GROUP 1	III.	"Bevea Fillide mia"	(Casone)
	IV.	"Dolcissimi legami"	(Tasso)
	V.	"Non giacinti o narcisi"	(Casone)
	VI.	"Intorno a due vermiglie e vaghe labra"	
GROUP 2	VII.	"Non sono in queste rive"	(Tasso)
	VIII.	"Tutte le bocche belle"	(Alberti)
GROUP 3	XI.	"S'andasse Amor a caccia"	(Tasso)
	XII.	"Mentr'io mirava fiso"	(Tasso)
	XIII.	"Ecco mormorar l'onde"	(Tasso)

The four madrigals of group 1 reveal an impersonal appropriation of Marenzio's canzonetta-madrigal reminiscent of the pastoral madrigals of Book I. We have already noted many features of this style in "Non si levava" (which, apart from its ambitious dimensions and the semidramatic dialogue of its *seconda parte,* shares much with the works of group 1): the quick, motivic melodies, featuring rhythms such as ♩♪♪♩♩ , ♩|♩.♪♩♩|♩ , and ♩♩♩♩♪♪|♩ ; the frequent use of reduced textures, especially of two and three voices, and the avoidance of true imitation in favor of the staggered alternation of such groupings; and the polarized texture of the villanella. To these we may add characteristics we have noted in the madrigals of Book I: a generally syllabic delivery of text, with few melismas and much declamation on eighth notes, brief Marenzian shifts to triple meter, and passages of four- and five-part homophony in the canzonetta rhythms enumerated above.

The most striking feature of the madrigals of group 1, however, is their bland treatment of the text. Aside from "Dolcissimi legami," where talk of "bonds" and "chains" inspired Marenzian pictorialisms reminiscent of the pastoral madrigals of the First Book, these works display little effort to project the meaning or rhetoric of their texts. (There is no question here, as we have noted, of the affective style of Book I. Languishing, drawn-out, dissonant music could have little place in setting such dispassionate texts.) It is true that Monteverdi's texts afforded fewer obvious opportunities for musical depiction than the pastoral rhymes of the First Book; but even when such opportunities arose Monteverdi was loathe to seize on them, passing without musical comment by such words as *fior, volan, stelle,* and *augei.* He seems consciously to have chosen here the largely neutral approach to the meaning and rhetoric of the poetry that is a debilitating feature of many canzonetta-madrigals. Only gradually, with texts more forceful in their expression of passion than these, did Monteverdi come to command the musical means to capture and heighten the rhetorical profile of his texts.

He took a hesitant step in this direction already in the two works I have placed together in group 2. Both employ striking harmonic disjunctions to convey important syntactic breaks in their texts: the move from C to E major at "Né il suon" in "Non sono in queste rive" (a move echoed later, with text-expressive intent, at "più dolce armonia") and the move from C to A major at the exclamation "Oh, perché non potessi" in "Tutte le bocche belle." In each madrigal the effect of disjunction is enhanced by an emphatic full cadence on C just before the surprising move. The technique anticipates the decisive harmonic reorientation midway through one of Monteverdi's most famous madrigals, "A un giro sol de' begli occhi lucenti" from the Fourth Book. But there Guarini's text, with its moving (if familiar) turn from the description of the serene natural surroundings to the contemplation of the poet's wretched state, allowed Monteverdi to sustain the emotional shift effected by his harmonic move till the end of the work. Here neither text permitted such encompassing musical rhetoric. In "Non sono in queste rive" and "Tutte le bocche belle" the unexpected moves turn out to be only momentary ruffles in the otherwise placid surface of unremarkable canzonetta-madrigals.

The second novel feature that sets these two pieces apart is their inclusion of many lengthy melismas. Here Monteverdi developed the brief melismas of the pastoral madrigals of Book I into extended florid passages, reminiscent of the "luxuriant style" that Anthony Newcomb has traced to the rise in popularity of the Ferrarese singing ladies in the early 1580s.[18] As in the First Book, these melismas are usually though not always employed with pictorial intent, at words like *l'aure, canto,* and *ch'intorno* (contrast *queste,* "these," in "Non sono in queste rive"); in this they increase the frequency of madrigalisms here over the works of group 1. But they affect Monteverdi's style in a more profound way as well. Once in each of these works he underlaid florid duets in the upper voices with slowly descending basslines (at "canto che m'ardi e piaci" in "Non sono in queste rive" and "ch'intorno a gli occhi miei" in "Tutte le bocche belle"). The result is a villanella-like texture without the homophony usual in the villanella; substituting for it is the Marenzian rhythmic independence we noted at the beginning of "Non si levava." The upper voices pursue their illustration of the text while the bass provides a clear structural underpinning for the texture. Monteverdi was quick to perceive the two-fold potential, at once expressive and structurally unambiguous, of this device. He exploited it, now with basslines plunging through an eleventh, in two of the canzonetta-madrigals of our group 3.[19]

"S'andasse Amor a caccia," "Mentr'io mirava fiso," and "Ecco mormorar l'onde" show Monteverdi's canzonetta-madrigal in its most mature state. The

---

18. *The Madrigal at Ferrara* 1:76–89.
19. Leo Schrade, *Monteverdi,* pp. 140–41, and Carolyn Gianturco, *Claudio Monteverdi,* pp. 22,
25–28, discuss this technique and other similar descending basslines in Book II.

three works are tailored, so to speak, from the same musico-poetic fabric. They all set madrigals by Tasso. They all exhibit the same tonal type, one not found before this in Monteverdi's works (soft hexachord, F final, identical normal cleffing of $C_1C_1C_3C_4F_4$). They cling to their common tonic of F with an obstinacy unprecedented in Monteverdi's madrigals—so much so that in "S'andasse Amor" not one of the six internal cadences-with-suspension is on any other hexachordal degree. (The two other works cadence away from F only slightly more frequently.) All three madrigals employ a contrapuntal texture new for Monteverdi, featuring prominent vertical combinations of distinct motives setting different phrases of text. To facilitate the writing of this double and triple counterpoint Monteverdi often used relatively slow, monotonal motives, which readily combine with the canzonetta motives of groups 1 and 2.[20] All three works extend the novelties of group 2: "S'andasse Amor" and "Ecco mormorar" exploit their florid writing, while "Mentr'io mirava" shares their move to distant harmonic areas for expressive ends (at "mille sospiri"). And, finally, two traits more difficult to define unite these madrigals: a structural coherence of a rigor unknown in Monteverdi's earlier works and a maturing ability to capture in music the meaning and syntactic organization of the text.

All these characteristics, and especially the last, are exemplified in the most famous madrigal of Book II, "Ecco mormorar l'onde." Its text is a fourteen-line depiction of a pastoral dawn—landscape poetry of a sort in which Tasso excelled:

Ecco mormorar l'onde,	Now the waves murmur,
e tremolar le fronde	and the boughs and the shrubs tremble
a l'aura mattutina e gl'arboscelli,	in the morning breeze,
e sovra i verdi rami i vagh'augelli	and on the green branches the pleasant birds
5 cantar soavemente,	sing softly
e rider l'oriente.	and the east smiles;
Ecco già l'alba appare	now dawn already appears
e si specchia nel mare,	and mirrors herself in the sea,
e rasserena il cielo,	and makes the sky serene,
10 e imperla il dolce gielo,[21]	and impearls the fields,
e gl'alti monti indora.	and gilds the high mountains:
O bell'e vagh'aurora,	o beautiful and gracious Aurora,
l'aura è tua messagiera, e tu	the breeze is your messenger, and you the
dell'aura	breeze's
ch'ogn'arso cor ristaura.	which revives each burnt-out heart.

(trans. Luciano Rebay, *Italian Poetry*)

20. The view of such motives as an anticipation of seventeenth-century monodic styles (see, for example, Einstein, *The Italian Madrigal*, pp. 722–23) is a distorting one; it at once underestimates the melodic variety of monody and ignores the frequent use of monotonal declamatory gestures throughout the history of the *frottola* and polyphonic madrigal.

21. Tasso's line is an *endecasillabo*—"e le campagne imperla il dolce gielo"—providing a direct object for "imperla" and making "il dolce gielo" the subject of lines 10–11. Monteverdi's version is syntactically tightened if less varied, with "il dolce gielo" as object and only one subject, "l'alba," for lines 7–11. I have altered the translation given here to reflect Monteverdi's version.

The text itself provides a clue to one source of the novel elements in Monteverdi's setting. It resembles in subject and wording another of Tasso's poetic landscapes, the description of the enchanted garden of Armida from *Gerusalemme liberata,* which Wert had set in his *Ottavo libro de madrigali a cinque voci* of 1586:

Vezzosi augelli infra le verdi fronde	The joyous birds, hid under greenwood shade
temprano a prova lascivette note.	sung merry notes on every branch and bough;
Mormora l'aura, e fa le foglie e l'onde	the wind, that in the leaves and waters play'd,
garrir, che variamente ella percote.	with murmur sweet now sang, and whistled now;
Quando taccion gli augelli, alto risponde;	ceased the birds, the wind loud answer made,
quando cantan gli augei, più lieve scote;	and while they sung it rumbled soft and low:
sia caso od arte, or accompagna, ed ora	thus, were it hap or cunning, chance or art
alterna i versi lor la musica 'ôra.	the wind in this strange music bore his part.
(XVI, 12)	(trans. Edward Fairfax, *Jerusalem Delivered*)

As in "Non si levava," the textual similarities inspired a musical relationship as well.[22] The tonal type of Wert's work is identical to that of Monteverdi's, and "Vezzosi augelli" also steadfastly adheres to its F tonic, cadencing only twice, in passing, on C. It opens with the same monotonal murmuring in the lower voices as "Ecco mormorar," suggesting a source for Monteverdi's frequent use of such single-note motives in our group 3. "Vezzosi augelli" also provides a model for two traits that set "Ecco mormorar" somewhat apart from its companions "S'andasse Amor" and "Mentr'io mirava": a prominent use of villanella texture and frequent E♭ inflections of the "F-major" tonality. Most important, "Vezzosi augelli" betrays unmistakably the heritage in Wert's works of Monteverdi's new techniques of multiple counterpoint, of simultaneously declaiming different text phrases set to distinct motives in a contrapuntal texture. Wert's opening beautifully juxtaposes the canzonetta-like delivery of the first two verses with the "murmuring breezes" of the third (Ex. 7). In similar fashion Monteverdi combined the motives setting verses 1–3 of "Ecco mormorar" in a spacious exposition lasting twenty-six measures.[23] In neither Wert's madrigal nor Monteverdi's is this procedure an example of the *laceramento della poesia* (laceration of the poetry) deplored by the Florentine theorist Vincenzo Galilei and Einstein alike. Quite the opposite: both composers realized, through their ability to present simultaneously text phrases describing different natural sounds, the composite sonorous nature picture that the poet could

22. Arnold, "Monteverdi and His Teachers," p. 108, has noted the connection between these two madrigals. For a modern edition of Wert's see Giaches de Wert, *Opera Omnia* 8:11–14.

23. Monteverdi's exposition also recalls other recent madrigals by Wert. I have noted its textual and musical relation to "Ecco ch'un altra volta" from the Ninth Book of 1588 (see Gary Tomlinson, "Madrigal, Monody, and Monteverdi's *via*

naturale alla immitatione," pp. 68–69n), and Carl Dahlhaus, in a lengthy analysis of "Ecco mormorar," has pointed out its more extensive similarities to Wert's "Io non son però morto" from Book VIII of 1586 (see "*Ecco mormorar l'onde,*" pp. 144–46). It seems clear that Monteverdi's musical conception took form under the influence, powerful if perhaps not entirely conscious, of various madrigals by Wert.

EXAMPLE 7

Wert, "Vezzosi augelli in fra le verdi fronde," beginning
(*Opera Omnia,* ed. MacClintock and Bernstein, 8:11;
quoted by permission of Armen Carapetyan)

only imply. Polyphony transcended a limitation of text, and an ostensibly anti-poetic device was turned to a text–expressive end. So Monteverdi's use of this technique is not, as Einstein maintained, an "instrumental element . . . not in harmony with the classical ideal [of the madrigal]."[24] Rather it was a new, structural means of semantic expression, outreaching by far the traditional pictorialisms of the canzonetta–madrigal.

Monteverdi, then, had much to learn from Wert, and in Book II he capitalized

24. *The Italian Madrigal,* p. 723; on Wert's *laceramento della poesia* see p. 516.

on his first lessons. As regards the structural integrity of his madrigals, however, he was already his own master, and extended and deepened the techniques he had learned from Ingegneri. In "Ecco mormorar" the bassline's descent of a sixth at the end of the first main section (mm. 21–24) is a transposition down two octaves of the descent in the *canto* near its beginning (mm. 7–10; the point is strengthened by near-octaves between bass and *canto,* where there had been near-fifths before). Both descending lines foreshadow the slower descent of an eleventh in the bass near the end of the madrigal (mm. 72–82). This musical structure reflects a poetic one: all three descending lines set a verse referring to the morning breezes (vv. 3 and 13). The strongest musical articulations in the piece, all full cadences on F, occur at the end of the long exposition in multiple counterpoint (m. 26) and at the two main syntactic breaks in the poem (after vv. 6 and 11; mm. 39 and 67). The cadence at measure 67 is elided to what follows, but Monteverdi insured a marked sense of articulation here by returning to the music that had begun the second period at measure 40 (compare "Ecco già l'alba appare" and "O bell'e vagh'aurora"). Finally, a thematic unity reminiscent of Ingegneri rules the piece even where literal repetition is absent: the themes setting verses 4, 6, and 9 are all variations on the same scalar ascent from F to C, and the longer line setting verse 11 seems to grow out of the last of these.

Such rigorously unified musical treatment was ideally suited to Tasso's "Ecco mormorar l'onde." (The same is not true for his "S'andasse Amor a caccia," where a similarly unified musical structure is evident.) Tasso's madrigal is a repetitive, paratactic listing of the refreshing attributes of the dawn, with virtually no syntactic variety until its final three verses. It makes its effect through insistent anaphora and isocolon, both broken off only at the last moment with an allusion to the poet's lovesick state. The sameness of Monteverdi's setting becomes in this context a compelling force in the communication of the poet's meaning (and it is tempting to suppose, with the similarly rigorous coherence of "S'andasse Amor" in mind, that Monteverdi appreciated this only gradually, as he adapted the style of the other group 3 works to this text). In addition, this overarching unity allowed the composer to indulge frequently in pictorial madrigalisms without fear of breaking down the work into a series of disconnected musico-poetic images. And for Tasso's twist at the end Monteverdi had a musical response at hand. The affective style of Book I, gentler now and purged of its awkward dissonances, here made its decorous entrance into Monteverdi's mature canzonetta-madrigal as a fitting musico-rhetorical peroration.

Six of the ten remaining madrigals of the Second Book take the style of the canzonetta-madrigal as their starting point, amplifying and enriching it according to the particular needs of their texts:

XIV. "Dolcemente dormiva la mia Clori" (Tasso)

XV. "Se tu mi lassi, perfida, tuo danno!" (Tasso)

XVI. "La bocca onde l'asprissime parole" (Bentivoglio)

XVII. "Crudel, perché mi fuggi?" (Guarini)

XIX. "Non m'è grave il morire" (Bartolomeo Gottifredi)

XX. "Ti spontò l'ali, Amor, la donna mia" (Alberti)

All six works occur near the end of the collection, and in style they suggest a later composition than that of the canzonetta-madrigals discussed above, one dependent on the advances won in those works. The neutral or at best pictorial approach to text expression in most of those canzonetta-madrigals gives way in these works to the new sensitivity to the musical projection of poetic syntax we have seen in "Ecco mormorar l'onde." Monteverdi has begun to understand that music can enhance the significance of poetry not only through stock iconic gestures matched to it but also through the projection of its rhetorical structure.

"Dolcemente dormiva la mia Clori," on Tasso's madrigal describing the stealing of a kiss from a sleeping shepherdess, is a work in the style of "Ecco mormorar" with two important additions: a new use of the trio of lower voices for striking pictorial representation at "Dolcemente dormiva" ("Sweetly was sleeping") and "Allor io mi chinai" ("Then I bent down"), and the use of emphatic four- and five-part homophony and staggered exclamations to reflect the poet's urgent desire. "Non m'è grave il morire" is an advanced structural essay, bridging the distance between "Ecco mormorar" and the famous "Ah dolente partita," published at the head of Book IV but composed by 1597. To the problem posed by Gottifredi's lengthy and pedestrian opening period—

Non m'è grave il morire,	It pains me not to die,
donna, per aquetar vostro desire,	lady, to soothe your longing,
anzi il viver m'annoia,	indeed my life's a bother
sapendo esser voler vostro ch'io moia	knowing that you desire that I die

—Monteverdi conceived an effective solution: a forty-measure exposition in the manner of "Ecco mormorar," superimposing musical statements of the syntactically dependent lines 1–4. (Monteverdi ingeniously enhanced the poet's amplification of line 1 in line 3 by juxtaposing contrasting motives setting these verses *before* the weaker, vocative line 2 is heard. Note here the typical contrast, as in "Ecco mormorar," between the slow-moving, monotonal motive setting line 1 and the canzonetta motives setting lines 2 and 3.) A homophonic recitation of the following two lines in canzonetta rhythms forms the brief middle section of the piece, and a lengthy affective peroration exaggerates the pathos of the last lines—"e vi vedessi a sorte / lagrimar per pietà de la mia morte" ("and if perchance I saw you / weeping out of pity for my death")—and provides a structural counterbalance for the huge exposition.[25]

"Crudel, perché mi fuggi?," the only setting of Guarini's verse in the Second Book, shows an oratorical use of the low-pitched trio of "Dolcemente dormiva" to declaim the poet's opening question, and extreme disjunctions of rhythm and style in the setting of the poem's punch line—"e doler non si pò chi non ha core!" ("and he who has no heart cannot feel pain!")—that extend the Luzzaschian style of Book I and anticipate Gesualdo. But most novel here is Monteverdi's discriminating use of homophonic declamation, in which the weight of each cadence is carefully attuned to poetic syntax (Ex. 8). The division of Guarini's question at its midpoint neatly underscores his alliteration: "Credi tu per fuggire, / crudel, farmi morire?" ("Do you believe by fleeing, / cruel one, you'll make me die?"). More important, the half cadence at "fuggire" thrusts us forward to its resolution at "morire," that is, to the completion of the question. And the phrase "Ah, non si pò morir" is made to follow breathlessly, a musical as well as poetic exclamation.

This same subtle use of homophonic declamation to reflect poetic syntax dominates "Se tu mi lassi, perfida, tuo danno!" This work, unique in Book II in its almost unbroken homophony, probably reveals a second facet of Wert's forceful impact on Monteverdi. For, as "Ecco mormorar" was Monteverdi's answer to the pastoral side of Wert's *Gerusalemme liberata* settings of 1586, "Se tu mi lassi" seems to reflect their more emotional aspects: the fury of the abandoned Armida that Wert portrayed in "Qual musico gentil, prima che chiara" and "Forsennata gridava."[26] In fact, in its passionate emotion "Se tu mi lassi" is exceptional among the Tasso lyrics of Book II. Monteverdi may well have chosen it with the outbursts of Wert's Armida in mind.

Monteverdi's style in this work shows numerous features borrowed from Wert. At "se miseria stimassi" his three-voice semichoir substitutes *fauxbourdon*-like parallel six-chords for the expected villanella texture of duet and independent bassline—a striking and archaic element of Wert's mature style that would play an increasingly prominent role in Monteverdi's subsequent madrigals. At "Misera e tu" Monteverdi enlivened his five-part homophony by staggering first one, then another of his voices, another technique typical of Wert's homophonic declamatory style. But most reminiscent of Wert is the rhythmic and harmonic profile of the homophony itself. It often moves now in fluid, additive rhythmic patterns of quarter and half notes, patterns carefully sculpted to the declamation of the text, instead of in the clipped, schematic rhythms of the canzonetta-madrigal. The declamatory rhythms of the text determine the musical rhythms in a manner reminis-

25. For a somewhat different conception of the structure of this work see Monteverdi, *Madrigali a 5 voci, libro secondo*, p. 27.
26. The homophonic style of "Se tu mi lassi,"

then, seems to me to have little to do with the Venetian style that Einstein offers as its source (*The Italian Madrigal*, p. 722).

cent of the *madrigale arioso* of the 1550s, and the strong sense of metric regularity typical of the canzonetta-madrigal is thus weakened (Ex. 9).

The harmonic progressions in Example 9 are dominated (except for the brief shift to the affective style at "misera") by root progressions of interlocking fourths and fifths that give to modern ears the impression of an easy vacillation between a minor key and its major relative. These progressions are also characteristic of Wert. In the next chapter we shall trace them to his earliest works and suggest that they represent there self-conscious echoes of improvisational harmonic schemes like the *passamezzo antico* and *Romanesca*.

The four remaining madrigals of Book II stand apart from those already discussed: they are not canzonetta-madrigals and owe little or nothing to the style of Marenzio. In his setting of the quatrains of Pietro Bembo's sonnet "Cantai un tempo, e se fu dolce il canto," which ends the collection, Monteverdi matched to the old-fashioned verse "an archaistic motet-like style," as Einstein noted, "with luxuriant melismas and an uninterrupted flow of the five voices, somewhat in the

EXAMPLE 8

Monteverdi, "Crudel, perché mi fuggi?," mm. 32–37

EXAMPLE 9

Monteverdi, "Se tu mi lassi, perfida, tuo danno!," mm. 7–15

style of the Rore of 1542 or 1544 or of Willaert's *Musica nova*."[27] Einstein's intuition did not lead him astray. "Cantai un tempo" seems to present yet another case of Monteverdi's youthful *imitatio*; it is modeled on the opening madrigal of Rore's First Book for five voices of 1542, "Cantai, mentre ch'i arsi, del mio foco."[28] The similarities of wording and theme of the two texts are manifest even in their *capoversi*, and the tonal types of the two works are identical: soft hexachord, G final, high clefs. Moreover, the particular system of clefs employed by Monteverdi ($G_2C_2C_3C_3F_3$) suggests the studied archaism of his music. For while it had been Rore's preferred high-clef system, occurring in fifteen of his seventeen five-voice madrigals written in high clefs, Monteverdi used it only three times in all his madrigals—here and in two of the other conservative works now under discussion. Finally, Monteverdi's opening point of imitation has the quality of a parody of Rore's. Rhythms and some pitches are changed, but the melodic profiles and order of entrance of the voices are retained. (Melodic similarities also occur later in the work but less tellingly. They could well be chance artifacts of the identity of tonal type of the two madrigals.)

The archaic style of "Cantai un tempo" and its imitation of Rore suggest that it was one of Monteverdi's student exercises with Ingegneri; the fact that he did not set (or at least did not bother to publish) the whole of Bembo's sonnet adds weight to the hypothesis. In any case, the work reveals Monteverdi's sure understanding of Rore's early style. It shows a preference for full imitative textures and long, non-motivic imitative subjects; an avoidance of homophonic texture and simultaneous text declamation; a composite rhythmic motion on almost every quarter note after the opening and infrequent or undercut cadential articulations; an avoidance of long melismas except for occasional madrigalisms (as on "canto"; compare "cantai" at the corresponding spot in Rore's work); and no declamation on notes shorter than the quarter note. For all its character of a student exercise, then, "Cantai un tempo" is a significant work. It tells us that Monteverdi was solidly grounded in the mid-sixteenth-century contrapuntal *ars perfecta* and that he appreciated the differences between this art and his own modern practices already by 1590, a decade before Artusi first attacked him.

"Donna, nel mio ritorno," "Quell'ombra esser vorrei," and "Questo specchio ti dono!" compose a final group of works that also shows most of these characteristics, though in less insistent form than "Cantai un tempo." (The first two of these works share with "Cantai un tempo" Rore's high-clef arrangement.) These madrigals too revert to a retrospective style: the largely text-neutral, uniform idiom of

27. *The Italian Madrigal*, p. 722. Pirrotta, "Scelte poetiche," pp. 16-17nn, sees in the choice of Bembo's poetry another manifestation of Casone's influence on Monteverdi.
28. For a modern edition see Cipriano de Rore, *Opera Omnia* 2:1–4. Martha Feldman, in a private communication, has identified the author of Rore's text as the Venetian poet Giovanni Brevio.

Ingegneri that Monteverdi had employed in the cycle "Ardo sì, ma non t'amo" from Book I. And, as these are the last works in which Monteverdi looked back to this style, so the Second Book was the last in which he styled himself "Discepolo del Signor Ingegneri" on the title page.

That Monteverdi should have chosen to set Tasso's madrigal "Donna, nel mio ritorno" in this unventuresome style is not surprising. The poem itself is retrospective, moving in the complex, reasoned periods of the mid–sixteenth-century discursive madrigal; its difficult semantic and syntactic structures hardly suggest any musical responses specifically reflective of them.[29] The situation is different with Girolamo Casone's madrigals "Quell'ombra esser vorrei" and "Questo specchio ti dono!" These poems are indistinguishable from the lyrics Monteverdi had set as canzonetta-madrigals near the beginning of Book II—poems like "Bevea Fillide mia" and "Dolcissimi legami." They all share the imagistic, dispassionate proto-Marinist style described above. And this poetic connection suggests a musical paradox: there is an underlying expressive affinity between Monteverdi's canzonetta-madrigals and his works in the style of Ingegneri. Both idioms, the old and the new, for all their obvious differences, provide largely neutral musical settings for their texts. They are different musical symptoms of the same literary malaise: poetry that, owing to its undistinctive rhetorical structure and especially to its imagistic content, is not susceptible of compelling musical expression.

Such poetry dominates the first half of Book II and may, as we have suggested, represent the temporary influence of Casone's poetic ideals on the young Monteverdi. It led the composer, in any case, to canzonetta-madrigals of an expressive neutrality rarely seen in Book I. "Ecco mormorar l'onde" breaks—indeed transcends—these bounds through a use of newly mastered techniques and a happy meshing of repetitive rhetoric in music and verse. From then on the poetry of the Second Book shows a widened range of style and situation, to which Monteverdi responded with a technical versatility building on the most advanced of the canzonetta-madrigals. The works near the end of Book II look to the future in their most salient features—the homophonic declamation of "Se tu mi lassi," the precise rhetorical projection of "Crudel, perché mi fuggi?," the structural play of "Non m'è grave il morire." Perhaps only this forward-looking stylistic breadth encouraged Monteverdi to make, in publishing "Cantai un tempo," a graceful bow to the past.

29. On the discursive madrigal see Ulrich Schulz-Buschhaus, *Das Madrigal,* chap. B.III, and chap. 4 below.

3

Wert, Tasso,
and the Heroic Style
(Book III)

ONTEVERDI'S APPRECIATION OF TASSO, hesitant and secondhand in Book II, matured notably by 1592, when he published his *Terzo libro de madrigali*. The work that fascinated him now was the epic poem *Gerusalemme liberata*. So much so that he put aside almost completely the "madrigalismo descrittivo" of many texts of Book II: there are no lyric poems by either Tasso or Casone here. The amorous trifling of 1590 gave way to amorous passion in 1592.

The Third Book was Monteverdi's first publication since leaving Cremona and the environs of his youth and entering the service of Duke Vincenzo Gonzaga of Mantua. It betrays in various ways the impact of his new surroundings. First of all, it is in Einstein's words "filled with the presence of the *tre dame*"—not, undoubtedly, the singing ladies of Ferrara as Einstein supposed but the rival *concerto* formed at Mantua in the late 1580s.[1] At least nine of its fifteen texts are the work of Guarini, whose ties to Duke Vincenzo dated back as far as 1579 and who resided sporadically at Mantua from December 1591 to July 1593.[2] Most important, Monteverdi's Third Book reveals even more explicitly than the Second the musical and literary tutelage of Giaches de Wert, by now the semiretired luminary of the Mantuan musical establishment.

Monteverdi was not untouched by Wert's music before he moved from Cremona; we have noted its impact in the multiple counterpoint and flexible homophonic declamation of certain works of Book II. But at Mantua Wert's influence quickly grew more profound. It revealed itself especially in Monteverdi's settings of *ottave* from Tasso's *Liberata*—six *ottave*, to be precise, in two cycles of three madrigals each, "Vattene pur, crudel, con quella pace" and "Vivrò fra i miei tormenti e le mie cure." In choosing these texts Monteverdi took his lead from Wert, who had published settings of fourteen *ottave* from Tasso's epic in his Seventh and Eighth Books of 1581 and 1586. With only two exceptions (the lyrical landscapes "Vezzosi

---

1. See Newcomb, *The Madrigal at Ferrara* 1:98–101.

2. Vittorio Rossi, *Battista Guarini ed Il pastor fido*, pp. 54, 79, 105–10.

augelli," which Monteverdi had taken as the inspiration for "Ecco mormorar l'onde," and "Usciva omai dal molle e fresco grembo") Wert had drawn these stanzas from emotionally climactic episodes of the poem: Erminia's plaints among the shepherds and over what she takes to be the corpse of Tancredi (cantos 7 and 19), Tancredi's lament at the tomb of Clorinda (12), and Armida's tirade at the betrayal and departure of Rinaldo (16). Monteverdi likewise chose his texts from the latter two episodes—though avoiding, no doubt deliberately, the *ottave* Wert had already set. He looked to Wert also for many particulars of his musical style in these settings, as Einstein and more recent commentators have noted. And in the process he achieved a musical *gravità* not found in any of his earlier works, a weightiness wholly in keeping with the heroic pretensions of the poetic genre from which his texts were drawn.

Tasso himself may have played a role in inspiring Monteverdi's heroic style, just as he seems to have prompted Wert's in the early 1580s.[3] For he lived in Mantua from March to November of 1591,[4] and though it is unlikely that the troubled poet would have had direct contact with a novice in Duke Vincenzo's musical staff, his presence itself at the court could hardly have escaped Monteverdi's notice. In any case, Tasso had written at length on the heroic style in poetry.[5] And in *La Cavaletta*, as we have seen, he had challenged composers to seek nobler musical idioms. In his *Liberata* settings of Book III Monteverdi responded to Tasso's challenge.

Wert, we have suggested, had responded some time before. His settings from Tasso's poem display one facet of a stylistic seriousness he pursued throughout the 1580s. (Another facet may be viewed in the imposing settings of Petrarch's verse in his Ninth and Tenth Books of 1588 and 1591.) But this was not the first time Wert had sought an appropriate musical idiom for epic verse. He had done so many years earlier, in 1561, in his only book of madrigals for four voices. Here he published settings from Ludovico Ariosto's *Orlando furioso* in an idiom that foreshadows his and Monteverdi's heroic style of the 1580s and 1590s. To trace the sources of Monteverdi's *Liberata* settings we must begin with these works.

Wert's *Primo libro de' madrigali a quattro voci* is, in Einstein's phrase, "an apotheosis of homophony."[6] Nowhere is the judgment more fitting than in reference to the Ariosto settings "Dunque baciar sì bell'e dolce labbia," "Il dolce sonno mi promise pace," "Ma di che debbo lamentarmi, ahi lassa," and "Era il bel viso suo qual esser suole." These works show almost strict homophony, loosened for the most part only to allow cadential suspensions at the ends of phrases, and enlivened by frequent syncopation. Textural reduction, indeed textural variety of any sort, is rare.

3. For this suggestion see Carol MacClintock, *Giaches de Wert, 1535–1596*, pp. 58–61.

4. Angelo Solerti, *Vita di Torquato Tasso* 1:676–86.

5. Especially in his *Discorsi dell'arte poetica e in particolare sopra il poema eroico*, published in 1587 but written before 1570, and the revised and enlarged version of these published in 1594 and entitled *Discorsi del poema eroico*.

6. *The Italian Madrigal*, p. 516.

The poetry is set line by line and syllabically, with simultaneous rests in all the voices between most lines.

In all these musical traits these works recall strophic reciting formulas of the sort published as much as fifty years earlier in some of Petrucci's books of *frottole*. And there is a poetic reason as well to link these pieces to the largely oral traditions of solo song reflected in such formulas: the texts of the first three of them are drawn from Bradamante's speeches giving vent to her anguish at the continuing travail of her love for Ruggiero. If we may judge by the later appearance in the printed repertory of the *Ruggiero* bassline, these were favored episodes in the tradition of solo recitation of passages from Ariosto's epic dating back undoubtedly to its first publication in 1516.[7] In short, the sketchy musical and literary evidence alike support Carol MacClintock's assertion that Wert's Ariosto settings named above "are really polyphonic versions"—or at least polyphonic reflections—"of *arie per cantar ottave*."[8]

The harmonic language of these works especially seems to link them to this sixteenth-century tradition of epic declamation. All four show minimal harmonic variety even by the modest standards of Book I à 4. "Dunque baciar" and "Il dolce sonno" in particular, both in the soft hexachord with G finals, circle incessantly around four triads, g, D, B♭, and F. ("Ma di che debbo" and "Era il bel viso," in the ♮ system with D finals, show a predilection only slightly weaker for the analogous triads d, A, F, and C.) It is probably no coincidence that these triads are exactly those central to harmonic variation schemes like the *Romanesca, folia,* and *passamezzo antico*. Such minor-mode patterns seem to have antedated major-mode analogues like the *Ruggiero* and *passamezzo moderno* and may trace their origins even to the fifteenth century. They were associated by 1550 not only with the dance but also with oral traditions of semi-improvised poetic recitation.[9] In taking over this

---

7. On the *Ruggiero* melody and bassline see Alfred Einstein, "Die Aria di Ruggiero" and "Ancora sull' 'aria di Ruggiero.' "

8. Wert, *Opera Omnia* 15:ix. The connection of Wert's four-voice Ariosto settings to recitational traditions undoubtedly involves also the *madrigale arioso* of the 1550s and 1560s, which shares many features with the pieces in Wert's Book I à 4; on this subgenre see James Haar, "The 'Madrigale arioso.'" One of the Ariosto settings in Wert's Book I à 4, the famous "Chi salirà per me, madonn'in cielo," had in fact already been published as a *madrigale arioso* by Antonio Barrè in 1558. This work, however, stands somewhat apart from the four Ariosto settings discussed here in its prevailing imitative texture and major-mode tonal orientation (soft hexachord, F final). The motivation for the stylistic difference is surely po-

etic: this *ottava* is not from an impassioned moment of the *Furioso* but is the poet's tongue-in-cheek invocation that opens canto 35. Wert's response is lyrical and nonrecitational, a style he would develop in later settings of descriptive stanzas from Ariosto's poem, "Non tant'il bel palazz'è sì eccellente" and "Vaghi boschetti di soavi allori." And these works look forward in turn to "Vezzosi augelli." The stylistic dichotomy of the Ariosto settings of Book I à 4, in other words, anticipates a similar one in the Tasso settings of the 1580s.

9. The best résumé of these oral traditions and of sixteenth-century solo song in general remains Einstein, *The Italian Madrigal*, chap. 12; see also the articles cited in n. 7 above. On the *strambottisti* of the late fifteenth century see Nino Pirrotta, *Li due Orfei: Da Poliziano a Monteverdi*, chap. 1

harmonic idiom Wert may well have sought to reflect in his madrigals the musical style preferred in the 1550s for the solo recitation of stanzas from *Orlando furioso*. His Ariosto settings of 1561, in other words, seem to evidence a fertile conjunction of oral and written musical traditions.[10]

A restricted harmonic vocabulary is not necessarily an ineffective one. The groups of chords set forth above lend themselves to energetic sequential motion by interlocking progressions of a fourth, toward the flat side of the circle of fifths (Ex. 10), toward the sharp side (Ex. 11), or even in both directions within the same phrase (Ex. 12). Wert was quick to exploit the rhetorical potential of such sequences, as in the imploring repetitions of the final line of "Il dolce sonno" (Ex. 13) or in the twelfth line of "Dunque baciar," where the energy of the rising sequence captures the forceful first half of the line ("That he who kills another . . ."), only to dissipate abruptly in the low-pitched retribution of its second half (". . . must be killed"; Ex. 14).

Wert's later settings of *ottave* from *Gerusalemme liberata* borrow important features from these early Ariosto settings. The first of them, the famous "Giunto alla tomba, ove al suo spirto vivo"—published in 1581 and the earliest setting from Tasso's epic by any composer—displays the connection most clearly. Its preferred texture is the supple recitational homophony of the Ariosto settings, apparent at many points in the work but especially in its gloomy opening measures (Ex. 15). The poetry is mostly set syllabically, often with simultaneous rests in the voices between phrases. Wert's overriding concern here, as in the Ariosto settings, was to shape a rhythmically effective declamation of the text.

But this concern did not keep him from expanding vastly the harmonic, textural, and expressive variety in these works over those setting Ariosto's verse. The homophonic texture is now usually not strict but relaxed by the staggering of one or more voices in relation to the others (see mm. 4 and 7–9 in Ex. 15). Occasionally it gives way to full-fledged imitation (for example, in "Giunto alla tomba" at "il pianto," end of the *prima parte*). Cadences are sometimes expanded into long poly-

---

(translated as *Music and Theatre from Poliziano to Monteverdi*). On the particular harmonic schemes mentioned here see, in addition to the writings of Einstein, Imogene Horsley, "The Sixteenth-Century Variation," and Claude V. Palisca, "Vincenzo Galilei and Some Links between 'Pseudo-Monody' and Monody."

10. This harmonic idiom is not, of course, restricted in Wert's output to his settings of Ariosto's stanzas, only used most consistently there; for a beautiful example of its use in other contexts see the opening of the popular "Cara la vita mia, egl'è pur vero" from Book I à 5 of 1558. Mon-

teverdi, as we have seen, associated this harmonic style with homophonic declamation already in his Second Book. With provocative results James Haar has begun to explore the impact of *arie* for singing Ariosto's *ottave* on the written repertory; see his "Arie per cantar stanze ariostesche." Although Haar is most concerned to isolate melodic patterns borrowed from the oral traditions, he notes (p. 35) that two of his examples (2c and 2e), from 1577 and 1552, show harmonic progressions bearing clear resemblances to the *passamezzo antico* and *Romanesca*.

EXAMPLE 10

Wert, "Ma di chi debbo lamentarmi, ahi lassa," mm. 4–7
(*Opera Omnia,* ed. MacClintock and Bernstein, 15:26;
quoted by permission of Armen Carapetyan)

EXAMPLE 11

Wert, "Dunque baciar sì bell'e dolce labbia," mm. 7–10
(*Opera Omnia,* ed. MacClintock and Bernstein, 15:19;
quoted by permission of Armen Carapetyan)

EXAMPLE 12

Wert, "Dunque baciar sì bell'e dolce labbia," beginning
(*Opera Omnia,* ed. MacClintock and Bernstein, 15:19;
quoted by permission of Armen Carapetyan)

EXAMPLE 13

Wert, "Il dolce sonno mi promise pace," mm. 21–24
(*Opera Omnia,* ed. MacClintock and Bernstein, 15:25;
quoted by permission of Armen Carapetyan)

EXAMPLE 14

Wert, "Dunque baciar sì bell'e dolce labbia," *seconda parte,*
mm. 7–10 (*Opera Omnia,* ed. MacClintock and Bernstein, 15:21;
quoted by permission of Armen Carapetyan)

phonic melismas (for example, at "un lagrimoso rivo" in the *prima parte*). Reduced textures are common, especially villanella-like trios of upper voices, although Wert was for the most part careful to avoid the harmonic vocabulary of this light genre (see the *seconda parte,* at "Deh prendi questi piant', e questi baci").

Wert used madrigalisms far more frequently here than in the settings from the *Furioso.* Usually these are what I have termed "affective" madrigalisms: harmonic cross-relations, unexpected progressions, dissonances, and long melodic leaps that constitute a direct translation of the emotional charge carried by the text into musical terms. Less frequent are neutral pictorial madrigalisms, which depend for their significance on a more-or-less straightforward visual correlation between musical gesture and textual meaning—for example, the octave leaps up at "il ciel prescrisse" ("heaven foretold"; these look back to one of the few madrigalisms of the

EXAMPLE 15

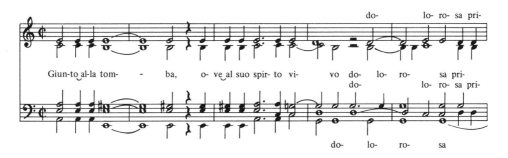

Wert, "Giunto alla tomba, ove al suo spirto vivo," beginning
(*Opera Omnia,* ed. MacClintock and Bernstein, 7:38;
quoted by permission of Armen Carapetyan)

works of 1561, at "Dal ciel cader" in "Ma di che debbo").[11] And sometimes Wert employed pictorial madrigalisms with such insistence that they transcend my classifications and take on the expressive resonance of affective ones (as in the melismas at "Al fin sgorgando"—"Finally, pouring forth").[12]

The harmonic style of these *Liberata* settings seems at first glance to have little to do with that of the Ariostian epic style. Nor is this surprising. Between 1561 and 1581 the *Romanesca*-like idiom of the Ariosto settings had taken on new generic

11. See Tomlinson, "Music and the Claims of Text," pp. 585–86n. In "Tasso, *La Gerusalemme liberata,* and Monteverdi," a provocative essay that reached me too late for thorough consideration here, Dean Mace suggests an ostensibly similar dichotomy between "naturalistic" and "symbolic" text setting (see pp. 133–34). However, he views the text-expressive dissonances and harmonic surprises of the mid-sixteenth-century madrigal as pictorial gestures, "with no *direct* relation between the meaning of words and

music"; this forces him to distinguish, in a manner I find unconvincing, between Monteverdi's "expressive" and earlier composers' "illustrative" uses of such devices (pp. 152–55). In general, Mace's argument seems to me to rely too much on old-fashioned, exaggerated notions of an expressive opposition between monodic and polyphonic practices around 1600.
12. The idea is Newcomb's, in *The Madrigal at Ferrara* 1:83.

associations, less high-flown ones linking it to the villanella, canzonetta, and canzonetta-madrigal (and arising, perhaps, from earlier associations of the *Romanesca* and other such harmonic patterns with dance music).[13] By the 1580s Wert could exploit this idiom in setting madrigal verse and even lyrical passages from the *Liberata* like "Vezzosi augelli," but he could hardly have retained it unchanged as the basis of his heroic style. Instead he adapted it, through a dual process of prolongation and increased complexity in the relations of its sonorities, to attain the new gravity he sought. To appreciate the far-reaching effects of this adaptation we may return to the opening measures of "Giunto alla tomba" (see Ex. 15 above).

The four triads employed here, A minor-major, E, C, and G, are the harmonic pillars of the *Romanesca* moved up a step. And the succession of triads setting the first two lines of text recalls the sequential pattern we have seen above: (a) $\to$ E $\to$ a (C) $\to$ G $\to$ C. But whereas in Examples 10–14 such sequences occupied at most two measures, usually with one triad per syllable, here the sequence has been prolonged through two lines of verse—a full seven measures of slow, somber declamation. The result of this wholesale slowdown of harmonic rhythm is an impressive harmonic stasis, its corollary a preponderance of unmoving, repeated-note melodies molded rhythmically to the declamation of the text—both features typical of Wert's *Liberata* settings. Sometimes Wert treated these monotonal melodies in imitation, creating a unique musico-poetic fabric of rhythmically lively declamation combined with restricted melodic motion and static or slowly shifting harmonies. This texture occurs especially in the Tasso settings of Book VIII (1586), as if Wert devised it after the composition of "Giunto alla tomba" in 1581 as an outgrowth of the stylistic novelties there. Examples are the first measures of "Sovente all'or che su gl'estivi ardori"—a double point simultaneously developing the first two lines of text—and, more dramatically, those of "Forsennata gridava 'O tu che porti.'" Most memorable (for us and, as we shall see, for Monteverdi) is the beginning of the *seconda parte* of "Misera, non credea ch'a gl'occhi miei," where the imitative treatment of the exclamation followed by a slowly drooping melody results in a likewise sagging harmonic movement. It is an opening point as unorthodox as it is expressive (Ex. 16).

Along with this slowing of harmonic rhythm comes an impression that the pairs of sonorities of the original *Romanesca*-like sequence have achieved a new independence from one another. Returning to Example 15, we may see that the individual harmonies here are no longer clearly equal partners in a single sequential process (E $\to$ a $\to$ G $\to$ C) as they had been in analogous passages from the early Ariosto settings. Instead, by inserting a C-major sonority between the units of the

---

13. The idiom is prominent, for example, in the villanelle of Giovanni da Nola and the canzonette of Monteverdi that they inspired. See Lionello Cammarota, *Gian Domenico del Giovane da Nola: I documenti biografici . . ., madrigali a 4 e 5 voci, canzoni villanesche a 3 e 4 voci.*

EXAMPLE 16

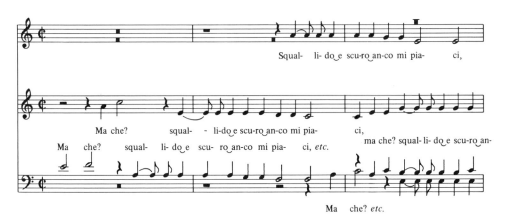

Wert, "Misera, non credea ch'a gl'occhi miei," *seconda parte,*
beginning (*Opera Omnia,* ed. MacClintock and Bernstein, 8:30–31;
quoted by permission of Armen Carapetyan)

original sequence and beginning the work with an analogous A-minor triad, Wert
asserted the larger hierarchical ordering of these harmonies as dominant-tonic pairs
(a → E → a / C → G → C). The result is a fluid system of independent, contrasting tonalities that modern analysts of Monteverdi's music (if not of Wert's)
have variously termed *Teiltonarten,* "parenthetical expansion" on individual hexachordal degrees, and "circumscriptive tonality."[14]

Wert's insertion of a C-major triad in the *Romanesca* formula introduced another novelty: a third relation, from A minor to C, not found in the original har-

14. See below, excursus 2, n. 4.

monic sequence. Both Wert and Monteverdi after him frequently employed this relation in their heroic style, where it served as an alternative to the root progressions by second, fourth, and fifth that by now dominated the villanella and canzonetta-madrigal. And such third relations, of course, suggested expressive cross-relations. In Example 15 Wert was quick to take up the suggestion in the shift from C major to A major of measures 7–8.

Occasionally, also, Wert reused in more literal fashion the harmonic sequences of the madrigals of 1561. Compare the surging conclusion of "Misera, non credea" in Example 17 with Example 14 above. Example 18, from the *quarta parte* of "Qual musico gentil, prima che chiara" (from Book VIII like "Misera, non credea"), runs the sequential pattern in both directions much in the manner of Example 12. Significantly, both these echoes of the four-voice style of 1561 are scored for what is now a reduced texture of four voices.

Monteverdi's two three-section *Liberata* cycles of 1592 exploit and develop all these features of Wert's heroic style. This is especially clear in "Vivrò fra i miei tormenti," a work that in its closer reliance on its models seems to reveal a lesser self-assurance than "Vattene pur." Not that "Vattene pur" shows no direct borrowings from Wert's *Liberata* settings. (One of these is its closing point of imitation, on "piango e m'assido," based on the setting of "il pianto" at the end of the *prima parte* of "Giunto alla tomba"; and we will note others below.) But "Vivrò fra i miei tormenti" borrows its tonal system (♮ hexachord, D final, high clefs) and so many other particulars from "Misera, non credea" that it suggests that Monteverdi had this particular work of Wert clearly in mind while he composed it. The poetic connection, as we would expect, is manifest: both texts present the speaker (Erminia in Wert's work, Tancredi in Monteverdi's) lamenting over a dead or presumed-dead loved one.

EXAMPLE 17

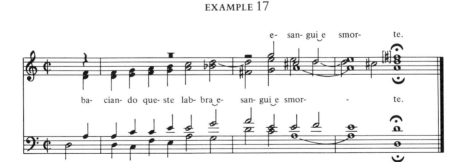

Wert, "Misera, non credea ch'a gl'occhi miei," *seconda parte,* end
(*Opera Omnia,* ed. MacClintock and Bernstein, 8:33;
quoted by permission of Armen Carapetyan)

EXAMPLE 18

quel- le ch'a mil- le an- ti- chi in pre- mio so - - no ne- ga- te,

Wert, "Qual musico gentil, prima che chiara," *quarta parte,*
mm. 19–21 (*Opera Omnia,* ed. MacClintock and Bernstein, 8:45;
quoted by permission of Armen Carapetyan)

To work backward: Monteverdi ended his cycle with the same sequential approach to the cadence Wert had used to end his (Ex. 19; compare Ex. 17 above). Such *Romanesca*-like harmonic successions occur frequently in Monteverdi's cycles, as they had in Wert's. Sometimes they take the form of quick-moving sequences with special text-expressive intent (as at "negl'ultimi singulti; udir ciò spero"—"in your last sighs; I hope to hear that"—in the second part of "Vattene pur"). More often they function, in the manner of "Giunto alla tomba," as the granitelike harmonic foundation for homophonic or imitative development of monotonal declamatory melodies (for example, the opening nine measures of "Vivrò fra i miei tormenti"). In this way Monteverdi's cycles embraced the special junction of harmonic stasis and frenetic rhythmic activity that had marked Wert's *Liberata* settings.

In the *seconda parte* of "Vivrò fra i miei tormenti" Monteverdi aped the most jarring of Wert's third-related chord progressions: the move from G minor to E major, entailing melodic chromaticism in two voices, at "s'odi il mio pianto" ("if you hear my lament") in the second part of "Misera, non credea." Monteverdi's Tasso settings, like Wert's, feature many less daring third relations as well. When these include melodic half steps or cross-relations they are usually employed with obvious expressive intent, as in the final bars of the *seconda parte* of "Vattene pur," where shifts from F to A major and from D major to F eerily depict Armida's lapse into unconsciousness.

Monteverdi profited also from a close study of Wert's novel textures. The second part of "Vivrò fra i miei tormenti" opens with a reworking of Wert's striking beginning of the same part of "Misera, non credea" (Ex. 20; compare Ex. 16 above). The similar text incipits ("Ma che?" versus "Ma dove?") suggested to Monteverdi a similarly interrogative opening, which he followed with Wert's imitative treatment of slowly descending repeated-note melodies. Monteverdi's version is if anything even more dispirited than Wert's because of its more single-

EXAMPLE 19

Monteverdi, "Vivrò fra i miei tormenti e le mie cure," *terza parte,* end

minded structural logic. All of Monteverdi's melodic lines descend after their exclamatory beginnings (Wert's tenor rises in its second statement of the motive); they are dragged down from below by the prolonged, dogged stepwise descent of the single bottom voice, the *basso* (Wert's descent is interrupted by the shift from tenor to bass as the lowest voice).

Monteverdi reused this particular harmonic-textural complex, more freely, to open the third parts of both his cycles. And in general the textural spectrum of his *Liberata* settings is just that which Wert had explored in his: strict homophony, which Monteverdi used less often than Wert and then only briefly; staggered homophony, usually with an inner voice anticipating the others (a much-used texture in these works); and imitative polyphony based on largely monotonal, declamatory subjects.

Repeated-note, recitational melodies figure centrally in all these textures and are especially prominent in the last two. In his use of such lines Monteverdi reveals perhaps the most important lesson he learned from Wert's *Liberata* settings: the tremendous potential of declamatory rhythm to profile sharply the meaning and syntax of the text. I have cited elsewhere examples from the monotonal melodies of "Vattene pur," melodies whose rhythms incisively capture the tumbling assonance

EXAMPLE 20

Monteverdi, "Vivrò fra i miei tormenti e le mie cure,"
seconda parte, beginning

of "indivisibilmente" or the repetitive syntax of "tanto t'agiterò quanto t'amai" ("I will bedevil you as much as I loved you").[15] These examples can easily be multiplied and usually involve either monotonal lines or lines whose melodic motion is sprung, so to speak, by repeated notes at their beginnings. Thus the text-expressive leap of a minor sixth on "crudel" at the beginning of "Vattene pur" releases the pent-up energy of the repeated notes before it, as does the pictorial melisma on "l'onde" at the end of the *prima parte.* (These madrigalisms look back, respectively,

15. "Madrigal, Monody, and Monteverdi," pp. 70–71. Such techniques are a central subject of Mace's "Tasso and Monteverdi" as well.

to the opening of Wert's "Forsennata gridava" and the florid setting of "Al fin sgorgando" noted above in "Giunto alla tomba.") Tasso's sometimes complicated syntax may even be clarified by Monteverdi's distinctive declamatory patterns. In the third part of "Vivrò fra i miei tormenti," the melodic leap on "tomba" after repeated notes leaves no doubt as to the subject of a phrase whose inverted order might otherwise have rendered its musical setting ineffective ("honorata per me *tomba* felice"—"tomb honored by me, and fortunate").

Not surprisingly, given the propensity to structural clarity we have noted in madrigals of Books I and II, Monteverdi recognized more clearly than Wert the potential of this forceful declamatory style to bind together the separate sections of his cycles. The minor sixth on "crudel" in "Vattene pur" returns in the *seconda parte* of the work (at "Per nom'Armida") and is then extended to embrace a full octave and allow for the imitative outcries on "chiamerai." (These echo Wert's setting of "T'ingannai, t'allettai" in the fourth part of "Qual musico gentil" but with surer expressive effect, since Monteverdi's music not only effectively declaims the text but also realizes its meaning—"you will cry out.") And distinctive declamation joins with harmony, texture, and tessitura in "Vivrò fra i miei tormenti" to create a structural reference point that returns in all three sections. At the first statements of "paventerò" and "temerò" (in part 1), "Dal furor" (part 2), and "honorata per me" (part 3) vigorous declamation of the new poetic lines, in a staggered homophonic texture, follows hard on the heels of a full cadence on F and, with the *canto* moving to the top of its range, turns the music back toward the harmonic region of D and A.

The heroic style of Monteverdi and Wert constitutes the fullest realization in the polyphonic madrigal of epic *gravità*. The need for such a weighty style, if not its specific connection with epic poetry, had been asserted in Tasso's *La Cavaletta,* and the poetic material to base it on supplied by his *Gerusalemme liberata.* In creating the style, Wert looked back to the oral tradition of solo recitation that had long been associated with epic verse in general and Ariosto's *Orlando furioso* in particular. The harmonic vocabulary and vibrant text declamation of his settings no doubt reflect important characteristics of this tradition.

The importance of Monteverdi's *Liberata* settings of 1592 lies partly in such musical traits. Here, in imitation of Wert, he experimented with techniques either new to his works or less surely used before: sequential progressions, jarring harmonic shifts involving cross-relations and melodic chromaticism, monotonal declamation followed by long melodic leaps, novel textural possibilities, and, especially, sharply chiseled declamatory rhythms.

But lists of innovative techniques do not explain the full significance of these works. The most important lesson Monteverdi gleaned from Wert was the more general truth that all these devices—and others, among them the harmonic stasis and structure-clarifying musical recalls of works like "Ecco mormorar l'onde"—could work in the service of truly serious musico-poetic expression. Wert's *Liberata* settings must have seemed a revelation to Monteverdi, one that showed him a path to affective utterance of an altogether more profound sort than is found in his adolescent Luzzaschian efforts of Book I or even his most forward-looking works of Book II. Monteverdi's imitations of Wert in the Third Book set the tone for his works of the next two decades, straight through the musico-dramatic triumph of *L'Arianna*. They galvanized him, led him to repudiate the emotionally neutral canzonetta style that had threatened to dominate Book II, and pushed him to seek more richly expressive idioms. He did not stop setting witty amorous verse after 1592, of course. But now he saw in such poetry levels of significance, and devised musical means to project them, that he would have missed without the eye-widening experience of Wert's heroic style in the early 1590s. It is as if Monteverdi's exploration of amorous sorrow in the *Liberata* settings helped him gain a deepened understanding of amorous play as well. In the next chapter we will examine the mature amorous styles that resulted.

4

Guarini and
the Epigrammatic Style
(Books III and IV)

Foreshadowings of the Style (Book III)

ASSO MAY HAVE INSPIRED the freshest idiom in Book III, but Guarini pointed the way to Monteverdi's future. The paradox here is more apparent than real. Monteverdi's settings of two cycles from *Gerusalemme liberata* contained much that the composer would develop in later works but were rooted in a repudiation of the canzonetta-madrigal of Books I and II—a repudiation required, as I have suggested, by the heroic style of Tasso's verse. Only with less exalted rhymes could Monteverdi pursue the implications of the most advanced canzonetta-madrigals of the Second Book. And with a decisiveness that is entirely typical he settled by 1592 on the verse of Guarini—his madrigals, and excerpts from *Il pastor fido*—as the stimulus for this extension of earlier styles.

The choice is not surprising. Guarini was one of Italy's two most celebrated living poets, having joined ranks with Tasso as a result of the immense popularity of *Il pastor fido,* circulated in manuscript and published in the late 1580s. He was, as we have noted, a frequent visitor to the Mantuan court from 1591 to 1593 and was by far the most luminous literary presence there after Tasso's departure in November 1591. And Vincenzo Gonzaga surely was Guarini's most ardent admirer among the rulers of Italy, nurturing throughout the 1590s a plan to stage his huge tragicomedy.

So Monteverdi's preoccupation with Guarini is not in itself remarkable. But its steadfastness over the following years certainly is. The nine settings of Guarini's verse in Book III form a modest prelude to nineteen more in the Fourth and Fifth Books of 1603 and 1605, not counting separate sections of multipartite works. In all, twenty-eight of the forty-seven madrigals in these three books set texts by Guarini, a concentration on a single poet unequaled in Monteverdi's remaining output. And the number might be higher still: some of the eleven texts in Books III,

IV, and V whose authors remain unidentified show clear stylistic affinities to Guarini's lyrics and could well be his work.[1]

In these collections two related but distinct styles emerge from Monteverdi's reading of Guarini. One is associated with many (though not all) of the texts excerpted from *Il pastor fido*. We shall consider this style in the next chapter. In many of its traits it reveals clearly its origin as a *stile rappresentativo,* its conception as stage music. But it builds also on the other style, a more lyrical idiom that Monteverdi perfected in his settings of Guarini's madrigals. These poems, at their best, frame the traditional Platonizing paradoxes of the lover's state in language that is original in its epigrammatic wit, brevity, and syntactic and semantic precision. And just these characteristics render unforgettable the best works in what I shall call Monteverdi's epigrammatic style.

The settings of Guarini in Book III do not yet embody the mature epigrammatic style. They are works of consolidation, deploying with increased confidence techniques that were new in the Second Book and in general showing a greater stylistic affinity to that collection than to Book IV. Nevertheless it would be a mistake to conclude, with Schrade, that these madrigals "present no stylistic changes."[2] For even when they reuse musical devices seen in Book II, they are apt to transform them or link them to the poetry in ways that give them a novel appearance. And in some of these madrigals distinctive devices and gestures that were beyond the range of Book II appear for the first time.

These may occur even in the most retrospective works in the book, "La giovinetta pianta," "Lumi miei, cari lumi" (Guarini), and "O rossignuol ch'in queste verdi fronde" (Bembo: the second and last poem of Pietro Bembo that Monteverdi ever set). These works look back all the way to the First Book in their combination of a♭-hexachord, G-final tonal orientation, an interspersing of lively canzonetta textures with slow-moving affective passages, and a somewhat schematic structural response to their texts. (The last feature is especially apparent in "La giovinetta pianta," where the alternations of three-voice and fuller textures have the character of varied reprises employed to underscore the syntactic parallelism of the text.) They look back beyond Book I to the *Canzonette* of 1584 in their predilection for high-voice trios. In this and their frequent indulgence in pictorial melismas, they suggest that they were intended for use by Duke Vincenzo's *concerto* and recall Newcomb's luxuriant style of the 1580s.[3]

---

1. Especially reminiscent of Guarini are "La piaga c'ho nel core" and "Longe da te, cor mio" in the Fourth Book.

2. *Monteverdi,* p. 179.

3. *The Madrigal at Ferrara* 1:81–89. As late as Book IV, two madrigals, "Io mi son giovinetta" and "Quell'augellin che canta" (Guarini), still display all these features, though with greater

melismatic panache than these works of Book III. Two more madrigals of 1592, "O come è gran martire" (Guarini) and "Sovra tenere herbette e bianchi fiori," share the canzonetta rhythms, love of trios of upper voices, and, in the second piece, luxuriant melismas of this style. Both, however, seem more advanced than the pieces we are discussing. They are written in a

Yet even a conservative piece like "O rossignuol" has its novel elements. Its barbed declamation of "può ristorar" breaks with the conventions of the canzonetta-madrigal and takes its lead instead from the stronger rhetoric of the *Gerusalemme liberata* settings. So does the rising sequence at the end of the work. More important still is a new treatment of dissonance adumbrated here. The sequence at the end of the work is only the final change rung on a contrary-motion figure heard in various arrangements in the forty previous measures. Some of these arrangements are free of unorthodox dissonance (Ex. 21a), but in others, especially as the end of the work approaches, Monteverdi employed the novelties of the *seconda pratica,* introducing struck dissonances—that is, nonsuspended dissonances—of just the sort Artusi would later condemn (Exx. 21b and 21c). In doing so Monteverdi revealed a subtle understanding of his materials. The individual lines in the chordal textures of Examples 21b and 21c, because their stepwise contrary motion is consistent and predictable, override any threat to coherence that the dissonance might pose. The vigorous melodic logic alone insures the clarity of the passage; it therefore lessens the obligation of the harmonies to do so and allows Monteverdi to exploit text-expressive dissonance more freely. This is the essence of Monteverdi's new treatment of dissonance. His ultimate answer to Artusi's charge of irrationality in this matter is simply that he earned the privilege of loosening his control of dissonance by tightening his control of other musical elements.

Throughout the Third Book (and often in the Fourth and Fifth Books) Monteverdi relied on similar homophonic structures, involving clearly directed contrary motion, to generate his most piquant dissonances. Thus in the opening point of "O dolce anima mia dunqu'è pur vero" the minor sevenths of Examples 21b and 21c are widened to a jarring major seventh in the major-mode context, closely anticipating an offending passage from "Cruda Amarilli" that Artusi would cite in 1600 (Ex. 22).[4] In the same madrigal Monteverdi increased the pungency of a passage in the affective style by articulating what would otherwise be suspended dissonances (Ex. 23; the overlapping of the rising and falling lines hardly obscures their emphatic contrary motion). More daring, finally, is an affective passage from "Occhi, un tempo mia vita" (Ex. 24) where the *canto* (the second line from the top) leaps to a dissonant B♭.

Such treatment of dissonance, though a harbinger of future developments, is still infrequent in the Third Book. More typical here is the adaptation of the most advanced contrapuntal techniques of Book II—the techniques of "Ecco mormorar

different tonal type (natural hexachord, A finals, high clefs) and move considerably beyond the G-final works in rhetorical efficacy; see, for example, the opening exclamations and five-voice homophonic outburst at "O soave mio ardore" in the first or the light-hearted ostinati and abrupt harmonic reorientation at "Onde lieta mi disse" in the second.

4. Compare the setting of "e più fugace" in "Cruda Amarilli." For Artusi's citation see *L'Artusi,* fol. 39v (p. 35 in Strunk, *Source Readings*).

EXAMPLE 21

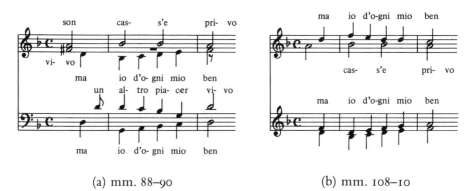

(a) mm. 88–90   (b) mm. 108–10

(c) mm. 113–15

Monteverdi, "O rossignuol, ch'in queste verdi fronde"

EXAMPLE 22

Monteverdi, "O dolce anima mia
dunqu'è pur vero," mm. 18–19

EXAMPLE 23

Monteverdi, "O dolce anima mia dunqu'è pur vero," mm. 34–42

EXAMPLE 24

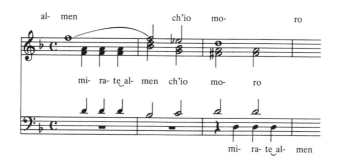

Monteverdi, "Occhi, un tempo mia vita,"
mm. 56–58

l'onde"—to diverse literary ends. In new poetic contexts these devices reveal unexpected expressive possibilities. And in exploring these possibilities Monteverdi achieved an ever closer accord of text and music.

The elaboration of the idiom of "Ecco mormorar" had begun already in Book II, of course, in the opening multiple counterpoint of "Non m'è grave il morire." In the Third Book just the same techniques of double and triple imitation form the structural basis of no fewer than five works:

    IV.   "O dolce anima mia dunqu'è pur vero"
    V.   "Stracciami pur il core"
    VII.   "Se per estremo ardore"
    XI.   "O primavera, gioventù dell'anno"
    XII.   "Perfidissimo volto"

Significantly, all five works set poetry of Guarini—four madrigals and one presumed excerpt from *Il pastor fido* ("O primavera").[5] In every case more than half the music is framed in double and triple points of imitation—much more than half in "O dolce anima mia," "Perfidissimo volto," and especially "O primavera," where seventy-five of eighty-four measures use this technique.

This last work well exemplifies the syntactic subtlety and versatility Monteverdi discovered in adapting his combinatory contrapuntal techniques to Guarini's verse. The text develops the Petrarchan antithesis of serene natural surroundings and the poet's lovesick turmoil, the opposition that Tasso had hinted at in "Ecco mormorar l'onde." It does so in a succession of syntactic parallelisms embracing semantic oppositions:

O primavera, gioventù dell'anno,	Oh springtime, youth of the year,
bella madre di fiori,	beautiful mother of flowers,
d'herbe novelle e di novelli amori:	of new grasses and new loves:
tu ben, lasso, ritorni,	well may you return but—
5 ma senza i cari giorni	alas!—without the hopeful days
delle speranze mie. Tu ben sei quella	so dear to me. Well may you be
ch'eri pur dianzi sì vezzosa e bella,	that which you were before, so charming and pretty;
ma non son io quel che già un tempo fui,	but I am not the same as I once was,
sì car'a gl'occhi altrui.	so dear to the eyes of another.

The semantic oppositions here work on various levels. Verses 4–6, while weakly advancing the contrast of poet and nature ("You return, but my happiness does

---

5. I say "presumed" because Monteverdi's text shows extensive differences from the analogous passage in *Il pastor fido* (III, i, 1–14). The text that Monteverdi set has the appearance of a poetic madrigal, and indeed Monteverdi set it in a style he ordinarily reserved for such lyric poems. It is not inconceivable that the text first circulated as a lyric poem, which Guarini then rewrote for inclusion in his tragicomedy. (Luzzaschi also set Monteverdi's version of the text, in his *Madrigali . . . a uno, e doi, e tre soprani*, published in 1601 but probably composed in the 1580s.) Nor is it impossible that Guarini or another poet extracted the lines from *Il pastor fido* and revised them to yield the more generalized feel of the lyric. Such after-the-fact revisions are suggested even more strongly in the case of "Quell'augellin che canta" from Monteverdi's Fourth Book. Here the text follows closely Linco's lines in the first scene of *Il pastor fido*, except that (1) three lines have been cut, apparently to avoid their reference to Silvio, the other character in the scene, and (2) a clumsy couplet of generalizing lyric import has been tagged to the end of the passage. A dramatic excerpt, in other words, has been recast as a lyric.

Monteverdi set this text too in a style he normally used for lyric poems—the conservative luxuriant style of "La giovinetta pianta" described above. The argument that Monteverdi considered these texts lyrics rather than dramatic excerpts—that perhaps they were given to him in the form of poetic madrigals—gains strength from a parallel case among the texts set by Benedetto Pallavicino in his Sixth Book of 1600. There "Vivrò io mai per altro amor contenta" follows closely Mirtillo's verses "Viver io fortunato / . . . / ogni voler, ogni poter mi sia" (*Il pastor fido*, III, vi). But according to *Delle opere del Cavalier Battista Guarini* 2:126 a version of the text closer to Pallavicino's than to that of the play was published as a poetic madrigal around the time Pallavicino set it. A final example of the same phenomenon may be Filippo di Monte's "O d'aspido più sorda e più fugace," from his Fourteenth Book of 1590. The text is ostensibly an independent, thirteen-line madrigal, but its clear connections to *Il pastor fido*, I, i have been pointed out by Brian Mann, *The Secular Madrigals of Filippo di Monte, 1521–1603*, p. 381.

not"), are opposed to the invocation of verses 1–3 ("Beautiful spring, / your return is unexpectedly sad"). Verses 6–9, parallel in syntax to verses 4–6, embody more explicitly than they the poet-nature opposition ("You're what you've always been, but I am changed"). Verses 6–7 also, however, contradict verses 4–6 and in doing so echo the sentiments of the opening invocation ("Your return is sad. / Nevertheless, you're what you've always been, i.e., beautiful spring").

What strikes us first in Monteverdi's setting is the increased assurance—the jaunty confidence, one might almost say—of the lengthy, three-motive exposition with which it begins. The three melodies associated with verses 1–3 are more distinctive than most of those used in earlier multiple-subject points; none is monotonal, and the first plunges through an entire octave. They are deployed in a plastic texture that seems almost unconstrained by laws of counterpoint, so freely are they combined and recombined.[6]

Guarini's rather paratactic invocation could have allowed Monteverdi to juxtapose the opening verses in random order, much in the manner of "Ecco mormorar l'onde." But the other texts of Guarini in Book III do not open with parataxis, and in "O primavera," as in those other works, Monteverdi was careful to respect the poet's syntactic order. He did so, ingeniously, by emphasizing first one verse then another in his multiple counterpoint—in the order in which they appear in the poem. The technique is apparent in the first eleven measures of "O primavera," for four voices, and clearer still in the seventeen-measure reelaboration of the same motives à 5 that follows the opening. It is easily perceived in a graphic rendering of the voice entries in these twenty-eight measures, in which the numbers 1, 2, and 3 represent not only the first three verses of the text but also the motives invariably associated with each of them (see table).

			Measure number							
	1	5		10		15		20		25
Canto	2	3	3		1		2 2		3		3 3
Quinto	1		1	2		1		2		3	
Alto	1	2		3	1		2		2		3
Tenore	1	2			3 3	2		3		3	3
Basso						2	1		2	3	

At measure 28 the canzonetta-like motion of Monteverdi's exposition abruptly ceases, and the lower three voices begin a slow, descending *fauxbourdon* setting of

6. Monotonal motives are not absent from all these madrigals of Book III, however; indeed in "Stracciami pur" and "Perfidissimo volto" they exhibit something of the declamatory vigor of the *Liberata* cycles.

the affective line 4. The emotional shift from lines 1–3 to line 4 is thus captured; but, within the limits of his affective style, Monteverdi had now also to project the poet-nature antithesis Guarini set forth in lines 4–6. He returned to combinatory contrapuntal techniques to do so. Against the slow descending lines derived from the first setting of line 4 he set a new motive, rising in quarter notes and setting lines 5–6. Gradually the music and text of line 4 give way entirely to a homophonic development of the quarter-note motive. As in the preceding exposition, clear communication of the words is not compromised.

The end of verse 6 and verse 7 call for the praises of spring to be sung again. The canzonetta rhythms and tumbling eighth notes of Monteverdi's double counterpoint here evoke the beginning of the piece and allowed him to set off starkly the second and stronger turn to the poet's sorrow at verse 8. Monteverdi divided this line down the middle ("ma non son io / quel che già un tempo fui"), provided it with two distinct motives appropriately reminiscent in their rhythmic character of those setting verses 4–6, and wrote yet another double point of imitation. He set verse 9 as the afterthought that it is, with a gently falling affective peroration in the manner of "Ecco mormorar l'onde."

In all this Monteverdi expressed in music the semantic richness of Guarini's text, its significant antitheses and balances, while respecting its syntactic structure through the simultaneous (or near-simultaneous) presentation of the phrases that make up each of its grammatical periods. And in a general way these two features—fidelity to the sense and structure of the text—are the dual hallmarks of Monteverdi's epigrammatic style. Their achievement in "O primavera" still depends on a quite limited number of textural and rhythmic devices (and is all the more remarkable in that harmonic variety is eschewed utterly; the F-major stasis of this work is still another characteristic that brings to mind "Ecco mormorar"). By the time of the epigrammatic works of the Fourth Book, Monteverdi would bring to bear on his texts a broader range of musico-poetic techniques.

A decisive step toward his consolidation of these is evident in two more settings of Guarini's verse in Book III, "Ch'io non t'ami, cor mio" and "Occhi, un tempo mia vita." In sheer variety of musical devices these madrigals outstrip any that Monteverdi had previously composed. It is as if he had consciously set himself to forge from the disparate influences on his young career a new idiom of unprecedented versatility. In the process many of the constituent elements were themselves transformed. And novel ingredients were introduced, especially from the new epigrammatic style developed in these years at Ferrara by Luzzasco Luzzaschi and others.[7]

The basic texture of these two works is Wert's homophonic declamation, more supple here than in works like "Se tu mi lassi" of Book II. (Note, for example, the

7. On this style see Newcomb, *The Madrigal at Ferrara*, vol. 1, chap. 7.

EXAMPLE 25

Monteverdi, "Occhi, un tempo mia vita," beginning

underlining of poetic parallelism through identical additive rhythms at the beginning of "Ch'io non t'ami.") The multiple-subject counterpoint of "O primavera" has all but disappeared, reserved now (as in "Occhi, un tempo") for closing a work with a contrapuntal peroration and pointing up similarities of wording in the final lines of its poem. Along with strictly chordal declamation come other, freer textures: the staggered homophony of the *Gerusalemme liberata* cycles (for example, at "Ma se tu sei" in "Ch'io non t'ami") and the melodies-plus-bassline trio of the villanella. The expanded text-interpretive possibilities of the latter are especially important. Monteverdi may still use it, in the Marenzian manner we have seen in "Non si levava" from Book II, to bind together one phrase of text with its semantic consequent. (See "Ch'io non t'ami," at the first setting of "Come poss'io lasciarti e non morire?"—"How can I leave you and not die?") But in the opening measures of "Occhi, un tempo," to capture Guarini's isocolon ("Occhi, un tempo mia vita, / occhi, di questo cor fido sostegno"), he put it to a new use (Ex. 25). The bassline of the homophonic presentation of verse 1 is repeated (transposed) as the bassline of the following trio, but at the same time the top voices introduce verse 2 to new music. Unlike Marenzio's technique, this altered usage moves beyond the level of a single musical phrase to link one idea, already presented, with a new and different one. It is, in short, a novel means to insure musical continuity. It affords a striking example of Monteverdi's growing skill in merging the structural and text-expressive aspects of his art.[8]

8. Though Monteverdi seems to develop this device through elaboration of Marenzio's villanella textures, it may also be viewed as an extreme simplification of his techniques of multi-subject counterpoint. This perspective is suggested by the madrigals of Benedetto Pallavicino, Monteverdi's predecessor as *maestro di cappella* at the Gonzaga court. In his Sixth and Seventh Books of 1600 and 1604 Pallavicino used the device six times, almost always as a way of initi-ating double points of imitation. In "Oh come vaneggiate" from Book VI, one of his most advanced works, the technique occurs twice, starting the double points that open and close the work. Books VI and VII are transcribed in Peter Flanders, "The Madrigals of Benedetto Pallavicino"; Book VI is now also available, along with Books I–V à 5, in Benedetto Pallavicino, *Opera Omnia*.

To achieve the fidelity of musical to poetic expression that characterizes the epi-grammatic style a precise control of musical continuity (and discontinuity) was re-quired. Monteverdi needed to respond to poetic articulations of different weights with an array of musical analogues. Some of these were at hand: he frequently ex-ploited staggered homophony, for example, to overlap musico-poetic phrases and avoid debilitating caesuras between them. Another such device, as we have just seen, he developed from a Marenzian technique he had used earlier. One more is the "false" resolution of the bassline in a full cadence to the third degree instead of the first. If the bassline begins the following poetic verse on this resolution, as at "Prima che questo sia / morte non mi perdoni" in "Ch'io non t'ami," an elision of both musical and poetic phrases results.

For still another new means to control musical continuity Monteverdi looked to the Ferrarese style of Luzzaschi. This is the "evaporated cadence," as Newcomb has called it: the undercutting of a cadence by means of a gradual textural reduction as it approaches. A modest instance concludes Example 25 above, but at the end of the opening section of "Occhi, un tempo" Monteverdi went further, reducing the texture in two steps from four to three to two voices, these last forming a unison (see Ex. 26). This cadence contrasts with the more emphatic cadences that typically conclude Monteverdi's multiple-subject expositions. Consider, for example, "O primavera," whose poetic organization is similar to that of "Occhi, un tempo," an invocation in the opening lines leading to second-person address in the following verses. But the too-final cadence at the end of the exposition (m. 28) does little to enhance this grammatical connection. In "Occhi, un tempo" the thinning of the texture to a unison G and the delaying of the resolution of the *basso* until the start of the next phrase both undermine the cadence. The rhetorically effective gesture of this depleted texture's resolving, so to speak, into the massed homophony that im-mediately follows—matched to the semantic "resolution" in the poetry, which be-

EXAMPLE 26

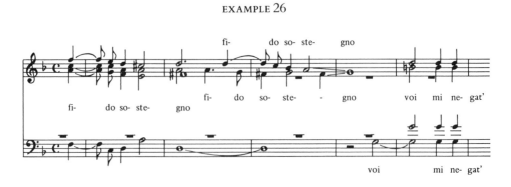

Monteverdi, "Occhi, un tempo mia vita," mm. 14–19

gins only with the "voi" of verse 3—echoed through Monteverdi's works as far as the *Sestina* of the Sixth Book.

The harmonic idioms of these two madrigals are as varied as their textures. Most fundamental, perhaps, are Wert's *Romanesca*-like progressions of interlocking fourths, evident in Examples 25 and 26 above. The forceful harmonic motion of these, whether embodied in sober declamatory homophony or the light motivic rhythms of the canzonetta, lent Monteverdi's epigrammatic works a tonal coherence rarely equaled in those of Luzzaschi or his Ferrarese colleagues Alfonso Fontanelli and Gesualdo. (Increased tonal coherence allowed for subtler shadings of harmonic continuity and discontinuity; we shall return later to Monteverdi's rhetorical use of tonality.) Enriching this basic vocabulary are more daring usages: the third-related triads, with cross-relation, of the heroic style, and the freer treatment of dissonance we have already noted in "Occhi, un tempo" (see Ex. 24 above). In "Chi'io non t'ami" Monteverdi experimented with the introduction of unorthodox dissonance in elaborated cadential decorations. Such uncanonical dissonance may be another sign of the impact of Ferrarese developments on Monteverdi at this time. Monteverdi even returned occasionally to Wert's *fauxbourdon*-like successions of first-inversion chords. Once again, the impression is of a vigorous creative mind straining to meld the techniques at its command into a musical alloy of new expressive versatility. It is not surprising, then, that the epigrammatic madrigals of the Fourth Book display a dazzling range of techniques and inspirations.

The Mature Musical Epigram (Book IV)

To compose the perfect epigrammatic madrigal Monteverdi needed the perfect epigram. The madrigals he set in Book III, both those by Guarini and those by other poets, do not in general measure up. By the standards of the madrigal they are almost all lengthy poems, from ten to fifteen lines long. (Only "O primavera," at nine lines, and "Occhi, un tempo," at seven, are shorter.) They treat their amorous subjects in a format that the German literary historian Ulrich Schulz-Buschhaus has termed "discursive": a reasoned, slow-paced thematic development in which each new period follows logically and straightforwardly from the last. Their complex syntax shows considerable hypotaxis, that is, grammatical subordination of one phrase to another. Their thought sequence typically requires three or more separate poetic periods for its elaboration, of which the first, announcing the theme of the poem, is usually the most distinctive. Their subject tends to be formulated in general conceptual terms rather than by means of concrete, specific situations.[9]

9. For this and the description of the epigrammatic style below see Schulz-Buschhaus, *Das Madrigal,* chaps. B.III, B.V, esp. pp. 59–65, 163–66.

Guarini's "Stracciami pur il core," set by Monteverdi in Book III, exemplifies all these traits:

Stracciami pur il core;	Tear up my heart, then;
ragion è ben, ingrato,	there is good reason, ingrate,
ché, se t'ho tropp'amato	if I've loved you too much,
porti la pena del comess'errore.	for it to bear the pain of my error.
5 Ma perché stracci fai de la mia fede?	But why do you make a tatter of my faith?
Che colp'ha l'innocente?	How is it at fault?
Se la mia fiamma ardente	If my ardent flame
non merita mercede,	does not deserve mercy,
ah, non la mert'il mio fedel servire?	ah, doesn't my faithful service deserve it?
10 Ma straccia pur, crudele;	But tear away, cruel one;
non può morir d'amor alma fedele.	a faithful spirit cannot die of love.
Sorgerà nel morir quasi fenice	My faith will rise in death, as if a phoenix,
la fede mia più bell'e più felice.	more beautiful and happier than before.

Its thirteen lines fall into three sections, lines 1–4, 5–9, and 10–13, developing rationally and in largely abstract terms the distinction between the lover's passion and his faithfulness. The first two sections have complex, hypotactic grammatical structures, and the first alone, especially in contrast to the halting final section, yields the beginning accentuation typical of the discursive style. Only the emotionally heightened rhetoric of the poem, evident particularly in its insistent questions, distinguishes it from countless discursive madrigals written in the first half of the sixteenth century. (And it was this heightened emotion, we may guess, that attracted Monteverdi to the poem.) "Stracciami pur" is, as we have suggested, typical of the lyrics of the Third Book, whether by Guarini (compare "O primavera," "O dolce anima mia," "Se per estremo ardore," "Perfidissimo volto," and "Lumi miei, cari lumi") or by other poets (compare Bembo's "O rossignuol" and the anonymous "La giovinetta pianta").

The discursive style of these lyrics contrasts utterly with the dominant poetic style of Book IV, Schulz-Buschhaus's "epigrammatic style." We may define it by reference to one of the best madrigals of Guarini set here:

Cor mio, mentre vi miro,	My love, while I look at you
visibilmente mi trasform'in voi	I am visibly transformed into you;
e trasformato poi,	and transformed, then
in un solo sospir l'anima spiro.	in one single sigh I expire.
5 O bellezza mortale,	Oh deadly beauty!
o bellezza vitale,	Oh life-giving beauty!
poi che sì tosto un core	since even as a heart
per te rinasce, e per te nato, more.	is reborn for you, for you born it dies.

The sprawling dimensions of "Stracciami pur" have been reduced to eight lines, mostly of seven syllables, a typical length for Guarini's epigrammatic madrigals. This conciseness has been achieved, syntactically, through an avoidance of wordy constructions and hypotaxis: carefully balanced structures of equivalent clauses dominate (in vv. 1–2 and 3–4, in vv. 5 and 6, and within v. 8). Guarini sought grammatical brevity in the streamlined participial usage of lines 3 and 8 ("trasformato," "nato")—Schulz-Buschhaus's *partizipiale Auflösungen,* taken over from the laconic Latin epigram.[10] Finally and most important, the poet achieved semantic brevity by substituting for the multipartite logical structure of the discursive style the two-part format of the classical epigram. This consists of a situation (*expositio* or *narratio*) and a closing "point" (*acumen*). In "Cor mio" verses 1–4 set an amorous scene, in concrete terms that would be exceptional in the discursive style, while verses 5–8 conceptualize this scene and resolve it in a witty paradox—the *acutezza* for which Guarini was especially revered in the early seventeenth century.[11]

Other lyrics by Guarini in Book IV adhere less strictly to the archetypal epigrammatic format but retain its essential brevity and *acutezza.* The most conventional of them returns to the Petrarchan contrast of lover and landscape we have seen in "O primavera":

A un giro sol de' belli occhi lucenti	At one turn of those pretty, gleaming eyes
ride l'aria d'intorno,	the air around us smiles,
e'l mar s'acqueta e i venti,	and the sea and winds grow quiet,
e si fa il ciel d'un altro lume adorno.	and the sky is adorned with a new light.
5 Sol io le luci ho lagrimose e meste.	Only I have sad and tearful eyes.
Certo quando nasceste,	Surely when you were born,
così crudel e ria	so cruel and wicked,
nacque la morte mia.	then was born my death.

But the treatment of the traditional topos is less discursive here and less repetitious than in "O primavera," even though the caesura between situation and point is blurred by the ambiguous, transitional function of line 5. (Monteverdi's music would settle any doubts as to his placing of this line in *expositio* or *acumen.*) In another example Guarini enlarged the *expositio* through repetitive structures reminiscent of his discursive madrigals but enlivened by straightforward isocolon (lines 3–6):

Voi pur da me partite, anima dura,	Thus you leave me, oh hard-of-heart,
né vi duol il partire.	nor does your leaving pain you.
Oimè, quest'è un morire	Alas, this is a cruel
crudele, e voi gioite?	death, and you rejoice?
5 Quest'è vicino aver l'ora suprema,	This is the approach of my most fatal hour,
e voi non la sentite?	and you don't feel it?
Oh meraviglia di durezz'estrema:	Oh miracle of exceeding harshness:
esser alma d'un core	to give life to a heart,
e separarsi e non sentir dolore!	and depart from it, and not feel the pain.

---

10. Ibid., p. 172.
11. Though the epigrammatic style is most evident in the lyrics of Book IV, three poems in Book III, all by Guarini, foreshadow it: "O come è gran martire," "Ch'io non t'ami, cor mio," and "Occhi, un tempo mia vita." The last two madrigals, as we have seen, inspired the most advanced musical idiom of the Third Book.

Finally, in one of his most exquisite lyrics Guarini merged *expositio* and *acumen*, extending the first through the entire poem while retaining the witty force of the second—all under the sway of an encompassing *gioco di parole:*

Oimè, se tanto amate	Alas, if you're so fond
di sentir dir "oimè," deh, perché fate	of hearing "alas" said, oh, why do you
chi dice "oimè" morire?	kill him who says "alas"?
S'io moro, un sol potrete	If I die, you'll hear but one
5 languido e doloroso "oimè" sentire;	languid and sad "alas";
ma se, cor mio, volete	but if, my dear, you wish
che vita abbia da voi, e voi da me,	that I take life from you, and you from me,
avrete mill'e mille dolci "oimè."	you'll have thousands and thousands of sweet "alases."

Most of Guarini's epigrammatic madrigals—most of his *rime* in general, perhaps—seem to have been written already in the 1580s.[12] Nevertheless, there is evidence that the poet had come by the mid-1590s to value epigrammatic wit and conciseness in his madrigals more highly than ever before. In these years, from at least the end of 1595, Guarini set himself to collect and revise his lyric poetry.[13] The collection was published by Giovan Battista Ciotti in May 1598, prefaced with a letter from the publisher that makes clear Guarini's important if belated role in its preparation and the extensive revisions that many of his poems underwent:

> These are those *Rime* of Signor Cavalier Guarini, my most gentle readers, so much requested and long desired by the world; . . . I set myself some time ago to bring together a goodly collection of them. . . . And when I believed myself to have finished that collection, and to be able to bring it forth to the world, I was apprised that the author had substantially altered them, so much so that one could better call them "transformed" than "corrected." Whence I was forced to alter my plans, and give my efforts over to obtaining [the poems] from the author himself. . . . Above all I publish here the true and legitimate texts according to the author.[14]

Of the 142 madrigals in the *Rime* of 1598, most are eight to ten lines long, and not one exceeds eleven lines.[15] These statistics alone are striking in view of the lengths of the eight madrigals by Guarini that Monteverdi had set in 1592: three of them are twelve, thirteen, and fifteen verses long, and only one has fewer than ten

---

12. Musical settings are often useful in establishing this point. They allow us, for example, to assign *termini ante quem* of 1582 to "Oimè, se tanto amate" (Marenzio's setting was published in that year) and 1584 to "Cor mio, mentre vi miro" and "Lumi miei, cari lumi" (Alessandro Striggio referred to his settings of these poems, now lost, in letters of that year; see Riccardo Gandolfi, "Lettere inedite scritte da musicisti e letterati, appar-

tenenti alla seconda metà del secolo XVI," p. 532).
13. Rossi, *Battista Guarini*, pp. 121–22.
14. *Opere di Battista Guarini*, p. 191.
15. This count does not include eight much longer poems set apart at the end of the section entitled "Madrigali"; these represent a distinct poetic genre, called by the eighteenth century the *madrigalessa*.

verses. Clearly Guarini prized brevity in selecting madrigals for inclusion in his *Rime,* omitting or abridging the most long-winded of his earlier lyrics.

He seems to have sought other traits of the epigrammatic style as well. Of the eight poems by Guarini in Monteverdi's Third Book, only four found their way into the *Rime.* Three of them are precisely the madrigals that in their two-section structure and final *acutezza* most closely approach the style of the texts of Book IV: "O come è gran martire," "Ch'io non t'ami, cor mio," and "Occhi, un tempo mia vita." The fourth, "Perfidissimo volto," is especially interesting: it was extensively abridged and revised by the poet for inclusion in the *Rime.* Guarini transformed it, in fact, from the sprawling discursive madrigal of fifteen verses set by Monteverdi into an exemplary epigram. The transformation provides a telling object lesson in the poet's madrigalian ideals around 1598. The version set by Monteverdi in 1592 reads:

Perfidissimo volto,	Most treacherous face,
ben l'usata bellezz'in te si vede,	plainly I see in you your wonted beauty,
ma non l'usata fede.	but not your wonted faith.
Già mi parevi dir: "Quest'amorose	Once you seemed to say to me, "These
luci, che dolcemente	amorous eyes, so beautiful and kind,
rivolgo a te sì belle e sì pietose,	that sweetly I turn on you—
prima vedrai tu spente	you'll see them spent before
che sia spento il desio ch'a te le gira."	the need with which they gaze on you is spent."
Ahi, ch'è spent'il desio,	Alas! the need is spent,
ma non è spento quel per cui sospira	but not she for whom
l'abandonato core.	my abandoned heart sighs.
O volto troppo vago e troppo rio,	Oh face too pretty and too wicked,
perché se perdi amore	why, if you lose love,
non perdi ancor vaghezza?	don't you also lose your charm?
O non hai pari a la beltà fermezza?	Or is your faith not equal to your beauty?

The version included in the *Rime* reads:

Perfidissimo volto,	Most treacherous face,
ben l'usata bellezza in te si vede,	plainly I see in you your wonted beauty,
che mi consuma il core,	which consumes my heart,
ma non l'usata fede.	but not your wonted faith.
Ah, se tu perdi amore,	Ah, if you lose love,
perché seco non perdi ancor vaghezza,	why don't you with it also lose your charm,
o non hai pari a la beltà fermezza?	or is your faith not equal to your beauty?

These data on the length and publication of Guarini's lyrics in Book III are reversed for Guarini's lyrics in Book IV. None of the six madrigals of Guarini here is longer than eleven lines, and four of them appear in the *Rime* of 1598. Of the two that do not, "Non più guerra, pietate" recalls clearly—much more clearly than the other five poems—the rhetorically heightened discursive style of "Stracciami pur il core" and may have been omitted for this reason. (We shall see that Monteverdi's music also recalls the style of Book III.) "A un giro sol" was excluded, perhaps, because its frank reuse of a Petrarchan theme is atypical in the late-sixteenth-century madrigal and in Guarini's output in particular.

At the very least, then, the *Rime* evidence Guarini's preference by 1598 for those of his madrigals that avoid discursive tendencies and embrace instead the concise *acutezza* of the epigram. Monteverdi's choice of texts in his Third Book reveals little awareness of this epigrammatic ideal, but by the time of Book IV his stylistic goals had come to mirror Guarini's. Monteverdi may have been encouraged to adopt the new ideal by Guarini himself in 1592–93, when the poet was a frequent resident of Mantua. It is more likely, however, that Monteverdi and Guarini participated independently in a general stylistic development affecting both music and poetry in the years around 1600. The Ferrarese musical style of the 1590s—that of Luzzaschi, Fontanelli, and Gesualdo—was after all predicated on similar poetic ideals.[16] And the spokesman for this style, the author of the famous dedication to Luzzaschi's Sixth Book of 1596, was none other than Alessandro Guarini, the eldest son of Giambattista. His words sum up the essence of his father's best lyrics:

> Skipping over all those other poetic forms that have changed only in subject matter—such as canzonas, sestinas, sonnets, ottavas, and *terze rime*—I shall say of the madrigal that it seems to have been invented just for music, and I shall speak the truth in saying that in our age it has received its perfect form—a form so different from its former one that, were the first versifiers to return to life, they would scarce be able to recognize it, so changed is it in the brevity, the wit [*acutezza*], the grace, the nobility, and finally the sweetness with which the poets of today have seasoned it.[17]

Six years after the appearance of Guarini's letter, a Venetian poet with close ties to the court of Vincenzo Gonzaga, Mauritio Moro, made explicit the connection of the modern madrigal and ancient epigram: "Finally you may read madrigals, the last-born child of this [Tuscan] tongue, which the divine Tasso, the singular Goselini, the noble and refined Manfredi, the most virtuosic and delightful Rinaldi, the gentle and most courteous Agostino Nardi, Simonetti, Guarini, and others have published up until now: which in their laconic brevity equal or rather surpass the Epigrams of the Latin poets."[18] Just in these years, too, the young Neapolitan poet Giambattista Marino was perfecting the language of image and *acutezza* that would bring him fame with the publication of his *Rime* in 1602. Marino was not one to acknowledge his poetic debts readily, but his praise for Guarini was warm: "He alone in this century (without any exceptions) seems to me to merit the title of poet,

16. On this style see n. 7 above and excursus 1 below.

17. Translated in Newcomb, *The Madrigal at Ferrara* 1:118. Newcomb gives the original on pp. 277–78.

18. *I tre giardini de' madrigali del Costante, Aca-*demico Cospirante, Mauritio Moro Vinetiano, p. 19. Moro dedicates his *Giardino primo* to Vincenzo Gonzaga and reveals in his letter of dedication that he had sent the duke an earlier version of it in manuscript.

for his lively expression of emotions and tender sentiments and for the vitality and delicacy of his style."[19]

So Monteverdi's turn to the epigrammatic style was not an isolated phenomenon, nor one that necessarily reflects the direct influence of Guarini. (Indeed we shall posit below the existence of a general Mantuan epigrammatic style in the late 1590s, akin to the contemporary Ferrarese style in its poetic ends if not its musical means.) But of the indirect influence of Guarini there can be no doubt, for the best examples of Monteverdi's new style are repeatedly inspired by the elegant epigrammatic lyrics of the Ferrarese poet.

Monteverdi in his music, like Guarini in his poetry, came to value conciseness in the 1590s. The average length of his single-section madrigals had grown steadily from fifty-four measures in Book I to seventy-seven measures in Book II to a huge ninety-three measures in Book III. This increase reflected Monteverdi's ever surer control of large musical spans, made possible by the mastery of such devices as the multiple-subject expositions that characterize Book III. Now, however, his expressive ideals were taking a new turn, and the average length of the madrigals of the Fourth Book dropped to seventy-five measures, slightly below the average for Book II. The most refined examples of the epigrammatic style fall short even of this average: "A un giro sol," seventy-three measures, "Sfogava con le stelle," seventy-one measures in spite of its thirteen-line poem, "Oimè, se tanto amate," sixty-seven measures, "Cor mio, non mori? E mori!," sixty-one measures, and "Cor mio, mentre vi miro," at forty-nine measures the tiniest madrigal Monteverdi had published since the First Book.

Such brevity depended on a matching of musical gesture to the syntactic and semantic aspects of the poetry more precise than Monteverdi had ever before achieved. To this end the composer employed all the devices we have observed in the most advanced works of the Third Book. In "Cor mio, mentre vi miro," for example, he captured the grammatical dependency of line 1 on line 2 by means of dovetailed phrases, achieved by staggering the homophony setting line 2 and rendered effective by a resonant eighth-note declamation of "visibilmente" (recalling that of "indivisibilmente" in "Vattene pur, crudel"; the text of "Cor mio" is given above). He conveyed the similar relationship of verses 3 and 4 by using the bassline of verse 3, with its original text, to support the upper-voice duet declaiming verse 4, in the manner of "Occhi, un tempo mia vita" (Ex. 27; compare Ex. 25). Whenever Monteverdi used this technique he was careful in the following measures to sound the newly introduced poetic line by itself (often, as here, in a *fauxbourdon* arrangement for the three lowest voices). Just as in his multiple-subject exposi-

---

19. Letter to Gaspare Salviani of 1612, cited in Rossi, *Battista Guarini*, p. 151.

EXAMPLE 27

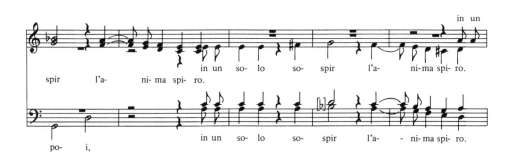

Monteverdi, "Cor mio, mentre vi miro," mm. 11–19

tions, he took pains when juxtaposing two or more poetic lines to guarantee the intelligibility of each line.

In "Cor mio" the crucial poetic caesura between *expositio* and *acumen* (after v. 4) is heralded by a textural reduction akin to an evaporated cadence—a pictorial rendering of the soul expiring ("l'anima spiro")—and confirmed by the massed homophony and disjunctive tonal shift that follows without pause. The rising sequential succession of cadences setting verses 5 and 6 (actually sequences within sequences, functioning at the level of both two- and four-bar units) propels us powerfully forward. The same upward sequence and text are then reiterated by the tenor, absent from the first exclamations, which acts as a bassline for duets declaiming verse 7 and the beginning of verse 8. (This musical technique again binds poetic lines that are closely dependent: the paradox of the contradictory exclamations of verses 5 and 6 is explained only by verses 7 and 8.) The passage culminates after seventeen measures in rapid chordal declamation of this last line and a half without verses 5–6, in which we recognize once again the interlocking sequential harmonies of the *Romanesca* tradition. The energy stored up in this long series of rising sequences carries us across the abrupt musical caesura at its end into the affective peroration on "e per te nato, more." Monteverdi thus insured the syntactic juncture of the parallel phrases of verse 8 while respecting, in his shift to affective counterpoint, the semantic contrast ("rinasce . . . more") that embodies the paradoxical *acutezza* of the poem. But the semantic contrast works even within the last phrase, embodied precisely in the final words of the poem: ". . . nato, more." So Monteverdi's concluding point of imitation, while contrasting with what came before, must also, in the manner of "O primavera," embrace internal contrast. It does so brilliantly, without recourse to multiple counterpoint, by cutting short the rising line in each voice on "nato" with a dying collapse of a seventh to express "more."

Abrupt tonal disjunction is an important rhetorical tool in these epigrammatic madrigals, especially when matched, as in "Cor mio," to the poetic division between situation and point. Usually it coincides, again as in "Cor mio," with striking changes of texture, rhythmic motion, and/or other musical elements. The technique appears already in "Ch'io non t'ami" of Book III (at "Ma se tu sei quel core"), and we have noted antecedents of it as far back as Book II (see chap. 2 above); but its most impressive use is in "A un giro sol de' belli occhi lucenti." The A-minor tonality of this piece moves off shortly after its start to C and G, where melismatic madrigalisms depict the natural surroundings described in verses 1–4 (see the text above). It returns wrenchingly at "Sol io . . ." (v. 5), tying this line unambiguously to the *acumen* and giving rise to a long, dissonance-ridden dual-subject peroration on verses 6–8.

In "Sfogava con le stelle" Monteverdi employed tonal disjunction with subtler semantic intent. Ottavio Rinuccini's thirteen-line lyric hardly seems at first glance to qualify as an epigram.[20] But a closer look reveals that its last nine verses consti-

---

20. The ascription of this madrigal to Rinuccini has been passed on unquestioningly in the musicological literature on the basis of Francesco Trucchi, ed., *Poesie italiane inedite di dugento autori* 4:112. Trucchi drew the poem and its ascription from the small manuscript miscellany Cl. VII.907 in the Biblioteca Nazionale of Florence; to my knowledge neither is found in any of the other, more extensive Florentine manuscripts of Rinuccini's poetry. This might seem to cast doubt on the ascription, especially since the madrigal is extraordinarily long by Rinuccini's usual standards. But other external evidence reinforces the ascription: (1) "Sfogava con le stelle" is modeled on Torquato Tasso's madrigal "Al lume delle stelle." I have shown elsewhere that Rinuccini turned to Tasso for just this sort of poetic guidance already in the 1580s ("Rinuccini, Peri,

Monteverdi," pp. 91, 113–26). The madrigals that resulted from this imitation of Tasso are, like "Sfogava con le stelle," generally longer than the madrigals later collected in Rinuccini's *Poesie* (Florence, 1622). (This suggests, by the way, that Rinuccini too participated in the turn to epigrammatic brevity of the 1590s discussed above.) (2) *Sfogare* is not a common verb in the late-sixteenth-century lyric. But a version in Rinuccini's hand in the Biblioteca Nazionale of the canzonetta "Non havea Febo ancora" (the text of Monteverdi's famous *Lament of the Nymph*) echoes its usage in "Sfogava con le stelle": "Si trà sdegnosi pianti / sfogava il suo dolor" (beside the second of these verses Rinuccini has entered the reading later published in his *Poesie*: "spargea le voci al ciel"; see MS Palatine 250, fols. 147v–48v).

tute in themselves a madrigal with epigrammatic as well as discursive tendencies, one introduced and given a semidramatic context by verses 1–4:

	Sfogava con le stelle	A lovesick man poured forth
	un infermo d'amore	to the stars
	sotto notturno ciel il suo dolore,	in the nighttime sky his grief,
	e dicea fisso in loro:	and said, his eyes fixed on them:
5	"O imagini belle	"Oh beautiful images
	de l'idol mio ch'adoro,	of my idol, whom I adore,
	sì com'a me mostrate	just as you show me,
	mentre così splendete	while you glisten thus,
	la sua rara beltate,	her rare beauty,
10	così mostrate a lei	so show her
	i vivi ardori miei;	my burning ardor;
	la fareste col vostr'aureo sembiante	with your golden semblance you might make her
	pietosa sì, come me fate amante."	kind, just as you make me lovelorn."

The epigrammatic caesura after verse 11 is weakened significantly by the hypotactic syntax of the five lines before it, which creates a rival caesura between the dependent clause of verses 7–9 and its consequent (vv. 10–11). This secondary caesura is all the stronger because the consequent forms a semantic antithesis to its antecedent ("As you show me her beauty, so show her my ardor").

With a sure hand Monteverdi turned this discursive feature of the poem to his advantage. He set off verses 10 and 11 as a major-mode tonal ellipsis, steadfastly cadencing three times on F and contrasting with the D-minor tonality that prevails before it. At the true epigrammatic caesura he shifted tonal gears again, back to the D tonic of the opening, thus rounding off the madrigal in the tonality with which it began.

Monteverdi marked this tonal return by reverting to the famous texture of the opening of "Sfogava con le stelle": unmeasured homophonic chanting in the manner of *falsobordone*. Just as composers of sacred music used *falsobordone* as a polyphonic means of moving rapidly through lengthy psalm texts, so Monteverdi evoked it here to declaim quickly verses 1–4. But his use of it had other, richer functions as well. It differentiated the poet's opening narration of the scene from the first-person epigrammatic complaint that follows.[21] And even as it enhanced the tonal return at line 12, its rapid declamation allowed an unusually effective musical rendering of Rinuccini's harsh enjambement: "la fareste col vostr'aureo sembiante / pietosa."[22]

21. See Schrade, *Monteverdi,* p. 191.
22. The probable Florentine provenance of Monteverdi's text has inspired much conjecture about connections between his *falsobordone* techniques and nascent Florentine monody, especially in the light of similarities of his setting to Giulio Caccini's, published in 1602 in *Le nuove*

musiche (see Imogene Horsley, "Monteverdi's Use of Borrowed Material in 'Sfogava con le stelle' "). We should tread carefully here, however. First, the dependence of Monteverdi on Caccini might also run in the opposite direction, given the extensive circulation of Monteverdi's madrigals in manuscript form around 1600 (see

EXAMPLE 28

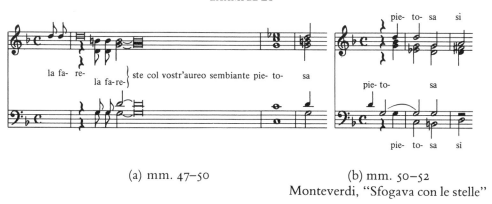

(a) mm. 47–50 (b) mm. 50–52

Monteverdi, "Sfogava con le stelle"

To enliven the plodding hypotaxis of verses 7–11 Monteverdi exploited his favored epigrammatic connective device, more insistently than anywhere else in his output. That is, he made the two syntactic groups (lines 7–9 and 10–11) internally coherent by repeating lines 7, 8, and 10 as basslines supporting the introduction of the next verses in duets above. Moreover, to bind together the two lines of the invocation of verses 5–6 he repeated, in varied and abbreviated form, the forceful rising lines of the exclamation "O" at "de l'idol mio."

Finally, to put across the affective locutions of the text Monteverdi indulged in more venturesome dissonances than we have encountered before, thus providing more grist for Artusi's mill. But in each case, as in Book III, the dissonances arise in passages whose structural logic is ironclad. At "il suo dolore" he introduced a minor seventh by prolonging the subdominant harmony in the lower voices (a sonority already heard, without dissonance, at "d'amore") against a stepwise descent in the *canto*. At the exclamation "O" the unequivocal melodic trajectories of all the voices render the fleeting dissonances they create expressive instead of subversive. And Monteverdi generated the grinding clashes at "pietosa sì" by a simple, stunning rearrangement of the voice leading of the perfectly consonant *falsobordone* progressions heard just before. Instead of rising a half step to take the third of the subdominant harmony while the bass drops a fifth (Ex. 28a), the top voice now repeats its note, forming a ninth over the drooping bass (and usually also a seventh over a middle voice following the bass in parallel thirds; see Ex. 28b). The clarity of the gesture is never in doubt and suffices to carry us through the introduction of a new motive (at "come me fate amante") and new dissonance in Monteverdi's adroit and expressive dual-subject peroration.

---

excursus 1 below). Second, Salomone Rossi, Monteverdi's colleague at Mantua, published his setting à 5 of "Sfogava con le stelle" a month before Caccini's appeared; it should certainly be taken into account. Finally, we must remember that *falsobordone* has in general no closer relation to monody than to any number of homophonic declamatory styles of the sixteenth century.

Our nagging sense that in "Sfogava con le stelle" Monteverdi needed to over-come certain discursive limitations in Rinuccini's poem is gone in "Oimè, se tanto amate." Monteverdi's setting of Guarini's fine lyric seems another example, like "Ecco mormorar l'onde," of the serendipitous meeting of uniquely congenial musical and poetic styles that characterizes the composer's oeuvre. In this poem Monteverdi found the perfect epigram. It enabled him to perfect his own epigrammatic style in music.

Guarini's fivefold repetition of the word "oimè" binds his eight verses tightly (the poem is given above). It also gives rise to less obvious rhetorical effects: the excited chiasmus of lines 1–2 ("oimè" — verb phrase / verb phrase — "oimè"), the parallel endings of the three syntactic periods of which the poem consists (" 'oimè' morire . . . 'oimè' sentire . . . 'oimè' "), and the languishing expansiveness yielded by the widening gaps between recurrences of the word after line 3 (it occurs in lines 1, 2, 3, 5, and 8).

Monteverdi seized first on the unifying force of Guarini's repetitiveness. Each time "oimè" returns in his setting it is declaimed by the most prominent voices to the drooping thirds that opened the piece (or to expanded variants of them: see the falling fourth, fifths, and seventh of measures 16–18).[23] The unorthodox, bitter-sweet dissonances of the first measures return with this motive, either undisguised (mm. 16–17, 27, 37, 54–55, and 64) or in the form of piquant cross-relations (mm. 49–51). Monteverdi's emphasis of Guarini's "oimè"'s by means of this recurring material projects as well the *allargando* effect of their less and less frequent repetition across the whole poem; the musical spaces between clustered statements of the word widen from two to five to nine and finally to eleven measures. Monteverdi reflected this slowdown on the local level as well, in the written-out ritard with which the madrigal closes. This wonderful transformation of the traditional affective peroration plays also on Guarini's use of a truncated, that is, end-accented, line to end his poem—the first such ending among Monteverdi's texts.

Monteverdi also underscored the wit of Guarini's final line in ways unavailable to the poet. He realized literally its "thousands and thousands of sweet 'alases' "—or nineteen of them, at any rate—in repetitions of droll insistence. The first group of these is built from an elaborated *fauxbourdon* descent or, more properly speaking, from two interlocking such progressions. Monteverdi's last-moment sidestepping of the implied $VII^6 \rightarrow I$ cadence (to C) yields, in the most inspired stroke of the

<hr />

23. Neither of the modern editions of the Fourth Book gives an acceptable text underlay for the *canto* in these measures, with the result that the falling fifth in this voice does not coincide in these editions with "oimè." In the first edition of 1603 the underlay is crowded but nonetheless clear. The only reading that observes proper po-etic elision and takes account of the hyphenation of "mori-re" (indicating nonsyllabic delivery) also sets "oimè" to the melodic descent:

chi di- ce "oi- mè" mo- ri- re?

work, the cadence with which it will ultimately end (Ex. 29). This combines a strong cadential bassline, the effect if not the fact of mild dissonance in its irregular harmonic resolution, and the falling third of the "oimè" theme. (How much less imaginative a cadence a lesser composer might have created, with a regular V → I resolution and the falling motive from the fifth to the third rather than the third to the first scalar degree.)

Monteverdi exploited his recurring "oimè" theme as well in his vivid rendering of Guarini's opening chiasmus (Ex. 30). Here he joined to it a surging harmonic sequence (g → D / Bb → F / . . . C → g), interrupted to accommodate the quick insertion of "se tanto amate / di sentir dir." The combination of the recurring motive on each "oimè," the hurried eighth-note declamation of the intervening syllables, and the rising sequential harmonies sweeps us through Guarini's chiasmic enjambement to the end of verse 2 ("deh, perché fate"). This phrase is also set as a rising sequence—a more hectically rising one—and reaches a cadence only with the next return of the sinking "oimè" theme, at the end of verse 3.

The epigrammatic caesura of Guarini's madrigal occurs between lines 5 and 6, in the middle of the *expositio* that, as we have noted, extends through the entire poem. Not surprisingly the caesura inspires a tonal leap, aided by a pause in all the voices and followed by livelier rhythms, from the G minor that has ruled the work so far to Bb. And, just as in "Sfogava con le stelle," this semantic and tonal departure in poetry and music affords the opportunity for semantic and tonal return a moment later. The music moves to a full cadence on Bb at the end of verse 7 and, as the poet returns in verse 8 to the subject of "oimè"'s, falls immediately back to G. With the tonality of the opening measures return also their unhurried rhythms and falling-third motives, and even their sequence seems to be alluded to in measures 54–57.

The tonal returns of "Sfogava con le stelle" and "Oimè, se tanto amate" are not entirely alike in poetic function, however. The poetic return that Monteverdi high-

EXAMPLE 29

Monteverdi, "Oimè, se tanto amate," mm. 47–52

EXAMPLE 30

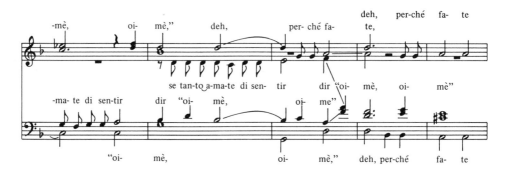

Monteverdi, "Oimè, se tanto amate," beginning

lighted in "Sfogava" was a vague one, a return to general thoughts of the beloved's cruelty that had already been indirectly evoked in the opening verses of the poem. This less-than-explicit literary context weakens the musico-poetic impact of Monteverdi's return, if not its effectiveness in rounding out the purely musical structure. In "Oimè, se tanto amate," on the other hand, the thematic and tonal return of Monteverdi's setting enhances the precise verbal reprise of Guarini's madrigal. The return of "oimè" at the end of the final line fulfills the epigrammatic promise of verses 1–3, where it was so prominently featured. The poet could only position the word perfectly in its context and leave it, his epigram complete. It was left for Monteverdi to transform it into the consummate *musikalischer Spass*.[24]

Monteverdi could not have done justice to Guarini's madrigal at the time of Books I–III. His rhetorical procedure there was one of musical juxtaposition matched to semantic contrast—a blunt tool but, as we have seen in works like "O primavera," one that Monteverdi could wield with considerable skill and ingenuity. It was not, however, merely a personal advance that Monteverdi achieved with

24. For a Schenkerian analysis of "Oimè, se tanto amate" that intersects only occasionally with mine, see Felix Salzer, "Heinrich Schenker and Historical Research."

his epigrammatic style. He also surpassed the expressive possibilities of all the various madrigalian styles practiced by his contemporaries. These idioms—from the Ferrarese style of abrupt contrast and free dissonance and chromaticism, to Benedetto Pallavicino's extension in his late works of Wert's manner, to Marenzio's exploration in his last two collections first of homophonic declamation, then of expressionistic counterpoint—were conceived as a succession of musical responses tailored more or less vividly to the declamation and sense of individual phrases of the text. Composers of these idioms rarely combined lines of poetry, preferring instead a verse-by-verse approach in which the boundary between one line and the next carried the full weight of musico-poetic syntactic coherence. At the same time, however, they only occasionally distinguished anything like Monteverdi's panoply of cadential emphases. Their rhetorical vision was therefore shortsighted, bound usually by the limits of a single verse or period. Their works tended, when they were invested with expressive gestures of great distinctiveness, to give as a whole a fragmented, unintegrated effect especially noticeable in madrigals by Gesualdo but apparent also in pieces by Marenzio, Luzzaschi, Pallavicino, and others.

Monteverdi's epigrammatic style was his most original means of dealing with this expressive weakness, which, it should be said, is not absent from his own output. (It is a structural weakness as well, and hence, as Schrade noted, structural coherence and expressive cogency are naturally merged in the best works of the Fourth Book.)[25] The success of the epigrammatic style depended on straightforward homophonic declamation, making frequent use of reduced textures, and the relegation of earlier, hard-won contrapuntal techniques to concluding perorations. In this simplified texture (a villanella-like texture, that is, and not the multisubject polyphony of Wert, Pallavicino, and Monteverdi himself in his Second and Third Books) Monteverdi sought new methods for combining successive poetic lines, thus significantly extending the rhetorical range of previous styles.

Most crucial to the success of the epigrammatic style, perhaps, was Monteverdi's self-imposed limitation in it of tonal variety. The harmonies in these madrigals revolve with the utmost clarity around the tonic chord, developing the *Romanesca*-like vocabulary of Wert's madrigals and lighter genres like the villanella. The rhetorical force of this harmonic lexicon, which Monteverdi had discovered in his study of Wert's *Liberata* settings, was now deepened. And this transparent tonal context allowed Monteverdi unequivocally to distinguish local effects from expression on broader levels. Moments of expressive dissonance and chromaticism are heard in these works as purely local phenomena, not, as often occurs in Ferrarese madrigals of these years, as local gestures that also redirect the larger musical flow in obscure and unpredictable ways. On the other hand, tonal reorientation, when it does occur, carries with it increased expressive force: it is a once-in-a-

25. *Monteverdi*, pp. 190–91.

madrigal event capable of conveying a decisive semantic shift at the caesura of an epigrammatic poem. When combined with an evaporated cadence followed by massed homophony, it lends these gestures a structural and rhetorical force barely adumbrated in their use by Ferrarese composers. And tonal clarity, finally, engenders a strengthened sense of tonal unity. The relationship of the falling motives in the opening and closing sections of "Oimè, se tanto amate" gains in musico-poetic efficacy from the major-mode hiatus between these sections.

In his epigrammatic style Monteverdi united techniques from all his earlier idioms to achieve a new sensitivity of musical response to words, one, it is tempting to add, unmatched in the previous history of Western polyphony. In the process he won his way for the first time to an original, mature, and utterly personal mode of musical oration.

EXCURSUS 1:
A Speculative Chronology of the Madrigals of Books IV and V

The epigrammatic style is not the only style in the Fourth Book. In fact, the collection as a whole stands out among Monteverdi's first six books for the wide variety of its music, as scholars have frequently noted. This diversity is hardly surprising, for the Fourth Book was not published until 1603, eleven years after the Third. Crucial years of stylistic maturation, from the end of Monteverdi's twenty-fourth year to the end of his thirty-fifth, separate it from his earlier collections. Indeed, the diversity of Book IV and the chronological gap between it and Book III together lead easily to the supposition that Monteverdi gathered here madrigals he had composed throughout the 1590s and first years of the new century—a supposition bolstered by the appearance of one piece from Book IV in an anthology of 1597 and by other external evidence. The case of the Fifth Book of 1605 is similar, even though its styles are not as varied as those of Book IV. External evidence enables us to place the composition of two of its madrigals back as far as 1598.

Both collections together, then, seem to preserve a chronologically unclear record of Monteverdi's development during the central years of his early maturity. If musicologists have been loathe to decipher this record, it is because the fragments of hard-and-fast evidence available to aid them are few, and because of their suspicion of chronology based primarily on musical style. But our understanding of the northern-Italian madrigal of the 1590s has grown remarkably in recent years, providing a more clearly focused stylistic background against which to view Monteverdi's personal development. In some cases this clarified context has invested the

sparse external evidence for the dating of his madrigals with novel and unexp(
significance. Add to this the strikingly, self-consciously directed growth that
seems to characterize that portion of Monteverdi's output for which a relatively
secure chronology is available—a growth that may lead us to suspend somewhat
our normally healthy suspicion of chronology based only on style—and the hesitancy to offer a hypothetical ordering of Monteverdi's madrigals from 1592 to 1603
should vanish. Recognizing the inherent limitations of my argument, then, and of-
fering as *apologia* the insight it might yield into Monteverdi's musical growth, I
suggest the following approximate chronology of the works of Books IV and V.

Works in Styles of the Third Book, circa 1592–96

Five madrigals from Book IV forcefully recall styles we have seen in the preceding
book. They show none of the techniques of the mature epigrammatic madrigals—
their new connective devices, evaporated cadences and abrupt tonal disjunction, uncanonical dissonance treatment, and so on. Nor do they show other elements of
style that may, as we shall see, be associated with Monteverdi's works of the late
1590s. Instead they ring changes on the florid and contrapuntal idioms of the Third
Book.

As we noted above, two of these madrigals, "Io mi son giovinetta" and "Quel-
l'augellin che canta," are in the pictorial, G-minor florid style of "O rossignuol"
and similar works in Book III, a conservative style already by 1592. They appear
together as numbers 13 and 14 of Book IV. Both pieces look back as far as the
canzonetta-madrigals of the Second Book in their predilection for slowly descending basslines supporting melismas in the voices above. And both (especially the
second) recall Monteverdi's settings from *Gerusalemme liberata* in their use of five-
part homophony with the tenor staggered in relation to the other voices.

The next piece, "Non più guerra, pietate," is in a different style. Its text, by
Guarini, is a ten-line amorous complaint in a rhetorically impassioned but nonetheless discursive style—that is, a madrigal along the lines of Guarini's "Perfidissimo
volto" (in its first version) and "Stracciami pur il core." Monteverdi set it, as he had
set these other lyrics, in the multiple-subject contrapuntal style that had dominated
Book III. He conveyed Guarini's intense rhetoric through cutting declamatory
rhythms especially reminiscent of "Perfidissimo volto."

Monteverdi's infatuation with multiple-subject polyphony culminated in
"Piagn'e sospira; e quand'i caldi raggi," the contrapuntal *tour de force* that ends the
Fourth Book. The placement of the work is not surprising: Monteverdi had ended
each of his previous books with pieces displaying some type of compositional vir-
tuosity, from the three-madrigal cycle on rival lyrics of Guarini and Tasso of Book
I, to the exercise in Rore's *stile antico* of Book II, to the Marenzian harmonic wan-

derings in the service of narrative depiction setting Livio Celiano's pastoral *partenza* "Rimanti in pace" of Book III. He would continue this practice in his later collections, concluding Books V and VI with works scored for nine and seven voices, and Books VII and VIII with lengthy ballets. (Only the Ninth Book, published posthumously in 1651, does not show this and other elements of self-conscious organization—a compelling argument, by the way, that Monteverdi himself specified the ordering of pieces in his madrigal books while he was alive.)

To call "Piagn'e sospira" a contrapuntal *tour de force* is not to exaggerate. Eighty-seven of its 110 measures comprise a mammoth multiple-subject exposition, setting six eleven-syllable lines of poetry to at least six strikingly distinctive melodies (the first a slow chromatic ascent). After such a beginning the setting of the final two lines of text could hardly avoid seeming perfunctory, even though Monteverdi treated them to vigorous sequential homophony with touches of expressive chromaticism.

If the musical style of "Piagn'e sospira" suggests a date of composition in the early 1590s, so does its text, an *ottava* by Tasso from the revised version of his *Liberata* entitled *Gerusalemme conquistata*.[1] That Monteverdi should have been interested in this work during these years seems logical. First, it is obviously related to the *Liberata,* which also occupied Monteverdi's thoughts at this time. Second, its publication, a much-touted, long-awaited literary event, took place in November 1593. Third, and most provocative, Tasso was hard at work on the *Conquistata* during his last stay in Mantua in 1591—a time when, even if Monteverdi did not actually meet the poet, he could hardly have been unaware of his presence at court.

Hardly less impressive than the exposition of "Piagn'e sospira" is that of "Ah dolente partita," which opens Book IV. This work too employs the multiple-subject contrapuntal style of Book III but with a new affective pathos obvious already in the chain of suspensions of its first measures. (Here as in "O primavera" and "Quell'augellin" Monteverdi set an excerpt from *Il pastor fido* in a lyrical style without dramatic connotations.) We can assign a more secure date to this madrigal than to any other in the Fourth Book. It was published, along with five pieces from the Second and Third Books, in Paul Kaufmann's Nuremberg anthology of 1597, *Fiori del giardino di diversi eccellentissimi autori*.[2] And it seems to have been composed after January 1594, for, as Einstein noted, it borrows features from Marenzio's setting of the same text published at that time.[3] Indeed, it may even have been written

---

1. The author and poetic source were identified by Pirrotta, "Scelte poetiche," p. 28.

2. RISM 1597[13]. The other works of Monteverdi included are "Non si levava" and "Dolcemente dormiva" from Book II and "La giovinetta pianta," "Sovra tenere herbette," and "Stracciami pur il cor" from Book III.

3. *The Italian Madrigal,* p. 726. Aside from the homophonic setting of "E sento nel partire" noted by Einstein, Monteverdi also borrowed Marenzio's half-note perpetual motion on "per far che moia immortalmente il core," enhancing its expressive charge with falling diminished fourths.

after August 1595, when Wert's "Ah dolente partita" was published at the head of his Eleventh Book, since Monteverdi's multiple-subject exposition, utterly unlike Marenzio's homophonic opening, looks to Wert for its ordering of vocal entries and for elements of the melodic and rhythmic character of its first themes. This second *terminus post quem* is less secure than the first because Monteverdi might well have had the opportunity to hear and study Wert's setting at Mantua before its publication. (Nor, of course, can we rule out the possibility that Monteverdi's setting was the earlier of the two.) But the connection of the two pieces inspires the attractive speculation that when Monteverdi, emulating Wert, placed his setting at the head of his next publication (even though it was in a style by now outmoded) the "dolente partita" he commemorated was the death of his Mantuan mentor in 1596.[4]

The question of influences on "Ah dolente partita" may be more complicated still. Its exposition also shows some similarity to that of Gesualdo's "Voi volete ch'io mora," notably in the shape and treatment of its fourth motive, at "E pur i' provo." (Compare Gesualdo's work at "Questa misera vita.") Gesualdo published "Voi volete" at the head of his Third Book, dedicated in March 1595; it is clear from another borrowing, noted below, that Monteverdi knew the work. But Gesualdo's multiple-subject exposition, with its vertical juxtaposition of three poetic lines, is unique in his Third Book and highly unusual in general in the Ferrarese style of the 1590s. It suggests, indeed, the influence of Mantuan idioms. Specifically, it recalls in its triple counterpoint, its opening motive descending through an octave, and the canzonetta-like rhythm of its second motive the exposition of Monteverdi's "O primavera" from Book III. So the lines of stylistic dependence seem to run from Mantua to Ferrara and back again, and the confluence of stylistic gesture in Monteverdi's "Ah dolente partita" connects Gesualdo, Wert, and Marenzio.

Works in Ferrarese and Mantuan Regional Styles, circa 1595–1600

The interaction of Monteverdi and Gesualdo described above raises the larger question of Monteverdi's familiarity with Ferrarese musical developments of the mid-1590s. We have already pointed out several signs of his earlier dependence on Luzzaschi's works of the 1580s, including the evaporated cadences of the most

---

4. In a private communication Robert Holzer has offered another plausible interpretation: the "dolente partita" refers to the death of Duke Alfonso d'Este of Ferrara, an event Monteverdi mentions in the dedication of Book IV. For an analysis of modal structures in "Ah dolente partita" from a modern reductionist perspective, see Susan Kaye McClary, "The Transition from Modal to Tonal Organization in the Works of Monteverdi," pp. 113–35.

advanced works of Book III. But Monteverdi's dedication of the Fourth Book to the Accademici Intrepidi of Ferrara suggests an even more direct involvement with the Ferrarese court in the mid-1590s:

> Since in previous years I was not able to present some of my madrigals in manuscript to the Most Serene Alfonso Duke of Ferrara, because of his death; now that there has arisen in that city a Prince, and Leader of a most noble group of beknighted friends and doers of virtuous deeds, gathered together in your large Academy, Most Illustrious Signori, . . . I have thought it appropriate not to leave the same city, to which I am much inclined, and to acknowledge the same Cavaliers, my Signori, with the gratitude I owe, presenting and dedicating to them as I now do with all my heart's affection the same and other new Madrigals published here.[5]

Duke Alfonso died in November 1597, and Anthony Newcomb has argued from documentary evidence that Monteverdi was not known at Alfonso's court before December 1594. These dates delimit the period of Monteverdi's first involvement with the Este court. Notably they place it precisely in the years when the ducal printer Vittorio Baldini was proclaiming Ferrarese musical preeminence with a series of madrigal collections by Luzzaschi, Gesualdo, and Fontanelli.[6] Hence it would seem likely that the madrigals of Book IV that most clearly employ Ferrarese idioms are at least some of those Monteverdi intended to present to Alfonso before November 1597.

Two works grouped together in Book IV (nos. 8 and 9) seem explicitly to evoke Gesualdo's Fourth Book, published by Baldini in 1596: "Luci serene e chiare" and "La piaga c'ho nel core." The first is a resetting of the text by the Ferrarese poet Ridolfo Arlotti that opens Gesualdo's collection—the only text in Monteverdi's Fourth and Fifth Books set by Gesualdo, Luzzaschi, or Fontanelli in the mid-1590s. (This striking paucity of shared texts suggests that, whatever contact Monteverdi may have had with the Ferrarese composers, he had little to do with the local poets who seem to have supplied most of their texts.)[7] In resetting the text, Monteverdi borrowed numerous textural and rhythmic details from Gesualdo, including the homophony at "nell'incendio, diletto" and "O miracol d'amore" and the eighth-note declamation of "alma ch'è tutta foco." He also took over Gesualdo's static and straightforward AA'BB' form (inspired by the strophic structure of the text) but transposed his A' up a whole step, raising the tessitura and with it the emotional intensity of his setting.

The opening of "La piaga c'ho nel core," with its slow, dissonant, chromatic

5. Claudio Monteverdi, *Madrigali a 5 voci, libro quarto,* ed. Elena Ferrari Barassi, p. 70.

6. See Newcomb, *The Madrigal at Ferrara* 1:208 and chap. 7. Domenico de' Paoli, *Monteverdi,* p. 101, has suggested that Monteverdi may have traveled to Ferrara seeking employment from Alfonso in mid-1596, when Vincenzo Gonzaga chose Pallavicino instead of him to replace Wert as *maestro di cappella* at Mantua.

7. Newcomb, *The Madrigal at Ferrara* 1:116–18, 130, discusses the local poetic style preferred by the Ferrarese composers. On p. 130n he identifies Arlotti as author of "Luci serene e chiare."

homophony, surely represents Monteverdi's most transparent assimilation of Gesualdo's more extreme expressive methods. It daringly imitates the first measures of such madrigals as "Sparge la morte," "Moro, e mentre sospiro," and "Ecco morirò dunque" in Gesualdo's Fourth Book. Monteverdi's following abrupt shift to quicker rhythms and imitative counterpoint to capture the poet's contrast of his state with his beloved's ("La piaga c'ho nel core, / donna, onde lieta sei"—"The wound I have in my heart, / my lady, which makes you happy") is also a clear reflection of the fragmentary emotional world of the Ferrarese madrigal of the 1590s. (Compare, for example, Gesualdo's "Ecco morirò dunque" or, with the emotional order reversed, Luzzaschi's "Gioite voi co'l canto, / mentr'io piango, e sospiro.")

Such individual gestures do not, of course, make these two madrigals thoroughly Ferrarese. Neither work, taken as a whole, could be mistaken for one by Gesualdo or Luzzaschi. This is true because the borrowed gestures are anomalous events superimposed on but not altering fundamentally the foundations of Monteverdi's own developing style. A final example of his dependence on Gesualdo, the opening of "Cor mio, non mori? E mori!," demonstrates this with particular clarity (Ex. 31a). Monteverdi borrowed the pungent dissonance of his second measure almost literally from the beginning of the *seconda parte* of Gesualdo's "Voi volete ch'io mora" (Ex. 31b). Obvious similarities of wording here undoubtedly in-

EXAMPLE 31

(a) Monteverdi, "Cor mio, non mori? E mori!," beginning

(b) Gesualdo, "Voi volete ch'io mora," *seconda parte*, beginning (*Sämtliche Madrigale,* ed. Weismann, 3:15)

spired Monteverdi's borrowing. Immediately after the dissonant suspensions, however, Monteverdi's and Gesualdo's paths diverged in directions characteristic of each composer. Gesualdo turned to an imitative texture that, according to Newcomb, is typically Ferrarese: spun from a fragmentary, tonally vague motive. Monteverdi, on the other hand, turned to a speechlike homophonic declamation foreign to the Ferrarese style.

And in general, except for occasional gestures specifically reminiscent of the Ferrarese dialect, Monteverdi's madrigals differ in style from works of Luzzaschi, Gesualdo, or Fontanelli. But this does not mean that his creative voice was yet the stunningly individual one of the mature epigrammatic style. Rather he shared his musical language with other composers around him in Mantua, notably Benedetto Pallavicino and Salomone Rossi. In so doing he participated in a distinctive "Mantuan style" of the mid- and late 1590s, a style rooted in the late works of Wert and showing, in its own way, as much internal linguistic consistency as Newcomb's Ferrarese idiom of the same years. Before we trace the development of this style into the most advanced idioms of Books IV and V, it will be useful to enumerate some of its features and contrast it with the contemporary Ferrarese style.[8]

The Mantuan style of 1595–1600 is above all a homophonic language of flexible, text-inspired declamatory rhythms. Here as elsewhere its dependence on the heritage of Wert's madrigals is manifest. Imitative textures are infrequent and usually reserved for final perorations, where double-subject counterpoint is common. Internal imitative passages generally either lapse quickly into homophony or are spun from brief declamatory motives with straightforward tonal implications. Reduced textures are common, most often moving in parallel first-inversion chords or villanella-style trios of duet plus bassline.

The Ferrarese style, in contrast, favors mercurial, single-subject imitation at quick rhythmic intervals. (As we have mentioned above, Wertian techniques of

8. For my generalizations on the Ferrarese style of the mid-1590s I am much indebted to Newcomb, *The Madrigal at Ferrara*, vol. 1, chap. 7. Over a number of years Professor Newcomb has also shared with me, with unfailing generosity, transcriptions of works in this style and personal observations on them. My description of Mantuan style ca. 1595–1600 relies on madrigals from Monteverdi's Fourth and Fifth Books that may be securely dated in these years (see below), on ten madrigals from Salomone Rossi's First Book à 5 of 1600, edited by Vincent d'Indy (*Choix de 22 Madrigaux à cinq voix*), and on Benedetto Pallavicino's Sixth Book à 5 of 1600, transcribed by Flanders ("The Madrigals of Pallavicino" 2:1–132). Flanders also transcribes Pallavicino's Seventh Book, issued posthumously by the composer's son in 1604, three years after his father's death; but these madrigals must be treated with caution as evidence of the style of the late 1590s because many of them—works like "Una farfalla cupida e vagante," "Né veder fuor de l'onde," and "Non son in queste rive"—are redolent of styles prominent in Monteverdi's Second and Third Books and probably date back to the early 1590s. Indeed, in the context of Monteverdi's developing style, all the features that distinguish Pallavicino's Seventh from his Sixth Book—its luxuriant writing, extravagant melodic leaps, contrapuntal complexities, and avoidance of unorthodox dissonance—indicate that the posthumous Book VII preserves a generally earlier repertory than Book VI (but see Flanders's opposite conclusion, vol. 1, p. 123).

multiple counterpoint are rarely utilized.) This polyphony may be built from sprightly motives that recall the canzonetta-madrigal or, more often, from those fragmentary, indistinct melodies that Newcomb has described (and that are evident in Example 31b above).[9] Textural reduction usually occurs in association with these points of imitation, less often with trios reminiscent of the villanella. Short homophonic passages often move in the sharply profiled rhythms of the canzonetta-madrigal (though on occasion Luzzaschi and Fontanelli exhibit a notable ability to reflect the more fluid rhythms of speech in their homophony; see, for example, Luzzaschi's "Se parti i' moro, e pur partir conviene" in Book V of 1595).

The varieties of harmonic progression that typify the Ferrarese style are conditioned by its textural preferences: its imitative tendencies, the participation of the bottom voices in this imitation, and its avoidance of stratified villanella textures. Ferrarese basslines thus tend to adopt the largely conjunct motion of the upper voices, weakening or evading $V \rightarrow I$ cadential progressions and producing nontonal harmonic movements that frequently sound wayward to modern ears. This undirected tonal feel is enhanced by Ferrarese composers' frequent indulgence in melodic chromaticism and harmonic cross-relations.

In the Mantuan style, on the other hand (and this is perhaps the fundamental difference between these two regional dialects), the bassline is more clearly distinguished from the other parts in its disjunct melodic motion and therefore free to function as harmonic foundation. This trait, descended again from Wert's works, underscores the close relation between the Mantuan madrigal and lighter genres like the villanella. It posed the danger that the madrigal might, in its use of their restricted harmonic vocabulary, lapse into harmonic blandness—skillfully avoided by Monteverdi and usually by Pallavicino, if not by Rossi. But its advantages outweighed this danger. Ultimately it enabled Monteverdi to construct the palpable long-range tonal structures we witnessed in the preceding chapter; as I suggested there, it also underpinned his increasing freedom in the treatment of dissonance. And, by clarifying *Romanesca*-like sequential harmonic successions that are rarely found in Ferrarese works, it provided him with a crucial device of rhetorical expression and formal articulation.

The use of melismas in the two styles yields a final reflection of their textural and harmonic differences. The Ferrarese composers typically restrict themselves to brief eighth-note melismas, almost invariably with clear pictorial intent, and distribute them imitatively throughout the five voices. Pictorial melismas also occur in Mantuan madrigals of these years, but they are most often deployed in only two or three voices, in parallel thirds or tenths, and in a texture whose manifest vertical orientation they do not obscure. Some Mantuan madrigals of the late 1590s extend earlier florid styles to include sixteenth-note melismas. Pallavicino employed such

---

9. *The Madrigal at Ferrara* 1:120–21.

roulades for a combination of text painting and cadential emphasis, much as Wert had used eighth-note melismas before him (Ex. 32a). Monteverdi, in a famous passage from "Cruda Amarilli" cited by Artusi, characteristically converted Pallavicino's pictorialism into an affective exclamation (Ex. 32b).[10]

Four of Monteverdi's madrigals in the Fourth and Fifth Books may be assigned dates of composition in the late 1590s on the basis of Artusi's criticism of them in his treatises of 1600 and 1603:

"Cruda Amarilli" (Book V) and "Anima mia, perdona" (and its second part, "Che se tu se' il cor mio"; Book IV). In the Ragionamento secondo of L'Artusi overo delle imperfettioni della moderna musica, which took place on 17 November 1598, Luca relates having heard "certi Madrigali nuovi" the evening before in a private concert involving Luzzaschi and other musicians. Of the nine excerpts quoted from these new works in the following discussion, seven come from "Cruda Amarilli" and two from "Anima mia, perdona."[11]

"O Mirtillo, Mirtill'anima mia" (Book V). Later in the Ragionamento secondo Luca describes a madrigal he heard "non molti giorni sono"; his naming of its text and description of its distinctive opening gesture allow conclusive identification of Monteverdi's work.[12]

"Era l'anima mia" (Book V). In the Seconda parte dell'Artusi of 1603, Artusi quotes a letter he wrote in response to one by a Ferrarese academician with the pseudonym l'Ottuso and a second letter by l'Ottuso in rebuttal of Artusi's response. Artusi states that l'Ottuso's first letter was delivered to him in 1599; his own letter must have followed quickly, judging by his pointed mention of the month delay between it and l'Ottuso's second letter. The entire correspondence, then, probably took place in 1599 (but at least in part after May since l'Ottuso's second letter discusses madrigals from Marenzio's Ninth Book, dedicated in that month). In his letter Artusi reproduces the opening measures of "Era l'anima mia."[13]

That the first three of these pieces were indeed "new madrigals" (as Luca put it) in late 1598, and not works composed for Duke Alfonso before his death a year earlier, is perhaps affirmed by the fact that they all set excerpts from Il pastor fido. In the summer and fall of 1598 Vincenzo Gonzaga sponsored three performances of Guarini's play in Mantua. These generated excitement in literary circles throughout Italy and abundant labor for Vincenzo's artistic staff. They also, it seems likely,

---

10. If this new florid style seems at times to anticipate gestures of certain monodic styles after 1600, so also do the frequent *accenti* that occur in Book IV for the first time in Monteverdi's works. For discussion of this ornament see Monteverdi, *Madrigali a 5 voci, libro quarto*, pp. 28–29.

11. *L'Artusi*, fols. 39r–40r; translated in Strunk, *Source Readings*, pp. 34–35. For modal-Schenkerian analyses of both these works see McClary, "The Transition," pp. 136–75.

12. *L'Artusi*, fol. 48v.

13. *Seconda parte dell'Artusi*, pp. 5–21.

EXAMPLE 32

(a) Pallavicino, "Se ben al vincer nacqui," mm. 18–19
(Flanders, "The Madrigals" 2:264; quoted by permission)

(b) Monteverdi, "Cruda Amarilli," mm. 11–14

inspired Monteverdi to begin a series of madrigals setting passages from the play in styles unlike those of "O primavera," "Ah dolente partita," and "Quell'augellin." Perhaps the first fruits of these labors were "Cruda Amarilli," "Anima mia," and "O Mirtillo." In any case, there can be little doubt that the most talked-about Mantuan musical imports to Ferrara toward the end of 1598 were works associated more or less closely with *Il pastor fido*.[14]

These four madrigals mentioned by Artusi exhibit the general features of Man-

14. We shall return to Monteverdi's *Pastor fido* settings of these years, and their possible associa- tion with performances of the play, in the next chapter.

tuan style enumerated above: they rely on homophonic declamation, simplified de-clamatory counterpoint (even in the double-subject perorations with which three of them end), and a restricted vocabulary of straightforward harmonic progres-sions. Some more specific features are also worth noting. Uncanonical dissonance is frequent, usually introduced in Monteverdi's characteristic, structurally unam-biguous fashion (as at "qual vendetta aver" in measure 61 of "Anima mia"). A new, effective rhetorical device is the leap of the top voice away from a suspended disso-nance. (See Example 33 below, at "se vedesti," and also the opening of "Anima mia" and "come se' tu cor mio" in "Era l'anima mia." The imitative texture of the end of Example 33, layered in parallel thirds, is typically Mantuan and reminiscent of Pallavicino's contrapuntal techniques of these years.)[15] And novel varieties of bassline motion emphasize the third instead of the fourth degree as the antepenulti-mate sonority before V → I cadences, allowing for the expressive dissonance that begins "Cruda Amarilli" and ends the *prima parte* of "Anima mia." (This technique too recalls Pallavicino.)

Transposed repetition of phrases is ubiquitous, and sequential harmonic struc-tures are occasionally used with conspicuous rhetorical force, as at "E tu perché ne strigni" of "O Mirtillo," or in the same madrigal's famous opening measures, branded by Artusi an "impertinentia d'un principio" (Ex. 33). Abrupt rhythmic disjunction appears for pictorial purposes in "Cruda Amarilli" (at "e più fugace"—"and more fleeting"—where its fragmenting, Ferrarese effect recalls "sì tosto passa"—"so soon passes"—in Luzzaschi's "Quando io miro me stessa" of 1594 and anticipates "che tosto fugge"—"which soon flies by"—in the chorus ending Act II of Monteverdi's own *Orfeo*); such disjunction is used for exclamatory force at "Deh, perché ti consumi?" in "Era l'anima mia" (as it was used by Pallavicino to open "Oh, come vaneggiate" in his Sixth Book).[16]

Finally, the syntactic devices of the epigrammatic style appear only sparingly and hesitantly in these madrigals. Decisive tonal shifts and evaporated cadences have little role. The important device of repeating one poetic line in the bass while introducing the next line above occurs twice, but in neither instance has Mon-teverdi yet fully appreciated its binding force. At the opening of "Anima mia" it appears in one of a series of textual repetitions, recalling Pallavicino's usage.[17] In "Era l'anima mia" it even cuts against the grain of the text: verses 4–6 are cleanly separated from verses 1–3, on which they depend, and instead bound to verses 7–8, a new period.

15. Monteverdi and Pallavicino both used this texture to set the line "Parean dir quei bei lumi" in "Era l'anima mia." For Pallavicino's setting see Flanders, "The Madrigals of Pallavicino" 2:74–79.

16. For Luzzaschi's madrigal see Newcomb,

The Madrigal at Ferrara 2:208–13; for Pallavi-cino's, Flanders, "The Madrigals of Pallavicino" 2:86–91. I have discussed Monteverdi's exclama-tory rhythmic shifts in "Madrigal, Monody, and Monteverdi," pp. 67–70.

17. See chap. 4 above, n. 8.

EXAMPLE 33

Monteverdi, "O Mirtillo, Mirtill'anima mia," beginning

The undated works that show the closest stylistic kinship to these madrigals mentioned by Artusi are all in Book IV. (It seems probable, therefore, that the three works that open Book V, "Cruda Amarilli," "O Mirtillo," and "Era l'anima mia," are the oldest in that collection.) These undated works are "Volgea l'anima mia," "Voi pur da me partite," "Anima del cor mio," "Longe da te, cor mio," and "Cor mio, non mori? E mori!" (which looks forward to the mature epigrammatic style more conspicuously than the others). In addition one madrigal, "Anima dolorosa, che vivendo," merges elements of the Mantuan idiom with clear Ferrarese traits, especially its sudden, fragmenting shifts of musical character matched to poetic contrasts (for example, "Anima *dolorosa,* che *vivendo* / tanto *peni e tormenti*"—"*Sad* soul, which, *living,* / knows such *pain and torment*"). In all likelihood these works, like those mentioned by Artusi, were composed at the end of the 1590s.

The Epigrammatic and Other Late Styles,
circa 1599–1603

We have seen that the mature epigrammatic style is not so much the product of new musical techniques as the result of a synthesis of devices already available, in the interests of projecting syntactic and semantic structures in the text. We may logically view the style, therefore, as Monteverdi's personal elaboration of the more general Mantuan dialect of the late 1590s (and of other traits in his earlier works as well). The madrigals that most clearly exhibit the style—"Cor mio, mentre vi miro," "Sfogava con le stelle," "A un giro sol," and "Oimè, se tanto amate"—would then be dated after 1598.

This late dating offers three advantages. First, it accords with a suggestion I have made elsewhere, on the basis of textual treatment in parallel musical passages, that "Cor mio, mentre vi miro" was composed after "O Mirtillo."[18] Second, it allows the attractive hypothesis that Monteverdi's first encounter with Rinuccini's poetry, in "Sfogava con le stelle," was one consequence of the increased artistic contact between the Mantuan and Florentine courts engendered in 1600 by the wedding festivities of Maria de' Medici and Henry IV of France.[19] Finally and most important, it might explain why Pallavicino, whose style clearly evolved through the 1590s along lines parallel to those of Monteverdi's development, remained largely untouched by the epigrammatic synthesis. If these works of Monteverdi had been known in Mantua by 1598 or 1599, we might expect Pallavicino's Sixth and Seventh Books of 1600 and 1604 more clearly to betray their impact, especially since these collections abound in settings of Guarini's epigrammatic verse.

One last madrigal from Book IV remains to be dated. This is "Sì ch'io vorei morire," a work as bold in conception as it is anomalous in Monteverdi's output as a whole. Its text may well be the work of the Venetian Mauritio Moro, though none of the five similar poems printed in his Tre giardini de' madrigali of 1602 resembles Monteverdi's text closely enough to allow positive identification.[20] Its music speaks an exaggerated, emphatic language, well attuned to the aroused eroticism of the text and sharing little with the urbane sprezzatura of the epigrammatic style. (One exception is the descending bassline "Ahi bocca, ahi baci, ahi lingua" in measures 68–71, reversed to support the rising sequential homophony that follows—a brilliant elaboration of epigrammatic connective techniques.)

Pallavicino provides the best clue for the dating of this madrigal. Its three different passages of rising and falling chains of suspensions (at "Ahi, cara e dolce lin-

18. "Madrigal, Monody, and Monteverdi," p. 68n.

19. Pirrotta, "Scelte poetiche," p. 32, suggests that Monteverdi may have traveled to Florence in Duke Vincenzo's retinue and met Rinuccini there.

20. See I tre giardini de' madrigali, Giardino secondo, pp. 201–3. Joel Newman first suggested Moro as author of the text in a Communication to JAMS 14 (1961), 418–19. The fact that all five of Moro's madrigals, like Monteverdi's text, begin and end with the line "Sì ch'io vorei morire" raises the possibility of some poetic competition

between Moro and another author, for gareggiamenti involving such shared lines from one poem to the next were common in the sixteenth century. In any case, the publication of Moro's poems in 1602 is not helpful in dating Monteverdi's madrigal because of the aforementioned textual disparities, because the preface to Moro's second Giardino states that his poems were written some time before their publication, and because the dedication of the first Giardino, to Vincenzo Gonzaga, attests to Moro's close ties to the Mantuan court before 1602.

gua," "che di dolcezza," and "deh, stringetemi") and its sequential repetitions of the same poetic line at the beginning and end are all features anticipated literally in his Sixth Book.[21] But in each case Monteverdi's dissonant chains are longer, his sequences leaner and more insistent than Pallavicino's. Indeed, Monteverdi's extension in this work of the older composer's techniques seems to border on intentional caricature. A date for "Sì ch'io vorei morire" after the publication of Pallavicino's Sixth Book in March 1600 seems likely.

Two works in Monteverdi's Fifth Book show a special liking for the extended sequential homophony of "Sì ch'io vorei morire," though not for its Pallavicinian handling of dissonance. These are "Che dar più vi poss'io" and "M'è più dolce il penar," the second setting an excerpt from *Il pastor fido*. Both madrigals make frequent use of epigrammatic connective devices, and the first briefly adopts the *falsobordone*-like free declamation of "Sfogava con le stelle."

Two more works, the lengthy *Pastor fido* cycles "Ecco Silvio colei ch'in odio hai tanto" and "Ch'io t'ami et'ami più de la mia vita," differ from these two in little but their less frequent indulgence in the sequences of "Sì ch'io vorei morire." They too display some trappings of the mature epigrammatic style. In his *Seconda parte* Artusi provides a *terminus ante quem* for "Ecco Silvio" of March 1603, the month in which Monteverdi's Fourth Book was printed. It would seem probable, then, that all but the continuo madrigals of Book V were composed by the time of Book IV.[22]

Two Fragmentary Madrigals

In 1608 two madrigals by Monteverdi were included, along with works by Giovan Giacomo Gastoldi, Paolo Virchi, and Antonio Taroni, in the posthumous Twelfth Book of madrigals of Wert.[23] A bass part book from this collection survives at the music library of the University of California at Berkeley. It is not found in the New Vogel; apparently no other part books have yet surfaced. The two madrigals by Monteverdi, "Pensier aspro e crudele, / ch'ogn'hor m'ascend'al core nova fiamma" and "Sdegno la fiamm'estinse, / e rintuzzò lo stral, e sciolse il nodo," are both for five voices and, like the other works in the book, without continuo. The text of the second was set also by three other composers: Filippo di Monte (XV à 5,

21. See Flanders, "The Madrigals of Pallavicino" 2:17, 41–42, 84–85, 88–89, 123–27.

22. On the dating of the continuo madrigals of Book V see chap. 6 below. Note that Book V opens with the four madrigals discussed by Artusi but not published in Book IV, in the order of Artusi's citation of them (and probably of their composition as well). Why had Monteverdi refrained from making this defiant gesture in his Fourth Book? Had his hopes that the controversy of 1600 would quietly die down been dashed by the appearance of Artusi's *Seconda parte,* dedicated just twenty-five days after Book IV?

23. *Il duodecimo libro de madrigali di Giaches d'Wert a 4. a 5. a 6. & 7. Con alcuni altri de diversi eccellentissimi autori* (Venice, 1608); the book was collected by Wert's son, Ottavio.

1592), Marco da Gagliano (III à 5, 1605), and Antonio il Verso (XV à 5, 1619). No settings of "Pensier aspro e crudele" are listed in the New Vogel, suggesting that the text was of local Mantuan origin. It may even have been the work of Duke Vincenzo Gonzaga, for Ottavio Wert, in dedicating his father's works to the duke, revealed Vincenzo's authorship of some of their texts: "Le parole di molti d'essi [madrigali] sono parto del Felicissimo ingegno di V. A."

These basslines yield much information about the style of the works, especially concerning their general layout—their ordering of contrapuntal and homophonic passages and their repetitions, transposed and rescored, of the latter—but also regarding the more specific nature of the lost music. The opening of "Pensier aspro e crudele," for instance, clearly suggests a four-bar, mainly homophonic phrase setting the first line of text for three or four voices without the bass, followed by a repetition of this material transposed and rescored for five voices (Ex. 34). The setting of "ch'ogn'hor m'ascend'al core" calls for a flurry of contrapuntal entrances involving all five voices by measures 16–17. And the following exclamation returns to homophony, perhaps with some staggering of the voices.

More specifically, the disjunct opening line (mm. 5–8) is strongly redolent of the first phrases of "Cruda Amarilli." It surely shared their unorthodox dissonance, perhaps with a C (descending from D) struck above the bassline's B, suspended over its F♯, and descending by step to provide the fifth for the final D-major chord. The following counterpoint would revert to normal dissonance treatment, ending abruptly on a first-inversion G chord, while the homophonic passage after it would entail expressive cross-relations and even linear chromaticism (C → C♯ → D at "gelosia").

EXAMPLE 34

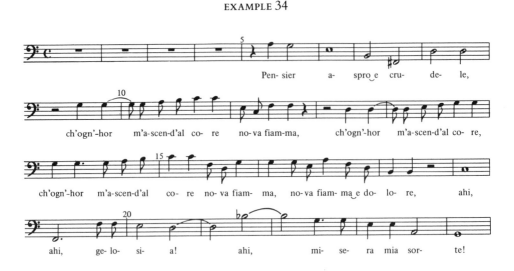

Monteverdi, "Pensier aspro e crudele," bassline, mm. 1–24

In these implied traits, and less hypothetically in its disjunctive melodic style and wide-ranging harmonic implications, the bassline of "Pensier aspro e crudele" suggests a date for the madrigal relatively close to its publication, at least after around 1598. So, more explicitly still, does the bassline of "Sdegno la fiamm'estinse." It features sixteenth-note and dotted-eighth-to-sixteenth-note melismas hardly ever found in the basslines of Books I–IV but reminiscent once again of "Cruda Amarilli" and of the continuo madrigals concluding Book V (Ex. 35). Both works undoubtedly date from the most mature years of Monteverdi's composition of madrigals without continuo.

EXAMPLE 35

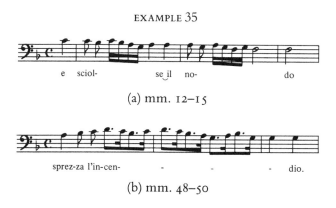

(a) mm. 12–15

(b) mm. 48–50

Monteverdi, "Sdegno la fiamm'estinse," bassline

5

Guarini, Rinuccini,
and the Ideal
of Musical Speech

From *Il pastor fido* to *L'Arianna*

N 1598 VINCENZO GONZAGA finally brought to pass the performance of *Il pastor fido* that he had cherished since 1584 and pursued actively since 1591. The play was staged three times in Mantua that year, in late June and early September and, most sumptuously, on 22 November during the visit of Margherita of Austria, on her way to wed Philip III of Spain. In all three performances, and also in those abandoned in various states of preparation in 1591–92 and 1593, music played a significant role. To limn a background for the predominant style of Monteverdi's Fifth Book we must attempt to define this role.[1]

On the subject of music, the documents published by the literary historian Alessandro d'Ancona concerning the preparations for *Il pastor fido* are laconic. They reveal, aside from the general importance of music in the staging of the play, little more than that Wert and Francesco Rovigo were the main composers for the abortive production of 1591–92 and that the *gioco della cieca* in Act III, scene ii was from the first conceived as a ballet, with the four speeches of the chorus set to music. Other documents tell us that the rather modest *intermedi* created for the 1591–92 production were to be sung throughout to the accompaniment of instruments deemed appropriate to the subject of each.[2]

---

1. It is now a century since Alessandro d'Ancona narrated the convoluted history of Vincenzo Gonzaga's attempts to stage *Il pastor fido* in "Il teatro mantovano nel secolo XVI." These articles were republished with some additions as an appendix to d'Ancona's *Origini del teatro italiano,* which I have used. The events have been retold in less exhaustive form by Rossi, *Battista Guarini,* pp. 223–32, and, among musicologists, by Mac-

Clintock, *Wert,* pp. 178–85; Adriano Cavicchi, "Teatro monteverdiano e tradizione teatrale ferrarese," pp. 143–51; Newcomb, *The Madrigal at Ferrara* 1:41–46, who corrects two misreadings of the documents in MacClintock; and Iain Fenlon, *Music and Patronage in Sixteenth-Century Mantua* 1:149–61.

2. Rossi, *Battista Guarini,* pp. 307–10, prints the manuscript synopses of these *intermedi.*

More helpful is a published account of the lavish *intermedi* depicting the wedding of Mercury and Philology that were written for the last performance of 1598, on 22 November.[3] The descriptions of all but one of the *intermedi* begin with locutions like "Dopo il secondo atto nel finir della musica," suggesting that the choruses ending the acts of *Il pastor fido* were sung. Indeed the description of the *licenza* or epilogue of the play even specifies the beginning of the text that Guarini's shepherds and nymphs sang: "Vieni, santo Imeneo." This line and four others following it recur six times in all in Guarini's last two scenes; in their final occurrence at least, and perhaps in the others before it, they were sung. None of this evidence is surprising, of course. We would expect that the choruses of *Il pastor fido* were sung on the basis of less direct evidence than the descriptions of its *intermedi,* in particular the dramatic theorist Angelo Ingegneri's discussion, also of 1598, of the use of music in pastoral dramas.[4]

None of the music for any of these choruses seems to have survived, but Giovan Giacomo Gastoldi's setting of the *gioco della cieca* for the November performance has come down to us in his Fourth Book of madrigals of 1602.[5] The obligation to provide music for the *gioco* had passed to Gastoldi because by 1598 both Wert and Rovigo were dead. Presumably Gastoldi alone did not compose all the music for the performance, which amounted to an elaborate set of *intermedi* and choruses for the end of each act. So Monteverdi's participation in the project is a likely possibility.[6] The intriguing question raised by this possibility, then, is whether any of his *Pastor fido* settings in the Fourth and Fifth Books were composed for use in the performances of 1598.

The notion is not unreasonable and has been endorsed more or less explicitly by

3. The account, of 1604, is reproduced by Achille Neri, "Gli 'Intermezzi' del 'Pastor fido.' " These *intermedi* acknowledge the famous ones performed in Florence in 1589 not only in their spectacular ostentation but also in more explicit ways. In the second of them, for example, the sailor's solo song with double echo recalls in situation and technique Arion's "Dunque fra torbid'onde" of 1589, by Ottavio Rinuccini and Jacopo Peri. Rinuccini and Peri's first musicodramatic collaboration, it would seem, was known in Mantua by 1598. (Intriguingly, Monteverdi suggested just such a song in 1617 for the *intermedi Le nozze di Tetide*; see Monteverdi, *Lettere,* p. 96. Could he be remembering here the song that he had heard in—or composed for—*Il pastor fido* nineteen years earlier?) The *intermedi* of 22 November were surely not those used in stagings of *Il pastor fido* earlier in 1598: their references to Margherita and Philip would have made no sense then. Perhaps the *intermedi* of 1591 were employed in the earlier 1598 performances.

4. Angelo Ingegneri, *Della poesia rappresentativa e del modo di rappresentare le favole sceniche,* pp. 536–37. The most pertinent passage is given in MacClintock, *Wert,* pp. 181–82.

5. Four madrigals there setting the appropriate texts from Act III, scene ii are entitled "Il Gioco de la cieca rappresentato alla Regina di Spagna nel Pastor fido." The first two are given in Newcomb, *The Madrigal at Ferrara* 2:22–30.

6. As indeed is the participation of other Mantuan composers like Pallavicino and Rossi. The parceling out of the *intermedi* to various composers would accord well with Florentine practice in 1589 and also with Mantuan practice for the *intermedi* of Guarini's comedy *L'Idropica* in 1608.

various scholars.[7] They also have noted the theatrical qualities of these madrigals, especially "O Mirtillo," "M'è più dolce il penar," and the long cycles of Book V. And in 1608 Aquilino Coppini, the editor of three volumes of spiritual *travestimenti* of Monteverdi's madrigals, termed the works of the Fifth Book "musica rappresentativa," perhaps with a knowledge of their genesis now lost. That these works are hardly suitable for the stage in their published form is no objection: Monteverdi could easily have revised them for publication, transforming them from some type of solo song into five-voice madrigals, just as he later reworked Ariadne's lament for inclusion in the Sixth Book.[8] Finally, the objection that *Il pastor fido* was a spoken drama, in which the choruses but not the dialogue might be sung, is anachronistically restrictive. Though we still know little about its specific uses, music evidently served many functions in sixteenth-century drama, particularly in pastoral and comic genres. (Its employment in tragedy was probably more narrowly circumscribed.) Guarini himself wrote in his *Compendio della poesia tragicomica* of 1601 that "all the Arcadians were poets, that their principal exercise was music, which they learned as infants."[9] The idea of Amarilli, Mirtillo, or the other protagonists of the 1598 *Pastor fido* bursting into song in the manner of *Singspiel* or modern musical comedy is not in itself farfetched.

There are, however, other, sounder objections to the hypothesis that Monteverdi's settings were sung in the performances of 1598. Most important is the fact that his texts are not those we presume were sung in the performance—that is, the choruses ending each act. *Il pastor fido* is a huge play; even after, by Giovanni Crescimbeni's later estimate, almost a fourth of it was cut in 1598, it remained over five thousand verses long, twice the length of many spoken dramas of the time and over four times as long as the longest of Rinuccini's music dramas.[10] Since the Mantuan performance was extended already by a ballet, sung choruses, and protracted, extravagant *intermedi,* it is difficult to believe that it was further lengthened by the protagonists' singing substantial portions of their soliloquies and dialogue.

Ingegneri's contemporary account of pastoral drama seems to confirm this

7. Notably Cavicchi, "Teatro monteverdiano," pp. 150–51, and Denis Stevens, *Monteverdi*, pp. 18–20. Stevens's assumption that solo song played a large role in *Il pastor fido* is probably encouraged by his belief that Francesco Campagnolo, a tenor who lived with Monteverdi and sang in various music dramas after 1600, played the part of Silvio in 1598 (see Stevens, ed. and trans., *The Letters of Claudio Monteverdi*, p. 130). But this confuses two Campagnolos. The one scheduled to take Silvio's part in 1591–92 (we do not know whether he actually realized the role in 1598) was named Evangelista and may, as d'Ancona suggests, have been Francesco's father (see

Origini, pp. 542–43, 551). There is no evidence that Evangelista was a singer. And in any case if Francesco was young enough to live with a music master after 1600 he certainly could not have been old enough to take part in *Il pastor fido* in 1591. This confusion is evident also in Rossi, *Battista Guarini*, p. 224, and MacClintock, *Wert,* p. 183n.

8. This point has been made by MacClintock, *Wert,* p. 181n.

9. Quoted from Pirrotta, *Li due Orfei,* p. 305.

10. Crescimbeni is quoted by MacClintock, *Wert,* p. 183n.

point. He writes of the free use of music only in speaking of comedies and pastoral dramas without choruses: "I come now to music, third and final part of dramatic presentations, which, in comedies and pastoral dramas without choruses, may be used in any manner [*ad arbitrio altrui*], to serve as *intermedi* or accompany them in another way so that they are rendered more delightful."[11] The implication here and elsewhere in Ingegneri's discussion is that, in plays with choruses, the music should be limited to these and the *intermedi*.

There is also an element of professional competition in Monteverdi's *Pastor fido* settings, one that militates against a view of these works as devised for a specific courtly spectacle. Six of the eight excerpts Monteverdi set in Books IV and V had already been set by Marenzio in his Sixth, Seventh, and Eighth Books of 1594, 1595, and 1598.[12] Marenzio's works were certainly not intended for use in a performance of the play. This seems clear from the musical style of most of them and clearer still from the changes made in their texts (especially the frequent substitution of "generic" pastoral names like Tirsi for the names of Guarini's protagonists). In resetting these texts, even though he remained closer than Marenzio to Guarini's originals, Monteverdi perpetuated what was for Marenzio a musico-poetic alliance without overt dramatic associations. And *Pastor fido* settings by Wert and Pallavicino reveal that Monteverdi was not the only Mantuan composer to do so. Wert may even have initiated the rivalry, for his "Cruda Amarilli" from Book XI (1595) shows clear musical connections to Marenzio's, published two months later, while Pallavicino's only two *Pastor fido* settings, "Deh, dolce anima mia" and "Cruda Amarilli" from Book VI (1600), both recall Marenzio's settings of the same texts in his Seventh Book.[13]

All these considerations distance Monteverdi's *Pastor fido* settings from the performance of the play in 1598. But they do not disqualify that event as the decisive source of inspiration for Monteverdi's music. After all, the *termini ante quos* offered by Artusi for "Cruda Amarilli," "Anima mia, perdona," and "O Mirtillo" suggest that these works date from 1598. They suggest, that is, that Monteverdi turned from his earlier, lyrical settings of madrigal-like excerpts from *Il pastor fido* ("O primavera," "Quell'augellin," and "Ah dolente partita") to new, more dramatic settings in the same year the play mounted the Mantuan stage.

Nor do the above considerations repudiate Coppini's description of the Fifth

---

11. Ingegneri, *Della poesia rappresentativa,* pp. 536–37.
12. Einstein, *The Italian Madrigal,* p. 851, also sees "a sort of competition with Marenzio" in Monteverdi's Fifth Book. But one of Monteverdi's *Pastor fido* settings, "Quell'augellin," may well have been composed before Marenzio's setting was published in 1595. See excursus 1 above.

13. There is thus a family of related settings of "Cruda Amarilli," including Wert's, Marenzio's, Pallavicino's, and Monteverdi's. See Flanders, "The Madrigals of Pallavicino" 1:169–82. In "Deh, dolce anima mia" Pallavicino, unlike Monteverdi, followed Marenzio's extensively altered version of Guarini's text.

Book as "musica rappresentativa." As has often been noted, "O Mirtillo" in particular adumbrates the novelties of Ariadne's lament a decade later[14] (as well as those of "Ecco Silvio," "Ch'io t'ami," and "M'è più dolce il penar," which we have placed in the years immediately after 1598). And the notion that these works may have originated as dramatic solo song with instrumental accompaniment gains support from the striking similarities of technique they bear to the five-voice version of the lament in Book VI—as if they resulted from the same process of polyphonic elaboration on simpler theatrical templates.[15]

We may easily imagine that the excitement caused by the performances of Il pastor fido in 1598 gave rise to a flurry of dramatic and semidramatic presentations of excerpts from the play, at court, in the Mantuan academies, or by the Jewish theatrical troupes for which the city was renowned.[16] Indeed one such presentation in neighboring Ferrara may be memorialized in Artusi's description of the concert where Luca heard Monteverdi's Pastor fido madrigals. In any such performance Monteverdi's "musica rappresentativa," arranged for one voice or five, might have found a ready audience. So in the end the distancing of Monteverdi's madrigals from the ducal stage in 1598 need not entail their dissociation from the stage in general.

The theatrical orientation of Monteverdi's Pastor fido settings is worth stressing because, as I have suggested, these works were the proving ground of a new language fully mastered only in L'Arianna of 1607–8. To be sure, they sometimes invoke contrapuntal techniques we have already discussed: epigrammatic juxtapositions of syntactically bound lines of text, polyphonic exclamations as in "Sfogava con le stelle," evaporated cadences, double-subject perorations, and so on. But beyond these occasional holdovers, the Pastor fido settings, especially "O Mirtillo" and the five-section dialogue "Ecco Silvio," present a homophonic façade at first forbidding in its austerity.

Monteverdi's choice thus to limit the technical and textural variety of his music (for it must have been a choice, even if these works originated as solo song, naturally more limited than five-voice polyphony) modified his approach to the poetry in subtle but profoundly important ways. It focused his attention on the conveyance of forward-moving, linear rhetorical tropes in his text, rather than the more conceptual syntactic dependencies that he had captured in the polyphonic juxtapo-

14. See, for example, Schrade, Monteverdi, p. 215; Guido Pannain, "Polifonia profana e sacra," p. 293; and Denis Arnold, Monteverdi, p. 72.
15. Some of the traits of the five-voice version of Ariadne's lament shared by the Pastor fido settings are its ubiquitous structural repetition of sections of text and music not repeated in the solo version (these repeated blocks are invariably transposed and rescored), its instance of epigrammatic juxtaposition of poetic lines obviously not juxtaposed in the solo version, and its stolid, four-square declamatory rhythms, restricted by demands of polyphonic writing.
16. On the Mantuan academies and Jewish troupes see Fenlon, Music and Patronage 1:35–43.

sitions of the epigrammatic madrigals. It caused him, in other words, to seek novel and effective musical means to project the repeated gestures, exclamations, questions, and verbal assonance of the poetry. And it diverted his thoughts from patterns of syntactic subordination that had depended for their expression on polyphonic devices in the epigrammatic style.

Another difference between the epigrammatic madrigals and the *Pastor fido* settings reflects general stylistic differences between their texts. The passages from Guarini's play that Monteverdi set around 1600 (as opposed to the madrigal-like passages he had set earlier) are less closed in their logic, more open-ended and discursive, than the lyrics that had inspired the epigrammatic style. This we would expect; the excerpts from *Il pastor fido* are, after all, excerpts. In setting these free-formed rhetorical passages Monteverdi moved away from the strict and manifest tonal logic of his epigrammatic works. His tonal organization is now looser, more varied, and wider-ranging. No better example of this new freedom may be cited than the "impertinent" opening (to use Artusi's epithet) of "O Mirtillo" in the soft hexachord (see Ex. 33 in excursus 1 above).

If in the course of these changes some expressive possibilities of the epigrammatic style were relinquished, their loss was in the service of a new and significant goal. For only by turning away from the polyphonic lyricism and narrowly circumscribed musico-poetic logic of his epigrams could Monteverdi achieve an oratorical and finally theatrical style of sung speech. Or, putting the matter the other way around, Monteverdi's attainment in the *Pastor fido* settings of a homophonic declamation more responsive to the free, discursive development of dramatic poetry than any earlier such style entailed the renunciation of text-expressive structures dependent on richer textures and stricter tonal logic.

The *Pastor fido* settings from around 1600 constitute the first substantial repertory in Monteverdi's output in which he turned resolutely away from the exploration of the expressive niceties available to a five-part texture to pursue the rhetorically effective declamation of dramatic texts. The novelty of these works is their emphatically linear expressive orientation. (Perhaps for this reason the treatise Monteverdi first conceived in these years before *Orfeo* and *L'Arianna* was later entitled *Melodia*. . . .)[17] In this, most crucially, they lay the foundations of the impassioned, pathetic, and grandiloquent melody of Ariadne.

Of course the effectiveness of such a restricted musical style depended greatly on the rhetorical efficacy of the text. If it was without distinctive and communicative structures, so in all likelihood would be the music. But there was little risk of such stagnancy in setting *Il pastor fido*. In passages like "O Mirtillo" Monteverdi

---

17. In a letter of 22 October 1633; see Monteverdi, *Lettere,* p. 321 (translated in Stevens, *The Letters,* p. 410).

found the emotion mirrored in a balanced, translucent, and musical syntax that remains the chief glory of the play four hundred years after its composition:

O Mirtillo, Mirtill'anima mia,	Oh Mirtillo, Mirtillo my love,
se vedesti qui dentro	if you could see herein
come sta il cor di questa	how stands the heart of her
che chiami crudelissima Amarilli,	you call most cruel Amarilli,
5 so ben che tu di lei	I know you'd feel for her
quella pietà, che da lei chiedi, avresti.	that mercy that instead from her you ask.
O anime in amor troppo infelici!	Oh spirits too unhappy in our love!
Che giova a te, cor mio, l'esser amato?	What use to you, my heart, to be thus loved?
Che giova a me l'aver sì caro amante?	What use to me, to have so dear a lover?
10 Perché, crudo destino,	Why, cruel Fate,
ne disunisci tu, s'amor ne strigne?	do you separate those whom Love has joined?
E tu, perché ne strigni,	And you, perfidious Love,
se ne parte il destin, perfido amore?	why join us two, if Fate drives us apart?
(III, iv)	

Admittedly, many techniques of Guarini's epigrammatic style remain clear enough in this passage—the pointed semantic reversals of verses 10–11 and 12–13, for example, and the witty conclusion to the complex hypotaxis of verses 2–6. But they stand alongside straightforward locutions that give eloquent expression to Amarilli's torment: the exclamations of verses 1 and 7 and the insistent parallelisms of verses 8–9 and 10–13. Such vivid rhetoric also characterizes the other excerpts Monteverdi set from *Il pastor fido,* especially "Ecco Silvio."

A decade later, in Ariadne's lament, Monteverdi found poetry that consumed even the lingering epigrammatic structures of *Il pastor fido* in a flame of emotion:

O Teseo, o Teseo mio,	Oh Theseus, oh my Theseus,
se tu sapessi, o dio!	if you but knew, oh God!
se tu sapessi, oimè! come s'affanna	if you but knew, alas, how wretched is
la povera Arianna,	the poor Ariadne,
5 forse, forse pentito	perhaps, perhaps repentant
rivolgeresti ancor la prora al lito.	you'd turn your ship around, back to the shore.
Ma con l'aure serene	But you, with placid breezes,
tu te ne vai felice, et io qui piango;	sail on your way content—while I complain.
a te prepara Atene	For you Athens makes ready
10 liete pompe superbe, et io rimango,	with happy, proudful pomp—while I remain,
cibo di fère in solitarie arene;	food for beasts on solitary sands.
te l'uno e l'altro tuo vecchio parente	With joy one and the other of your parents
stringerà lieto, et io	will clasp you to their breasts—while I
più non vedrovvi, o madre, o padre mio.	will not see you again, oh mother, oh father.
(vv. 801–14)[18]	

The similarities to Guarini's passage are obvious: the opening exclamation leading to conditional hypotaxis (lines 2–6) and the parallel syntactic structures of lines 7–

18. Verse numeration for Rinuccini's and Striggio's music dramas is taken from Angelo Solerti, *Gli albori del melodramma,* vols. 2, 3.

14. But the epigrammatic features of Guarini's lines have disappeared completely. Rinuccini's hypotaxis unfolds in affective repetitions and exclamations and conveys a thought moving enough to embody Ariadne's sorrow but not so complex as to dilute it with clever phrasemaking. Even the parallelisms of the last seven lines speak more personally than Guarini's analogous lines, foresaking his abstract appeal to the conflict of love and destiny for concrete comparisons of Ariadne's woe and Theseus's happy triumph. In Ariadne's lament (if not, perhaps, in the whole of *L'Arianna*) Monteverdi found a poetic idiom whose chief aim was the pure rhetorical formulation of passion. It was, given Monteverdi's own expressive goals in the years around 1600, the ideal *poesia per musica*.

Monteverdi's settings of "O Mirtillo," "Ecco Silvio," and to a lesser degree "Ch'io t'ami" and "M'è più dolce il penar," ring with anticipations of Ariadne's eloquence. The opening of "O Mirtillo" is often cited in this regard (see again Ex. 33 in excursus I). The long descending leap with which the *canto* begins, setting the exclamation "O" in stark relief, foreshadows one of the most frequent and expressive gestures of the lament. There as here it is associated with exclamations: "se tu sapessi, *oimè!* come s'affanna," "*o* padre mio," "*ah* Teseo mio," and so on. (Monteverdi had used this device already to open "O come è gran martire" in Book III, and ultimately it is derived from the text-expressive melodic leaps he had taken over from Wert in his *Gerusalemme liberata* settings.)

A closely related technique is found in measures 5–8 of "O Mirtillo," where the melodic high point of the *canto* is accentuated both by the motion of the *basso,* which renders it dissonant, and by the following downward leap. Here the result is a clumsy misaccentuation of "vedesti"; but in "Ecco Silvio" Monteverdi reused the gesture with more rhetorical skill, and it returns often, associated with similar poetic locutions and sometimes yielding even more wrenching dissonance, in *L'Arianna* (Ex. 36).

The opening bars of "O Mirtillo" display, in their harmonic sequence mirroring Guarini's backtracking syntax, an important rhetorical device of Monteverdi's representative style. In his *Pastor fido* settings and later in *Orfeo* and *L'Arianna* he deployed such structures ever more flexibly to project repetitive tropes in the text. Already in "O Mirtillo" they show considerable subtlety; for example, Guarini's lines "Che giova a te, cor mio, l'esser amato? / Che giova a me l'aver sì caro amante?" inspire sequences within sequences. Each line is divided into two sequential units at its infinitive ("l'esser," "l'aver"), and the whole setting of the first line is transposed up a fourth to accommodate the second (Ex. 37).

Monteverdi applied similar structures to repeated questions in the *terza parte* of "Ch'io t'ami," to the witty parallelisms of "M'è più dolce il penar" (at "ciò voglia il mio volere / o possa il mio potere"), and to numerous repetitive locutions in "Ecco Silvio." Most notable in the last-named work is the setting of "Bramastila ferir:

EXAMPLE 36

(a) Monteverdi, "Ecco Silvio
colei ch'in odio hai tanto,"
terza parte, mm. 43–45

(b) Monteverdi, Ariadne's lament,
excerpt from third part

(c) Monteverdi, Ariadne's lament,
beginning

(d) Monteverdi, Ariadne's lament,
excerpt from third part

ferita l'hai; / bramastila tua preda: eccola preda; / bramastila alfin morta: eccola a
morte" ("You sought to wound her—see her wounded here; / you sought to prey
on her—here's your prey; / you sought at last to kill her—here she dies"), where
the end of the third sequential unit is redirected, with an *Arianna*-like melodic collapse in the *canto,* to convey the "morte" of the last line (Ex. 38). Guarini's rhetoric
here prefigures Rinuccini's at "Ma con l'aure serene" in the section of the lament
quoted above. And Monteverdi's response to Rinuccini's verse shares much with
Example 38, even though he employs varied repetition on the same pitch instead of
sequential transposition.[19]

These sequences from the *Pastor fido* settings are motivated by repeated syntactic and poetic patterns in the text, and the technique, to be sure, is not without precedent in the first four books of madrigals. But Monteverdi's sequences there had
more often functioned independently of the text, spinning out florid roulades on
neutral poetic structures (as near the end of "Ecco mormorar") or, especially, repeating locutions not repeated by the poet (as in the opening and closing bars and

19. For detailed discussion of this passage see below, pp. 127–29.

EXAMPLE 37

Monteverdi, "O Mirtillo, Mirtill'anima mia," mm. 41–51

EXAMPLE 38

Monteverdi, "Ecco Silvio colei ch'in odio hai tanto,"
prima parte, mm. 18–28

elsewhere in "Sì ch'io vorei morire"). We should also distinguish from Monteverdi's new rhetorical sequences another technique frequently used in both the *Pastor fido* settings and earlier madrigals: the repetition of blocks of text and music transposed and rescored. (See, for example, "O Mirtillo," at the repetitions of "se vedesti qui dentro" and "E tu, perché ne strigni.") All these techniques advance the musical argument while momentarily suspending that of the poetry. In the sequences of the *Pastor fido* settings, on the other hand, text and music move forward together. Again, this musico-poetic bond is only possible because of the distinctive rhetorical structures built into Guarini's verse. Monteverdi would exploit such rhetoric even more consistently in Ariadne's lament, where his musical structures faithfully reflect Rinuccini's poetic ones.

Still other techniques of the *Pastor fido* settings would later reappear in *L'Arianna*. They are especially prominent in the dialogue "Ecco Silvio." At the beginning of the *terza parte* of this cycle Monteverdi enhanced the alliterative resonance of Guarini's "se mia non sei / se non quando ti perdo" through quick eighth-note declamation. The gesture looks back to declamatory patterns first developed in the heroic style and forward to the treatment of locutions like "parlò la lingua sì" in the lament.[20] In the *prima parte* of "Ecco Silvio" the abrupt harmonic fall to the flat side and rhythmic slowdown for the exclamation "Ah garzon crudo!" also looks forward to *L'Arianna* and backward to polyphonic *Gerusalemme liberata* settings—this time those of Wert.[21] As he would in the lament, Monteverdi completely avoided pictorial madrigalisms in "Ecco Silvio," even at locutions that traditionally would have elicited them (for example, "Ecco gli strali e l'arco"—"Here are my arrows and bow"—in the *quarta parte*). And finally, as he would in the lament, Monteverdi built on distant textual echoes in "Ecco Silvio" a loose musical refrain that binds together two of its parts: the lengthy sequence beginning at "ferisci il petto" in the fourth part returns at "ferir io te" in the fifth (though Monteverdi manages this second, briefer sequence only by adding a repetition of the phrase not found in Guarini's verse).

In many particulars, then, the *Pastor fido* settings of the Fifth Book adumbrate more or less distinctly the expressive world of *L'Arianna*. But their musico-rhetorical language is everywhere deepened and diversified in the great lament. Their melodic-harmonic exclamations stand now beside subtler melodic formulas attuned to fleeting poetic parallelisms, and their declamatory rhythms are loosened to approach more closely the changing cadence of stylized stage speech. Their flexible sequences join forces with an array of repetitive structures to convey an equally wide range of repeating poetic formulations. Their dissonances and unexpected harmonic turns are emboldened as Monteverdi seeks more and more incisive emo-

20. See below, pp. 130–31.
21. For Monteverdi's direct reuse of a Wertian musico-poetic complex in Ariadne's lament see

Tomlinson, "Madrigal, Monody, and Monteverdi," pp. 71–75.

tional characterization, and the harmonic twists are given new coherence, framed in a broader tonal context of absolute clarity and simplicity (one building on the tonal consolidation of the epigrammatic style). The modest musico-poetic refrain of "Ecco Silvio" is reworked into a fine-spun web of musical and textual reminiscences and associations, some of them almost subliminal in their connective force, extending across the whole of the lament.

All these techniques combine in Ariadne's lament to create a musical speech of unprecedented oratorical eloquence. Here, for example, is the beginning of the second section (see also Ex. 39):

O Teseo, o Teseo mio,	Oh Theseus, oh my Theseus—
sì che mio ti vo' dir, ché mio pur sei,	for I still call you mine, since mine you are,
benché t'involi ahi crudo! a gli occhi miei;	although you steal away (cruel!) from my eyes—
5 volgiti, Teseo mio,	turn back, my Theseus,
volgiti, Teseo, o dio!	turn back, Theseus (oh God!),
volgiti indietro a rimirar colei	turn back to look again at her
che lasciato ha per te la patria e il regno,	who left for you her homeland and her kingdom,
e in queste arene ancora,	and now upon these sands,
cibo di fère dispietate e crude,	food for heartless, cruel beasts,
10 lascierà l'ossa ignude.	will leave her bones picked bare.
O Teseo, o Teseo mio,	Oh Theseus, oh my Theseus,
se tu sapessi, o dio! . . .	if you but knew, oh God! . . .

(vv. 791–802)

The tremulous repetition in Rinuccini's first line elicits a melodic sequence from Monteverdi, variants of which will occur frequently in the lament at similar poetic locutions. Its triadic rise to d″, the melodic peak of the first period (vv. 1–3), gradually invests Ariadne's speech with a minimal vitality, enough for her to oppose weakly, in verse 2, the desolate reality of her situation. But her protest falls off immediately, despondently—a descent broken only to reflect the syntactic duplication of verse 2 ("che mio . . . che mio . . .") and the dissonant sigh "ahi" of verse 3 (an extension of devices we have seen in Example 36 above).

Ariadne's second period (vv. 4–10) is longer and bolder, as she summons Theseus back to her. It begins, as the first period had, with repeated locutions (vv. 4–5); for these Monteverdi invoked his sequential refrain but now with notably quickened declamation. The exclamation "o dio!" brings the melodic line again to d″ (this time by means of an ornamental *accento* reminiscent of Book IV), but this melodic high point now falls to g♯′ instead of g′, as the bass moves by step to the root of an E-major chord not previously heard. The harmonic surprise boosts Ariadne's musical and emotional pitch to new heights, widening the skeletal sequence f′–a′–d″ of verses 1–2 to f′–a′–e″ for verses 4–6. Ariadne's leap to e″ coincides with her command to Theseus. Her high note is immediately rendered discordant by the motion of the bassline; resolution of the discord initiates a long, dissonant descent

EXAMPLE 39

Monteverdi, Ariadne's lament, second part, beginning

to the cadence on A that ends the period. Along the way Monteverdi's excited, monotonal declamation and flashes of dissonance illuminate subtleties of Rinuccini's prosody: the alternating assonance of line 7 ("che la*scia*to ha per *te* la *pa*tria e il *re*gno"), the fierce, onomatopoetic -ta- of "dispietate," and the liquid alliteration of line 10, stressed by the offbeat, dotted rendering of "lascierà l'ossa." After a pause the heroine starts up once more, falling back easily from the tonicized A to D and returning to the sequential refrain setting her earlier appeals to Theseus.

In this example Monteverdi derived the overall organization of his music from the rhetorical shape of Rinuccini's three periods, matching their parallel beginnings (vv. 1, 4–5, and 11–12) with the varied repetition of his rising sequence. He filled out this structure with gestures reflecting the poet's finer rhetorical details: the parallelism within verse 2, and the exclamations of verses 3, 5, and 12 (the last two set to identical music), and the alliteration and assonance throughout. Of course this distinction of two levels, one structural and the other attuned to rhetorical detail, is artificial. On all levels the music responds to the syntactic structure and rhetoric of the text. And, just as in nonmusical speech, the gestures of one level interact with those of another in creating affect and meaning. Thus the refrain setting verses 4–6, for example, not only recalls verses 1–2, the beginning of the first period, but also captures in its sequential structure the local anaphora "volgiti . . . / volgiti . . . / volgiti. . . ."

But the distinction of levels is useful if only to point up the wide variety of ways in which Monteverdi's music projects the rhetorical essence of Rinuccini's poetry. The complex interaction of syntactic and semantic levels that makes up Rinuccini's oratory speaks loud in Monteverdi's setting. His musical speech enhances the lyricism of dramatic poetry without sacrificing any of its linguistic richness. Aside from scattered moments in earlier Florentine dramatic monody and Monteverdi's own *Orfeo* (to both of which we shall return), it was the first solo song that could claim so much.

Other examples clarify the point. The last eight lines of the second section of the lament, lines 7–14 on page 120 above, form three equivalent periods (vv. 7–8, 9–11, and 12–14), each contrasting Theseus's joyful homecoming with Ariadne's woe. The parallelism of the first two is underlined by their matching metric structures and rhyme (note that the rhyme of verses 8 and 10 extends back into the verse: "et io qui piango . . . et io rimango"); but the second period runs over through verse 11, slowing the pace in anticipation of the third period, also of three verses.

Monteverdi set the three references to Theseus to variations of the same music, each time abruptly veering away from a solid cadence on G as Ariadne turns to consider her own plight (Ex. 40). The composer highlighted Rinuccini's rhymes in verses 7–10 through melodic and rhythmic equivalences, though the setting of verse 10 moves off in a tonal direction different from that of verse 8, creating an unsettled effect (matched to the poet's enjambement) that propels us to the conclu-

EXAMPLE 40

Monteverdi, Ariadne's lament, second part, end

sion of the period in verse 11. Verse 12, an *endecasillabo,* needs more music than the analogous verses 7 and 9, both *settenari;* Monteverdi contrived to combine their opening gestures to accommodate its greater length. The final turn to Ariadne's woe (vv. 13–14), concluding this section of the lament, brings a recomposed version of the music that opened and closed the first section—Ariadne's famous cry "Lasciatemi morire!" This is yet another of the recurring musical gestures that bind the lament together as a whole. Here the hesitant rise of the melody and its final collapse capture the dejected poetic pace of Ariadne's invocations of her parents and project the enervating effect of Rinuccini's extension of the period from two to three verses (an effect avoided in the setting of the second period by the quick declamation of verse 11).

Monteverdi captured Rinuccini's more energetic rhetoric as well, as in these verses from the third section of the lament:

Son queste le corone,	Are these then the crowns
onde m'adorni il crine?	that you'd place on my head?
Questi gli scettri sono,	Are these the scepters,
queste le gemme e gli ori:	these the gems and riches:
5 lasciarmi in abbandono	to leave me abandoned
a fêra che mi strazi e mi divori?	to beasts that will rend and devour me?

(vv. 822–27)

The foreshortening technique here, as the question in lines 1–2 is shortened to analogous one-line questions in lines 3–4, propels the speaker through line 5 to the end of line 6. And Monteverdi was not insensitive to the effect (Ex. 41). His setting captures both the foreshortening of lines 1–4 and its lasting effect straight through to the end of the passage. The omission after the third question of the pause that had followed the first two complements perfectly the accelerating rhythmic drive of the text, as does the rise to the dissonant melodic peak on "lasciarmi." The tumbling

EXAMPLE 41

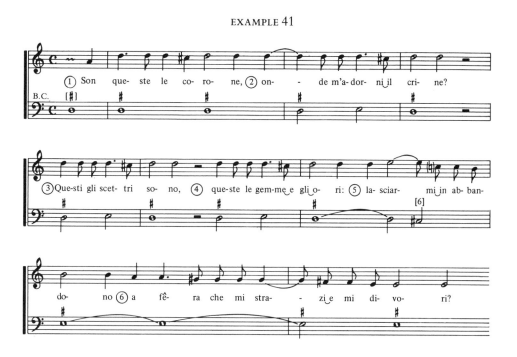

Monteverdi, Ariadne's lament, excerpt from third part

declamation after this climax increases the pace through lines 5 and 6 by means of a repeated rhythmic germ, itself foreshortened from ♩ ♪ ♪ ♪ ♪ ♪ ♩ ♩ to ♩ ‖: ♩. ♪ ♪ ♪ :‖ ♩ ♩.

A final example, from the end of the fourth section, shows Monteverdi's sensitivity to Rinuccini's musical assonance (see also Ex. 42):

O Teseo, o Teseo mio,	Oh Theseus, oh my Theseus,
non son, non son quell'io,	it was not, was not I,
non son quell'io che i fêri detti sciolse:	it was not I who spoke such wicked words:
parlò l'affanno mio, parlò il dolore;	my woes spoke, and my anguish spoke;
5 parlò la lingua sì, ma non già'l core.	my tongue spoke, yes, but not indeed my heart.

(vv. 844–48)

After her last, disconsolate cry to Theseus, returning for the last time to the musico-poetic refrain of Example 39, Ariadne gradually regains some degree of composure. Her poetry reflects this returning control in its progression from the hesitant half starts of verses 2–3 to the more coherent assertions of verses 4–5. Monteverdi's music captures Ariadne's hesitancy and her final blurting out of verse 3. The rapid declamation here enhances Rinuccini's assonance ("non son") and sets off starkly the text-expressive dissonant halt on "fêri" (a combination of dissonances, actually, more venturesome than any in the *Pastor fido* settings). Mon-

EXAMPLE 42

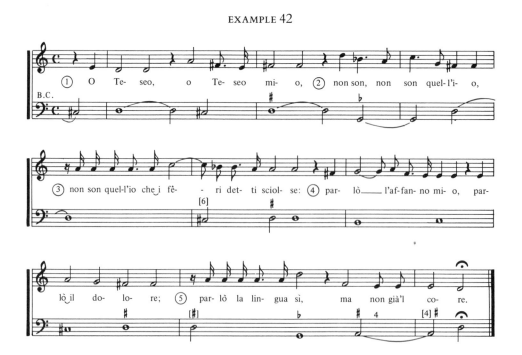

Monteverdi, Ariadne's lament, fourth part, end

teverdi projected Ariadne's growing composure in the loose sequence setting verses 4–5; its individual units correspond to the parallel locutions of Rinuccini's half verses. At verse 5 the quickened declamation of verse 3 returns, emphasizing the poet's liquid consonance ("parlò la lingua"), as it had earlier pointed up his assonance. This time, however, Ariadne reaches the high tonic note she had fallen short of in verse 3, and the melody sinks back in the dignified, dejected cadential formula we noted already at the end of Example 40.

From L'Euridice to Orfeo

To this point I have taken pains to emphasize the connection of L'Arianna to the Pastor fido settings of the late 1590s. We shall return below to the strong family resemblances of style among these works and in particular to the underlying generic similarities they manifest. Nevertheless, the differences between the Pastor fido settings and L'Arianna remain obvious enough. The former have come down to us as five-part madrigals, while the preserved theatrical version of Ariadne's lament (though not, we shall see, its original version) is monody, solo song with continuo accompaniment. The Pastor fido settings, if they ever had a true dramatic function, were songs imbedded within a mostly spoken drama; the lament was the musical climax of a fully sung drama. L'Arianna, in short, was an opera and hence connected in the minds of its creators not only with the settings from Il pastor fido but also with the Mantuan and Florentine operas of the preceding decade. These provide another line of stylistic ancestry for the lament and an additional source of fertilization for Monteverdi's music in general.

The best of them by a composer other than Monteverdi, and the work from which he learned the most, was Jacopo Peri's setting of Rinuccini's Euridice of 1600. And the earliest surviving work of Monteverdi to reveal the lessons of Peri is Orfeo, composed a year before L'Arianna on a text by the Mantuan poet and bureaucrat Alessandro Striggio and first performed early in 1607.

Monteverdi and Striggio's emulation of Peri and Rinuccini is evident throughout Orfeo.[22] In the texts, first of all, the similarities between the two works often cannot be ascribed to the common reliance of the two authors on the ancient sources of the Orpheus myth or on the more recent tradition of Orphic drama stemming from Poliziano's Orfeo (1480). They may take the form of a rough identity of content, as in Acts I and II of Striggio's and Rinuccini's works; they may also present a more precise resemblance of dramatic organization, as in Striggio's mes-

22. On the poetic and musical similarities of L'Euridice and Orfeo see also Nino Pirrotta, "Monteverdi e i problemi dell'opera"; Barbara Russano Hanning, Of Poetry and Music's Power; and Anna Maria Monterosso Vacchelli, "Elementi stilistici nell'Euridice di Jacopo Peri in rapporto all'Orfeo di Monteverdi."

senger scene, structured in most particulars after the same scene in *L'Euridice*. Or a character introduced in *L'Euridice*, extraneous to the myth itself and not found in Rinuccini's sources, may have a dramatic counterpart in *Orfeo*: Venus, Rinuccini's Dantesque escort for Orpheus on his journey to the underworld, is renamed Speranza by Striggio, who points up the connection to Dante's Virgil by quoting the line "Lasciate ogni speranza, voi ch'entrate" from the *Inferno*.

Some of the most important speeches in *Orfeo* correspond closely in content and even in locution to their counterparts in *L'Euridice*—most strikingly the messenger's narration of Euridice's death and Orpheus's response to the news in Act II.[23] Still other speeches in *Orfeo*, not strictly analogous to any in *L'Euridice*, nevertheless reveal their dependence on the earlier work. Thus in Act III Orpheus's speech following Charon's rebuff of his formal plea borrows its structure of long, madrigal-like strophes unified by a refrain from Rinuccini's "Funeste piaggie."[24] Striggio's refrain itself, "Rendetemi il mio ben, tartarei numi" ("Give me back my love, Tartarean gods"), is clearly styled after Rinuccini's "Lagrimate al mio pianto, ombre d'inferno" ("Weep at my lament, infernal phantoms"). Striggio took "Funeste piaggie" also as the starting point for Orpheus's long lament opening Act V of his work, as is evident from a number of similarities of locution between the two speeches.[25]

Monteverdi's debt to Peri in the music of *Orfeo* is as apparent as Striggio's to Rinuccini in the verse. Monteverdi sometimes borrowed a simple but dramatically effective musical device from Peri, for example the low, growling tessitura of his underworld choruses. On one occasion he derived a more sophisticated musico-dramatic technique from his predecessor, Peri's eloquent characterization of Orpheus and Pluto by tonal and melodic means. In the lengthy exchange in which Orpheus convinces Pluto to return Euridice to the living, Peri had consistently contrasted Orpheus's fluid declamation in and around G minor with Pluto's four-square, often triadic melodies in and around F major. The repeated tonal juxtaposition and contrast in melodic style define the affective charge of each key—F major unyielding and bright, G minor plaintive, soft.[26] Echoes of this tonal and melodic dichotomy sound throughout the two underworld acts of *Orfeo*. In Act III Charon's strophes hover mainly around F and C, though they cadence in D minor, and his triadic, rhythmically direct melodic style is much indebted to that of Peri's Pluto. Orpheus's "Possente spirto" is in G minor, and his later refrain, "Rendetemi il mio ben," cadences in the same key. In Act IV Monteverdi brilliantly extended Peri's conception to embrace a more subtle dramatic distinction: here Proserpina,

23. See *Orfeo*, vv. 218–37, 246–55; *L'Euridice*, vv. 190–222, 226–36.

24. *Orfeo*, vv. 387–410; *L'Euridice*, vv. 418–47.

25. See especially Striggio's vv. 567–68, 571, and 572 (compare *L'Euridice*, vv. 424, 436–37, and 425) and Orpheus's apostrophe to Euridice in the final section of this passage (vv. 594–611; compare *L'Euridice*, vv. 436–47).

26. See the facsimile edition of *Le musiche di Jacopo Peri . . . sopra L'Euridice* (hereafter *L'Euridice*, facs. ed.), pp. 32–34.

who argues on Orpheus's behalf, sings in G minor (with a prominent admixture of Bb major), while Pluto's responses waver between F and C. But Monteverdi's final use of Peri's G-minor–F-major contrast is his most poignant. As Orpheus turns back to gaze on Euridice, defying Pluto's condition for her release, he begins to sing on G minor, quickly veering off to cadence on A as his "dolcissimi lumi" begin to fade from view. An infernal spirit, singing on F and then cadencing on C, harshly confirms Orpheus's failure: "Rott'hai la legge, e sei di grazia indegno." Euridice's final, exquisite speech, "Ahi, vista troppo dolce e troppo amara!," follows and reverts once more to the plaintive G minor in which Orpheus and Proserpina had won her resurrection.

In following the lead of Peri, Monteverdi also sometimes emulated the general structural outlines of large musical units in *L'Euridice*. He borrowed, for example, the organization of his lamenting chorus at the end of Act II from Peri's analogous composition. Striggio, like Rinuccini, structured this chorus in strophes unified by a short refrain. Monteverdi, like Peri, employed the full chorus only for the refrain, setting the strophes for reduced vocal forces over a repeating but varied bassline. (Monteverdi set his two strophes as duets, while Peri set his three strophes as two solo *arie* over a varied bassline, followed by a vocal trio.)

Finally, and most important, where Striggio's speeches show extensive similarities to analogous speeches in *L'Euridice* there are almost invariably strong reminiscences of Peri's setting in Monteverdi's. These analogous passages reveal Monteverdi's substantial debt to Peri in his recitative. Compare the two composers' settings of the messengers' narrations of Euridice's death (Exx. 43a and 43b). We should note first of all that the dramatic situation is not precisely equivalent in the two works at this point: in Rinuccini's libretto Orpheus is not informed of Euridice's death until the end of the messenger's long monologue describing how it occurred, while in Striggio's work Orpheus is told of Euridice's death almost immediately, responds briefly (but to good effect in Monteverdi's setting), and only then listens, stunned, to the messenger's narration. So Peri could begin his setting in an unruffled major mode and with a serenely flowing melody as the messenger describes the delight of Euridice and her frolicking companions (not quoted here); only later would the composer introduce darker harmonies and an impassioned melodic style. Monteverdi, on the other hand, had to set the tragic tone from the beginning of the narration. His messenger declaims somberly over a long-held pedal, rising through the notes of the minor harmony with passing emphasis on nonharmonic tones—a simple technique adumbrated at various points in Peri's score.[27] Monteverdi modeled the tonal shift at verse 5 of his setting, as the messenger first speaks of the insidious viper hidden in the grass, on Peri's tonal break at the

27. Especially similar is Peri's opening of Orpheus's plea to the gods of the underworld, "Funeste piaggie"; see *L'Euridice*, facs. ed., pp. 29–30. Peri's setting of the present messenger's narration also begins with this technique, though for the reasons mentioned the emotional color of the passage contrasts markedly with that of Monteverdi's opening.

EXAMPLE 43

(a) Peri, *L'Euridice,* excerpt from Daphne's narration

(b) Monteverdi, *Orfeo*, Act II, excerpt

analogous point of his setting ("quand'ahi, ria sorte acerba!"; Striggio's text, here as elsewhere in this passage, bears strong resemblances to Rinuccini's). Both composers moved abruptly up a whole tone, a prominent minor seventh resolving to the fifth of the new chord. Peri shifted from C to D major, Monteverdi from D major to E minor, delaying the arrival of E major until, at verse 7, he reached it by a plagal cadence analogous to that concluding verse 4. Peri continued up another whole step to an E-major chord, and this section of his monologue, like the analogous verses 5–7 in Monteverdi's, centers on E and A.

Monteverdi's harshest harmonic juxtaposition in this passage, the E-major-to-G-minor shift at verses 7–8, is a familiar expressive means in Peri's score.[28] Here it imitates the milder G-major-to-E-major juxtaposition that Peri employed, like Monteverdi, to depict Euridice's deathly pallor (at "come raggio di sol che nube adombri"). Again the musical similarities arise especially where the texts resemble each other most closely, as if Monteverdi associated Rinuccinian locutions in Striggio's text automatically, even unconsciously, with Peri's music.

Similarities such as these reveal Monteverdi's dependence on *L'Euridice* in composing the recitatives of *Orfeo*. This is not to say that Monteverdi had not encountered many of the devices of Peri's recitative in other musical contexts and even exploited them in his own earlier five-part madrigals. But Peri and Rinuccini's *Euridice* offered him a compelling object lesson in the incorporation of such techniques in a vivid rhetoric of monodic music-speech. And the passages in Peri's score that most captivated him, to judge by the evidence of his reliance on them, are just those climactic moments in the new *stile rappresentativo* that still command first attention today: the messenger's narration, Orpheus's response, "Non piango, e non sospiro," and Orpheus's plea to the underworld, "Funeste piaggie." For the first two Striggio provided Monteverdi with speeches analogous in dramatic function and content; it was natural for the composer to follow the lead of his predecessor in the music as well. And, although *Orfeo* lacks a direct analogue to "Funeste piaggie" in the underworld, substituting for its rhetorical eloquence the musical virtuosity of "Possente spirto," reminiscences of Rinuccini and Peri's great recitative lament abound in Monteverdi's score, especially in Orpheus's recitatives of Acts III–V.

Thus Monteverdi's *Arianna* and *Orfeo* look back on interrelated but distinct traditions: on the solo song with instrumental accompaniment of sixteenth-century *intermedi* and semimusical drama—reflected, at least, if not actually embodied, in

---

28. See *L'Euridice*, facs. ed., p. 17 (Orpheus's response to the news of Euridice's death), systems 2, 3–4. At Daphne's entrance (to report Euridice's death) Peri renders this juxtaposition even more wrenching by suspending the B♭ of the G-minor triad over the E-major triad (see p. 13, system 1); usually, however, he prefers the less harsh G-major-to-E-major progression seen in Example 43a.

the settings from *Il pastor fido*—and on the monodic recitative of Florentine opera. To say more than this, to assess the relative importance of each of these traditions in the stylistic formulation of *Orfeo* and *L'Arianna,* we must first distinguish these two works and define the traits that set the recitative of one apart from that of the other.

Some of the distinctive features of the recitative of *Orfeo* must be viewed as shortcomings in light of the styles of both the later lament and the earlier *Pastor fido* settings. These weaknesses arose usually as musical reflections of rhetorical deficiencies in Striggio's text; hence they are of little aid in measuring Monteverdi's reliance on earlier styles. They include the breakdown of the poetic structure of the text under the strain of Monteverdi's attempt to invest it with expressive vitality, the rambling, seemingly arbitrary melody at certain points, and occasional lapses into iconic rather than rhetorical expression through the use of pictorial madrigalisms.[29]

Other differences between the recitative of *Orfeo* and that of *L'Arianna,* however, are less solecistic and less easily traced to Striggio's inadequacy. Most important among these is the greater rhythmic complexity of the recitative of *Orfeo*. In comparison with Ariadne's lament its juxtaposition of contrasting rhythmic values is sharper, its use of declamation on sixteenth notes more frequent, and its syncopation more pronounced. These characteristics of the vocal part are reflected also in the bassline: it moves less smoothly, with more disjunction of rhythm and pitch, than in the lament.

Also, Monteverdi's harmonic style is less orthodox in *Orfeo* than in *L'Arianna.* The harmonic vocabulary, first, is less restricted, resulting at moments of high emotion in progressions of a poignant eccentricity not encountered in the later work (see, for example, the end of the Messenger's narration in Act II, at "piena il cor di pietade e di spavento"). The treatment of dissonance in *Orfeo* involves struck discords harsher than those in the lament (for example, the major seventh near the beginning of Orpheus's "Tu se' morta" in Act II).[30] And in general the introduction of dissonance reveals its connection to sixteenth-century practice—its origin, that is, in polyphonic suspension techniques—less clearly in *Orfeo* than in *L'Arianna.*

These rhythmic and harmonic characteristics affect the melodic style of the recitative of *Orfeo* as well. It is less symmetrical, less predictable in its trajectories, less even in its forward motion—in a word, less lyrical—than Ariadne's melody. (As we have noted, such melodic features, more than the harmonic and rhythmic ones just enumerated, arise in part from infelicities in Striggio's rhetoric.)

All these differences between *Orfeo* and *L'Arianna* may be viewed as manifestations of the different performance circumstances of the two works and, ultimately,

29. I discuss these difficulties more fully in "Madrigal, Monody, and Monteverdi," pp. 77–78n, 80–86.

30. For these two passages see Claudio Monteverdi, *L'Orfeo favola in musica,* facs. ed., pp. 38, 39.

of their subtly different genres. For it is a fact usually ignored that Ariadne's lament was not originally accompanied monody in the manner of *Orfeo* but solo song with a polyphonic accompaniment of viols.[31] This we know from one of the few specific accounts we have of its performance, the report written one day later by the Estense ambassador in Mantua to his superiors at Modena: "Then the Comedy in music was presented . . ., and all the beautifully dressed actors played their parts very well, but best of all the comedienne Ariadne. It was the story of Ariadne and Theseus, and in her lament in music accompanied by viols [*accompagnato da viole et violini*] she made many weep at her sad state."[32] In other words, the monodic version of the lament that has come down to us in manuscript sources and in the print of 1623 is not the original version. It is as much a homophonic reduction of that original as the five-voice version in Book VI is a polyphonic elaboration of it. The lament sung in 1608 undoubtedly stood somewhere between the two versions we possess. It was not monody at all but "pseudo-monody."[33]

This interpretation reveals the close connection between Ariadne's lament and a common style—probably the most common style—of dramatic and semidramatic solo song in the sixteenth century. In this style the voice was accompanied by a consort of instruments, each with separate written-out parts, together playing more-or-less polyphonic music, rather than by one or two continuo instruments realizing a fundamentally homophonic accompaniment. The one type of accompaniment starts from a polyphonic conception but often exploits simpler homophonic textures, while the other is conceived homophonically but frequently indulges in simple improvised polyphony. The *intermedi* for *Il pastor fido* of November 1598 involved numerous solo songs of this pseudo-monodic sort.[34] And if Monteverdi's *Pastor fido* settings originated as solo songs, they were undoubtedly also in this semipolyphonic style.[35]

31. A fact ignored in, among other writings, my own.

32. Quoted from Solerti, *Gli albori del melodramma* 1:99. I have interpreted the ambassador's "violini" to mean the treble members of the consort of viols. Federico Follino, the official Mantuan chronicler of the events, is less specific about the manner of performance of *L'Arianna,* though his mention of "the instruments placed behind the scene, accompanying her continuously and changing their sound with the changes in the music," recalls the musical practices of countless sixteenth-century *intermedi*; see Solerti, vol. 2, p. 145.

33. The term is Einstein's; see *The Italian Madrigal,* chap. 12, and also Palisca, "Vincenzo Galilei and Some Links."

34. This much is evident from the contemporary account of them; see n. 3 above.

35. Innumerable instances of such solo songs in a theatrical context are described in the published accounts of Florentine *intermedi* from 1539 to 1589. See Pirrotta, *Li due Orfei,* chaps. 4, 5. The music for some of these songs has survived; for examples see Pirrotta, Exx. 32, 33, 35, 39, 40, 44. For complete examples from *intermedi* of 1565 and 1589 see Howard M. Brown, "Psyche's Lament," and D. P. Walker, ed., *Musique des intermèdes de "La pellegrina."* Piero Strozzi's "Song of Night" from the Florentine carnival masquerades of 1579 (Pirrotta, Ex. 39) is especially relevant to the present discussion since its original polyphonic accompaniment must be reconstructed from a version for voice and continuo preserved in the Biblioteca Nazionale Centrale of Florence (MS Magliabechiano XIX, 66). Pirrotta also reproduces a description of a performance of a tragedy in Reggio Emilia in 1568 in which the

The need to synchronize four or five parts in such solo song placed greater restrictions on the declamatory freedom of the vocal part than in true accompanied monody. It is these restrictions that led in *L'Arianna* to a rhythmic style less complex than that of *Orfeo* and as a happy corollary to an arioso melodic idiom of sustained emotional force. The original lament owed its unique power partly to Monteverdi's ability to turn the limitations of this old style to his advantage, and it was the final and greatest monument to the vital traditions of music drama of the sixteenth century. Its wide circulation in monodic form to become the standard against which seventeenth-century music drama was judged reflects the deep dependence of the new order on the old.

Why did Monteverdi choose this style for *L'Arianna* and not for *Orfeo*? Undoubtedly because he considered the two to be different dramatic genres.[36] *Orfeo*, like its model, Rinuccini and Peri's *L'Euridice*, was written for intimate performance in front of aristocratic academies or in the private chambers of royalty. Like *L'Euridice*, it was called simply a *favola*, or "mythological story," and made no claim to the privileged status of Aristotelian dramatic genres of the late sixteenth century. *L'Arianna*, on the other hand, was one of the premier events in a season of spectacular courtly festivities. It was performed before four to six thousand courtiers and foreign guests (the chroniclers differ on the exact count) and proclaimed its Aristotelian pretensions in calling itself a tragedy. Five days after this musical tragedy was performed, Guarini's comedy *L'Idropica* took the stage, with elaborate *intermedi* in the traditional manner (for which Monteverdi composed the Prologue). In all these features the festivities of 1608 extended the most lavish tradition of sixteenth-century courtly entertainment. They looked back, that is, on events like the performance of *Il pastor fido* in November 1598. We tend, with selective musicological hindsight, to link the composition and performance of *L'Arianna* with those of *Orfeo* a year earlier. But Monteverdi's own associations may well have run instead to the festivities of a decade before.

Monteverdi's evocation of an earlier style of dramatic song was, in these circumstances, a logical choice. Ariadne's polyphonic solo song tapped a time-honored tradition of courtly ritual; its immediate, immense success was probably partly due to the appeal of its conventional musical surface. Its semipolyphonic ac-

---

choruses at the ends of the acts were presented as solo song (pp. 224–25). This, together with the fact that one Giacomo Guidoccio was assigned the role of *coro* in the *Pastor fido* preparations of 1592 (d'Ancona, *Origini*, pp. 550, 552), suggests that the main choruses of Guarini's play could also have been sung in this fashion. It seems more likely, however, that the Reggio Emilia performance was an extraordinary one, that Guidoccio was engaged in 1592 to speak the lines

for *coro* within the acts of *Il pastor fido,* and that the choruses ending each act were sung *à più voci*. Nevertheless, the account of 1568 reminds us once again not to circumscribe too narrowly the possible uses of music in sixteenth-century drama.

36. For a general discussion of the first operas in respect to genres of spoken drama of the time, see Tomlinson, "Rinuccini, Peri, Monteverdi," chap. 3.

companiment, dignified melodic arioso, and orderly harmonic idiom achieved a tragic decorum entirely in keeping with the generic claims of Rinuccini's play. And, not least, its full instrumentation sounded through a hall large enough to accommodate four thousand, where the "clavicembano" or the wooden portative organ of *Orfeo* would not have carried.

Orfeo, in contrast, was a chamber drama. Like all chamber music, it could afford to speak a more complex language, to paint, as it were, with a finer brush. In the face of *L'Arianna* its intricate adaptation of Peri's Florentine monody amounts to a melodramatic *ars subtilior*—one that did not long persist in the later development of opera. Imitations of Ariadne's lament abound in operas of the next half century, while echoes of Orpheus's plaints are few and far between.[37]

So the monody of *Orfeo* looks back more clearly to *L'Euridice* than to the *Pastor fido* settings, while *L'Arianna* must have brought to Monteverdi's mind first the festivities of 1598 and only after these the new Florentine music drama he had essayed in *Orfeo*. These stylistic and generic discriminations, however, need not obscure the fundamental unity of expressive intent that links Monteverdi's first two operas. Both works aimed for an unprecedented fluency of rhetoric, a musico-poetic language with the flexibility and affective force to enable the protagonists to convey their emotions in musical speech of stylized realism.

Behind this ideal, in both works, urging Monteverdi on in spirit or fact, stood Rinuccini. Striggio had modeled *Orfeo* on his *Euridice,* after all; and *L'Arianna* was his own. There is every reason to believe that Monteverdi's collaboration on the latter work with Rinuccini was close, and satisfying for musician and poet alike.[38] Rinuccini's advice, and the tacit guidance of his verse, must have encouraged rhetorical tendencies that Monteverdi had nurtured already in the *Pastor fido* settings and *Orfeo*. Poet offered composer an ideal dramatic *poesia per musica,* one that Monteverdi had probably admired in Peri's *Euridice* and hoped for in his collaboration with Striggio.

In *L'Arianna, L'Euridice,* and *La Dafne* (his earliest libretto), Rinuccini had also perfected the dramatic framework within which his lyrical language of emotion could operate to best effect. He called the latter two dramas *favole,* or mythological stories. As such their plots —and the plot of *L'Arianna* as well, for all the tragic pretensions of that work—showed a simplicity rarely found in spoken drama of the period. They eschewed the Aristotelian techniques of recognition and *peripeteia* carefully built into the plots of pastoral dramas like *Il pastor fido,* Tasso's *Aminta,* or

---

37. Exceptional examples are provided, significantly, by Peri himself in the music he supplied for the role of Clori in Marco da Gagliano's *Flora* of 1628. See pp. 89–106 of the facsimile edition of this opera for numerous echoes of *Orfeo*.

38. See Tomlinson, "Madrigal, Monody, and Monteverdi," pp. 86–87, and James H. Moore, review of *The Letters of Claudio Monteverdi,* by Denis Stevens, pp. 563–64.

Guidobaldo Bonarelli's popular *Filli di Sciro*. Instead they offered the unadorned rhythm of myth: Apollo loves Daphne, she flees; Euridice dies, Orpheus seeks to bring her back to life; Theseus betrays Ariadne, she laments. These are hardly plots at all, in the sense gleaned by sixteenth-century dramatists from Aristotle's *Poetics* and Sophocles' *Oedipus Rex*. Instead they are static situations, dramatic tableaux framed only to stimulate the emotions of the protagonists and then allow their unconstrained expression.

The theatrical impulse here is Senecan. Rinuccini's dramas convey their subject, the emotional reaction of the protagonist to his or her situation, by means of simplified action and stylized soliloquies. The characters speak their passions to the audience more than to each other. Hence the plays' orientations are as much oratorical—concerned with affective speechifying—as they are, properly speaking, dramatic—depicting the interactions of the characters onstage. The emotive soliloquies that dominate the dramatic landscapes of all three works—the laments of Apollo and Ariadne, Orpheus's plea to the underworld, and the many messengers' narrations of offstage events—share with the speeches of Seneca's tragedies a strong Ciceronian impulse to impassioned oration. And this impulse, not surprisingly, merges smoothly with the expressive capabilities of Rinuccini's Petrarchan verse.[39]

In such dramas as these, Monteverdi was quick to perceive, emotion counted for all. They were, in their aim and scope, the perfect theater for Monteverdi's music, deepening and clarifying his own expressive ideals. Add in Rinuccini's heightened rhetoric, easily joined to the syntax of Monteverdi's music, and the rich resulting mixture realized as never before a fundamental goal of humanist musicians: to speak in music.

EXCURSUS 2:

The Reconciliation of Dramatic and Epigrammatic Rhetoric in the *Sestina* of Book VI

The contrasting rhetorical approaches of the epigrammatic madrigals on the one hand and the *Pastor fido* settings and *L'Arianna* on the other join in a remarkable truce in the *Lagrime d'amante al sepolcro dell'amata* from the Sixth Book of 1614. Even in the best of circumstances this rapprochement could not have been perfect. For the clear distinction that Monteverdi drew in his works of 1598–1608 between two contrasting rhetorical modes—the polyphonic (lyric, epigrammatic) and linear

---

39. For a discussion of Peri and Rinuccini's "Funeste piaggie" from this Ciceronian perspective, see Tomlinson, "Rinuccini, Peri, Monteverdi," pp. 252–61.

(dramatic, monodic) syntaxes we have described—was too final, too essential to admit ever again their full reconciliation. It recognized and exalted two disparate expressive impulses that had created a latent tension in Monteverdi's oeuvre almost from the first. Once he had isolated these syntaxes, Monteverdi was disinclined to reunite them, preferring in Books V–IX to exploit them individually or seek new solutions altogether to the composition of madrigals.

Scipione Agnelli's inept text for the *Lagrime,* however, left Monteverdi little choice. It coerced him to attempt the reconciliation he might otherwise have avoided. This was so partly because it partakes of both poetic modes. It is dramatic in presenting, without narration or other lyric mediation, the plangent words of the shepherd Glauco over the tomb of his beloved nymph Corinna—a promising subject for Monteverdi, with resonance in earlier works like *L'Arianna* and Tancre-di's plaint at the tomb of Clorinda in Book III. (And resonance in his personal expe-rience as well: the poem commemorates Caterina Martinelli, his young protégée who had begun to rehearse the role of Ariadne shortly before her death in March 1608.)[1] Agnelli's poem is also lyric, in its revival of the strictest, most virtuosic *forme fixe* of Petrarch's *Canzoniere,* the *sestina.*

This is a purely formal lyricism, of course. In spite of it Monteverdi might have been able to set the poem as a dramatic lament, like "O Mirtillo" or "Ecco Silvio" with the addition of a few epigrammatic trappings, were it not for the syntactic clumsiness of the verse itself. For Agnelli had overreached his poetic abilities. In order to arrange his six rhyme words even approximately in the scheme dictated by Petrarchan and sixteenth-century *sestine* alike,[2] he tangled himself in a syntax knot-ted with Byzantine word orders, non sequiturs, lengthy periods often built by the piling up of brief, ineffective phrases, and other infelicities. Monteverdi seems to have turned back to the polyphonic techniques of the epigrammatic style chiefly to aid in smoothing out the kinks of this text. His solutions are sometimes brilliant, endowing the work with a rhetorical potency hardly hinted at in the poetry. Where, on the other hand, the text speaks more clearly, Monteverdi relies on the straightforward musico-poetic oratory of his dramatic style. The result is an amal-

---

1. Duke Vincenzo himself, who seems to have had his own, nonartistic reasons for lamenting Martinelli's death, requested Monteverdi's set-ting of it. The composer complied in mid-1610, during the same months that saw his polyphonic elaboration of Ariadne's lament. See the letter of Don Bassano Casola of 26 July 1610, given in Emil Vogel, "Claudio Monteverdi," p. 430, which also reveals Monteverdi's intent at this time to set Giambattista Marino's *canzone* on Hero and Leander (*La lira,* pt. 2, *canzone* 9); see chap. 6 below. On Vincenzo's probable liaison with Martinelli see de' Paoli, *Monteverdi,* pp. 218–19.

2. The second and fifth rhyme words of the first stanza are reversed from their proper order (or, conversely, those rhyme words in the first stanza are reversed from their proper order in all the following stanzas). Denis Stevens, *Musicol-ogy,* p. 204, and *Monteverdi,* p. 35n, recognizes the presence of formal irregularities in Agnelli's poem but not their full extent. He wrongly at-tributes them only to Monteverdi's reordering of the text in his setting.

EXAMPLE 44

Monteverdi, *Sestina,* beginning

gam, unique in Monteverdi's output, that fluctuates between the mature linear and polyphonic rhetorical modes of Books IV and V and Monteverdi's first operas.

The flexible homophonic declamation of the *Pastor fido* settings and earlier works returns at many points in the *Sestina,* usually with the expressive power we have come to expect of it. It opens the *prima parte,* for example, setting Glauco's invocation of the "Incenerite spoglie, avara tomba" ("Ashen remains, greedy tomb") in a somber manner that recalls the first measures of Wert's "Giunto alla tomba" (Ex. 44; see Ex. 15 above). Its expectant rise through twelve measures to a half cadence is balanced by the polyphonic collapse that follows on "Ahi lasso!" (The abrupt contrast here again brings to mind "Giunto alla tomba"; and Monteverdi reused this exclamation near the end of his cycle, in the *sesta parte* at "Ahi morte!") After these three lines, however, Agnelli's syntax grows unwieldy:

> Con voi chius'è il mio cor a' marmi in seno,   My heart is closed within your breast of marble,
> 5   e notte e giorno vive in pianto, in foco,[3]   and night and day the anguished Glauco lives
>   in duol', in ira il tormentato Glauco.   in weeping, in torment, in pain, in wrath.

In order to bind together the loosely knit phrases of this period (especially in lines 5 and 6, characterized by rhetorical *dissolutio*), Monteverdi resorted to epigrammatic

---

3. Monteverdi set this line as given here. The poetic form, however, requires the reversal of its final phrases: "e notte e giorno vive in foco, in pianto." See Stevens, *Musicology,* p. 204.

techniques: a series of textual juxtapositions in multiple counterpoint of lines 4 and 5, 4 and 6, 4, 5, and 6, and 5 and 6.

In the *seconda parte* Monteverdi again attempted to set the poet's opening invocation to homophony (this time more freely staggered), but the awkwardness of Agnelli's verse frustrated him:

Ditelo, o fiumi, e voi ch'udiste Glauco	Say it, oh rivers, and you who heard Glauco
l'aria ferir di grida in su la tomba,	rend the air above the tomb with cries,
erme campagne; e'l san le Ninfe e'l	abandoned fields; the nymphs and heavens
Cielo:. . . .	know it: . . . .

The obscure grammatical identity of "voi" and "erme campagne" in verses 1 and 3 is entirely lost in Monteverdi's music—indeed it is hard to imagine how it might be projected in music without a wholesale restructuring of the text—and the pause on "Glauco" undermines his semantic role as subject of the infinitive phrase in verse 2. Far more satisfactory is Monteverdi's solution for the last three lines of this stanza:

a me fu cibo il duol, bevanda il pianto,	my food is sorrow and my drink is tears,
5 letto, o sasso felice, il tuo bel seno,	my bed, oh fortunate stone, your cherished breast,
poi ch'il mio ben coprì gelida terra.	since frozen earth has covered up my love.

Monteverdi isolated line 6 as a refrain for two voices enlivened by piquant suspended dissonance. He introduced it early, sounding line 6 before line 5, and alternated it with the other lines, alone or in contrapuntal juxtaposition, as follows:

$$4 \quad 6 \quad \frac{4}{5} \quad 6 \quad \frac{5}{6} \quad 6 \quad 6$$

Thus Monteverdi brought the logical antecedent of the period, given by Agnelli in reversed order only in line 6, into more telling association with its consequents listed in lines 4 and 5.

The first five lines of the third strophe present a sprawling, run-on period that would seem to defy effective musical conveyance:

Darà la notte il sol lume alla terra,	The sun will light the earth at night,
splenderà Cintia il dì, prima che Glauco	the moon will shine all day, before Glauco
di baciar, d'honorar lasci quel seno,	will cease to kiss and honor that bosom
che nido fu d'amor, che dura tomba	where once lived love, and now a rigid tomb
5 preme; *né sol d'alti sospir, di pianto*	weighs heavy; nor will heaven and the spheres
prodighe a lui saran le sfere e'l Cielo.	alone lavish loud sighs and tears upon it.

Monteverdi framed this *parte* with passages of homophonic declamation (setting the italicized words above), in both cases stating the text first for three voices and then, transposed, for five. His attempt to bind the opening two clauses of the strophe to their semantic consequent ("prima che Glauco . . .") and weld together the many phrases of verses 2–5 is, at least, ingenious. Each homophonic statement of lines 1–2 traces a descending tetrachord ($8 \rightarrow 5$) and leads to a half cadence, first in D minor, then in A minor. In the magisterial setting of "prima che Glauco" that follows (mm. 11–15), the *canto* resumes this descent in whole notes, falling from E to A and completing the A octave begun in the second statement of lines 1–2. The *canto* line, with its text, is immediately taken over by the bass, now transposed to fill in the fifth A to D (and thus reverse the transposition scheme of the first measures). Meanwhile the upper parts, in quicker motion, spin out sequences matched to the repetitive syntax of the text they declaim (vv. 3–5). The whole process ends in an evaporated cadence, appropriately on "che dura tomba / preme," and then is repeated in varied form.

The final three strophes provide less coarse grist for Monteverdi's mill. He treated stanza 4 mainly to homophonic declamation, with little textual juxtaposition until the adroit peroration in double counterpoint. (The B♭-major tonal ellipsis at the beginning of this *parte,* expressive of the heavenly vision of verse 1 and abruptly diverted back toward D minor with the terrestrial woes of verse 2, accounts for the flatted key signature, unique in the cycle.)[4]

The fifth stanza is the most compelling in Agnelli's poem, reminiscent of Ariadne's lament in its insistent and straightforward rhetoric:

Ochiome d'or, neve gentil del seno,
o gigli de la man, ch'invido il Cielo
ne rapì: quando chiuse in cieca tomba,
chi vi nasconde? Oimè! povera terra
5 il fior d'ogni bellezza, il sol di Glauco
nasconde? Ah, muse qui sgorgate il pianto!

Oh hair of gold, fair snowfall of her breast,
oh lily-white hands, that envious heaven
stole away: closed in this blind tomb,
who hides you? Alas! humble earth
the flower of all beauty and Glauco's sun
hides? Ah Muses, here pour forth your tears!

Monteverdi matched the parallelism of Agnelli's first two and a half lines to repeated phrases of staggered homophony (mm. 1–7 and 8–14) and the query of lines 3–4 to chordal declamation with a questioning, offbeat cadence that recalls Book

---

4. The case is somewhat similar to that of "O Mirtillo," also with a D final but opening on B♭. The assertion of this similarity runs counter to Carl Dahlhaus's description of a qualitative change in Monteverdi's tonal usage between the *Pastor fido* settings of Book V and the *Sestina* (*Untersuchungen über die Entstehung der harmonischen Tonalität,* pp. 257–86). Dahlhaus's change involves a shift from the "composing out" of individual, independent hexachordal steps, resulting in what he calls *Teiltonarten,* to a hierarchical harmonic organization, in which the harmonies are related functionally to a single, preeminent tonal center. But in my view Dahlhaus overstates the extent of this shift, partly, it would seem, as a result of not considering any madrigals from before the Fifth Book. (His distinction of earlier "paratactic" and later "hypotactic" musical syntaxes does not stand up to such a consideration.) This is not to deny that Monteverdi's tonal structures evince a growing sense of hierarchical order across his long career. On this evolution see, aside from Dahlhaus, McClary, "The Transition"; her concepts of "circumscriptive tonality" and the "parenthetical expansion" of modal degrees are closely related to Dahlhaus's *Teiltonarten.* But the evolution was gradual and irregular, and our understanding of it should be qualified by closer attention to the structural and syntactic prerequisites of individual genres. There are striking moments of hierarchical tonal thinking in Monteverdi's early works—to which Dahlhaus and McClary do not perhaps do justice—just as the latest pieces frequently recall the flexibility of earlier varieties of tonal motion.

EXAMPLE 45

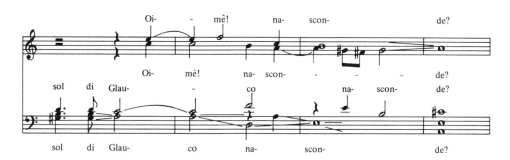

Monteverdi, *Sestina, quinta parte,* mm. 23–30

IV. In the next question (lines 4–6) Agnelli's short-lived rhetorical prowess collapses, beaten down by the contorted word order needed to place the rhyme words properly. Here for once, however, Agnelli's choppy syntax played into Monteverdi's hand: he set the individual phrases of the period ("povera terra," "il fior d'ogni bellezza," "il sol di Glauco") in the three lower voices, leaving the *canto* and *quinto* to articulate them with repeated cries of "Oimè!" (Ex. 45).[5]

This technique returns in the *sesta parte,* where Monteverdi isolated the cry "Ahi Corinna!" and repeated it piercingly in the upper voices against the parallel clauses of line 5 in the low trio:

. . . Ecco l'afflitto Glauco	. . . Here the wounded Glauco
fa rissonar "Corinna" il mar e'l Cielo.	makes sea and heaven echo with "Corinna."
5 Dicano i venti ogn'hor, dica la terra:	Let the winds say always, let the earth say:
"Ahi Corinna! Ahi Corinna! Ahi morte! Ahi tomba!"	"Ah Corinna! Ah Corinna! Ah death! Ah tomb!"

5. The device is not new in the *Sestina*; indeed this passage is elaborated from Monteverdi's setting of Petrarch's "Oimè il bel viso, oimè il soave sguardo," published with the *Sestina* in Book VI but in all likelihood composed in 1607 (see chap. 6 below). But the music better reflects the text in "Oimè il bel viso" than here because Petrarch, like Monteverdi but unlike Agnelli, insistently repeats *oimè* through his first five lines. (This truer reflection of poetic structure in music in the Petrarch setting suggests that it was written before the *Sestina*.)

The beauty of this arrangement is that it placed the exclamation "Ahi Corinna!" in close proximity to lines 3–4, realizing in music the echoes of Glauco's sorrow described there and controverting with genuine emotion the poetic license that would ascribe them in line 5 to the earth and winds. This is a quintessentially epigrammatic musical technique, disassembling the text and then reshaping it in polyphonic song that brings across its levels of meaning in ways unavailable to the poet.

From this emotional peak—the high point of the *Sestina* as a whole—the music falls back abruptly, exhausted, with fading exclamations of "Ahi morte! Ahi tomba!" that recall the *prima parte* and evanesce in an evaporated cadence. The three-line envoy that ends the poem is set entirely in homophony, dispirited and low of tessitura. Thus Monteverdi ends as he had begun the longest and perhaps the last of his *a cappella* madrigals.

THE
EMERGENCE
OF NEW IDEALS

6

Marino and
the Musical Eclogue
(Book VI)

IN JULY 1612, shortly after the death of Vincenzo I Gonzaga, Monteverdi was summarily released from his position at the court of Mantua. He returned to the environs of his youth—first to his father's house at Cremona and then to nearby Milan, where he seems to have spent part of the next year directing concerts in aristocratic salons. But this was probably not steady work and surely not a position of esteem for a composer of Monteverdi's fame at the height of his career. So he must have rejoiced in August 1613 to receive an invitation to audition for the position of *maestro di cappella* of St. Mark's in Venice. His trial was a success, and around the end of September he took up his new duties as a servant of *la Serenissima*. He would relinquish those duties only at his death, thirty years later.

Already in his first year at Venice Monteverdi found time to gather together a book of his madrigals for publication. This Sixth Book saw the light in 1614—we cannot securely assign it any more precise date since it, alone among Monteverdi's madrigal books, bears no dedication, as if to signify Monteverdi's newfound independence from princely patrons.[1] It is with the continuo madrigals of this book that we shall be concerned in the present chapter. But before discussing them we must briefly retrace our steps to Book V of 1605, for at the end of that collection Monteverdi had included his first continuo madrigals.

In fact Monteverdi supplied a *basso continuo* for all the madrigals of his Fifth Book. But in the title of the collection he carefully distinguished between the works that demanded instrumental support for their performance and those conceived as *a cappella* music: *Il Quinto Libro de Madrigali a cinque voci . . . col Basso continuo per il Clavicembano, Chittarone, od altro simile istromento; fatto particolarmente per li sei ultimi, et per li altri a beneplacito.* For the *a cappella* madrigals the optional instrumental line

---

1. On grounds of external evidence Stevens, *The Letters*, p. 95, suggests that it was published in June or July.

151

was a simple *basso seguente,* following at all times the lowest part of the vocal complex. The last six pieces, however, are true continuo madrigals. In writing them Monteverdi began to explore the novel expressive and structural capabilities of the new medium. Gradually that exploration would lead him away from the oratorical ideals of his youth.[2]

To Monteverdi the continuo offered, first, a new clarity of musical structure. In allowing extended passages for one or two voices with little sacrifice of harmonic fullness, it provided the opportunity for striking contrasts of texture—even more striking than those he had used to such good effect in earlier works without continuo. These contrasts could be exploited in turn to articulate with utmost lucidity blocklike forms rarely encountered in the *a cappella* madrigals. The procedure is clear in Monteverdi's setting of "Troppo ben può questo tiranno amore," a madrigal by Guarini whose straightforwardly segmented structure (as Pirrotta has noted) recalls a *ballata* lacking its *volta.*[3] Monteverdi seized on the division of the poem into three periods, the last two of which are rhetorically parallel, to support a musical form that may be represented ABB′ + coda. The A section is a fine introductory point of imitation for five voices, in which the instrumental part is merely a *basso seguente.* But each of the B sections begins with a lengthy solo for *canto* and true continuo, only later, in a closing point, swelling to five voices. Thus the end of the first B section contrasts in texture with the beginning of the second just as the A section had contrasted with it.

Even when the poetry did not present such ready-made structural articulations it could be manipulated to accommodate them. In setting Guarini's madrigals "Ahi, com'a un vago sol cortese giro" and "E così a poco a poco" Monteverdi employed the final line of each as a refrain. In the first he referred directly to Pallavicino, borrowing the setting of his refrain line, "Ah, che piaga d'amor non sana mai!," from Pallavicino's setting of the same text, published in his Sixth Book of 1600.[4] But Monteverdi did not find the refrain structure itself in Pallavicino's madrigal—this was all his own. The refrains of both works recur at the important syntactic divisions of each poem and stand out, by virtue of their fuller textures for three, four, or five voices, from the vocal duets that they separate. The reordering of the poetry entailed in this procedure is noteworthy: never before, except in passages of multiple counterpoint, had Monteverdi stated a line of text out of order. Now, however, structural possibilities suggested by his musical materials encouraged him to alter radically the profile of his text.

2. This break with the expressive goals of his epigrammatic and, to a somewhat lesser degree, his dramatic styles suggests that Monteverdi composed these continuo madrigals after the other works of Books IV and V—that is, after early 1603. This speculation may be corroborated by the absence of any reference to the continuo madrigals in Artusi's treatises of 1600 and 1603.

3. "Scelte poetiche," p. 227.

4. See Flanders, "The Madrigals of Pallavicino" 1:160–64, 2:40–46.

The straightforward formal procedures of these continuo madrigals are found also in other works of this time—in *Orfeo*, for example, with its frequent strophic variations and rigorous sectional organization, and in the Vespers of 1610, with its segmented structures and extensive use of variation techniques.[5] Such procedures are especially significant in the *Scherzi musicali* of 1607. Here the strophic forms are linked, for the first time in Monteverdi's works, with the metric novelties of the Anacreontic canzonette of Gabriello Chiabrera. Eleven of the sixteen poems set in the book are Chiabrera's, and Monteverdi even borrowed the poet's term for these lyrics, *scherzi,* for his title. All Monteverdi's earlier canzonette had set texts of *settenari* and *endecasillabi*. But now his music took on the special rhythmic vitality of four-, five-, six-, and particularly eight-syllable lines, arranged in strophes that betray Chiabrera's study of Ronsard and other French poets:

Damigella,	Little maiden,
tutta bella,	oh so pretty,
versa, versa quel bel vino;	pour and pour that lovely wine;
fa che cada	make fall
la rugiada	that dew
distillata di rubino.	distilled from rubies.

(*Twenty more strophes follow*.)

Dolci miei sospiri,	My sweet sighs,
dolci miei martiri,	my sweet torments,
dolce mio desio,	my sweet desire,
e voi dolci canti,	and you, sweet songs,
e voi dolci pianti:	and you, sweet tears,
rimanete, a Dio.	remain here; good-bye.

(*Six more strophes follow*.)[6]

Through the first half of the seventeenth century canzonette like these came to occupy an ever more prominent position in Italian poetry. And from 1607 on Monteverdi's tendency toward straightforward formalism was closely associated with the new Chiabreresque canzonetta.[7]

---

5. On the latter see Jeffrey G. Kurtzman, *Essays on the Monteverdi Mass and Vespers of 1610,* chap. 3.

6. I cite these poems from *Delle poesie di Gabriello Chiabrera,* II, 67–71, 62–63. For a recent consideration of the sources of Chiabrera's style and its impact on composers of monody see Silke Leopold, "Chiabrera und die Monodie."

7. I will return to such canzonette in chaps. 7 and 8 below. Chiabrera's poetic style may also be associated with French musical elements in Monteverdi's *Scherzi*; see Pirrotta, "Scelte poetiche," pp. 36–38, where the difficult issue of Monteverdi's "canto alla francese" is aired in exemplary fashion. This French manner, by the way, explicitly involves three other works of Monteverdi, each marked "alla francese": the Guarini settings "Chi vol haver felice e lieto il core" and "Dolcissimo usignolo" from Book VIII (1638) and the third *Confitebor* from the *Selva morale e spirituale* (1640), closely related in music to "Chi vol haver felice." All three works show stylistic links to the *Scherzi* of 1607 and may well date from Monteverdi's last years in Mantua.

A second trait facilitated by the presence of the continuo in Book V is vocal virtuosity. The solos and duets with continuo of all but one of these pieces abound in roulades and florid passagework only occasionally found in Monteverdi's *a cappella* madrigals, and in "Troppo ben può" and "E così a poco a poco" such virtuosity extends even to the sections for five voices. Again, it was probably the possibility of lengthy passages for one or two voices, gained by the use of the continuo, that led Monteverdi to this personal extension of the old-fashioned luxuriant style (which, after all, had been associated with a texture of one, two, or three voices and instrumental accompaniment ever since Luzzaschi had composed works for such forces for the Ferrarese *concerto di dame* in the 1580s). Monteverdi may even have turned to vocal display as a way to alleviate the textural uniformity of such passages.

Vocal acrobatics and repetitive, schematic formal arrangements have little to do with the various rhetorical means we have perceived in the *a cappella* madrigals of Books IV and V. They are, rather, more purely musical features. They tend to distance the music from the poetry, to break the intimate rhetorical link of text and music that Monteverdi had taken pains to create in his earlier works and that he would return to throughout his career in the most affective passages of his music dramas and madrigals. At the end of Book V, in other words, Monteverdi began to turn his back on his poets, enticed away by the musical constructive potential of a new medium.

It is not surprising, then, that his choice of poetry turns on different criteria here than elsewhere in Books IV and V. The madrigals by Guarini mentioned above show little of the epigrammatic brevity and wit of the lyrics set in the Fourth Book; nor do they ply the dramatic oratory of the excerpts from *Il pastor fido* in Book V. Instead they show traits well suited to Monteverdi's new architectonic tendencies. We have already noted the *ballata*-like form of "Troppo ben può," reflected in Monteverdi's musical form. "Ahi, com'a un vago sol cortese giro" and "E così a poco a poco" are placed together, linked in style and subject, in Guarini's *Rime*.[8] Both end with one-line morals that are not epigrammatic in effect, because they do not spring in witty or paradoxical fashion from the rather discursive material before them. On the other hand, these morals are perfect for use as refrains throughout the settings of the poems.

Ahi, com'a un vago sol cortese giro	Ah, at one pretty and graceful turn
di duo begli occhi, ond'io	of two lovely eyes, whence I
soffersi il primo e dolce stral d'amore,	was wounded by the first sweet arrow of Love,
pien d'un novo desio,	how quickly my heart,
sì pronto a sospirar torna il mio core!	full of new desire, sighs once again!

8. They appear on fols. 60v and 61r of the edition of 1599 and form a group, on the subject "Recidiva d'amore," with the intervening madrigal, "Oimè, l'antica fiamma."

Lasso, non val ascondersi, ch'omai	Alas, it is no good to hide, for now
conosco i segni che'l mio cor m'addita	I recognize the signs that my heart shows me
de l'antica ferita;	of the old wound;
et è gran tempo pur ch'io la saldai.	and it is long indeed since it was healed.
Ah, che piaga d'amor non sana mai!	Ah, a wound of Love is never cured!

This discursive, nonepigrammatic style characterizes all but one of the poems for the continuo madrigals of Book V. The exception is another of Guarini's madrigals, with sharper epigrammatic features than the lyrics mentioned above:

"T'amo mia vita," la mia cara vita	"I love you, my life," my dear life
dolcemente mi dice; e in questa sola	sweetly says; and in this single
sì soave parola	word so sweet
par che trasformi lietamente il core,	it seems she transforms willingly her heart,
per farmene signore.	to make me master of it.
O voce di dolcezz'e di diletto!	Oh words of sweetness and delight!
Prendila tost'Amore,	Seize it quickly, Love,
stampala nel mio petto,	etch it in my breast,
spiri solo per lei l'anima mia:	let my spirit breathe for her alone:
"T'amo mia vita" la mia vita sia!	let "I love you, my life" my life become!

In setting this poem, Monteverdi again used the procedures of the refrain madrigals just described. He assigned Guarini's opening phrase to the *canto* solo with continuo accompaniment and reintroduced it in this fashion three more times during the poem (after lines 2^1/2, 5, and 6^1/2) before developing it à 5 in a contrapuntal setting of the last line. Between these interjections the lower three voices declaim the rest of the poem with *seguente* accompaniment. (The *quinto* is not heard at all until the final point.) But Monteverdi's setting of the refrain " 'T'amo mia vita' " for solo voice is strikingly different in effect from the refrains for chorus of "Ahi, com'a un vago sol cortese giro" and "E così a poco a poco." It endows the madrigal with a dramatic immediacy not found in Guarini's lyric. Monteverdi's *canto* seems clearly to assume the role of the beloved herself, whispering the welcome phrase to her lover, who finally, in the polyphonic peroration, takes it over and repeats it again and again. The composer has forcibly interpreted Guarini's lyric poem, in which the beloved's words are remembered (imagined?) and exalted by the poet, as a poem mixing lyric and dramatic modes.

Guarini's " 'T'amo mia vita' " barely hints at this mixture of modes, but poems that more explicitly join lyric (or narrative) with dramatic utterance are not unknown in Monteverdi's earlier output and certainly not uncommon in the sixteenth-century madrigal as a whole. Examples are Rore's famous "Dalle belle contrade" or, among Monteverdi's works, "Non si levava" from Book II and "Rimanti in pace" from Book III. Moreover, we have seen that Monteverdi found novel means to project the shift from narration to actual speech in Rinuccini's mixed-mode madrigal "Sfogava con le stelle." It is hardly surprising, then, that in Book V Monteverdi immediately perceived the potential of the instrumental accompaniment to clarify modal shifts in the text. The *basso continuo*, he realized before any of his contemporaries, allowed him to isolate at will a dramatic persona from his ensemble of five voices, to merge an imaginary music drama with the polyphonic commentary and narration of the madrigal. The fact that Monteverdi's reading of Guarini's " 'T'amo mia vita' " distorts it into a somewhat uncongenial shape, from an epigrammatic lyric into a semidramatic *scena* for soprano with lyric comment by the lower voices, matters less than his discovery here of a new, mixed musical genre. He would invoke this genre in some of his best later continuo madrigals.

The lessons Monteverdi learned in his first use of the continuo, then, were three. He perceived in it the opportunity for an enhanced, even schematic, clarity of musical form, unlike the fluid, rhetorical formal patterns that predominate in his *a cappella* madrigals. It led him also to a new emphasis of vocal virtuosity, far more pronounced than the occasional earlier instances of the luxuriant style in his works. And, finally, he derived from it the means to inject a novel representational realism and immediacy into the traditional madrigalian framework of five voices. As we have repeatedly seen, Monteverdi was not one to waste the lessons he learned through compositional experience. He would extend the lessons of Book V in the continuo madrigals of the Sixth Book.

Monteverdi's strengthened urge to schematic structural clarity did not operate only within single madrigals. It is evident as well in the internal organization of his Sixth, Seventh, and Eighth Books. The *Sesto libro de madrigali* of 1614 falls into two sections, articulated by a series of lengthy madrigals that act as structural pillars at its beginning (the polyphonic adaptation of Ariadne's lament), middle (the *Sestina*), and end (a dialogue setting Giambattista Marino's miniature *canzone* "Presso un fiume tranquillo"). The first two of these works are conceived for voices alone, and each is followed by a setting of a sonnet of Petrarch, likewise *a cappella* ("Zefiro torna e'l bel tempo rimena" and "Oimè il bel viso, oimè il soave sguardo"; all four works are underlaid with *bassi seguenti* in the original print). "Presso un fiume tranquillo" is a continuo madrigal, like the remaining five works of the collection. These are all settings of sonnets, four of them by Marino and one by an author who remains unidentified ("Una donna fra l'altre honesta e bella").

Although the Sixth Book was not published until 1614, it undoubtedly preserves a repertory dating from the composer's last years in Mantua. "Una donna fra l'altre" had already been published, in a spiritual contrafactum by Monteverdi's Milanese friend Aquilino Coppini, in May 1609.[9] A letter of Bassano Casola of July 1610, as we noted in excursus 2, reveals that Monteverdi was at work at that time

9. *Il terzo libro della musica di Claudio Monteverde a cinque voci fatta spirituale da Aquilino Coppini* (Milan, 1609).

on the *Sestina* and the polyphonic *Lamento di Arianna*.[10] And Denis Stevens has offered the plausible hypothesis that Monteverdi's two settings of Petrarch in the Sixth Book are the sonnets to which the composer referred in a letter of 28 July 1607.[11]

All this leaves undated only the five settings of Marino's verse in Book VI. For various reasons, including their authorship by a single poet, their selection from a single poetic collection (Marino's *Rime* of 1602), and numerous musical and musico-poetic similarities among them, these works should be grouped together and viewed as a single, extended creative gesture. Schrade considered them the newest works of Book VI; Pirrotta agrees and suggests that Monteverdi's attention may have been drawn to Marino's poetry by the arrival in Mantua of the Neapolitan diva Adriana Basile and her husband, the Marinist poet Giambattista Basile, toward the end of June 1610.[12] The fact that Casola's letter of the next month links Monteverdi's name with Marino's for the first time lends credence to the supposition. In all probability Monteverdi composed the settings of Marino's verse in the Sixth Book after June 1610 but before July 1612, when he was dismissed from service at the Mantuan court.[13]

We have noted that the poems of Marino that Monteverdi chose are four sonnets and a *canzone*. With seven sonnets, a *sestina*, a *canzone*, and a dramatic excerpt among its texts, Book VI marks a new direction in Monteverdi's literary predilections. It alone among his books of musical madrigals contains none of the actual poetic madrigals that had dominated his first five books. For Book VI he chose instead poetic genres more rigorous in form.

Monteverdi's musical purpose in selecting these *formes fixes* is clear: they afforded him schematic poetic structures to match the architectonic musical forms he

---

10. It seems highly unlikely that Monteverdi ever completed the third work mentioned by Casola, a setting of Marino's *canzone Leandro*. Had he finished it, this piece would certainly have suggested itself as the perfect counterpart of the other two laments and probably have ended Book VI instead of "Presso un fiume tranquillo."
11. *The Letters*, pp. 50–51. Pirrotta, "Scelte poetiche," p. 232, places these two works, without reference to this letter or other evidence, in late 1607 or early 1608—that is, after the death of Monteverdi's wife, Claudia (on 10 September), and in the middle of his arduous compositional efforts for the wedding festivities of 1608. Pirrotta also suggests (p. 233n) that "Una donna fra l'altre" is one of the sonnets Monteverdi discussed in his letter of July 1607; but what then is the second sonnet? Pirrotta's chronology arises from his evident desire to endow these Petrarch

settings with special personal significance for Monteverdi, but the acceptance of Stevens's hypothesis militates against this view. "Zefiro torna" and "Oimè il bel viso" would seem to have been *scelte poetiche* not of Monteverdi but of his patron. My discussion below will suggest that, whatever our estimation of their respective poetic merits, Marino's sonnets suited Monteverdi's musical and literary goals at this time better than Petrarch's.
12. Schrade, *Monteverdi*, p. 280; Pirrotta, "Scelte poetiche," p. 234.
13. The setting of Marino's sonnet "A quest'olmo, a quest'ombre, et a quest'onde," published in the Seventh Book (1619), may also date from this period, though the other settings of Marino's verse in that collection are undoubtedly post-Mantuan works. See chap. 7 below.

had already essayed in the continuo madrigals of Book V. This is true even of the *a cappella* works in the Sixth Book: the quatrains of "Zefiro torna" and the terzets of "Oimè il bel viso" inspired more or less varied musical repetitions in their settings. (Monteverdi allowed himself more freedom, with obvious expressive dividends, in the fine peroration of "Zefiro torna" and in the opening bars of "Oimè il bel viso," which, as we have seen, look forward to the *Sestina*.) In the continuo madrigals the similarity of technique to Book V is even closer. The trio of lower voices that concludes the first quatrain of "Una donna fra l'altre" gives way abruptly to the *canto-quinto* duet that declaims the second; the terzets elicit extensively varied repetition à 5, as in "Oimè il bel viso." The poetic divisions of Marino's sonnet "Qui rise, o Thirsi, e qui ver me rivolse" allow Monteverdi to reuse the structure he had applied in Book V to "Ahi com'a un vago sol cortese giro."[14] The last line, set for five voices as a homophonic refrain, follows each of the quatrains and the last, five-line section, punctuating their virtuosic music for one, two, and three voices. Shifts of scoring at the midpoints of both quatrains further enhance the formal symmetry.

But Monteverdi seems also to have had more purely literary reasons for selecting these fixed forms and grouping them together in the Sixth Book. The collection as a whole is in its poetic themes the most unified of all his books, suffused with a warm glow of pastoral sorrow and nostalgia. It is, one might say, Monteverdi's pastoral romance—his *Arcadia* or, to anticipate by six years Marino's essays in the genre, his *Sampogna*. The relatively recent poetic type of the madrigal was hardly fitting in tone or dimension to this atmosphere, for whose expression Jacopo Sannazaro had set the standard more than a century before in measured *capitoli, canzoni,* and *sestine*. Obviously Monteverdi could not publish a collection setting only lengthy poems such as these, so he interspersed the three longer poems in Book VI with sonnets, venerable also but of more manageable proportions.[15]

The texts of the Sixth Book return again and again to the traditional topoi of the eclogue. Agnelli's *sestina* is nothing other than a pastoral elegy, with historical antecedents reaching back through Sannazaro and Virgil all the way to Theocritus. The four sonnets by Marino are all drawn from the *rime boscherecce* (woodland rhymes) of part 1 of his *Rime*. "Qui rise, O Thirsi" and "Batto, qui pianse Ergasto: ecco la riva" are remembrances of amorous adventures, narrated by one shepherd to another—a common subject and narrative arrangement for eclogues. Ergasto, Batto, and Thirsi (which Marino was careful to spell with a classicizing *h*) are among the most generic of pastoral figures, drawn from Sannazaro, Virgil, and

14. Arnold, *Monteverdi,* p. 82, and Pirrotta, "Scelte poetiche," p. 236, note the similarities of these two works.
15. Monteverdi's attention was drawn at least once to Sannazaro's *Arcadia* at this time. His only setting of an excerpt from it, "La pastorella mia spietata e rigida" (eclogue I, lines 91–105), was published in his *Scherzi musicali* of 1607.

Theocritus. "A dio, Florida bella, il cor piagato," "Misero Alceo, dal caro albergo fore," and the *canzone* "Presso un fiume tranquillo," all also by Marino, relate the separations or contemplations of pairs of pastoral lovers—themes ever present in sixteenth-century pastoral verse, if infrequent in the ancient eclogue.[16] Even Ariadne's lament, detached from its dramatic surroundings, and Petrarch's "Zefiro torna" ring with pastoral overtones; both might easily enough be regarded, even without the context of the Sixth Book to second the notion, as extensions of the traditional bucolic love-lay. Only "Oimè il bel viso" and "Una donna fra l'altre" display no pastoral trappings. We might guess that the first was included as the compositional twin of "Zefiro torna" and the second because it had already appeared in print in spiritual guise.

Aside from their crystalline fixed forms and their eclogue-like content, Marino's five *rime boscherecce* carried an additional bonus for Monteverdi. Like countless earlier eclogues, all but one of them indulged in the mixture of narrative and dramatic modes discussed above. "A dio, Florida bella," "Misero Alceo," "Batto, qui pianse Ergasto," and "Presso un fiume tranquillo" all offered Monteverdi the opportunity to perfect the musical distinction of narration and speech that he had attempted in "'T'amo mia vita'" of Book V. Indeed they, unlike Guarini's madrigal, are true mixed-mode lyrics, so Monteverdi could treat them as such without danger of garbling the poet's own utterance.[17]

Of these four works, "Batto, qui pianse Ergasto" realizes Monteverdi's new semidramatic conception least clearly. But then so does its text:

Batto, qui pianse Ergasto: ecco la riva	Batto, here wept Ergasto; here's the shore
ove, mentre seguia cerva fugace,	where Clori, following after a fleeing hind,
fuggendo Clori il suo pastor seguace,	and fleeing also from her following shepherd—
non so se più seguiva, o se fuggiva.	I can't say whether more she followed or fled.
5 "Deh mira" (egli dicea) "se fuggitiva	"Ah, look," he said, "if you like so much
fera pur saettar tanto ti piace,	to shoot at fleeing beasts,
saetta questo cor, che soffre in pace	shoot me in my heart, which silent suffers
le piaghe, anzi ti segue, e non le schiva.	such wounds, indeed pursues you and doesn't flee.
"Lasso, non m'odi?" E qui tremante, e fioco	"Alas, won't you listen?" Here trembling and faint

16. For some typical examples see the *Sonetti pastorali* of Pietro Angelio published in *Poesie toscane dell'Ilustriss. Sign. Mario Colonna, et di M. Pietro Angelio*, pp. 134–41.

17. This discussion may have reversed the order of the attractions of Marino's sonnets for Monteverdi, for it is possible that he decided to set them only because they encouraged the extension of the musical experiments of Book V, with no plans at first to publish them, with other works already composed, as a set of eclogues. Bassano Casola's letter of 1610, however, which refers to Monteverdi's projected "muta di Madrigali a cinque voci, che sarà di tre pianti," suggests that the composer already envisaged an overall thematic unity for his next book, albeit one that subsequently underwent some change of emphasis. These dual conceptions—the pastoral ethos of Book VI and its further development of the novelties of Book V—probably grew up together in Monteverdi's mind, both stimulated by his exposure to the poems of Marino's *Rime*.

10 e tacque e giacque. A questi ultimi accenti
l'empia si volse e rimirollo un poco;
    all'hor di nove Amor fiamme cocenti
l'accese. Hor chi dirà che non sia foco
l'humor che cade da duo' lumi ardenti?[18]
	he stopped and fell. And at these words
	the wicked one turned and threw him a glance;
	    then Love burned him anew with hot
	flames. Now who will say that it is not fire,
	the humor falling from two ardent eyes?

The poem participates in a classic topos of the eclogue—one shepherd tells another about the amorous experiences of a third. By employing this format Marino distanced the words of Ergasto from the dramatic present of his readers. This present is occupied instead by Batto and the unnamed narrator who relates Ergasto's plaint. In other words, "Batto, qui pianse Ergasto" is a mixed-mode poem that dramatizes the narration of its central event instead of the event itself.

Monteverdi seems to have recognized this extra representational dimension in Marino's sonnet. By setting Ergasto's lovelorn plea to Clori (lines 5–9) for *canto* and *quinto* with continuo and the surrounding lines for five voices, he distinguished the narrative from the dramatic sections of the poem. But his use of a duet of sopranos to "play" the role of Ergasto sacrificed the dramatic immediacy that a solo setting of the same lines might have yielded. It distanced the persona of Ergasto from the audience much as had the middle level of Marino's poem, at once narrative and dramatic. Monteverdi probably calculated his avoidance of the solo voice in the work to reflect the special complexity of this miniature eclogue.

The idea is supported by Monteverdi's consistent use of solo voice in the remaining three poems, "A dio, Florida bella," "Misero Alceo," and "Presso un fiume tranquillo." All three present simpler mixtures of literary modes than "Batto, qui pianse Ergasto," unnamed narrators setting the stage for characters to deliver their own lines in the perpetual present tense of the drama. And in all three Monteverdi gave the lines of dramatic speech over to individual singers, high or low in range according to the gender of the characters they play, while entrusting the narration to the full ensemble. This distinction of dramatic and narrative roles is most rigorous in "Presso un fiume tranquillo," set for seven voices so that the singers representing the lovers Filena and Eurillo could stand completely apart from the five-voice narrative chorus. The soloists join with the narrators only in the peroration, a repetition of the lovers' last lines stated earlier à 2.[19]

"A dio, Florida bella" begins almost exactly as " 'T'amo mia vita' " had and shares with the other continuo madrigals of Book V their tendencies to overly sche-

---

18. In line 5 Marino has "deh ninfa" instead of "Deh mira," obviously a better reading than Monteverdi's. My sources for Marino's poetry are *Rime di Gio. Battista Marino . . . parte prima* (Venice, 1602), *Rime del Marino. Parte seconda* (Venice, 1602; these volumes were republished in 1608 as *La lira*, pts. 1 and 2), and *Della lira del Cavalier Marino. Parte terza* (Venice, 1614). "Batto, qui pianse Ergasto" appears in pt. 1 of the *Rime* on p. 88.

19. Monteverdi altered the second line of Marino's last strophe from "la ninfa allor riprese" to "l'un e l'altro riprese" to allow both lovers to deliver the final four lines of the poem.

matic form and frequent outbursts of vocal virtuosity. Its two florid moments come at the ends of the quatrains, each of which is delivered by a single singer since they recount the words of the lovers Floro and Florida, respectively:

"A dio, Florida bella; il cor piagato
nel mio partir ti lascio, e porto meco
la memoria di te, sì come seco
cervo trafitto suol lo strale alato."

"A dio, beautiful Florida; my wounded heart
I leave you at my departure, and take with me
my memory of you, just as with it
a transfixed hind is wont to take the winged
arrow."

"Caro mio Floro, a dio; l'amaro stato
consoli Amor del nostro viver cieco;
ché se'l tuo cor mi resta il mio vien teco
com'augellin che vola al cibo amato."

"My dear Floro, a dio; let Love console
the bitter condition of our blinded life;
for if your heart stays here, mine goes with you,
like a bird that flies to its beloved food."

(*Rime,* pt. 1, p. 89)

It is easy to see why Monteverdi resorted to roulades at the ends of these quatrains. The labored similes here are figures of thought, not of speech, and entail no marked rhetorical features susceptible of musical formulation. Marino's undistinguished rhetoric forced Monteverdi to resort to pictorial madrigalisms, much as Striggio's occasionally had in the recitative of *Orfeo*. It is a problem that would recur frequently in Monteverdi's settings of Marinist verse; we shall return to it in the following chapters.

Easily the most powerful of these works is "Misero Alceo":

Misero Alceo, dal caro albergo fore
gir pur convienti, e ch'al partir t'apresti.
"Ecco, Lidia, ti lascio, e lascio questi
poggi beati, e lascio teco il core.
5   Tu, se di pari laccio e pari ardore
meco legata fosti e meco ardesti,
fa che ne' duo' talhor giri celesti
s'annidi e posi ov'egli vivi e more.
Sì, mentre lieto il cor staratti
accanto,[20]
10 gl'occhi lontani da soave riso
mi daran vita con l'umor del pianto."
Così disse il pastor dolente in viso;
la ninfa udillo; e fu in due parti intanto
l'un cor da l'altro, anzi un sol cor,
diviso.

Wretched Alceo, away from your dear home
you must turn, and make ready to depart.
"Now Lidia, I leave you, and leave these
blessed hills, and leave with you my heart.
"If of equal bonds and equal ardor you
are bound together with me and with me burn,
allow my heart in your two heavenly eyes,
where it lives and dies, to nest and rest.
"Thus while my heart stands near you,
happy,
my eyes, far away from your sweet smile,
will give me life with their tears."
Thus spoke the shepherd, sadness in his face;
the nymph listened; and meanwhile in two parts
their two hearts—rather, just one heart was
split.

(*Rime,* pt. 1, p. 89)

The dark homophonic beginning of this madrigal and its two-voice setting of lines 12–13, both strikingly reminiscent of passages in the *Sestina*, suggest that it was

20. Monteverdi has "more" instead of "mentre"; I restore the reading from Marino's *Rime*, pt. 1, p. 89.

written along with that work in the summer of 1610.[21] Its unceasing expressive gravity reinforces this connection and even inspires the speculation that Monteverdi may have turned to this poem when he abandoned his plan to set Marino's version of Leander's lament. In that case "Misero Alceo" would have become the third plaint of the Sixth Book mentioned by Casola, alongside the *Sestina* and Ariadne's lament.

Whatever its genesis, "Misero Alceo" represents both a loosening of the schematic forms of Monteverdi's continuo madrigals and a deepening of the pathos of their dramatic dimension. Monteverdi set Alceo's speech in lines 3–11 as recitative—the supplest, most affecting use of the *stile rappresentativo* in Book VI. Behind this seemingly free declamation is a structure of rigorous if inconspicuous logic: a repeating musical unit of melody and bassline. It is stated three times, altered to fit not only Alceo's changing declamatory patterns but also the different lengths of his three syntactic periods (lines 3–4, 5–8, and 9–11; the first statement of the unit is given in Example 46). The drooping chromaticism of the repeating bassline—the ostinato, we might as well call it—carries the perfect expressive charge for the protagonist's sorrow. It enables Monteverdi to make his form-clarifying gesture a bearer of musico-poetic emotion as well. And it anticipates operatic laments of Cavalli written three decades later.[22] Indeed, "Misero Alceo" as a whole is prophetic of Monteverdi's own later works. Its use of a repeating bassline for a combination of structural and expressive ends and its overall organization as a dramatic *scena* framed by polyphonic narrative passages look forward to his greatest mixed-mode continuo madrigal, the *Lament of the Nymph* of Book VIII.

But Monteverdi looked also to the past for the deepened expression of this work. Alceo's *stile rappresentativo* abandons the pictorial virtuosity of Floro and Florida for a music-speech reminiscent of Ariadne. Monteverdi adjusted the repeating bassline under it to match the unbalanced periods of Alceo's speech, rather than forcing these to march to the rigid step of literal musical repetition. The flexible homophonic techniques of the madrigal's opening measures had of course been developed in numerous *a cappella* works, as had the double counterpoint setting line 2 (a setting that nevertheless lacks the marvelous fluency of many earlier multiple points, falling rather uncomfortably into three small segments).[23] And the set-

---

21. Compare the opening measures of the *Sestina* (Ex. 44 above) and the setting of "poi ch'il mio ben coprì gelida terra" in its *seconda parte*. Monteverdi's pronouns in line 2 of "Misero Alceo" differ from Marino's (his *Rime*, pt. 1, p. 89, reads "conviemmi" and "m'apresti"), making lines 1–2 a narrative comment rather than a part of Alceo's self-pitying speech. This allowed Monteverdi to use his full narrative texture symmetrically to begin and end his setting.

22. See, for example, Cassandra's strophic aria "L'alma fiacca svanì" from *La Didone* (1641), partially reproduced by Pirrotta in *Li due Orfei*, pp. 306–8.

23. The overlapping entries in even quarter-note motion recall the similar texture used to good effect in the *prima parte* of the polyphonic lament of Ariadne—perhaps further evidence that "Misero Alceo" was composed at the same time as the *Lamento* and the *Sestina*.

EXAMPLE 46

Monteverdi, "Misero Alceo, dal caro albergo fore,"
mm. 26–34

EXAMPLE 47

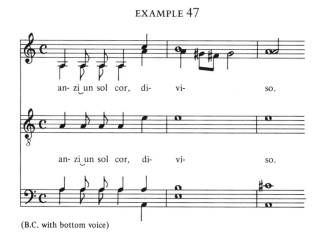

(B.C. with bottom voice)

Monteverdi, "Misero Alceo,
dal caro albergo fore," mm. 72–74

ting of "un sol cor, diviso" at the end of the work, bursting from a five-voice unison (!) to a chord spaced through more than two octaves on "diviso," recalls many
forceful and imaginative gestures in earlier works that transcended the realm of pictorialism (Ex. 47).

In "Misero Alceo," in other words, Monteverdi recouped some of the affective
eloquence of earlier years by resisting the temptation to foursquare structures and

vocal virtuosity with which he had experimented in his other early continuo madrigals. The seductive promise of the *basso continuo* tempted him in most of these works to provide simplistic, reproducible solutions to the problems of musico-poetic structure, as if one such musical solution might be blithely applied to any number of texts. There can be little doubt that works like "Qui rise, o Thirsi" or "A dio, Florida bella" cost Monteverdi fewer birth pangs than "Ecco mormorar l'onde," "Oimè, se tanto amate," or Ariadne's lament.

The inevitable result of such musical simplification—inevitable, at any rate, given the oratorical premises of Monteverdi's formative years and their musical ramifications—was expressive impoverishment. Through the remainder of Monteverdi's career an essential tension would arise again and again in his works between straightforward musical process and the more complex, free-formed rhetorical reflection of the wide variety of emotion in his texts. This tension is fundamentally different from the duality of epigrammatic and dramatic methods we have perceived in Monteverdi's *a cappella* madrigals, a duality of two expressive methods contrasting in musical and even rhetorical means but allied in their broadest oratorical and poetic goals. Monteverdi's urge to reconcile the opposed forces of the new tension is evident throughout his late works. Sometimes the reconciliation is almost complete, with hegemony granted to the rhetorical impulses of Monteverdi's early years and structural balances doubling as affective gestures in the manner of "Misero Alceo." Often, however, expressive and structural concerns coexist less easily, creating a patchwork of contrasting artistic aims, some exegetic of the text and others more exclusively musical. And in the weakest of his late works Monteverdi would seek the musical means to render the expression of human passion as schematic as he could already make the construction of musical form.

7

Marinism
and the Madrigal, I
(Book VII)

The New Poetics of Book VII

Tempro la cetra, e per cantar gli onori
di Marte alzo talhor lo stil e i carmi,
ma invan la tento, ed impossibil parmi
ch'ella già mai risuoni altro ch'amori.

I tune my lyre, and to sing the honors
of Mars sometimes I uplift my style and songs;
but in vain I strive, and it seems hopeless to me
that it will ever resound with anything but love
songs.

N 1614 MARINO had announced the themes of the third part of *La lira* with these Anacreontic lines. Five years later, set to music in the guise of an operatic prologue complete with instrumental *sinfonie* and ritornelli, they signaled the novel poetic themes and musical styles of Monteverdi's *Concerto. Settimo libro de madrigali a 1. 2. 3. 4. et sei voci, con altri generi de canti.*

At first thought, love may hardly seem a noteworthy new subject in Monteverdi's music. But in fact most of the amorous "carmi" of Book VII treat it in a way that sets this collection apart from Book VI. They abandon the laments, brokenhearted separations, and nostalgic remembrances found there and rejoice instead in carefree ruminations on Cupid's pleasures. The suffering and loss of Book VI have given way to stylized flames flickering in happy, refined souls—as in this feeble madrigal, placed right after "Tempro la cetra" seemingly in order to confirm and extend its program:

Non è di gentil core
chi non arde d'amore.
Ma voi che del mio cor l'anima sete,
e nel foco d'amor lieta godete,
gentil al par d'ogn'altre havete il core,
perch'ardete d'amore.

He is not of gracious heart
who does not burn with love.
But you, the spirit of my heart,
happily frolicking in the flame of love,
you have a heart as gracious as any other,
because you burn with love.

165

Dunque non è, non è di gentil core	Thus he is not, is not of gracious heart
chi non arde d'amore.[1]	who does not burn with love.

The reappearance of poetic madrigals like this one among Monteverdi's texts of 1619 is symptomatic of the new orientation. As we have seen, they had been entirely absent from Book VI, displaced there by the weightier genre of the sonnet. Also revealing of new trends is the fact that nine of the seventeen madrigals set in Book VII are by Guarini and Marino. Guarini had been completely absent from the Sixth Book; indeed that collection stands alone among the eight madrigal books Monteverdi published during his lifetime in this lacuna, an especially striking fact if, as seems likely, two of the Guarini settings published in Book VIII (1638) were composed before 1614.[2] We shall see below how this return to Guarini in Book VII betokens a new musico-poetic direction rather than a simple return to the epigrammatism of the Fourth Book.

The role of Marino's lyrics in determining this new orientation also needs qualification since his eclogue-like sonnets had done so much to set the very different tone of Book VI. Only two of Marino's six poems in Book VII are sonnets, however: "Tempro la cetra," the dedicatory lyric that proclaims Marino's and Monteverdi's amorous *stil novo,* and "A quest'olmo, a quest'ombre, et a quest'onde," a *sonnetto boschereccio* reminiscent of Book VI in poetic theme and musical setting. Perhaps Monteverdi set this text in Mantua, or just after he arrived in Venice, while still occupied with the publication of the Sixth Book. In any case, there is no doubt that it breathes the nostalgic pastoral ethos of that earlier collection and stands out as a striking anomaly among the other works of Book VII.

The remaining four poems by Marino are all madrigals of the most modern and fashionable sort: miniature lyrics enumerating through varied situation and conceit the erotic delights of the kiss. Monteverdi's settings of these poems—"Vorrei baciarti, o Filli," "Perché fuggi tra' salci," "Tornate, o cari baci," and "Eccomi pronta ai baci"—mark his principal encounter with the Marino cherished by his younger contemporaries. In Book VI Monteverdi had explored a more tradition-bound side of Marino's poetic personality, lyrics that attracted him for the serendipitous formal possibilities they offered, for their evocation of rich pastoral topoi, and for their melancholic cast. Now, at fifty, he was initiated into the sensual transcendence of sixteenth-century Petrarchism that is so distinctive a feature of Marino's achievement.[3] He turned to the Marino of current fashion, in the process revealing

---

1. Pirrotta's attribution of this *ballata*-like lyric to Guarini ("Scelte poetiche," p. 240) is a slip of the pen, repeated by Stevens (*Monteverdi,* p. 53). But the more usual attribution to Francesco degli Atti is also undoubtedly mistaken; see John Whenham, *Duet and Dialogue in the Age of Monteverdi* 2:77.

2. See chap. 6 above, n. 7.

3. Lorenzo Bianconi, *Il seicento,* p. 22, has also noted Monteverdi's relatively slow adoption of Marino's poetry and the idiosyncratic nature of his Marinist poetic choices in Book VI.

the powerful urge to keep abreast of new developments that would sustain him throughout the last years of his career—and in the process, one cannot but feel, substituting at least in part the dictates of fashion for those of a deeply held expressive ideal.

There can be no question, in any case, that Marino's *bacio* madrigals were enormously popular among musicians of Monteverdi's and younger generations. The four madrigals named above show the trend. A total of forty-one settings of them were published by other composers from 1603 to 1643; twenty-nine of these appeared before Monteverdi's settings of 1619. (In contrast, the four eclogue-sonnets in Book VI and "A quest'olmo" in Book VII found little favor among other composers: three of these poems inspired no published settings except Monteverdi's, while the remaining two were set a total of seven more times.) And Monteverdi would have seen firsthand evidence of the popularity of Marino's madrigals when he reached Venice. There Marc'Antonio Negri, his vice-chapelmaster at St. Mark's from his arrival until 1620, had published in 1611 a volume of *Affetti amorosi* on Marino's poetry, including settings of nineteen madrigals and one *canzone* (but no sonnets). Among the madrigals found here are all four of the poems later set by Monteverdi. His poetic choices in Book VII must surely have been affected by Negri and his music.[4]

Monteverdi's choice to set Marino's avant-garde madrigals was bound to alter his approach to the joining of text and music. For in these seemingly unpretentious lyrics Marino stepped out of the Petrarchan literary mainstream in whose currents Monteverdi's rhetorical preoccupations had been gradually shaped. Sixteenth-century Petrarchism had been a self-consciously restricted poetic mode. It aimed to illuminate the paradoxical emotions of the lover as they had been codified in a long tradition of courtly lyrics, ratified philosophically in the fifteenth-century Neoplatonic thought of Marsilio Ficino and promulgated in popular sixteenth-century *trattati d'amore* such as Pietro Bembo's *Asolani* and Castiglione's *Courtier*. To achieve this end, especially after Bembo's influential linguistic and poetic treatise *Prose della volgar lingua* appeared in 1525, Petrarchan poets built on the foundation of subject, imagery, and language that they found in Petrarch's own *Canzoniere*. This lexicon, restricted in situation and vocabulary, served well the restricted descriptive aims of the Petrarchan program.

But we should not underestimate the expressive potency of this program. Though it was limited in subject, its creative impulse came from within, its expressive mode was introspective, and its poetic range embraced the charted reaches of the psyche. Though restricted in language, it could call on the whole of ancient and

---

4. The only two pieces in Negri's collection not on texts by Marino set verses by Guarini: the madrigal "Donna, voi vi credete" and the famous soliloquy from *Il pastor fido* (III, vi) "Udite, lagrimosi / spirti d'Averno. . . ." The latter work is not by Negri but by Lucia Quinciani, his "discepola."

modern rhetorical practice to frame its vocabulary in affective and resonant periods. The fluid rhetorical exploration of the psychology of love in a conventional and precisely delimited linguistic context is the defining trait of late-sixteenth-century Petrarchism. This bond between impassioned oratory and introspective emotion united Armida, Amarilli, and Ariadne, three protagonists bred true to the Petrarchan tradition. It was as well the cultural link that attracted Monteverdi to all three in the years of his first maturity.

In Marino's poetics of *meraviglia,* on the other hand, there was little place for introspection.[5] Marino satisfied his overweening urge to dazzle his readers only by breaking down the painstakingly plotted boundaries of the Petrarchan tradition. Expanding the narrow range of amorous situations that served as the basis for most earlier love lyrics, he broached new, unexpected possibilities, participating in the "thematic revolution" in the Italian lyric that Giovanni Getto has described.[6] Petrarch's celebrations of Laura's eyes gave way to Marino's apostrophe to his lover's mole; her hair is golden by comparison to the hair net she wears, her hands as white as the *bianco umor* of the goat she milks. Often Marino supplanted conventional Petrarchan metaphors and similes with more farfetched figures in his search for *acutezza;* the famous picture in *L'Adone* of the nightingale as "una piuma canora, un canto alato" ("a melodious feather, a winged song") is only one, especially felicitous example.[7] And Marino welcomed new words and expressions to his poetic vocabulary, ones not found in the elite Tuscan glossary that sixteenth-century poets had culled from Petrarch. This is evident even in his well-known statement of poetic program, "È del poeta il fin la meraviglia / (parlo dell'eccellente, non del goffo): / chi non sa far stupir, vada a la striglia"—"The poet's aim is the marvelous / (I speak only of the excellent, not of the inept): / let him who cannot amaze work the stables." Here the colloquialisms *goffo* and *vada a la striglia* are hardly Petrarchan locutions.[8]

And most of all, at once arising from and giving rise to all the above-named traits, Marino's verse teems with objects from the real world—gems, minerals,

---

5. On Marino and the *marinisti* I have found particularly helpful Alberto Asor Rosa, introduction to his selection of Marino's *Opere;* Carlo Calcaterra, *Il parnaso in rivolta,* chap. i and passim; Calcaterra, introduction to *I lirici del seicento e dell'Arcadia;* Giovanni Getto, *Barocco in prosa e in poesia,* chaps. 1, 2; and Ottavio Besomi, *Ricerche intorno alla "Lira" di G. B. Marino.* These works present a tradition of scholarly revisions and *approfondimenti* reaching back to Benedetto Croce's classic *Storia dell'età barocca in Italia.* See also Franco Croce, "Gian Battista Marino"; James V. Mirollo, *The Poet of the Marvelous;* and Gianni Eugenio Viola, *Il verso di Narciso.* I have compared Marino's style to Ottavio Rinuccini's

Petrarchan idiom in "Music and the Claims of Text," pp. 566–79. For my sources for Marino's poetry see chap. 6 above, n. 18. Among the many modern anthologies, Calcaterra's *I lirici* gives a particularly extensive selection of the poems most favored by musicians, the madrigals and *canzoni* of pt. 2 of the *Rime.*

6. *Barocco,* pp. 67–88.

7. Besomi, *Ricerche,* passim and pp. 231–38, has warned against overstressing this aspect of Marino's style.

8. For further, less colloquial examples of Marino's "materia lessicale stravagante" see Getto, *Barocco,* p. 21.

flowers; birds, insects, and other animals; instruments of music, war, and even science. These are occasionally brought into resonant relation with his ostensive subject matter but more often juxtaposed with it almost arbitrarily, in the manner of superabundant, virtuosic musical ornamentation. It is this love of glittering description, this irresistible (or unresisted) temptation to detail the gaudy, seductive reality around him, that gives Marino's huge *Adone* its peculiarly objective stamp (not to mention much of its bulk). Marino's epic is no epic at all but, in Getto's phrase, an encyclopedic "compendio di tutto il poeticamente dicibile." The same imagistic impulse is revealed in *La galeria* of 1619, a collection of lyric poems conceived as companion pieces to pictures by renowned artists of the day. Marino owned many of these pictures and collected them avidly. He planned at first to publish his lyrics next to engravings of the pictures they concerned.[9]

This tendency to objectify poetic utterance, to seek inspiration in external image, led Carlo Calcaterra to label Marino the "poet of the five senses" and to single out his failure to instill with subjective emotion the ornate reality he depicted.[10] For in distancing himself from his Petrarchan forebears, in overreaching the linguistic and situational limitations of their vision, Marino had left behind as well the flame of impassioned introspection that flickered on through the end of the sixteenth century and illuminated (if at times dimly) their verse. Without this glowing nucleus the basic terms of the Petrarchan anthropology had to be redefined. Reality (and in particular nature) no longer served as a mirror of emotions but was reduced to a pretext for ornamental description, a rich source of objects to enumerate.[11] Love itself was no longer viewed primarily as the stimulus and determinant of these emotions. Instead it provided a garden of sensory and sensual delights, whose individual blossoms, in particular the many species of kiss, might be dissected, scrutinized, and classified with as much panache and little passion as are found in Marino's frequent catalogues of real flowers. And rhetoric, finally, was no longer a medium of heartfelt communication and persuasion but a tool to be wielded in the hammering out of virtuosic spangles. This last shortcoming was not lost on all Marino's contemporaries; the irascible writer Nicola Villani noted it expressly when in 1631 he entered the polemic over *L'Adone*. For him Marino represented the end point of a development toward rhetorical finery destructive of true emotion, one evident also in Tasso, Guarini, and other modern poets: "Using the farfetched conceits [*concetti ricercati*] and witty phrases [*arguzie*] of detached and dispassionate minds," he wrote, "it is no wonder that they do not sway and move others."[12]

9. Marino's *Lettere . . . gravi, argute, e facete* (first published in 1627; I use the expanded edition of Turin, 1629) abound in requests for paintings, drawings, and engravings. For one of these requests and for his first conception of *La galeria*, see the letter to Bernardo Castello, pp. 181–82.
10. *Il parnaso*, chap. 1.

11. Getto, *Barocco*, pp. 37–41; Asor Rosa, introduction to Marino's *Opere*, pp. 68–70.
12. From Villani's *Consideratoni di messer Fagiano sopra la seconda parte dell'occhiale del cav. Stigliani* (Venice, 1631); quoted from Benedetto Croce, *Storia*, p. 26. On Villani see also pp. 180–81, 205–9.

Marino was not, of course, without antecedents; and in certain respects, as Villani knew, both Tasso and Guarini were among them.[13] Tasso, Marino's Neapolitan compatriot, adumbrated in his lyric poems the thematic novelties that the younger poet would soon affirm. Tasso's language, too, admits many expressions outside the Petrarchan canon—so many, in fact, that in the 1580s the Florentine Accademia della Crusca bitterly criticized the linguistic obscurities and improprieties of *Gerusalemme liberata*.[14] And we have seen in chapter 2 that one facet of Tasso's lyric output is a descriptive, ornamental sort of madrigal redolent of Marino's later poetic vision. This was the side of Tasso that Girolamo Casone may have introduced to Monteverdi in the years before 1590. The composer repudiated it decisively, in favor of the more luminous emotional vistas of the *Liberata,* by 1592.[15]

We have seen also, in chapter 4, that Marino had high praise for Guarini. Marino's words are not specific enough to reveal exactly what traits he prized in the older poet's verse, but Guarini's epigrammatic *acutezza* must have ranked high among them. So the epigrammatic madrigals of Guarini might seem closely linked to Marino's and not the most promising place to seek the outgrowths of the Petrarchan tradition. But their subject matter, the contradictory torments of love, remains within that tradition, as does the inward-turned poetic eye that analyzes it. And, most important, their masterful embodiment of amorous paradox in paradoxical rhetoric is essentially Petrarchan. Monteverdi recognized this full integration of content and syntax and exploited it in the musico-rhetorical triumphs of Book IV.

Marino's madrigals often tend toward Guarini's two-part epigrammatic structure of situation and point. But just as often his predilection for image making disrupts the clear logical sequence of the epigram, and thus breaks down the Petrarchan link of subject and expression as well. The point is strikingly demonstrated in "Vorrei baciarti, o Filli," set by Monteverdi in Book VII, where the *expositio* of lines 1–3 is distanced from the final *acumen* by seven lines composed mainly of ornamental metaphors:

Vorrei baciarti, o Filli,	I'd like to kiss you, oh Filli,
ma non so come, ove'l mio bacio	but don't know how, or where my lips should
scocchi,[16]	smack,

---

13. Pirrotta, "Scelte poetiche," pp. 237, 239, notes the connections among these poets. On Tasso and Marino see Getto, *Barocco*, pp. 30–35, and Besomi, *Ricerche,* chap. 2; on Guarini and Marino, Asor Rosa, introduction to Marino's *Opere,* pp. 28–32.

14. See Weinberg, *A History of Literary Criticism,* pp. 1008–9.

15. Besomi's conclusion on Tasso's lyrics expresses well their proximity to the concrete, objective world of Marino: "The greatest novelty of the poetry of Tasso . . . is its elaboration of a new type of woman, less abstract than that offered by Petrarchan lyrics because it is bound to a domestic and often detailed reality; this separation [from the Petrarchan lyric] is evident also in the particular attention given to objects in the world—a world of which they often become nucleus and emblem" (*Ricerche,* pp. 82–83).

16. Marino has "prima" for Monteverdi's "come."

ne la bocca, o ne gl'occhi. on your mouth, or your eyes.
Cedan le labbra a voi, lumi divini, Let her lips give way to you, divine lights,
5 fidi specchi del core, faithful mirrors of the heart,
vive stelle d'amore. living stars of love.
Ah, pur mi volgo a voi, perl'e rubini, Ah! and yet I turn to you, pearls and rubies,
tesoro di bellezza, treasure of beauty,
fontana di dolcezza, fountain of sweetness,
10 bocca, honor del bel viso: mouth, highest honor of her face:
nasce il pianto da lor, tu m'apri il riso. from them is born her tears, you offer her smile.
     (*Rime,* pt. 2, p. 23)

Another of Marino's madrigals set in Book VII, on the Guarinian theme of the stolen kiss, shows a similar awkwardness in fulfilling its epigrammatic promise:

Perché fuggi tra' salci, Why flee among the willows,
ritrosetta ma bella, my shy but beautiful,
o cruda de le crude pastorella? cruelest of the cruel shepherdesses?
Perché un bacio ti tolsi? Because I stole a kiss?
5 Miser più che felice! The more wretched I!
Corsi per sugger vita, e morte colsi. I ran to suckle life, but found death.
Quel bacio, che m'ha morto, That kiss that killed me,
tra le rose d'amor pungente spina, a piercing spine amid roses of love,
fu più vendetta tua, che mia rapina. was rather your vengeance than my theft.
     (*Rime,* pt. 2, p. 18)

Here the situation hurries to a debilitating, premature point in verse 6. The last three verses, the true point, seem tacked on, artificially enlivened by the metaphor of verse 8. The remaining two madrigals by Marino in Book VII, "Tornate, o cari baci" and "Eccomi pronta ai baci," show no epigrammatic tendencies at all. The first is a celebration of the kiss vague in syntax and significance, the second a miniature dramatic *scena.* Clearly Monteverdi did not select Marino's lyrics with an eye to exploiting their epigrammatic rhetorical form.

 The madrigals of Guarini that Monteverdi set in the Seventh Book, like Marino's madrigals, seem oddly unsatisfactory when measured by the standards of his epigrams featured in Book IV. "Dice la mia bellissima Licori" shows only a weak epigrammatic pacing. Its true, Marino-like motivation is its image of Love as a "spiritello, / che vaga e vola e non si può tenere" ("a little spirit, / that wanders and flies and can't be caught"). Stronger epigrammatic tendencies are thwarted in "Con che soavità, labbra odorate" by discursive long-windedness and in "Se'l vostro cor, Madonna" by the complexities of an opening dependent clause five lines long—complexities Monteverdi would have been hard-pressed to surmount even with the versatile polyphonic techniques of the Fourth Book. "Parlo misero, o taccio?" suffers, like Marino's "Perché fuggi tra' salci," from premature epigrammatic closure. And the *acumen* of "O come sei gentile" is undercut by the clumsily overstated parallelisms that make up its *expositio.*

 The point here, of course, is that Monteverdi did not measure all these poems by the standards of Book IV. He did not ask epigrammatic logic of Marino. And his experience of this poet seems to have altered his reading of Guarini as well by 1619. Now Monteverdi was less attracted by Guarini's epigrammatic side and valued him more as a maker of images in Marino's fashion, a Marinist *avant la lettre*. He chose "O come sei gentile" not for its ungainly epigrammatism but for the opportunities for brilliant pictorial melismas that its talk of birds and bird song afforded. The central image of "Dice la mia bellissima Licori," not its weak concluding point, inspired Monteverdi's lively setting.

This change of emphasis had profound musical implications. In turning away from Guarini's epigrammatism Monteverdi relinquished also the tight union of syntax and sense it embodied. To exploit and enhance that bond of emotion and rhetoric, the defining trait of sixteenth-century Petrarchism, had been the unmistakable aim of Monteverdi's art at least from the *Liberata* settings of Book III through the *Sestina* of 1610. And, to be sure, the composer would reassert this goal, sporadically, in Book VII and throughout the remainder of his career. But his new emphasis of Guarini's lively imagery and his turn to Marino's ornamental objectivity signaled Monteverdi's partial acceptance of the reigning poetic order. This acceptance entailed a loosening of the tightly woven fabric of musical and poetic rhetoric he had spun in earlier works. It resulted frequently in an indifference of musical syntax to textual rhetoric and an extension of the independence of musical form found in the continuo madrigals of the Fifth and Sixth Books. And objective, image-laden description in his texts quickly led Monteverdi to impassive musical depiction: pictorial madrigalisms, which play but a small part in the Fourth, Fifth, and Sixth Books, return in full force in Book VII.[17]

Thus Guarini's madrigals in the Seventh Book proclaim Monteverdi's new musical Marinism as resoundingly as Marino's own lyrics. So also do other texts in the collection. Claudio Achillini, friend and epigone of Marino, appears among Monteverdi's poets for the first time. His love letter "Se i languidi miei sguardi" displays (to Monteverdi's disadvantage, we shall see below) the full ornamental panoply and lackluster rhetoric of much Marinist verse, though his *sonnetto di partenza* "Ecco vicine, o bella tigre, l'ore" remains more closely bound to Petrarchan models.[18] The shepherdess of the anonymous sonnet "Io son pur vezzosetta pastorella" compares her beauty to such typical Marinist appurtenances as mirrors, roses, jasmin, and necklaces of coral (but also dimly recalls Petrarchan models in her turn to self-pity in the final lines: "E non saranno a te punto graditi, / caro Lidio, i miei sguardi; e sempr'in fallo / ti pregherò, crudel, che tu m'aiti"—"And my

---

17. A tendency in this direction, to be sure, is apparent already in Book VI. There the occasional distinctive pictorialisms occur, significantly, in the settings of Marino's verse; Pirrotta labels them "marinismi musicali" ("Scelte poetiche," p. 237).

18. Claudio Gallico first noted Achillini's authorship of "Se i languidi miei sguardi," in "La 'Lettera amorosa' di Monteverdi e lo stile rappresentativo." Achillini's two poems appear on pp. 128–32 and 139 of his *Rime e prose*.

glances will not be welcome to you, / dear Lidio; and always to my shame / I'll call to you, cruel one, for you to save me").

Monteverdi also found Marinist image making in the verse of Gabriello Chiabrera. This is surprising, perhaps, in the light of received literary-historical notions. But the conventional placement of Chiabrera and Marino at opposite stylistic poles has too infrequently been questioned since its introduction by anti-Marinist polemicists at the end of the seventeenth century.[19] They are similar in many respects, especially in their common urge to escape from Petrarchan self-contemplation to a gaudy and decorative world of impersonal, external beauty and hedonistic sensual vitality.

Two of the madrigal-like lyrics Chiabrera called *scherzi* are included in Book VII, "Soave libertate" and "Vaga su spina ascosa." The second presages Marino's imagistic style especially clearly:

Vaga su spina ascosa	Hidden amid spines
è rosa rugiadosa,	is the pretty, dewy rose,
ch'a l'alba si diletta,	which thrives at the dawn,
mossa da fresca auretta;	brushed by fair breezes;
ma più vaga è la rosa	but prettier still's the rose
su la guancia amorosa,	on your enamored cheeks,
ch'oscura e discolora	which darkens and discolors
le guancie de l'aurora. . . .	the cheeks of the dawn. . . .
(*Delle poesie*, II, 4)	

Both Chiabrera's poems are made up entirely of *settenari*. This short-breathed metric regularity distinguishes them from most true madrigals and links them to Chiabrera's popular canzonette—the light-hearted strophic poems, written in various mixtures of four-, five-, six-, seven-, eight-, and eleven-syllable lines, that Monteverdi had set in his *Scherzi musicali* of 1607. The sunny disposition and prosodic predictability of these poems link them also to the two anonymous canzonette that Monteverdi included among the "altri generi de canti" of Book VII, "Chiome d'oro, bel tesoro" and "Amor, che deggio far." This was the first time that Monteverdi had allowed poetic canzonette to brush shoulders with higher literary genres in his madrigal books, though such mélanges had become commonplace in the monody books of younger composers and in the *canzonieri* of contemporary poets. The mixture is another sign of Monteverdi's bow to new fashions in Book VII and underscores the growing importance of Chiabreresque canzonette in his output as a whole.

19. For three exceptions see Benedetto Croce, *Storia*, pp. 277–78; W. Theodor Elwert, "La poesia barocca nei paesi romani," pp. 65, 69–70; and especially Getto, "Gabriello Chiabrera poeta barocco," in *Barocco*, pp. 123–62. Marino himself expressed his high regard for Chiabrera several times in his letters and at least once sent him poetry for his consideration. See, for example, Marino, *Lettere*, pp. 132, 134, 224.

Not that all the poems of the Seventh Book flash with Marinist glitter. A stylistic subplot runs through the collection, involving a smaller group of texts, retrospective in outlook and Petrarchan in resonance, that often recalled Monteverdi to the impassioned rhetoric of his earlier works. We have noted (with some surprise) that Achillini's sonnet "Ecco vicine, o bella tigre, l'ore" is one of these poems, a description of a lover's separation from his beloved that looks back beyond Marino's frigid exercises on this theme to echo faintly Tasso's moving sonnets, madrigals, and *canzone* "alla sua donna lontana." Guarini's sonnet "Interrotte speranze, eterna fede," cataloguing the woes of Petrarchan unrequited love, takes its start from an even older poem, Sannazaro's sonnet "Interditte speranze e van desio." (Another catalogue sonnet of the same type in Book VII, more schematic and less urgent in its rhetoric than Guarini's, is "O viva fiamma, o miei sospiri ardenti.")[20] From the middle of the sixteenth century comes Bernardo Tasso's anguished *ottava* "Oimè, dov'è il mio ben, dov'è il mio core?," undoubtedly the oldest text in the collection and one chosen to fulfill the literary requisites of its musical genre (see p. 196 below). The madrigals "Ah, che non si conviene" and "Non vedrò mai le stelle," their poets still unidentified, bring a distinctly un-Marinist weightiness to the lyrics of Book VII in this genre. The second of them resembles in its subject (a lover's complaint to the stars) and its mixture of narrative and dramatic modes Torquato Tasso's "Al lume delle stelle," also set here, which had earlier provided the poetic model for Rinuccini's "Sfogava con le stelle."[21] And, finally, Rinuccini himself weighs in, as if to signify that Monteverdi had not forgotten the years of *L'Arianna,* with his disconsolate *partenza amorosa* "Se pur destina e vole / il cielo."[22]

There is, then, a polarity of Petrarchan and Marinist expressive ideals in Book VII, one reflected, it hardly need be said, in Monteverdi's music. A comparison of works from these opposed poles, the settings of Rinuccini's "Se pur destina" and Achillini's "Se i languidi miei sguardi," will help to define some effects of Marinist poetry on Monteverdi's music. Superficially the two works are twins, in poetry as well as music. The texts are long monologues, 108 and 78 lines respectively, expressing a lover's grief at his separation from his beloved. The settings are dramatic recitatives—"in genere rappresentativo," as Monteverdi put it—for solo voice and continuo, the only such chamber monodies among Monteverdi's surviving works. But beneath the surface the differences of the two pieces are apparent enough.

20. Pirrotta, "Scelte poetiche," p. 242n, notes the close similarity of this poem to Petrarch's "O passi sparsi, o pensier vaghi et pronti." The poem is attributed to G. A. Gesualdo in the New Vogel.

21. See chap. 4 above, n. 20.

22. The poem is ascribed to Rinuccini in MS. Cl.VII.902 of the Florentine Biblioteca Nazionale, fol. 99v–100r; thematic and stylistic links between it and Rinuccini's other lyrics and music dramas confirm the ascription.

From its beginning Achillini's poem evinces a rhetorical lifelessness that too often characterizes Marinist verse:

Se i languidi miei sguardi,	If my languid gazes,
se i sospir interrotti,	if my broken sighs,
se le tronche parole	if my halting speech
non han sin hor potuto,	have not till now been able,
5 o bel idolo mio,	oh my lovely idol,
farvi de le mie fiamme intera fede,	to tell you truly of my passion,
leggete queste note,	read these words,
credete a questa carta,	believe this letter,
a questa carta, in cui	this letter that
10 sotto forma d'inchiostro il cor stillai.	distills my heart in ink.

Achillini concentrates his energies on enumerating his lover's glances, sighs, and broken speech and on the climactic image of verse 10 instead of working for a vivid rhetorical portrayal of loneliness and sorrow. Like Marino, he emphasizes conceits and images at the expense of impassioned syntactic structure. Grammatical units correspond with disconcerting regularity to the versification (even the infrequent *endecasillabi* are used only to accommodate phrases of extra length), and the strict parallelisms of lines 1–3 and 7–8 are therefore ploddingly underscored. Monteverdi dutifully reflected these parallelisms in his music, producing harmonic stasis and melodic redundancy (Ex. 48). He could do little to project in dramatic music Achillini's images, figures of thought with no vital rhetorical ramifications in the syntactic structure. By line 10 he retreated to an iconic setting, matching a long melisma to the word "cor."

EXAMPLE 48

Monteverdi, "Se i languidi miei sguardi," beginning

For his poem Rinuccini chose a strict scheme of rhyming couplets of *settenari*;[23] but even within these metric strictures the author of *L'Arianna* contrived to speak a more passionate language than Achillini:

Se pur destina e vole	If indeed heaven
il cielo, almo mio sole,	destines and wills, my beloved sun,
ch'in tenebre mi viva,	that I live in darkness,
ascolta alma mia diva	hear, my dear goddess,
5 ciò che potrà ridire	what, amid such misery,
fra cotanto martire	the cold, trembling lips
di sconsolato amante	of a disconsolate lover
lingua fredda e tremante.	can say once more.

The impetuous enjambement of lines 1–2 staves off from the outset the debilitating coordination of syntax and prosody of Achillini's poem and blurs and enriches the parallelisms of lines 2 and 4. Monteverdi tailored his melodic phrases not to the line units but to the enjambement (the unstressed rhyme "vole . . . sole" remains to assert subliminally the metric shape of the poetry); and he underlined Rinuccini's parallelism ("almo mio sole . . . alma mia diva") through fleeting rhythmic similarities (Ex. 49).

The rhythmic and harmonic variety of Example 49, much greater than that of Example 48, depends directly on the rhetorical vitality of Rinuccini's verse. He avoided Achillini's conceits and instead recalled the direct, anguished idiom we have seen in Ariadne's lament:

O pensier' vani e folli!	Oh vain and foolish thoughts!
Che speri? oimè! che volli?	What do you hope? Alas, what do you want?
Già dibattendo l'ale	Already high on wing
giunge l'ora fatale	draws near the fatal hour
dell'aspra dipartita.	of bitter departure.

This allowed Monteverdi to pursue an agitated, exclamatory style unattainable in setting a poem like "Se i languidi miei sguardi" (Ex. 50). Even Rinuccini's parallel locutions are structured in a livelier fashion than Achillini's: instead of repeating a full grammatical unit (as in Achillini's "Se i languidi miei sguardi, / se i sospir interrotti," etc.), Rinuccini suggested syntactic identity with a brief anaphora, then moved off in a new grammatical direction: "a voi, tremante e muto, / a voi dimando aiuto." (Note Rinuccini's enhancement of his false parallelism with the as-

---

23. It is a scheme referred to as a *frottola* in the early sixteenth century (see the *Opere di Girolamo Benivieni Firentino* [Florence, 1524]) and revived by various Florentine or Florence-connected po-ets around 1600, including Chiabrera (his "Vaga su spina ascosa," partially quoted above, is a short example of the type) and Michelangelo Buonarroti *il giovane.*

EXAMPLE 49

Monteverdi, "Se pur destina e vole / il cielo," beginning

EXAMPLE 50

Monteverdi, "Se pur destina e vole / il cielo," mm. 70–71

sonance "tre*mante* . . . di*mando.*") At times literal anaphora is suppressed in favor of a carefully wrought play of assonance:

O del cor luce e speme,	Oh light and hope of my heart,
odi le voci estreme,	hear my last words,
odile e del bel seno	hear them and bathe
una lagrima almeno	with one tear at least
bagni la viva neve.	the living snow of your breast.

Such "developing parallelisms," in contrast to Achillini's static repetition, elicited from Monteverdi dynamic, forward-moving settings in keeping with the aroused emotions of the protagonist (Ex. 51).

EXAMPLE 51

Monteverdi, "Se pur destina e vole / il cielo," mm. 106–12

The emotional frigidity of Achillini's poem is evident above all in its long central apostrophe to the hair, eyes, and mouth of the beloved, a conceit-ridden passage occupying more than three-quarters of the poem's original 141 lines. Monteverdi saw the problems posed in setting such a text in the *genere rappresentativo*. To overcome them he deleted the fifty-six lines describing the eyes and mouth of the beloved and even seven of those describing her hair. But the remaining forty-five lines praising her hair still proved excessive. Here Achillini's extended metaphor and kaleidoscopic imagery offered little to the composer of *L'Arianna*:

Dolcissimi legami,	Sweetest bonds,
belle mie piogge d'oro,	my beautiful rains of gold,
qual hor sciolte cadete	when you, loosened, fall
da quelle ricche nubi	from those rich clouds
onde raccolte sete,	where you are gathered,
e cadendo formate	and falling form
preziose procelle	a precious tempest
onde con onde d'or bagnando andate	whence with waves of gold you bathe
scogli di latte e rivi d'alabastro. . . .	reefs of milk and shores of alabaster. . . .

Monteverdi set this text to lifeless declamation over harmonies of a tiresome immobility never encountered in "Se pur destina": no fewer than eight measures of D minor followed by three of A minor before the harmonic rhythm resumes a less moribund pace. The *genere rappresentativo* had no power to enliven the cold *concettismo* of Achillini's poem.

Necessarily so, perhaps. A dramatic work like "Se i languidi miei sguardi" was bound to show the effects of Marinism in the worst light, since Monteverdi's conception of music drama had been defined from the first in terms of the one feature most glaringly absent from Marinist verse: compelling, introspective emotion. Marinist idioms in dramatic texts could not help but dilute the potent rhetoric, joining poetry and music, that Monteverdi had mastered in Ariadne's lament; this was a problem the composer would face again in his late operas, *Il ritorno d'Ulisse in patria* and *L'incoronazione di Poppea*. In lyric works, however, Marinist poetry could often interact more successfully with music and even encourage Monteverdi to develop vital new styles. It is to these works, this facet of Monteverdi's musical Marinism, that we now turn.

The New Madrigal of Book VII

In 1619 Monteverdi adopted a new madrigalian style as fashionable as his conspicuous Marinist poetic orientation. Pointedly, it seems, none of the madrigals here employs the conventional forces of five voices, with or without continuo. Even the retrospective "A quest'olmo" is scored for six voices, pairs of violins and recorders, and continuo. And the vast majority of the remaining works, nineteen of twenty-eight in all, call for two or three voices and continuo.[24]

Fifteen of these nineteen works are duets with continuo. The prevalence of this new texture in Book VII represented a radical and surprising departure for the fifty-year-old composer. Here for the first time he applied the term *madrigal* to pieces that broke decisively with the textural conventions of the genre. More striking still, he chose for his new madrigal a texture whose associations with the lighter genres of the late sixteenth century—the canzonette, villanelle, and *scherzi* of which Monteverdi himself had by now produced two collections—must have been plain to him and his contemporaries. Yet at the same time he published these works in part books, the traditional manner of presenting five-voice madrigals, rather than in the modish full scores of the monodists.[25] Monteverdi's Seventh Book embodies a

---

24. In Monteverdi's practice (and that of many other composers of the period) these two textures are essentially related since the bottom voice of the trios is usually a bass and follows the instrumental bassline closely. The instrumental foundation of the trios, in other words, remains close to the earlier *basso seguente,* while that of the duets is more often a truly independent *basso continuo.* For this reason declamatory, recitative-like episodes (which entail rhythmic independence of voices and bassline) occur much less frequently in Monteverdi's trios than in his duets. If continuo duet and trio are twin textures, however, Monteverdi's two madrigalian experiments for four voices and continuo in Book VII, "Tu dormi, ah crudo core" and "Al lume delle stelle," stand apart. In both Monteverdi returned to earlier polyphonic preoccupations, most notably the multiple-counterpoint expositions of Book III, their features now finely chiseled and marvelously attenuated with the aid of the continuous instrumental support. (Pirrotta also has called attention to these traits; see "Scelte poetiche," pp. 28–29.) An interesting testament to this retrospective cast in "Tu dormi" is the double point at "Io piango . . .," seemingly derived from the famous opening of Marenzio's "Solo et pensoso i più deserti campi" (Book IX à 5, 1599); it also anticipates the chromatic chorus of Seneca's followers in *Poppea.*

25. This significant distinction, which probably carried generic overtones in the early seventeenth century to which we are now little attuned, is discussed by Whenham, *Duet and Dialogue* 1:8–9.

breakdown of established generic distinctions in music as portentous as that of *Il pastor fido* in drama, and all the more significant since it was carried out by the acknowledged master of the madrigal in its time-honored five-voice guise.

Just as Monteverdi may have been led to the fashionable lyrics of Marino by his assistant Negri, so this new type of madrigal was probably suggested to him by another of his subordinates at St. Mark's, Alessandro Grandi. In August 1617 Grandi left his position as chapelmaster of the cathedral of Ferrara to become a singer of the *cappella marciana* of St. Mark's. Three years later he succeeded Negri to the position of vice-chapelmaster there. Both the initial appointment and the promotion were probably made by the procurators only after they had obtained Monteverdi's blessing; they imply his approval of Grandi's talents.[26] In the spring of 1615, before moving to Venice, Grandi had journeyed there to see his *Madrigali concertati a due, tre, e quattro voci* through the presses of Giacomo Vincenti. This was only the second publication in part-book format to include two- and three-voice continuo madrigals.[27] It was the first to do so that linked Monteverdi's terms *concerto* and *madrigale* on its title page. Its seven duets and two trios included three texts by Guarini and one by Marino. And—as Monteverdi undoubtedly noticed—it was immediately popular, achieving three reprints even before Monteverdi's Seventh Book was published and two more soon after.

All this suggests that Grandi's volume helped pave the way for Monteverdi's acceptance of the duet with continuo as a valid texture for the madrigal, or at least that it encouraged the continuation of madrigalian experiments he had already performed with this texture.[28] Nevertheless, the three-part texture was not new for Monteverdi in the Seventh Book. He had used it first as the basic texture of his canzonette (and, later, of his *scherzi*), and we have seen that it played an important and recurrent role in his *a cappella* madrigals for five voices. Its development took a new turn in the concerted madrigals of the Fifth Book, with their frequent sections for two voices and continuo. In these works the instrumental bassline, freed from the exigencies of text declamation, was more than ever before independent of the upper parts. This sort of continuo duet took to the stage in *Orfeo* and, in 1610, to the church in the psalms and motets of the Marian Vespers.

The duets of Book V, *Orfeo,* and the Vespers are especially important in the prehistory of the Seventh Book. Indeed three of the four few-voice motets in

26. On Grandi see James H. Moore, *Vespers at St. Mark's,* 1:5–11. Moore suggests that Monteverdi approved Grandi's promotion; the letter of Monteverdi he cites in support of the suggestion probably applies to Grandi's initial appointment as well.

27. The first was Giovanni Francesco Anerio's *Recreatione armonica* of 1611; see Whenham, *Duet and Dialogue* 1:8n, 9.

28. Whenham, *Duet and Dialogue* 1:165, has asserted that Grandi's duets conditioned Monteverdi's in more specific stylistic traits as well. Grandi's influence is particularly evident in the works that I shall distinguish below as Marinist in inspiration.

the Vespers, "Pulchra es," "Duo seraphim," and "Audi caelum" (excluding only the solo motet "Nigra sum"), were given the generic title in the original print that would reappear at the head of Book VII: *Concerto*. In these early continuo duets Monteverdi traded on the independence of the voices from the instrumental accompaniment to transcend the limited textural possibilities of the villanella and canzonetta. Their basslines move more slowly than the voices, extending the rhythmic stratification foreshadowed in Monteverdi's earlier use of the villanella texture in madrigals, but nevertheless usually maintain greater lyric interest than their counterparts in recitative. The voices interact in a variety of ways, sometimes declaiming in homophony, often joining in free imitation, and, perhaps most characteristically, exulting in lengthy melismas (which typically begin imitatively and end in parallel thirds or sixths). In this last trait *Orfeo* and the Vespers of 1610 give abundant further evidence of the link we saw in Monteverdi's five-voice continuo madrigals between duet texture and the luxuriant style (see chap. 6 above).

And this florid style persists in Book VII. Indeed the virtuosic gestures of its duet "O come sei gentile" are literally prefigured in the one through-composed duet of *Orfeo* and at various points in the Vespers (Exx. 52–54).[29] These extensive parallels might suggest that "O come sei gentile" was written before 1610, and in fact no traits of its musical syntax contradict so early a date. (Even its walking bass, in Example 53c, was anticipated in Orpheus's strophic song "Qual honor di te sia degno" of Act IV and in the odd-numbered strophes of "Laetatus sum" in the Vespers [Ex. 53b].) But it seems more likely that Monteverdi composed it nearer to the time of its publication, especially in the light of his probable preoccupation in the years around 1610 with the weightier expressive world of the Sixth Book. It is hard to imagine Monteverdi dashing off this frothy first example of what was for him a new kind of madrigal before he had seen Book VI to the printer. In this admittedly

29. The chronology of these works is anything but clear. The duet of Orpheus and Apollo "Saliam cantando al cielo" (Exx. 52a and 53a) comes from the version of Act V published in the score of 1609; its text is not in the libretto issued at the time of the performances of early 1607. It therefore probably represents an alteration of the music drama made sometime between 1607 and 1609. As to the Vespers, I agree with Kurtzman's suggestion (*Essays*, p. 10) that the movements of the work may well have been composed over an extended period. Stylistic connections to Books IV and V, the *Scherzi* of 1607, and especially to *Orfeo* suggest a range of ca. 1603–7, though some movements, in particular the motets "Pulchra es" and "Audi caelum" and the *Sonata*, probably fall closer to 1610. This does not mean that the Vespers were not gathered for publication with the possibility of a complete performance in mind, including the motets in the place of antiphons; on this question see *inter alia* Stephen Bonta, "Liturgical Problems in Monteverdi's Marian Vespers." Nor does it disallow the possibility, raised by Iain Fenlon in "The Monteverdi Vespers," that the Vespers were performed in May 1608 for the inauguration of a new knightly order in Mantua. But Fenlon's suggestion that the Vespers were *written* for this celebration seems to me untenable, given the composer's taxing preparations in these months for *L'Arianna, L'Idropica,* and the *Ballo delle ingrate*. If Monteverdi had also composed a thirteen-movement Vespers service at this time, he certainly would have adduced it as further evidence of overwork in his well-known complaining letter of 2 December 1608.

EXAMPLE 52

(a) Monteverdi, *Orfeo,* Act V, excerpt

(b) Monteverdi, Vespers, "Laetatus sum," mm. 74–76
(*Tutte le opere,* ed. Malipiero, 14:183)

(c) Monteverdi, "O come sei gentile," mm. 1–4, 10–12

EXAMPLE 53

(a) Monteverdi, *Orfeo,* Act V, excerpt

(b) Monteverdi, Vespers, "Laetatus sum," mm. 24–25
(*Tutte le opere,* ed. Malipiero, 14:176)

(c) Monteverdi, "O come sei gentile," mm. 50–54

sketchy scenario, then, "O come sei gentile" would become an example of delayed self-modeling, in which Monteverdi, essaying the two-voice madrigal for the first time (perhaps even after the publication of Grandi's volume in 1615), reverted reflexively to the florid duet style he had mastered in earlier continuo madrigals à 5, in *Orfeo,* and in the Vespers.

At any rate, "O come sei gentile" is not alone among the duets of Book VII in its luxuriant style. Two similar duets, "Non è di gentil core" and "O viva fiamma," are placed with it at the beginning of the collection. Significantly, these three works, stylistically retrospective by 1619, are grouped around "A quest'olmo," which, we have seen, also looks back—to the pastoral sorrows of Book VI. The group includes, finally, the duet "Io son pur vezzosetta pastorella," much like the other three duets in constructive technique and especially like "O viva fiamma" in its crestfallen conclusion, although it does not share their melismas. All

EXAMPLE 54

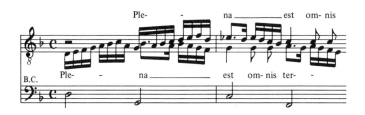

(a) Monteverdi, Vespers, "Duo seraphim," mm. 34–37
(*Tutte le opere,* ed. Malipiero, 14:192)

(b) Monteverdi, "O come sei gentile," mm. 68–72

these works probably constitute the earliest chronological layer of the Seventh Book. (The setting of "Tempro la cetra" for solo tenor that precedes these works and opens the collection, on the other hand, was surely one of the latest works in it. Its particular florid style, with its wide tessitura, long leaps, offbeat anticipations, and notated trills, looks forward to certain moments of the *Combattimento di Tancredi et Clorinda* of 1624. Its position "out of order" is of course required by its programmatic function as prologue to the collection.)

There is other evidence that these florid duets were Monteverdi's first two-voice madrigals. All three, along with "Io son pur vezzosetta pastorella," are scored for two sopranos and continuo, the same forces Monteverdi had employed in the motet "Pulchra es" from the Vespers.[30] But after the first four duets in Book VII Monteverdi never returned to this scoring in his madrigals, either in the ten remaining through-composed duets of 1619 or in the seven additional such works he published later, in 1624, 1632, and 1638. Instead of sopranos, fifteen of these seventeen works, including all seven published after 1619, call for two tenors and continuo.

Nor did Monteverdi frequently return in his later two-voice madrigals to the sustained melismatic style of these early soprano duets. The two cases in which he did are exceptional enough to prove the rule. They are the famous *ciaccona* "Zefiro torna, e di soavi accenti" (1632), on a sonnet by Rinuccini, and "Mentre vaga Angioletta" (1638), on a *madrigalessa* or extended madrigal by Guarini. The texts of both these works afforded Monteverdi the opportunity to catalogue the madrigal composer's pictorial devices, and it is to this end that he ingeniously exploited the florid style in each.

Monteverdi seems, then, to have associated melismatic luxuriance with soprano voices in his duets. And the same conclusion might be drawn from his five through-composed trios with continuo. Of these only one, "Parlo misero, o taccio?" of Book VII, involves sopranos (two of them, with bass and continuo). It is by far the most virtuosic of the five, stringing out a series of wayward melismas in the voices with little text-expressive or structural rationale. It bears all the earmarks of an early experiment in an unfamiliar medium.[31] The suspicion arises, in fact, that Monteverdi may have abandoned soprano scoring in his secular duets and trios out of a desire to avoid the virtuosity he associated with it. Perhaps this desire was nurtured by his quick discovery, after his first essays in the new madrigalian genre, of richer expressive possibilities open to it. In any case, the remaining ten duets in Book VII reserve melismas for occasional pictorial displays or, in "Non vedrò mai le stelle," for a florid *exclamatio* marking off the modal shift in the poem in the manner of "Sfogava con le stelle." (This gesture returns in the quartet with continuo "Al lume delle stelle"—Monteverdi's musical acknowledgment of the similarities of Rinuccini's and Tasso's poems.)

These nonmelismatic duets of Book VII, most likely composed after the melismatic ones, fall into two groups, intersecting at certain points along the way to

30. He used it also in the florid motet "Cantate Domino," the single work of Monteverdi published in 1615 in the anthology *Parnassus musicus Ferdinandeus* (RISM 1615[13]).

31. The remaining three trios in Book VII are scored for tenors and bass. Two of them, "Vaga su spina ascosa" (Chiabrera) and "Augellin, che la voce al canto spieghi," bear strong musical similarities to each other: they are somewhat melismatic but show a more confident musico-poetic logic than "Parlo misero, o taccio?" The last trio, "Eccomi pronta ai baci" (Marino), is the most assured of the group. Like the duet settings of Marino's verse, it is nonmelismatic. It too has a companion piece, similar in structure and expression: "Taci Armellin, deh taci," published in 1624 in the anthology cited below in chap. 8, n. 1. We shall return to both these works.

their expressive goals. Their divergent musical styles correspond to the contrasting idioms, Marinist and Petrarchan, of the texts they set:

I

"Vorrei baciarti, o Filli" (Marino)
"Dice la mia bellissima Licori" (Guarini)
"Perché fuggi tra' salci" (Marino)
"Tornate, o cari baci" (Marino)
"Soave libertate" (Chiabrera)

II

"Ah, che non si conviene"
"Non vedrò mai le stelle"
"Ecco vicine, o bella tigre, l'ore" (Achillini)
"Se'l vostro cor, Madonna" (Guarini)
"Interrotte speranze, eterna fede" (Guarini)

In his Marinist duets Monteverdi created a musical language that vividly conveys the ornamental hedonism of his texts. It does so especially through animated syllabic declamation, characterized by repeated eighth notes in greater profusion than anywhere in Monteverdi's earlier works, of the sort that begins "Perché fuggi tra' salci" (Ex. 55). The conclusion of this patter song nicely underscores Marino's polyptoton—"o *cruda* de le *crude* pastorella"—but for the most part, typically, the song relies on tireless repetitions of the poet's words and phrases. Note that this lively declamation allows Monteverdi to make abrupt, effective changes of pace, as here at "o cruda."

EXAMPLE 55

Monteverdi, "Perché fuggi tra' salci," beginning

The walking bass that begins Example 55 is another frequent trait of Monteverdi's Marinist style, one associated with its rapid declamation. (We have noted it already in the duets for sopranos, where it is usually employed instead to underpin vocal melismas.) It links all these works to the light-hearted world of the canzonette near the end of Book VII, "Chiome d'oro" and "Amor, che deggio far." Its most successful usage, perhaps, occurs in "Dice la mia bellissima Licori." Here it supports the long central depiction of the "sprite that walketh, that soars and flies" (to quote Nicholas Yonge's translation from *Musica transalpina*), differentiating this episode from those around it.

The *scherzando* character of this passage returns briefly later in the piece, at "ma nol posso toccar," in a new guise: an eight-bar interpolation in quick triple meter. Such interpolations occur likewise in "Perché fuggi tra' salci," where they emphasize, in languid Marinist fashion, the phrase "Quel bacio." They first appear in Monteverdi's duets in "Pulchra es" of the 1610 Vespers.

Monteverdi insured the rhythmic vitality of these duets also through offbeat and even syncopated entrances at the level of the eighth note. These underline, for example, the lover's repeated entreaties at the beginning of "Tornate, o cari baci" (Ex. 56). Syncopated exclamations of "baci, baci" in parallel thirds form a refrain later in this work, proclaiming in music Marino's obsession with the word. (These exclamations recall the staggered cries "corsi, corsi" in "Perché fuggi tra' salci," where they presage the abrupt shift, on "e morte colsi," to an affective style reminiscent of Book I.) In "Vorrei baciarti" an offbeat entrance combines with the alternation of two distinct themes—it can hardly be called a double point in this attenuated texture—to convey the two choices of the poet, to kiss the eyes or mouth of his lady (Ex. 57).

The spirited alternation of short motives evident in Examples 56 and 57 is a final distinctive feature of Monteverdi's Marinist duets. Relying on his wealth of experience with more complex counterpoint, Monteverdi easily combined the motivic fragments of these works into extended musical paragraphs. In the process he derived a textural variety from his modest performing forces unforeseen by his contemporaries. This variety in turn allowed him to construct longer, more elabo-

EXAMPLE 56

Monteverdi, "Tornate, o cari baci," beginning

EXAMPLE 57

Monteverdi, "Vorrei baciarti, o Filli," mm. 25–33

rate forms than they, to distance his duets from the lyrical strophic *arie* that often echo in theirs and approximate the structural proportions of his madrigals for five voices.

And occasionally to approximate their text-expressive capacities as well, for Monteverdi was by no means helpless in the face of Marino's image-laden syntax. This is obvious in "Tornate, o cari baci," where four lines of metaphors separate the "Voi" of line 4 from its verb "pascete" in line 8:

Tornate, o cari baci,	Return, oh dear kisses,
a ritornarmi in vita,	to bring me back to life,
baci, al mio cor digiuno esca gradita.	kisses, welcome food for my famished heart.
Voi di quel dolce amaro,	You, with that bittersweetness
5 per cui languir m'è caro,	for which I gladly languish,
di quel dolce non meno[32]	with that sweetness, no less
nettare, che veleno,	nectar than poison,
pascete i miei famelici desiri;	you satisfy my ravenous desires;
baci, in cui dolci provo anco i sospiri.	kisses, in whose sweetness I taste also sighs.

(*Rime,* pt. 2, p. 23)

Here, in the manner of the *seconda parte* of the *Sestina,* Monteverdi worked a wholesale reconstruction of his text. He interpolated one voice's statement of line 8 between the other's renditions of lines 4, 4–5, and 6–7, each time with an increase of rhythmic pace and a wrenching harmonic shift that seem calculated to expose the earthy reality behind Marino's dreamy metaphors (Ex. 58).

32. Marino has "vostro" instead of "dolce."

EXAMPLE 58

Monteverdi, "Tornate, o cari baci," mm. 24–49

EXAMPLE 59

Grandi, "O chiome erranti, o chiome," mm. 23–29
(Whenham, *Duet and Dialogue* 2:229–30; quoted by permission)

It is this text-expressive constructive skill that most clearly distinguishes Monteverdi's duets from those of his contemporaries, including his colleague Grandi. Example 58 is a case in point, for it recalls a passage from Grandi's "O chiome erranti, o chiome," the single setting of Marino's poetry in his *Madrigali concertati* (Ex. 59).[33] Monteverdi's harmonic and rhythmic disjunctions between his two themes are more explicit than Grandi's, yielding greater expressive force. And Monteverdi adapted Grandi's techniques to a poetic passage that required them for

33. Transcribed in Whenham, *Duet and Dialogue* 2:228–30; Whenham notes the connection of these two passages (vol. 1, p. 165 and note).

EXAMPLE 60

(a) Monteverdi, "Soave libertate," beginning

(b) Grandi, "Udite lagrimosi / spirti d'Averno," beginning
(Whenham, *Duet and Dialogue* 2:231; quoted by permission)

its effective setting, while Grandi used them to bind the last two lines of Marino's poem but excluded the beginning of the final syntactic period, in the antepenultimate line, thus weakening the poet's epigrammatic point ("Well may you wander playfully, / and your waywardness is sweet, / but you do not stray when it comes to entwining hearts"). And Monteverdi contrived, through the skillful written-out ritard on line 8 that ends his passage, to avoid the arbitrary cadential virtuosity that ends Grandi's.

Monteverdi's finer craftsmanship is evident also in the opening measures of "Soave libertate," which echo those of Grandi's "Udite lagrimosi / spirti d'Averno" (Ex. 60).[34] Grandi's static bassline adds nothing to his opening exclamations, while Monteverdi's bassline, beginning with a first-inversion chord and in-

34. Grandi's piece is transcribed by Whenham, *Duet and Dialogue* 2:231–34; its text is the same soliloquy from *Il pastor fido* that had appeared in Negri's *Affetti amorosi* in 1611 (see n. 4 above).

volving the voices above in suspended dissonance, carries a charge of languishing sweetness from the start. His voices enhance this expectant hush with their rise of a fifth—hinting at the cadential fall to come—while Grandi's imitation at the lower fourth suggests sixteenth-century polyphonic rigors that remain half stated. Finally, Grandi's invocation trails off with no harmonic return to D (indeed with tonicizations of G and A instead); Monteverdi's falling voices and rising bass converge on the root-position tonic that had been denied at the beginning (and undercut by the quickened bass motion of measure 2). Monteverdi's easy mastery of the new madrigal and his prehensile sensitivity to its languid Marinist emotional world are apparent in this deceptively simple invocation of "Soave libertate."

The joyous sensuality of the Marinist duets finds little place in the works of our second group, pieces of grave expressive intent on texts of Petrarchan profile. The Marinist duets look back in their walking basses and lively declamation to strophic songs, canzonette, and the lyrical *madrigali* à 2 of Grandi. But these weightier "Petrarchan" duets (if the term may be applied to works setting no poems by Petrarch) are descended from different stock: from the five-voice madrigalian style of Books IV–VI and especially from Monteverdi's recitative.

Four of these works (the exception, "Ah, che non si conviene," is exceptional in other ways as well) prominently feature a *stile rappresentativo* little less austere than that of the *lettera* and *partenza amorose* that come later in Book VII. This idiom relies on a rock-solid, unmoving bassline controlling mostly minor-mode harmonies; slow, monotonal declamation with occasional struck dissonances in the voices; and, to accommodate the extra voice in the duets, frequent homorhythmic parallel thirds. (It thus represents a synthesis of two distinct styles in Monteverdi's earlier works, recitative per se and the choral homophonic declamation of the five-voice madrigals.) These traits are exemplified by the beginnings of "Ecco vicine," "Interrotte speranze," and "Non vedrò mai le stelle." The sullen opening of the last is especially nice (Ex. 61).

For the most part these works eschew the patter-song declamation, short motives, incessant repetition of brief text phrases, and quick *Stimmtausch* of the Marinist duets. Their declamation is impassioned rather than jaunty, as in the falling dotted rhythms, borrowed from the *Sestina,* of Example 62. (Compare the end of the *quinta parte* of the *Sestina.*) And their voice exchanges are slower, sometimes coupled with affective harmonies and evoking the contrapuntal complexities of thicker textures (Ex. 63). Occasionally these contrapuntal passages recall five-voice madrigals even more explicitly, as in the marvelous distillation of earlier double-subject perorations that ends "Non vedrò mai le stelle."

The formal organizations of these works also recall those of earlier madrigals, albeit with important modifications. We might expect "Non vedrò mai le stelle" to look back to "Sfogava con le stelle" of Book IV since its text matches Rinuccini's poem in its theme and mixture of modes:

Non vedrò mai le stelle	I'll never see the stars
de' bei celesti giri,	in the lovely celestial spheres,
perfida, ch'io non miri	treacherous one, without seeing
gl'occhi che fur presenti	the eyes that were present
5 alla dura cagion de' miei tormenti,	at the harsh beginning of my torment,
e ch'io non dica allor "o luci belle,	and without saying then, "Oh lovely stars,
deh, siate sì rubelle	ah, be as dim to her
di lume a chi ribella è sì di fede,	of light as she is untrue to faith—
ch'anzi a tanti occhi e tanti lumi ha core	she, who could before so many eyes, so many lights
10 tradir amante sotto fe d'amore."	betray her lover even while swearing love."

Indeed, "Non vedrò" echoes "Sfogava" in several features: in the somber homophonic declamation of its opening section (recitative à 2 now, instead of the earlier *falsobordone*; see Ex. 61); in the florid monodic exclamation, reduced from the polyphonic melisma of "Sfogava," and tonal disjunction that mark its shift from narration to dramatic speech; and in the affective double point with which it ends.

But in its central section "Non vedrò" diverges from the rhetorical, epigrammatic premises of "Sfogava." It deploys first a bouncy patter song in dotted rhythms and then a thirty-eight-bar triple-meter arioso extending the first tenor to the top of his range. This arioso section brings to mind the Marinist duets, but there such episodes were constructed on a much smaller scale. Here the section in triple

EXAMPLE 61

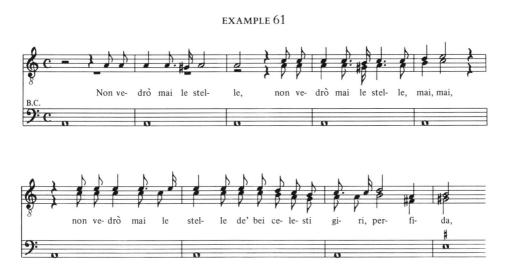

Monteverdi, "Non vedrò mai le stelle," beginning

EXAMPLE 62

Monteverdi, "Se'l vostro cor, Madonna," mm. 27–30

EXAMPLE 63

Monteverdi, "Non vedrò mai le stelle," mm. 12–19

meter dominates the formal landscape. More important, it joins with the melismatic exclamation and patter song before it to give the effect of an ecstatic musical celebration of the central image of the poem, the "luci belle" of verse 6. (The effect is reminiscent of "Dice la mia bellissima Licori," with its central "spiritello.") The musical expression of poetic syntax, carefully achieved in the opening recitative and in the contrapuntal peroration, is ignored during this display (fortunately and intentionally so, perhaps, since its text, lines 6–8 of the poem, is contorted and vacuous). The epigrammatic musical syntax of "Sfogava," and even the cruder demarcations by scoring changes in the mixed-mode eclogues of Book VI, have given way to the Marinist exaltation of poetic image. In "Non vedrò mai le stelle" Monteverdi's conflicting Petrarchan and Marinist inclinations met head-on.

No such collision marks the famous "Interrotte speranze." Instead it remains true throughout to the Petrarchan patrimony of its text, seeking out novel rhetorical possibilities of the two-voice texture. There is nothing new in its building-block structure, which looks back to the schematic sonnet settings of Book VI, and especially to "Zefiro torna e'l bel tempo rimena" in its reuse of the music of the first quatrain for the second. Monteverdi probably regarded such repetition as especially appropriate to these sonnets since their second quatrains merely continue the listings begun in their first four lines (listings of the beauties of spring in Petrarch's poem, of the woes of love in Guarini's). Indeed the two other sonnets with such listings that Monteverdi set also inspired repetitive musical schemes: the ostinato in Rinuccini's Petrarchan imitation "Zefiro torna, e di soavi accenti" and, in "O viva fiamma," one of the soprano duets of Book VII, an arrangement whereby every second line of the quatrains is sung to a restatement of the melody of the preceding line.

The essential novelty of "Interrotte speranze" lies elsewhere, in its rigorous control of pitch throughout the quatrains and first terzet. The voices begin each quatrain together with the continuo on a unison D; then the first voice rises slowly through an octave, with the second following it, before falling back to a cadence on A. The setting of the first terzet screws the pitch even higher up to E, and with it the extraordinary tension inherent in the agonized ascent, before the melodies collapse to the same cadence on A. The effect is of a single trajectory determining the melodic shape of the first thirty-eight measures of the piece. It is just the sort of long-range control of pitch found in Ariadne's lament and depends on the special emphasis of line characteristic of monody. The recitative-like style of "Interrotte speranze" allowed Monteverdi to introduce this formal technique of his monody into the madrigal.

It is a rhetorical technique as well, of course. The long rises in pitch take us in three sweeping affective gestures through Guarini's whole litany of lovesickness, eleven lines of poetry in all. Then the poet finally addresses the source of his sorrows: "Questi, ch'a voi quasi gran fasci invio, / donna crudel, d'aspri tormenti e fieri, / saranno i trofei vostri e'l rogo mio" ("These things I send you, like a great bundle, / cruel woman, of harsh and bitter torments, / will be your trophies and my funeral pyre"). And here Monteverdi shifted gears, loosing the voices from each other for the first time and eloquently juxtaposing "Questi" with the vocative "donna crudel." He released the pent-up emotion of the long opening section, finally, with an almost too playful contrapuntal peroration.

These Petrarchan duets of Monteverdi may well have been prompted by the serious duets in Marco da Gagliano's *Musiche a una dua e tre voci* (Florence, 1615), much as his Marinist ones took their start from Grandi's *Madrigali concertati*. Denis Arnold, at any rate, has noted several similarities of content and organization between Book VII and Gagliano's *Musiche,* to which may be added the use in both of a sonnet as programmatic proem to the collection.[35] But this stylistic link is of a general sort: even Gagliano's most serious duets do not show the austere *stile rappresentativo* of Monteverdi's, and altogether they tend rather to the florid ornamentation

35. *Monteverdi,* p. 84. But note the difference between Gagliano's tone, set by Bembo's "Cantai un tempo, e se fu dolce il canto," and Monteverdi's! I find less convincing than Arnold's connections Pirrotta's suggestion of similarities between Book VII and Monteverdi's own *Canzonette* of 1584; see "Scelte poetiche," p. 238. For a modern edition of Gagliano's *Musiche* see *Music for One, Two, and Three Voices.*

of the monodists than to Monteverdi's distilled reminiscences of polyphonic practice.

The link to Gagliano is important mainly in suggesting yet again the close attention Monteverdi paid to the styles of younger composers during the 1610s, a period of radical stylistic transformation in his own works. And one more duet in Book VII provides a final, unmistakable example of this attention. This is the well-known "Oimè, dov'è il mio ben, dov'è il mio core?," not a madrigal at all but a set of strophic variations on the *aria di Romanesca*. It was surely prompted by the series of such *arie,* mostly for two voices and continuo, written by the Roman composer Antonio Cifra from 1613 on. Cifra's poetic choices for these *arie,* like Monteverdi's, reflect the heritage of such settings in sixteenth-century recitational traditions: all are *ottave,* ten from *Gerusalemme liberata,* three from *Orlando furioso,* and one by Bernardo Tasso, the author of Monteverdi's text.[36] The new styles and genres of Book VII, Marinist as well as Petrarchan, bespeak Monteverdi's fertile receptivity to and searching comprehension of novel idioms around him. Both features would remain with the composer, helping to determine the stylistic avenues he would explore in the works of his last years.

36. Two of Cifra's duets are transcribed by Whenham, *Duet and Dialogue* 2:334–44; for commentary on the genre see vol. 1, pp. 132–38.

8

Marinism
and the Madrigal, II
(Developments after Book VII)

The Later Continuo Duets

FTER THE FOURTEEN through-composed duets of the Seventh Book, we noted in the preceding chapter, Monteverdi published only seven more works of this type. He included one in an anthology of 1624 ("O come vaghi, o come cari sono"),[1] two more in the *Scherzi musicali* of 1632 ("Zefiro torna" and "Armato il cor d'adamantina fede"), and four in the Eighth Book of 1638 ("Se vittorie sì belle," "Mentre vaga Angioletta," "Ardo e scoprir, ahi lasso, io non ardisco," and "O sia tranquillo il mar, o pien d'orgoglio").[2] In sheer numbers, then, Monteverdi's interest in the genre seems to have waned rapidly after the publication of Book VII. And this impression is strengthened by the tentative chronology we may advance for these last seven duets. For there is reason to believe that "Armato il cor," "Se vittorie sì belle," "Ardo e scoprir," and "O sia tranquillo il mar" (if not the virtuosic showpieces "Zefiro torna" and "Mentre vaga Angioletta") may have been composed long before their publications in 1632 and 1638.

The evidence for this assertion is purely stylistic in the cases of "Ardo e scoprir" and "O sia tranquillo il mar." These works, first published next to each other in Book VIII, form an intimately related pair. Both follow closely the serious style of "Non vedrò mai le stelle" and "Interrotte speranze," suggesting that they were written soon after the publication of Book VII. (Their exclusion from the collection of 1632 poses no obstacle to the hypothesis: their grave expressive demeanor and

---

1. *Madrigali del signor cavalier Anselmi nobile di Treviso posti in musica da diversi eccellentissimi spiriti a 2. 3. 4. 5. voci* (Venice, 1624; dedication dated 23 December 1623; RISM 1624[11]); Monteverdi included here also the trio "Taci Armellin, deh taci."

2. "Armato il cor" was reprinted in Book VIII; "Zefiro torna," "Se vittorie sì belle," "Armato il cor," "Ardo e scoprir," and "O sia tranquillo il mar" were all reprinted in the posthumous Ninth Book of 1651.

EXAMPLE 64

Monteverdi, "Ardo e scoprir, ahi lasso, io non ardisco," end

through-composed nature might together have disqualified them from inclusion in a volume of musical *Scherzi*.)

"Ardo e scoprir" and "O sia tranquillo il mar" recall the serious duets of Book VII in their use of two-voice recitative, rendered even more plangent here than in previous works. They look back specifically to "Interrotte speranze" in their D-minor tonality and in their tendency to align (more subtly, indeed, than the earlier work) syntactic and poetic units of their texts with repeated musical blocks developing from static tonic harmonies to a full cadence (see mm. 1–15 and 16–24 in "Ardo e scoprir," mm. 1–14 and 15–27 in "O sia tranquillo il mar"). Both works also recall "Non vedrò mai le stelle" in turning to triple-meter passages near or at their conclusions. But these triple-meter sections are of a new sort: in place of the jarring Marinist celebration of poetic image in "Non vedrò," Monteverdi attempted now to involve his arioso passages in the prevailing sorrowful sentiments of their texts. The huge triple-meter episode in "O sia tranquillo il mar" is affective gesture rather than glittering image, an effusive *exclamatio* on the words that form the crux of the poet's Ariadne- and Armida-like plight: "ma tu non torni, o Filli. . . ." The smaller such passage that ends "Ardo e scoprir" renders the lover's paralyzed speechlessness in the face of his lady in an inventive and effective fashion (Ex. 64). This affective use of triple meter in "Ardo e scoprir" and "O sia tranquillo il mar" suggests that Monteverdi perceived the inefficacy of the mixture of Petrarchan and Marinist expressive modes in "Non vedrò mai le stelle."[3]

Like these two works, "Armato il cor" and "Se vittorie sì belle" are musical and poetic twins, although first published six years apart.[4] Their poems, first of all,

3. In commenting on "Ardo e scoprir" Wolfgang Osthoff, *Das dramatische Spätwerk Claudio Monteverdis*, p. 44, suggests that the emotional heightening of its recitative gives it a novel gestural quality ("Der Affekt ist hier aus dem Stadium der blossen Gefühlsaufwallung in das der sinnlichen Gebärde übergegangen") and likens the "Bewegungsimpulse" of the work to "körperliche Haltungen." But the looseness of terminology here obscures an important distinction between the linguistic and rhetorical gesture of "Ardo e scoprir" and the "Gebärdenhaftigkeit" that Osthoff finds in a pictorial exercise like the *ciaccona* "Zefiro torna" (see p. 38).

4. They, like "Ardo e scoprir" and "O sia tranquillo il mar," were placed next to each other in

are identical in theme, length, rhyme scheme, prosody (except for their first lines, which differ in length), and even some wording:

Armato il cor d'adamantina fede,	My heart armed with adamantine faith,
nell'amoroso regno	I go to serve as soldier
a militar ne vegno.	in the realm of Love.
Contrasterò con ciel e con la sorte;	I'll struggle with the heavens and with Fate;
pugnerò con la morte;	I'll fight with Death,
ch'intrepido guerriero,	for, brave warrior,
se vittoria non ho, vita non chero.	if I don't gain victory, I don't cherish life.
Se vittorie sì belle	If wars of Love have
han le guerre d'amore	such wonderful victories,
fatti guerrier, mio core.	make yourself a soldier, my heart.
E non temer degli amorosi strali	And don't fear mortal wounds
le ferite mortali.	from amorous arrows.
Pugna; sappi ch'è gloria	Fight on; and know there's glory
il morir per desio della vittoria.	in dying for desire of victory.

Clearly, one of these madrigals was modeled on the other; probably they were written as a pair by the same poet. John Whenham has recently identified Fulvio Testi as the author of "Se vittorie sì belle"; so "Armato il cor" may well be his work also.[5]

The connection of Monteverdi to Testi (1593–1646) is notable in two respects. First, it adds another poet to Monteverdi's Marinist Parnassus. Testi was in his earliest lyrics—among which "Se vittorie sì belle" must belong—a fervent follower of Marino.[6] Both this madrigal and "Armato il cor," with their prosaic elaborations on Marino's favored metaphor likening love to war, revolve securely in the Marinist orbit of Monteverdi's poetic world system. Second, the connection of Monteverdi and Testi may help us assign a date to these two madrigals. Testi served the Estense at Modena as diplomat and poet throughout most of his adult life. Monteverdi's connection to Modena grew especially close in the years 1622–24, when he sent madrigals and canzonette to Prince Alfonso III d'Este and Duke Cesare I d'Este on several occasions. Either the prince or the duke may well have supplied

---

Book VIII. Schrade, *Monteverdi*, p. 333, notes their similarities and suggests that their style "goes back to the early twenties, to the time of the seventh book."

5. *Duet and Dialogue* 2:141. "Armato il cor" has often been ascribed to Ottavio Rinuccini, but I can find no basis for the ascription either in Rinuccini's *Poesie* (Florence, 1622) or in many Florentine manuscripts containing his work (of which the most important are MSS Palatine 249 and 250 in the Biblioteca Nazionale). Rinuccini did write a madrigal beginning "Armata il cor di fede" (*Poesie*, p. 293), but after its *capoverso* this poem shows no relation to the text set by Monteverdi.

6. Testi omitted his Marinist lyrics (published in Venice, 1613, and Modena, 1617) from later editions of his works (of which I read his *Opere* of Venice, 1663, and *Poesie liriche* of Modena, 1636). For a sample of these early lyrics see Calcaterra, *I lirici*, pp. 305–9; on Testi see Getto, "Irrequietezza di Fulvio Testi," in *Barocco*, pp. 163–98.

EXAMPLE 65

(a) Monteverdi, "Se vittorie sì belle," mm. 70–73

(b) Monteverdi, "Armato il cor d'adamantina fede,"
mm. 41–43

verses by Testi for these settings. The poetic evidence, then, points to 1622–24 as a plausible date for "Se vittorie sì belle" and "Armato il cor."[7]

So also, more emphatically, does the musical evidence. One of the many similarities between these two madrigals is their treatment of the word *pugnare,* which occurs in both poems (Ex. 65). This musical figure reappears in two other duets by Monteverdi, the motet "Fuge, anima mea," published in a Venetian anthology of 1620,[8] and the madrigal "O come vaghi, o come cari sono," an image-ridden Marinist exercise on Giovanni Battista Anselmi's verse published in an anthology of early 1624.[9] It appears again, finally, in a setting of "Armato il cor" by the Veronese composer Antonio Marastone, published late in 1624, which shows other resemblances to Monteverdi's setting as well.[10]

7. On Monteverdi's connections with Modena see Henry Prunières, *Monteverdi,* p. 217n; Stevens, *The Letters,* p. 283; and especially Paolo Fabbri, "Inediti monteverdiani." The letters to Monteverdi that Fabbri has unearthed even refer specifically to two pairs of madrigals requested from the composer.

8. Alessandro Vincenti, ed., *Symbolae diversorum musicorum . . . Ab admodum reverendo D. Laurentio Calvo . . . in lucem editae* (RISM 1620²). See mm. 1–3 of the work, in Monteverdi, *Tutte le opere,* vol. 16, pt. 2, p. 444.

9. For the title of this anthology see n. 1 above. See mm. 17–21 for the passage in question, in Monteverdi, *Tutte le opere* 9:103.

10. Marastone's collection is entitled *Concerti a due tre, et quattro voci* (Venice, dedicated 9 November 1624). "Armato il cor" is transcribed by Whenham, *Duet and Dialogue* 2:256–59; see mm. 29–33, and compare also mm. 49–51 with mm. 57–59 of Monteverdi's setting. This is the only published setting of "Armato il cor" other than Monteverdi's; there are no other settings of "Se vittorie sì belle."

EXAMPLE 66

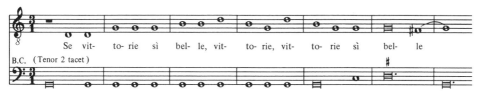

Monteverdi, "Se vittorie sì belle," beginning

EXAMPLE 67

Monteverdi, "Armato il cor d'adamantina fede," beginning

This congeries of musical correspondences strongly associates "Armato il cor" and "Se vittorie sì belle" with the early 1620s and suggests that the former work circulated in manuscript in time for Marastone to emulate it at the end of 1624. The appearance of Testi's verse implies a more specific date, 1622–24. And one more feature of both madrigals suggests these same years. It is yet another novel usage of the triple-meter sections of the Book VII duets, this time to capture the poet's metaphor of love-as-war in bellicose repeated chords and fanfare-like triadic melodies (Ex. 66). In "Armato il cor" the fanfare motives extend into the sections in duple meter, mingling there with a martial melisma (Ex. 67). These are, of course, all characteristic features of Monteverdi's famous *stile concitato*. And Monteverdi tells us in the preface to Book VIII that he first presented this style to the public in the *Combattimento di Tancredi et Clorinda*—in 1624.[11]

"Armato il cor" and "Se vittorie sì belle," then, are in all likelihood two of the

11. For a facsimile reprint of this preface see Monteverdi, *Tutte le opere,* vol. 8, pt. 1, p. [iii]; for a translation see Strunk, *Source Readings,* pp. 53–55.

"diversi côpositioni altre così Ecclesiastiche, come da Camera" in which, according to Monteverdi's preface, he pursued the experiments first undertaken in the *Combattimento*. But neither work seems to embody the mature *stile concitato*, omitting in particular the repeated sixteenth notes that Monteverdi singled out as the special novelty of the *Combattimento*. For this reason we might also view the beginnings of these two duets as preliminary approximations of the new style, composed before its careful rationalization in the *Combattimento* and conceived simply as warlike pictorialisms.

In either case the association of "Armato il cor" and "Se vittorie sì belle" with the *Combattimento* points up the link between the nascent *stile concitato* and the Marinist expressive premises of the Seventh Book. The new style was born of the concern, revitalized in Book VII, to depict in iconic musical gesture the images of the poetry. It was nurtured by the love-as-war metaphor widespread among the poems of Marino and his followers like Testi; for this reason the *stile concitato* is almost invariably not a depiction of simple anger, the *ira* Monteverdi discussed in his preface of 1638, but a portrayal of the hostilities of war. This Marinist metaphor also provided Monteverdi with the dialectical organization of Book VIII: *Madrigali guerrieri, et amorosi*. Two sonnets elaborating on it, one by Marino and one in explicit imitation of him, served as the proems to the matching halves of the collection:

Altri canti d'Amor, tenero arciero,	Let others sing of Love, the youthful archer,
i dolci vezzi, sospirati baci,	his sweet embraces, sighed-for kisses;
narri gli sdegni e le bramate paci,	others narrate the rages and hoped-for truces
quand'unisce due alme un sol pensiero;	when one single thought unites two souls;
di Marte io canto. . . .	I sing of Mars. . . .
Altri canti di Marte e di sua schiera	Let others sing of Mars, and of his legions
gli arditi assalti e l'honorate imprese,	the daring attacks and famous deeds,
le sanguigne vittorie e le contese,	the bloody victories and struggles,
i trionfi di morte horrida e fera;	the triumphs of Death, horrid and cruel.
io canto, Amor, di questa tua guerriera. . . .	I sing, Love, of this your she-warrior. . . .

(Rime, pt. 1, p. 1)

Image and Mimesis in the Last Madrigal Books

The *Combattimento* is a composition in the *genere rappresentativo* and thus is distinguished from the "canti senza gesto" ("songs without gestures") to which Monteverdi referred on the title page of Book VIII.[12] But it does not exemplify the nor-

12. The full title is *Madrigali guerrieri, et amorosi Con alcuni opuscoli in genere rappresentativo, che saranno per brevi Episodii frà i canti senza gesto. Libro ottavo di Claudio Monteverde Maestro di Capella della Serenissima Republica di Venetia. Dedicati Alla Sacra Cesarea Maestà Dell'Imperator Ferdinando III con privilegio . . . in Venetia, Appresso Alessandro Vincenti. MDCXXXVIII.*

mal "dramatic genre" of Monteverdi's music dramas or the monodies of Book VII, for the stanzas from *Gerusalemme liberata* that make up its text (XII, 52–62, 64–68) call for a narrator in addition to Tancredi and Clorinda. It is, in short, a mixed-mode work, resembling in this the eclogues of Book VI and its counterpart in the second half of Book VIII, the *Lament of the Nymph*.[13]

Monteverdi gave careful instructions for the staging of the *Combattimento*. He suggested that it be sung after several *madrigali senza gesto*. Clorinda should be armed, Tancredi armed and mounted; together "they must perform the movements and gestures in the manner expressed in the text, and nothing more or less. . . . [They should] observe carefully the tempi, sword-thrusts and movements, and the instrumentalists the music now excited, now soft, and the Narrator the words pronounced in time, so that these creations may converge in a unified imitation."[14] The full panoply of the *stile concitato* is presented by the narrator and by the instrumentalists, who play a consort of viols and continuo, while the protagonists act out the combat thus depicted. Performed in this manner, the pictorialisms of the *stile concitato* are endowed with a new mimetic dimension. They are no longer simple musical images, "senza gesto." Their gestural energy is fully realized in the choreography of actors onstage.[15]

This mimetic method, it must be said, remains to some degree bound by the limitations of Marinist image making. It does not very directly touch the emotions of Tancredi or Clorinda. For these, whether expressed by the protagonists themselves or by the narrator, Monteverdi returned to lyric monody or to the introspective rhetoric of recitative. And it is these moments, as Nino Pirrotta has put it, that "make the deepest impression on the minds of the listeners."[16] But Monteverdi's new mimetic method is nonetheless an ingenious attempt to turn the static Marinist emphasis of image to spirited representational ends. It is not surprising, then, that he first adumbrated this approach in setting Marino's madrigals in Book VII. These works are, of course, *madrigali senza gesto*, not intended to be staged or acted out. But Marino's text of "Perché fuggi tra' salci" suggests an action—the nymph's flight—that occurs even as the poet speaks (see chap. 7 above, p. 171). This gives its breathless opening a special depictive immediacy: it portrays not an object, an image, or even an image of an action but the action itself (see chap. 7, Ex. 55). The

13. Resembling even more closely, undoubtedly, the lost composition *Armida*, to which Monteverdi referred in letters from 1 May 1627 to 4 February 1628, and which he described in the first of these (see Monteverdi, *Lettere*, p. 241, and Stevens, *The Letters*, pp. 310–13; Monteverdi's text probably extended four lines farther than the couplet Stevens quotes on p. 310). To judge by Monteverdi's mention of *ira* in his letter, *Armida* made prominent use of the *stile concitato*. We can only guess why the *Lament* was published in Book VIII in the position we might have ex-

pected to be occupied by *Armida*, apparently the true twin of the *Combattimento* in poetic source, dimensions, and musical means. Perhaps the huge collection simply could not accommodate another work as long as the *Combattimento*.

14. *Tutte le opere*, vol. 8, pt. 1, p. 132.

15. Osthoff, *Das dramatische Spätwerk*, pp. 23–31, emphasizes this mimetic dimension (his term is *Gebärdenvorstellung*) and especially the independent role of the instrumental consort in its creation.

16. "Scelte poetiche," p. 32.

incident that occurs during another of Marino's lyrics in Book VII is even more explicit:

Eccomi pronta ai baci;	Here I am, ready for kissing;
baciami, Ergasto mio, ma bacia in guisa	kiss me, my Ergasto, but kiss so that
che de'denti mordaci	your biting teeth
nota non resti nel mio volto incisa,	leave no signs etched upon my face,
5 perch'altri non m'additi, e in esse poi	whence others might point at me and in these
legga le mie vergogne e i baci tuoi.	read my shame and your kisses.
Ahi! tu mordi e non baci!	Ah! you're biting, not kissing!
Tu mi segnasti ahi, ahi!	You've scarred me, alas, alas!
Possa io morir, se più ti bacio mai!	I'll die before I'll ever kiss you more!

(*Rime,* pt. 2, p. 24)

The action here is precisely located in the poem: between verses 6 and 7 Ergasto is permitted to kiss his lady; he bites. In the final verses the smitten lover vents her outrage and shame. Monteverdi's well-known setting captures her response with deadly mimetic accuracy: a pause for the bite, then excited exclamations, quick text repetitions, and staggered polyphony, leading finally to melting, mortified chromaticism.

Such mimetic depiction presupposes poems that imply or describe actions simultaneous with their reading or recital. And Monteverdi sought out several of these after Book VII. One was Giovanni Battista Anselmi's "Taci Armellin, deh taci," published in 1624, in which the poet tries in vain to keep his sleeping lady's dog from barking. (Monteverdi's setting is an indifferent rehearsal of devices from "Eccomi pronta.") Another was the *Combattimento,* of course, with its enactment of epic combat. A third, also in Book VIII, was Ottavio Rinuccini's canzonetta "Perché t'en fuggi, o Fillide," whose fleeing nymph recalls "Perché fuggi tra' salci."[17] Finally, the sylph of "Ninfa che scalza il piede e sciolta il crine" in Book VIII also flees from the speaker, showing that Monteverdi repeatedly turned this conventional pastoral topos to his new mimetic ends. He probably saw action lyrics like these as a fruitful alternative to the descriptive, image-laden verse more typical of the *marinisti.*

The investigation of the musical mimesis of simultaneous action seems to have captivated Monteverdi in dramatic compositions of the 1620s other than the *Combattimento.* It lies behind his famous fascination with Giulio Strozzi's minidrama *Licori finta pazza innamorata d'Aminta,* recorded in numerous letters of 1627 to Alessandro Striggio.[18] Monteverdi's ideas for setting this text at times seem to refute utterly the rhetorical premises of his youth. Individual words, not extended syntac-

---

17. I have identified the poem from fols. 22v–23r of MS Palatine 250 in the Biblioteca Nazionale of Florence, an unsigned but partially autograph manuscript of poetry by Rinuccini. On Monteverdi's setting see Lorenzo Bianconi, "Struttura poetica e struttura musicale nei madrigali di Monteverdi." Schrade, *Monteverdi,* p.

337, plausibly suggests a date of the late 1620s for the work.

18. See Monteverdi, *Lettere,* pp. 240–76, 284–85, and Stevens, *The Letters,* pp. 309–47, 354–57, 361–62. I have discussed Monteverdi's views on this work also in "Madrigal, Monody, and Monteverdi," pp. 101–2.

tic patterns, now dictate the musical organization: "The imitation of this feigned madness, being concerned only with the present and not with the past or future, consequently must be based on the single word rather than the sense of the phrase [*sopra alla parola et non sopra al senso de la clausula*]. When, therefore, war is mentioned, it will be necessary to imitate war, when peace [is mentioned], peace, when death, death, and so on." The continuous psychological development of Ariadne is replaced by a disjunctive mélange of "vivid gestures and separate passions," for the singer playing Licori must quickly transform her demeanor to meet the changing demands of the text: "And because the transformations and imitations happen in the shortest space of time, whoever takes on the leading role, which should arouse both laughter and pity, must be a woman who can lay aside every sort of imitation except the immediate one dictated by the word she is speaking."[19]

Most revealingly, perhaps, Monteverdi complains that the passages of Licori's role with no obvious pictorial suggestions for the music will be ineffective; he contrasts these with moments of more iconic text setting:

> I think, however, that three places should work to good effect: first, when the camp is being set up and the sounds and noises similar to those imitated in her words are heard offstage (this, it seems to me, will not fail); second, when she pretends to be dead; and, third, when she pretends to be asleep, where it will be necessary to use music imitating sleep. But in some other places, where the words cannot be imitated by gestures, noises, or other obvious sorts of imitation, I worry that the preceding and following passages might fall flat.[20]

Musical syntax matched to poetic rhetoric has given way here to musical emblems coinciding with the actions and images they represent. A pictorial conception of the joining of text and music has replaced an oratorical one. *Licori finta pazza*, had Monteverdi ever completed it, would have been Marinist music drama par excellence.[21]

19. These quotations come from Monteverdi's letter of 7 May 1627. See also his letter of 10 July: "It will only remain for Signora Margherita [Basile, scheduled to sing the title role] to become a brave soldier, to be fearful and bold by turns, mastering completely her own gestures without fear or timidity, because I am aiming to have lively imitations of the music, gestures, and tempi represented behind the scene; and I believe it will not displease Your Lordship, because the shifts from vigorous, noisy harmonies to soft, sweet ones will take place quickly, so that the words will stand out very well" (*Lettere*, pp. 264–65; Stevens's translation, *The Letters*, pp. 335–36).

20. Letter of 24 May (*Lettere*, pp. 251–52; Stevens, *The Letters*, pp. 320–21). In these excerpts I have used Stevens's translations as the basis for my own.

21. Bianconi, *Il seicento*, pp. 39–40, basing his interpretation on the first two excerpts from Monteverdi's letters quoted above, argues that the madness of Licori is a special case and that Monteverdi devised his new manner of imitation, a self-conscious departure from his normal musico-poetic practice, solely to depict her madness. But this interpretation does not account for my third excerpt, where the music is said to imitate things extrinsic to Licori's madness—camp sounds, feigned death, and sleep—and where Monteverdi doubts the effectiveness of passages of text not suggesting such imitation. *Licori* may indeed be a special case, but clearly it only led Monteverdi to an extreme statement of a conception of musical imitation manifested frequently in his late works.

Monteverdi never actually composed *Licori,* and his other new dramatic works of these years, *intermedi* and a tourney for Parma (1628) and the opera *Proserpina rapita* (1630), are for the most part lost.[22] Nevertheless, there is one work in Book VIII that betrays the impact of his iconic ideal of musical expression on the *genere rappresentativo* in this period: *Il ballo delle ingrate.* It may seem surprising to link this ballet with the years of *Licori,* since it was originally composed in 1608, on a text by Rinuccini, for the same Mantuan wedding celebrations that witnessed *L'Arianna.* But Denis Stevens has pointed out that the work was revived in 1628 at the imperial court in Vienna, and the text of the version published in Book VIII preserves the small alterations made in Rinuccini's poetry to fit that occasion.[23] There can be no doubt that Book VIII preserves as well Monteverdi's substantial musical revisions for the Viennese performance. And these relate *Il ballo* as a whole to the stylistic mainstream of his works of the 1620s.

This point has not been noted by students of Monteverdi and needs some emphasis. Whole sections of the ballet show a closer stylistic affinity to the madrigals of Monteverdi's Seventh and Eighth Books and to his late operas than to *L'Arianna* and *Orfeo*; these are most likely the result of large-scale revisions in 1628. The *sinfonia* repeated near the beginning of *Il ballo,* for example, in its stately rhythmic pace recalls the *sinfonia* that opens Book VII and anticipates the *sinfonie* of later Venetian operas.[24] The precipitous leaps and wide-ranging melismas of Pluto's role look forward to Seneca and Neptune in the last operas, not back to Charon and Pluto in *Orfeo.* And the abrupt chorus of infernal spirits shows none of the gravity of such choruses in *Orfeo,* presaging instead the narrators of Monteverdi's later *Lament of the Nymph* who describe the protagonist trampling flowers in her garden (p. 327; for the *Lament* see p. 287).

Other portions of the score undoubtedly were revised less extensively. These include the moving duet for Venus and Cupid (pp. 330–31), echoing, at times literally, the duets ending Act II of *Orfeo*; the final "Addio" of one of the ingrates (pp. 345 and 347), with its reminiscence of "Sì ch'io vorei morire" from Book IV; and the refrain of the ingrates (pp. 346 and 347), invoking in text, music, and formal organization the similar choral threnody of Jacopo Peri's *L'Euridice.*[25] But even at these moments the reviser's touch is occasionally apparent—as in the slurred exclamations, entering on offbeat eighth notes, of Venus and Cupid, gestures that first entered Monteverdi's recitative at one of the most affecting points of the *Combattimento* (compare the settings of "o," pp. 330–31 and 146).

---

22. On *Licori,* see Gary Tomlinson, "Twice Bitten, Thrice Shy." Thomas Walker has identified one surviving excerpt from *Proserpina rapita*; it is preserved in Monteverdi's Ninth Book of 1651. See "Gli errori di 'Minerva al tavolino,' " p. 13.

23. Denis Stevens, *"Madrigali Guerrieri, et Amorosi,"* pp. 231–32, 235.
24. For this passage see Monteverdi, *Tutte le opere,* vol. 8, pt. 2, p. 316. Further page references will be given in the text.
25. See *L'Euridice,* facs. ed., pp. 19–20.

Indeed, minor emendations like this one are conspicuous throughout the recitative of *Il ballo,* yielding a mixed style redolent at one moment of *L'Arianna,* at another of the *Combattimento* or even *Poppea.* Many of these revisions are affective ones, like the exclamations cited above, or Venus's sequential rendering of the exclamations in Example 68a, borrowed from a similar moment in the *partenza amorosa* of Book VII, "Se pur destina e vole / il cielo" (Ex. 68b). Many other revisions, however, endow the recitative with a pictorial quality probably less marked or lacking altogether in its original form. These are the alterations that reveal Monteverdi's iconic predilections in the years around 1628 and relate the revised *Ballo* to the ideals of *Licori* and other works of the time. They most often take the form of pictorial melismas on words like *arde* (burns), *strali* (arrows), and *superbe* (proud). (These melismas, in their wide tessituras and sixteenth-note anticipations tied to longer notes, are reminiscent of "Tempro la cetra" in Book VII and the *Combattimento* rather than of Orpheus's florid song "Possente spirto"; see Ex. 69). But not all the depictive gestures of *Il ballo* are fioriture. Indeed at one point Rinuccini anticipated in his verse the favorite Marinist mingling of images of love and war; and here, in 1628, Monteverdi could not resist a brief excursion into the full-fledged *stile concitato* (Ex. 70).

The preoccupation with musical image in the dramatic music of the 1620s, from the *Combattimento* and the *Licori* project to *Il ballo delle ingrate,* continues in the grand *concertato* madrigals of Book VIII, "Altri canti d'Amor," "Or che'l ciel et la terra e'l vento tace," "Ardo, avvampo, mi struggo, ardo; accorrete," and "Altri

EXAMPLE 68

(a) Monteverdi, *Il ballo delle ingrate,* mm. 187–90

(b) Monteverdi, "Se pur destina e vole / il cielo," mm. 68–72

EXAMPLE 69

(a) Monteverdi, *Il ballo delle ingrate,* mm. 309–12

(b) Monteverdi, "Tempro la cetra, e per cantar gli onori,"
mm. 49–52

(c) Monteverdi, *Il combattimento di Tancredi et Clorinda,*
mm. 130–33

EXAMPLE 70

Monteverdi, *Il ballo delle ingrate,* mm. 172–82

canti di Marte," as well as the trios "Gira il nemico, insidioso arciero" and "Ogni amante è guerrier; nel suo gran regno." All these works exploit the *stile concitato*. From political references in their texts it is clear that "Altri canti d'Amor" and "Ogni amante è guerrier" brandish their martial apparatus in tribute to the dedicatee of the collection, the recently crowned Emperor Ferdinand III.[26]

But none of these madrigals (with the qualified exception of "Gira il nemico") incorporates the mimetic dimension of the *stile concitato* in the *Combattimento*. They are *madrigali senza gesto,* and their martial images, mainly furious melismas and fanfare melodies over repetitive harmonies, are simple pictorial madrigalisms—and tedious ones, at that. Such bellicose bluster shows to worst effect in conjunction with the sterile virtuosity of "Ogni amante." It mars even the otherwise deeply felt setting of Petrarch's sonnet "Or che'l ciel." Here Monteverdi's pretext for the *stile concitato* is the line "guerra è'l mio stato, d'ira e di duol piena" ("war is my state, full of rage and suffering"); the twenty-one bars of musical hostilities depicting it do much to undermine the probing, introspective portrayal of the preceding choral homophony. Had he approached this text thirty years before, at the time of the five-voice "Zefiro torna," we may easily imagine the dissonant counterpoint with which Monteverdi would have emphasized the poet's emotions rather than his images.

Even when they are not employing the pictorialisms of the *stile concitato* these late madrigals tend to fall into a series of discrete musical images, demarcated by unequivocal formal divisions. This is especially true of the four grand *concertato* madrigals, all settings of sonnets, which unite their pictorial approach with the propensity to schematic block forms of the sonnet settings of Book VI. "Altri canti d'Amor" is typical. Monteverdi set its first, "amorous" quatrain for three voices and two violins over two languorous ostinati, the second a descending minor tetrachord. Sixty-two measures of *stile concitato* compose the next, contrasting section, setting the second quatrain of the poem for six-voice chorus and two violins over repeated chords of D, G, and C.[27] The terzets elicit further novel scorings. They are

26. Monteverdi's dedication suggests that he had originally planned to present the volume to Ferdinand II, emperor until December 1636; hence most of the works in Book VIII were probably composed by that time. This includes "Altri canti d'Amor," whose invocation to "Fernando" probably originally referred to Ferdinand II. But "Ogni amante," as Stevens has pointed out, specifies "Fernando Ernesto," that is, Ferdinand III, and was therefore either added to the collection or at least revised after 1636 (see *"Madrigali Guerrieri, et Amorosi,"* pp. 242–44; Pirrotta, "Scelte poetiche," pp. 245–46, identifies Rinuccini as the author of its text). On the basis of their similar styles and scoring (large vocal ensembles with obbligato instruments and continuo), I am inclined to link together the grand *concertato* madrigals as four of the latest works in Book VIII (therefore ca. 1634–36). "Gira il nemico," on a canzonetta of Giulio Strozzi, shows instead a more mimetic approach to the text; it may date from 1627–30, the years of Monteverdi's close collaboration with Strozzi on the projected *Licori* and the completed *I cinque fratelli* (1628) and *Proserpina rapita* (1630).

27. For a general discussion of the effects of such static harmonies on Monteverdi's madrigal style in Book VIII see McClary, "The Transition," pp. 236–40.

initially sung by bass alone, accompanied by the full string consort (two violins plus four *viole*) in its first appearance. Then the second terzet, replete with *concitato* and other madrigalisms, is restated in a slightly varied and expanded form, combining the full string band with all six voices for a sonorous close.

The other three madrigals in this group ring many changes (none of them fundamental) on this sort of form building. In "Altri canti di Marte," the counterpart of "Altri canti d'Amor" at the head of the *canti amorosi,* the *stile concitato* is concentrated in the opening seventy-one measures, setting the first quatrain. The rest of the piece consists of a series of often melismatic images arranged over basslines descending in stepwise fashion (interrupted only at the final terzet, sung first, as in "Altri canti d'Amor," by the bass solo).[28] "Or che'l ciel" introduces double counterpoint in its *seconda parte,* and the close of "Ardo, avvampo" evaporates unexpectedly in a cadence for two tenors and continuo (depicting the words "lascia che'l cor s'incenerisca, e taci"); but the first piece never fulfills the expressive promise of its opening choral homophony, and neither one avoids the debilitating formal caesuras that characterize all these works.

These sonorous, grandiloquent, but after all hollow works are not, perhaps, a gratifying summation of a madrigalian career that had witnessed the wonders of "Ecco mormorar l'onde," "Vattene pur, crudel," "Oimè, se tanto amate," and the *Sestina.* The syntactic suppleness and expressive imagination of these earlier pieces echo here only rarely and faintly. But in their iconic, almost antisyntactic treatment of text these last madrigals voice clearly the expressive goals of Marino and his age. And in their penchant for transparent formal clarity they extend a tendency evident in Monteverdi's oeuvre from the start, one given decisive impetus, as we have seen, by his adoption of the continuo in Book V and by his turn to new poetic forms and styles in the *Scherzi* of 1607 and in Book VI.

And one given free reign, it should be added, in the delightful and numerous canzonette and strophic songs of Monteverdi's late years.[29] These works too voice the new expressive ideal, and we may touch on them by way of concluding this survey of Monteverdi's Marinism. Monteverdi had, to be sure, composed such

28. The *ballo* at the end of the *canti guerrieri,* setting two sonnets of Rinuccini (see Pirrotta, "Scelte poetiche," pp. 246–47), employs this technique of long, repeated basslines to mark off the divisions of its second poem—a kind of strophic variations for five-voice chorus.

29. Aside from the *Scherzi musicali* of 1632, Book VIII, and Book IX (*Madrigali e canzonette a due, e tre, voci,* published posthumously in 1651), these works are preserved in Carlo Milanuzzi et al., *Quarto Scherzo delle ariose vaghezze* (Venice,

1624; three works by Monteverdi) and the anthology *Arie de diversi raccolte da Alessandro Vincenti* (Venice, 1634; RISM 1634[7]; two works). Stevens has assigned one more canzonetta, "Ahi, che si parti," preserved in manuscript at the Biblioteca Estense in Modena, to the mid-1620s (see *The Letters,* p. 283), but in style it resembles Monteverdi's *Canzonette* of 1584 more than his later strophic works and probably dates from before 1600.

light-hearted works before. But he apparently devoted increasing attention to the type in the 1620s and 1630s, no doubt under the sway of the burgeoning popularity of the Chiabreresque canzonette that supplied their texts. These poems turned away from Petrarchan rhetoric to embody instead the cool, graceful formalism we noted above in Chiabrera's *scherzi* (see chap. 6). In setting them Monteverdi abandoned most pretense to serious musico-poetic expression, substituting for it a Marinist world of charming, innocent hedonism. The chromatic sorrows into which these canzonette often dissolve are fleeting and in any case never so heartfelt that they are not immediately dispelled by the happy opening of the next strophe.

Of course Monteverdi had rarely turned to strophic forms for serious utterance, and with good reason: they usually placed severe limitations on his rhetorical response to his text. Too incisive and specific a setting of one strophe would fit uneasily to the next. So Monteverdi's late preoccupation with canzonette involved, in a different way than the Marinist madrigals in Books VII and VIII, a retreat from the compelling oratory of his youth. It is, finally, another of the Marinist tendencies of his late works—or at least, to avoid overtaxing our terminology, a trend arising from the same cultural ideals, the same flight from deep introspective expression, that fostered the Marinist poetic vision.

This is not to discount the sheer exuberance of musical creativity in many of these works, nor yet to ignore the ingenious means Monteverdi sometimes devised to overcome the expressive limitations of strophic texts. Both are evident in the delightful aria "Eri già tutta mia" from the *Scherzi musicali* of 1632 (see also Ex. 71):

Eri già tutta mia,	Once you were all mine,
mia quel alma e quel core.	your soul mine and your heart.
Chi da me ti desvia,	Who has led you away?
novo laccio d'amore?	A new bond of love?
5 O bellezza, o valore,	Oh beauty, oh valor,
o mirabil constanza, ove sei tu?	oh marvelous faithfulness, now where are you?
Eri già tutta mia, or non sei più.	Once you were all mine, but now you're gone.

(*Two more strophes follow.*)

Monteverdi deployed lines 1–4 in guileless melodic phrases over an ostinato bass; the bassline capitalizes still on the *Romanesca*-like sequential progressions present in Monteverdi's earliest works, while the phrase structure captures the strong-weak accentual pattern ending each line in its offbeat cadences. For the lover's exclamations in lines 5–6 Monteverdi shifted abruptly to affective recitative, complete with an unexpected turn toward minor harmonies. Line 7 brings back the music of line 1 in varied form, leading (or led, rather, by its suddenly hyperactive bassline) to a cadence; the two clauses of line 7, contrasting blissful past and wretched present, are separated by a pause in the vocal line.

This much would have satisfied a lesser composer, who at this point might have added a brief ritornello to lead into the next strophe. But Monteverdi milked

EXAMPLE 71

Monteverdi, "Eri già tutta mia," first strophe
(*Tutte le opere,* ed. Malipiero, 10:80)

the poet's final, all-important clause for more. The singer bursts into self-pitying repetitions of "non più," in quickened declamation over a new walking bass; these culminate in a marvelous melismatic exclamation, still over the insistently descending bassline. Monteverdi's lover is guileless, to be sure, but nonetheless touchingly downcast for it.[30]

30. I have deliberately omitted the last words of the song, "Ah, che mia non sei più," from my strophe in an attempt to work back from the text given in the music to what I consider the most likely original poetic form. My final couplet of truncated *endecasillabi* is a far more common closing gesture for canzonetta strophes than such a couplet followed by a *settenario tronco* would be. This suggests that "Ah, che mia non sei più!" is Monteverdi's own elaboration on the poet's closing "or non sei più." Canzonette like this one often admit differing scansions. My two lines 6 and 7, for example, could also be divided into four lines in the metric sequence 7–5 truncated–7–5 truncated. For a different reconstruction of the text along these lines see Osthoff, *Das dramatische Spätwerk,* p. 36. Osthoff rightly points up the anticipation of techniques of Monteverdi's late operas in the closing measures of the song (p. 37).

Such precise reflection of the expressive gestures of the text is unusual in strophic forms, as I have suggested. In "Eri già" it works because the rhetorical structures of the second and third poetic strophes mirror those of the first. Each strophe turns to exclamations at its fifth verse ("O fugaci contenti!," "O dispersi sospiri!"), and each ends with line 7 of the first strophe, a refrain. Such congruence of affective structure among strophes is common in seventeenth-century *canzonette per musica*. Monteverdi was not the only composer to use it as the basis for strophic settings of higher-than-usual expressive specificity.[31]

For every generalization about Monteverdi's works, it sometimes seems, there is an exception of distinctive creative vigor. The exception to the rule of Monteverdi's Marinist use of Chiabreresque canzonette is not to be found in the unassuming, insouciant emotional world of "Eri già" and the other musical *Scherzi*. It was published instead among the madrigals of Book VIII and is at once one of the greatest, most influential, and most famous of all Monteverdi's works: the *Lament of the Nymph*. Its text is an undistinguished canzonetta with refrain by Rinuccini, a mixed-mode poem presenting a nymph's complaint at her lover's betrayal. The first and fourth strophes run as follows:

Non havea Febo ancora	Phoebus had not yet
recato al mondo il dì,	brought day to the earth
ch'una donzella fuora	when a maiden came forth
del proprio albergo uscì.	from her house.
Miserella, ahi! più no, no;	Wretched girl, ah, no more!
tanto giel soffrir non può.	She cannot bear such scorn.
. . . .	. . . .
"Amor," diceva, il piè,	"Love," she said, stopping
mirando il ciel, fermò,	and gazing at the sky,
"dove, dov'è la fè	"where, where is the faith
che'l traditor giurò?"	that the traitor swore to me?"
Miserella, ahi! più no, no;	Wretched girl, ah, no more!
tanto giel soffrir non può.	She cannot bear such scorn.

(Six more strophes follow.)[32]

The poem had elicited nothing more than strophic songs from earlier composers,[33] but Monteverdi discovered other possibilities in it. Its mixture of literary modes,

31. For an example by another composer similar in many respects to "Eri già" see Sigismondo d'India's "Torna il sereno zefiro," from his *Musiche . . . libro quinto* (Venice, 1623). For another example by Monteverdi, this time involving the *stile concitato*, see the canzonetta "O mio bene, o mia vita" from Book IX.

32. For the complete poem see Rinuccini, *Poesie,* pp. 223–24.

33. See, for example, the settings of Antonio Brunelli (1614), modern edition in Putnam Aldrich, *The Rhythm of Seventeenth-Century Italian Monody,* p. 166, and Johann Hieronymus Kapsberger (1619), modern edition in Whenham, *Duet and Dialogue* 2:332–33.

with strophes entirely for the narrator at beginning and end, recalled the *Combattimento* and the musical eclogues of Book VI and suggested a musical organization like that of the setting of Marino's sonnet "Misero Alceo" there. Monteverdi set the narrative strophes (1–3 and 10) for three male voices; they flank symmetrically the central lament (strophes 4–9). This, like Alceo's plaint, unfolds over a repeating bassline, but of a new sort: the triple-meter descending tetrachord that Venetian composers and others used with increasing frequency through the 1620s and 1630s, in its touching minor-mode version.[34]

The flowing arioso that Monteverdi built over this ostinato achieves its expressive force through its rhetoric, now hesitant with misery, now pressing forward with impulsive grief—Ariadne's rhetoric transposed from recitative to aria, so to speak. It makes its effect also by its contrast with the sympathetic music of the narrators; they interject their refrain at unpredictable time intervals, between the protagonist's phrases or along with them. And of course it derives affective power from the staggered and dissonant relationship of all the voices to the inexorable tetrachord below.[35]

But none of this reveals the essential, astonishing novelty of the *Lament*: here, for the first time in his career, Monteverdi effaced utterly the form of a strophic lyric. There is hardly a trace left of the poem's formal outline in his woebegone setting. Even the refrain is camouflaged, omitted entirely from the opening and closing narrative sections, deployed irregularly throughout the nymph's song, and stated only twice in its entirety—one of these times by the bass alone, along with the middle lines of one of the nymph's strophes. What has been achieved here is a blurring of generic distinctions in music and poetry alike. From a poetic canzonetta Monteverdi has spun a through-composed dramatic *scena*; from light, formalist verse he has elaborated a musico-poetic lament of immense expressive force. Only the descending tetrachord, with its attendant triple meter and arioso melodies, remains as a dim reflection of the slight genre of the text. The *Lament*, in other words, is a brilliant anomaly. In it, from a foundation of Marinism, with materials touched by memories of lighter styles, Monteverdi erected an enduring monument to the Petrarchism of his youth.

---

34. On this ostinato and the *Lament* in general see Ellen Rosand, "The Descending Tetrachord." On p. 352n Rosand suggests a plausible date of ca. 1632 for the composition of the *Lament*.

35. To appreciate Monteverdi's skill in exploiting his ostinato one need only compare the *La-* ment to works by other Venetian composers using the same bassline. See, for example, Martino Pesenti's continuo duet "Ardo, ma non ardisco il chiuso ardore" (1638), transcribed in Whenham, *Duet and Dialogue* 2:311–21, and Apollo's lament from Cavalli's opera *Gli amori d'Apollo e di Dafne* (1640), facs. ed., fols. 85v–87r.

9

The Meeting of Petrarchan and Marinist Ideals (The Last Operas)

N THE MADRIGALS, *arie,* and canzonette of 1614–38 Monteverdi evolved new modes of musical expression and structure to accommodate the new poetics of Marinism. He created, in effect, a Third Practice, largely independent from the rhetorically inspired, Petrarchan Second Practice of the period 1592–1610. But at the same time he never relinquished the Petrarchan goals of those earlier years, and thus he was torn by the lure of two contrasting expressive ideals throughout his last decades. We have seen that he juxtaposed these ideals, more or less uneasily, in the late books of madrigals and even in individual works like "Misero Alceo," "Non vedrò mai le stelle," "Or che'l ciel et la terra," and the *Lament of the Nymph.* So it is not surprising that in his great final operas, *Il ritorno d'Ulisse in patria* (1640) and *L'incoronazione di Poppea* (1642), he attempted more resolutely than ever before to synthesize the divergent musical idioms now at his command and to merge the contrasting artistic objectives behind them.[1]

The attempt was especially crucial in these operas because to a composer like

1. On the vexing source problems of these operas see especially the writings of Wolfgang Osthoff, "Die venezianische und neapolitanische Fassung von Monteverdis 'Incoronazione di Poppea,' " "Zu den Quellen von Monteverdis 'Ritorno di Ulisse in patria,' " and "Neue Beobachtungen zu Quellen und Geschichte von Monteverdis 'Incoronazione di Poppea,' " and also Alessandra Chiarelli, " 'L'incoronazione di Poppea' o 'Il Nerone.' " The incomplete and equivocal sources for both works raise more questions than they answer, to the point of casting doubt on Monteverdi's authorship of the famous final love duet of Nero and Poppea (see Chiarelli, pp. 149–51). Nevertheless, it seems clear on stylistic grounds that most of the music of both operas not called into question by the sources could have been written by no one but Monteverdi; it is, in its variety, its versatility, and especially its gestural distinctiveness, unrivaled by any other midcentury idioms. (Comparison with the musico-dramatic gestures of Cavalli's early operas, which often superficially resemble Monteverdi's, is especially illuminating.) For a defense of Monteverdi's authorship of *Il ritorno* see Osthoff, *Das dramatische Spätwerk,* sec. D; for my early dating of this opera—still occasionally assigned to 1641—see Osthoff, "Zur bologneser Aufführung von Monteverdis 'Ritorno di Ulisse' im Jahre 1640." (The shift of one year is not without importance, for it resolves in Monteverdi's favor questions of stylistic priority posed by intriguing connections between *Il ritorno* and Cavalli's *Didone* of 1641.)

Monteverdi an exclusively Marinist dramaturgy could not have seemed a viable conception. From his first operas Monteverdi had realized that music drama was uniquely qualified to portray emotions profoundly and compellingly; he had, simply, defined his music drama in Petrarchan terms, the terms of Guarini, Rinuccini, and Striggio. Without a large admixture of Petrarchan introspection and passion Monteverdi's music drama would have lost its vital emotional core—the presentation of its characters' responses to the situations enacted—and been reduced at best to the iconic pantomime of portions of the *Combattimento*. The anti-introspective outlook of the Marinist vision was, in Monteverdi's terms, fundamentally antidramatic as well.

But the librettists of Monteverdi's last operas, Giacomo Badoaro and Gian Francesco Busenello, both much younger than he, were nurtured by Marinism. From this arises some of the special tension inherent in both *Il ritorno* and *Poppea*. The texts of these operas facilitated Monteverdi's adoption of Marinist musical devices and idioms but left less room for effective Petrarchan expression. They tipped the scales of Monteverdi's stylistic rapprochement away from impassioned, inward-looking rhetoric. Monteverdi's desire to redress the balance speaks most clearly in the many small rhetorical revisions he made in setting both dramas (but especially *Poppea*); to these we shall return.

It would be facile, however, to trace the Marinist tendencies in these operas to their librettists alone. After all, the surviving documentation strongly suggests that Monteverdi worked closely and on friendly terms with Badoaro to achieve a text for *Il ritorno* to his liking.[2] And though we know nothing of Monteverdi's relations with Busenello, the numerous liberties he took in setting *Poppea* indicate that he felt free to alter the text to suit his needs.[3] In each opera the final product seems to reflect a viable compromise of the interests of composer and librettist more than the struggle of a composer victimized by an unsatisfactory text. The Marinisms of *Il ritorno* and *Poppea* are Monteverdi's work as well as their poets'—which is only to repeat that the dichotomy of expressive aims apparent in both works reflects the ambivalence of their composer, not only the stylistic temperaments of their poets.

The obverse face of this ambivalence is the dazzling variety of styles and gestures in Monteverdi's music for *Il ritorno* and *Poppea*, a diversity that sets them apart from any other operas of the time—and from most operas of other times as well. Monteverdi's attempt to meld contrasting musical idioms into a coherent world

---

2. See Badoaro's letter of dedication to Monteverdi in the manuscript libretto of *Il ritorno* at the Biblioteca del Museo Correr, transcribed in Osthoff, "Zu den Quellen," pp. 73–74.

3. These liberties, much more frequent and substantial in Busenello's drama than in Badoaro's, suggest that Monteverdi took little or no part in preparing the libretto of *Poppea*—that he was given the text in finished form and manipulated it in his setting as best he could. I find Francesco Degrada's assignment to Monteverdi of a larger role in the preparation of the libretto unconvincing; see his generally admirable survey of Busenello's life and work, "Gian Francesco Busenello e il libretto della *Incoronazione di Poppea*."

onstage was not new in these late music dramas but reached all the way back to *Orfeo*. And in some ways the musical variety served the same ends in the 1640s as it had in 1607, only on an expanded scale. The extensive use of differing styles for character delineation in *Poppea* and *Il ritorno,* for example—the melismatic and wide-ranging virtuosity of the gods, the serious declamatory recitative of the protagonists, and the lyric tunefulness of the secondary and comic characters, to state the differences in general terms—finds a precedent in the musical characterizations of *Orfeo*: the angular, forbidding profile of Charon, the melting lyricism of Proserpina, and the virtuosity of Apollo.[4] And in both *Orfeo* and the late operas Monteverdi deploys a wide spectrum of formal types, including strophic and modified strophic structures, walking basses, and ostinati, to lend organizational coherence to lengthy stretches of dramatic time and set off freer passages of recitative.

But on the most general level the interaction of musical variety and drama in *Il ritorno* and *Poppea* is fundamentally different from that of *Orfeo*. In *Orfeo* divergences from the recitative style that is the backbone of the work either occur in conventional dramatic structures, the reflective choruses that end each act, or are motivated by the action. The choral round dance in Act I and the strophic songs of Orpheus and the shepherds in Act II constitute a true-to-life part of the wedding celebrations; "Possente spirto" (III) is the demonstration of musical virtuosity (if not oratorical persuasiveness) required to win back Euridice; "Qual honor di te fia degno" (IV) is Orpheus's joyful apostrophe to his victorious lyre; and the duet "Saliam" accompanies the apotheosis that ends the action in Act V. All these closed musical forms, in other words, may reasonably be viewed as stage songs, and most of them gain in verisimilitude by being rendered by Orpheus, a singer of legendary powers. When characters sing songs, they sing. When they speak, they simply speak—in the language of recitative. (And note that most of the distinctions of musical characterization in *Orfeo,* unlike those of the last operas, function within a single style that we recognize as recitative.) The illusion of musical speech is consistently maintained.[5]

---

4. Charon's portrayal builds on a similar characterization of Pluto in Jacopo Peri's *Euridice,* as we have seen in chap. 5 above. On musical characterization in *Il ritorno* and *Poppea* see Anna Amalie Abert, *Claudio Monteverdi und das musikalische Drama,* pp. 45–59, 68–92.

5. Pirrotta goes farther than this, arguing that the creators of the first operas chose renowned singers for their protagonists in order to justify the whole notion of musical speech (*Li due Orfei,* pp. 302–4; *Music and Theatre,* pp. 262–64). It seems to me, however, that such a pragmatic demand for realism was not at issue around 1600— that Pirrotta's interpretation imputes to the earli-

est operas a more self-conscious distinction of musical and poetic speech than was yet relevant. (It would grow more important already by 1640; see below.) It is true that Orpheus's legendary musical powers helped to justify, in a narrower sense, individual musico-dramatic gestures, set pieces like "Possente spirto" and "Qual honor." But for the concept of musical speech itself— recitative—no more justification was needed than the general mythic, pastoral ethos of the dramas in which it served. The point is confirmed by *L'Arianna,* none of whose characters was associated with special musical powers.

We do not have enough of *L'Arianna,* or of any of Monteverdi's other music dramas before *Il ritorno,* to know whether he sought in them the sort of musico-dramatic verisimilitude found in *Orfeo* (though it seems probable that he did so in *L'Arianna*). In the last two operas, at any rate, he did not. There the style of un-adorned recitative is no longer the central language that all characters speak, depart-ing from it only in special dramatic circumstances. It is rather one of many parallel languages of roughly equal prominence. Songs are not usually legitimized by the action; instead they are asserted as the primary mode of speech of certain characters, and indulged in by all in a fashion that seems to abandon the more verisimilar musico-dramatic standards of *Orfeo.*

In the last operas, in other words, musical speech as a matter of accepted con-vention, little touched by the demands of verisimilitude, has replaced music as a rhetorical heightening of speech credible in its well-defined mythical context. The humanist ideal of music and poetry as two sides of a single language, brought to its dramatic culmination in *Orfeo* and (to judge only by its lament) *L'Arianna,* has given way to a modern suspension of disbelief in the face of the anti-rational anom-aly of characters speaking in song. It is an *Entzauberung des Musikdramas* reminiscent of Max Weber; the last mythic fog of the Renaissance vision of real musical speech, redolent of lost pastoral ages, has dissipated. Humanist *dramma per musica* has been supplanted by spoken drama that happens to be set to music.

Thus much of the touted realism of *Il ritorno* and *Poppea*—their mixture of comic and serious elements, for example, and the everyday tone of some of their action—masks a more profound unreality, a self-conscious stylization of discourse. (Such stylization brings along with it the uneasiness of all self-conscious utterance: complaints about the capricious unreality of sung drama, still echoing today, were first heard in the 1640s. The need to suspend disbelief makes possible the refusal to do so.) Monteverdi's more realistic operas are *Orfeo* and, probably, *L'Arianna*—realistic because they present a vision of an Arcadian reality still cherished by late-Renaissance culture. The stylization of *Il ritorno* and *Poppea* betrays newer cultural premises, according to which language is not so immediate a translation of per-ceived reality, not so clear a window on the feelings associated with this perception. These operas manifest a delight in musical language itself, in the versatile and vir-tuosic manipulation of its varied linguistic devices. They reveal Monteverdi's fasci-nation with the trappings of style and structure, at times almost to the exclusion of the emotions and meaning such elements were made to convey in his earlier works. They threaten to substitute surface structure and ornament for deeper expression, virtuosity for introspection. They bear, in short, many of the earmarks of Marinist poetics.

The broad stylistic diversity of *Il ritorno* and *Poppea* disrupts the illusion of a unified musico-poetic language on the local level as well. It fosters a musical speech more fragmentary than that of *Orfeo* or *L'Arianna,* a discourse in which individual words and images tend to be singled out by abrupt changes of style in the music setting them. The seamless emotional evolution characteristic of Ariadne's lament is often replaced by a disjointed succession of discrete images and emotions. The remarks of the unidentified author of *Le nozze d'Enea con Lavinia*—Monteverdi's third opera of the 1640s, the music of which has not survived—on the quick emotional shifts in his text seem to signal Monteverdi's new outlook: "Changes of affection . . . please our Signor Monteverde very much, since they allow him to display with various emotions the marvels of his art."[6] The stylistic marvels of the music itself, rather than the emotions portrayed, seem to occupy Monteverdi's attention.

And often Monteverdi's shifting styles do not so much reflect changing passions as give iconic or mimetic treatment to individual images: pictorial expression, as we have seen, is a central feature of the new idioms of Monteverdi's late years. Thus in the eleven-measure span of Example 72 the guard's affective recitative, portraying Octavia's sorrow, gives way to the pictorialisms of the *concitato genere* and finally to mimetic laughter over a canzonetta-like walking bass. (This excerpt provides an interesting demonstration of the exteriorization of emotion often associated with Monteverdi's iconic techniques. The soldier experiences no feelings of his own but rather reenacts in detached fashion the actions of Nero and the rebelling states of the empire. In the affective recitative at the beginning of the excerpt, we may at least believe that he feels sympathy for Octavia.) Such a patchwork of styles, with its attendant pictorialisms, is not restricted to secondary characters or comic moments. Elsewhere I have called attention to it in Octavia's famous soliloquies "Disprezzata regina" and "A dio Roma" (*Poppea*, I, v and III, vii).[7] It may be witnessed as well in Ulysses' narration "Io greco sono" in *Il ritorno*, I, viii. This passage is especially interesting since, apart from its pictorialisms, it bears numerous similarities to Daphne's narration of Euridice's death in Act II of *Orfeo*, "In un fiorito prato." The same dramatic topos may be compared in its pre- and post-Marinist guises, and the comparison highlights the move from a fluid rhetorical convergence of musical and poetic syntaxes to a rhetoric repeatedly interrupted by pictorial expression. In all these examples, and others that might be adduced, immediacy of emotion is sacrificed to the requisites of iconic musical depiction, fluency of rhetoric to the distinguishing of discrete images by means of varied musical styles.

This tendency toward a fragmented and iconic style, like the more general styl-

6. From the "Argomento e scenario" of *Le nozze*; quoted from Osthoff, "Zu den Quellen," p. 75. Walker argues convincingly that the author of *Le nozze* was not, as long supposed, Badoaro; see "Gli errori," pp. 11–12, 19–20.

7. "Music and the Claims of Text," p. 587; see also Tomlinson, "Madrigal, Monody, and Monteverdi," pp. 100–101. Octavia's second soliloquy appears as III, vi in Busenello's libretto, followed by Arnalta's solo scene; in the score the order of the scenes is reversed.

EXAMPLE 72

Monteverdi, *L'incoronazione di Poppea,* I, ii, excerpt

ization of musical dramaturgy described above, reveals the Marinist orientation of *Poppea* and *Il ritorno.* And this orientation was encouraged, as we have noted, by various traits of Busenello's and Badoaro's dramas. Busenello for his part did not hesitate to proclaim his Marinist loyalties. Already in 1623 he wrote Marino a letter of ecstatic praise after poring over a manuscript copy of *L'Adone* (sent by the author to his Venetian publisher). And when Tommaso Stigliani criticized Marino's poem in the following years, Busenello sprang to its defense with two collections of viciously satirical sonnets.[8] Thirty years later Busenello's tastes had not changed. In one of his two letters of 1656 discussing his music drama *La Statira,* he professed to have followed, "if at a great distance, the style of the best modern [poets]"; and at the top of his list was Marino, whose metaphors and circumlocutions, Busenello said, were imitated even by his detractors; "whose fantasy was equal if not superior to Ovid's; who has been the most wondrous [poet] of our times, faultless in all

8. See Arthur A. Livingston, "Gian Francesco Busenello e la polemica Stigliani-Marino."

thoughts and feelings; who has lifted up Tuscan poetry to unapproachable heights; and who has initiated style into the most recondite delights that could ever be imagined by the entire chorus of Muses.'"[9] Badoaro was a close friend of Busenello and seems to have esteemed his literary accomplishments.[10] *Il ritorno* reveals that he shared, if perhaps with slightly less enthusiasm, Busenello's admiration of Marino.

The Marinism of *Poppea* and *Il ritorno* is most burdensomely apparent in their *concettismo*.[11] Both dramas—but especially Badoaro's—abound in moral, political, and philosophical maxims. Every character, from the gods down to the nursemaids, seems to have his or her own two cents to add concerning the principles of life. The protagonists too often converse in platitudes, as if the sententiousness of the chorus in Rinuccini's and Striggio's music dramas had by now infected the whole of dramatic discourse. Occasionally, authentic wit sparkles in these sayings:

> Non ti fidar giammai di cortigiani,   Don't ever put your faith in courtiers,
> perché in due cose sole   because Jove is powerless
> Giove è reso impotente: to do only two things:
> ei non può far che in cielo entri la morte,   he cannot make death enter into heaven,
> né che la fede mai si trovi in corte.   nor can he make the truth reside at court.
>   (Arnalta, *Poppea*, II, xii)

Or they rephrase a conventional trope with undeniable vitality:

> Chi pria s'accende   He who's lit with love
> procelle attende   can expect storms
> da un bianco sen;   from a white breast;
> ma corseggiando   but buccaneering on
> trova in amando   he'll find in loving
> porto seren.   a calm port.
> (Melanto, *Il ritorno*, I, ii)

Or they reveal a glimmer of Marinist verbal *acutezza*:

> Le corone eminenti   The crowns of power
> servono solo a indiademar tormenti.   serve only to bejewel torments.
>   (Seneca, *Poppea*, I, vii)

Most often, however, they exhibit only the ponderous cadence of weighty *sententiae*:

> Imparino i Feaci in questo giorno   Let the Phaeacians today learn
> che l'humano viaggio   that the human journey,

---

9. Quoted from Arthur A. Livingston, *La vita veneziana nelle opere di Gian Francesco Busenello*, pp. 374, 376.

10. See Livingston, *La vita veneziana*, pp. 119–22.

11. For the poetic texts of these dramas I have relied on the published edition of *Poppea* in Bu-

senello's *Delle hore ociose* (Venice, 1656) and *Il ritorno d'Ulisse in patria tragedia di lieto fine del signor Giacomo Badoaro . . . in Venetia l'anno MDCXLI* (MS Cicogna 192, No. 3330, Biblioteca del Museo Correr). Photocopies of both were generously supplied to me by Professor Ellen Rosand.

quand'ha contrario il ciel non ha ritorno. (Neptune, *Il ritorno,* I, vi)	when made contrary to the heavens, has no return.
È vita più sicura della ricca et illustre la povera et oscura. (Eumete, *Il ritorno,* I, xi)	The poor and obscure life is safer than the rich and illustrious.
Non vive eterna l'arroganza in terra; la superbia mortal tosto s'abbatte. (Ulysses, *Il ritorno,* II, x)	Arrogance does not live forever on earth; mortal pride is soon laid low.
Troppo egli è ver che gli huomini qui in terra servon di gioco agli immortali dei. (Penelope, *Il ritorno,* III, v)	It is too true that mortals here on earth serve as playthings of the immortal gods.
L'infamia sta gl'affronti in sopportarsi, e consiste l'honor nel vendicarsi. (Nutrice, *Poppea,* I, v)	Shame is forebearance at all affronts, and honor is found in getting even.
Chi nasce sfortunato di se stesso si dolga, e non d'altrui. (*Poppea,* I, xi)	He who's born unlucky should complain to himself and not to others.

The examples could easily be multiplied.

The problem such aphorisms posed for Monteverdi arose from their purely conceptual nature. Inevitably they involved no passion that might manifest itself in their rhetorical structure, allowing Monteverdi to strike up a syntactic congruence between text and music. (Their use in the lively stichomythia of Nero and Seneca in *Poppea,* I, ix was a happy exception that Monteverdi was quick to exploit.) At the most they might suggest some pictorial treatment—a playful melisma on Penelope's "gioco" or *concitato* fanfare motives for the Nutrice's "vendicarsi." They offered, in short, only meager opportunity for a meaningful connection to their setting. The music of most of them was left to fend for itself, a largely neutral conveyance of the text.

Closely related to the aphoristic inclinations of Badoaro and Busenello, and even more revealing of their Marinist orientation, is their love of imagery of all sorts.[12] Like Marino, they tend to objectify poetic utterance through reference to things in the real world. Their protagonists foresake the unmediated emotional ex-

---

12. This love is more emphatic in *Poppea* than in *Il ritorno*; Busenello more than Badoaro partook of the Marinist aesthetic of *acutezza.* (For this reason most of the examples below will be drawn from *Poppea.*) The difference hints at a basic di-chotomy of dramatic and poetic type between Monteverdi's last operas. And, though this is not the place to discuss it, we may at least note that the poetic drabness of *Il ritorno* is compensated by a richness of action onstage not found in *Poppea.*

pression of Orpheus and Ariadne and often seem unable to voice their feelings except by comparison to natural objects or objective concepts. Ottone returns to Poppea "qual linea al centro, / qual foco a sfera, e qual ruscello al mare" ("Like a radius to the center, / like fire to the heavens, and like a brook to the sea"; I, i). Once aware of her betrayal, he combines aphorism with objective imagery to denounce feminine treachery in a passage that Monteverdi, it seems, elected not to set:[13]

Ahi, chi ripon sua fede in un bel volto,	Ah, he who puts his faith in a pretty face
predestina se stesso a reo tormento,	preordains his fate of evil torment;
fabrica in aria, e sopra il vacuo fonda,	he builds on air, his cornerstone's a vacuum,
tenta palpare il vento,	he tries to catch the wind,
ed immobil afferma il fumo, e l'onda.	and thinks that smoke and waves are solid rock.

(I, xi)

Penelope's longing for Ulysses' homecoming inspires her not to "un giusto lamento" (as Monteverdi had once described Ariadne's plaint) but to a twenty-seven-verse enumeration of the things in nature that unfailingly return—eleven verses of which Monteverdi omitted from his setting (I, i). The poetic gesture is devoid of true sentiment and reminiscent of the empty, repetitive description that deadens Marino's own version of Ariadne's lament.[14] And Nero's love for Poppea takes on the permanence—and stolidity—of a Euclidean axiom: "Io non posso da te viver disgiunto / se non si smembra l'unità del punto" ("I could not live away from you / unless the unity of a point were divided"; I, iii).

Profound emotion, in fact, is nowhere much evident in Nero's passion. His is, rather, a quintessentially Marinist ardor, superficial, sensual, and luxuriating in the physical charms of its object. Two of the four scenes for the lovers (I, x and II, vii) are largely devoted to the rehearsal of these charms. No music has survived for the second of them, suggesting that Monteverdi found its amorous blandishments repetitive—as well he might, especially after the preceding scene, a lyric hymn to Poppea's beauties divided in the libretto among Nero, Lucan, Petronius, and Tigellinus. Monteverdi recognized this latter scene as lyric, not dramatic, poetry. He set it as a continuo madrigal, reducing the *dramatis personae* to two, Nero and Lucan, and exploiting the duet style first developed in Book VII, with its florid pictorialisms, walking basses, and arioso triple-meter passages (one of them, celebrating Poppea's mouth with languishing sweetness, organized over a repeating descending tetrachord). This was undoubtedly Monteverdi's last continuo duet, and

13. The words are set only in the Neapolitan manuscript of the score. I agree with Osthoff's conclusion, reached on stylistic grounds, that their music is not by Monteverdi; see "Die venezianische und neapolitanische Fassung," p. 106.

14. For a comparison of Marino's *Arianna,* published in his *Sampogna* of 1620, with Rinuccini's, see Tomlinson, "Music and the Claims of Text," pp. 577–79.

fittingly so. There could have been no more appropriate swan song for a genre he had often associated with the imagistic poetics of Marino.[15]

Other types of Marinist imagery are especially common in *Poppea,* rarer in *Il ritorno.* Simpler metaphor, of the sort that might be found in almost any libretto of the time, is frequent, as for example when Poppea calls Nero "l'incarnato mio sole, / la mia palpabil luce, / e l'amoroso dì della mia vita" ("my sun incarnate, / my light made palpable, / amorous daytime of my life"; I, iii) or in this similar exchange from *Il ritorno*:

Ulysses: Sospirato mio sole!	Ulysses: My sighed-for sun!
Penelope: Rinnovata mia luce!	Penelope: My restored light!
Ulysses: Porto quieto e riposo!	Ulysses: Calm port of repose!
(III, x)	

On other occasions Busenello attempted to avoid such commonplaces by delving far into the "recondite delights" of Marinist *meraviglia.* In a modest example, Ottone dressed as Drusilla is transformed into a serpent:

Eccomi trasformato	Here I am transformed
non di Ottone in Drusilla,	not from Ottone to Drusilla
ma d'huomo in serpe, il cui veneno, e rabbia	but from a man to a snake, whose rage and poison
non vide il mondo, e non vedrà simile.	has never before been seen, nor ever shall be.
(II, xiv)	

Octavia's tears over Nero's betrayal inspire a *translatio* that is even more farfetched and less emotionally gripping:

Il frequente cader de' pianti miei	The frequent falling of my tears
pur va quasi formando	is forming, almost,
un diluvio di specchi, in cui tu miri	a flood of mirrors in which you see
dentro alle tue delitie i miei martiri.	my torments reflected in your crimes.
(I, v)	

Most bizarre of all, perhaps, is Nero's passion-drunk wish, in one of his love scenes with Poppea, to be turned to air:

Deh, perché non son io	Ah, why am I not
sottile, e respirabile elemento,	a rarified and breathable element
per entrar, mia diletta,	entering, my delight,
in quella bocca amata;	in that beloved mouth;
ché passerei per uscio di rubino	so that I'd pass over a ruby threshhold
a baciar di nascosto un cor divino!	to kiss in secrecy a divine heart!
(II, vii)	

15. Monteverdi returned to this style once in *Il ritorno* as well, for the love duet of Melanto and Eurimaco in I, ii. The opening duple-meter section of this piece shows its ancestry in Book VII even more clearly than the duet for Nero and Lucan. It ends, like the later duet, with a section

An overdose of scholastic physiology seems to have narcotized the hallowed Neo-platonic notion of the eyes as gateway to the soul.

Monteverdi did his best to enliven the metaphors of Ottone and Octavia. He invested Octavia's phrasemaking with some emotion through cross-relations on "de' pianti miei"[16] and especially through the hesitant, dissonant repetition of "i miei" leading to the cadence on "martiri." His transmutation of Ottone's text is more radical. He rewrote its beginning to include a vacillation that vividly betrays Ottone's torment at the thought of murdering Poppea: "Eccomi trasformato d'Ottone in Drusilla . . . no! non d'Ottone in Drusilla, no, no, ma d'huom in serpe. . . ." It is no longer poetry, but it is effective psychological portrayal. In both cases Monteverdi evidently felt the need to alter and enrich the rhetorical profile of the poetry—a need entirely typical of his response to Busenello's and Badoaro's dramas, as we shall see. As for the third passage, Nero's oozy somatic image, it must surely have strengthened Monteverdi's resolve to skip the scene that contains it.

Sometimes Busenello combined metaphor with conceptual *acutezza,* as in Ottone's musings over the sleeping Poppea:

Passeran le tue luci	Will your eyes pass
dal dolce sonno, ch'è una finta imago,	from sweet sleep, which is but a reflection,
al vero originale della morte?	onto the true original of death?
E le palpebre tue, che fan cortina	And your eyelids, which make curtains
a due stelle giacenti in grembo al sonno,	to two reclining stars in the bosom of sleep,
saranno hor hora tenebrosi avelli	will they become now darkened tombstones
a' due soli gemelli?	for two twin suns?

(II, xiv)

Monteverdi's patience had never known saintly reaches; he cut these lines and three more before them from his setting. But he retained other, less metaphorical attempts at epigrammatic *acutezza,* as in Poppea's well-known lines from I, iii:

Signor, sempre mi vedi,	Signor, you always see me—
anzi mai non mi vedi.	and yet you never see me.
Perché s'è ver che nel tuo core io sia	For if it's true that I am in your heart,
entro al tuo sen celata,	concealed within your breast,
non posso da' tuoi lumi esser mirata.	I cannot then be looked at by your eyes.

These lines are famous not for their poetic qualities, of course (contrast their lame, repetitive cadence with the delicate touch of Guarini's epigrams!), but for the lively

---

over an ostinato. For a good discussion of Monteverdi's rhetorical sensitivity here see Osthoff, *Das dramatische Spätwerk,* p. 185.

16. The musical reading at these words in the Venetian manuscript of *Poppea* is corrupt and Malipiero's emendation incorrect (see Monteverdi, *Tutte le opere* 13:52). The correct reading, with Octavia singing g'–f♯'–g♯'–g♯' and the bass moving in half notes from d to e, is found in the Neapolitan manuscript of the opera (information supplied by Professor Ellen Rosand).

canzonetta setting Monteverdi gave them. The music, however, has little to do with the labored conceit or stilted rhetoric of the words; and text and music together have even less to do with the langorous, sensual characterization of Poppea throughout the rest of the scene.

Further examples of such images and conceits could be cited, and some adduced even from *Il ritorno*. But that would belabor the simple point I have tried to make: the poetic Marinism of *Poppea* and *Il ritorno* consists fundamentally in their authors' frequent recourse to adages, images, and conceits. All these are conceptual more than emotional modes of discourse, and their significance is rarely embodied in any distinctive way in rhetorical formulations that might interact with the syntax of Monteverdi's music. At most, they offered him the opportunity for Marinist pictorialism. At least, he was left to contrive affective passages of recitative for passionless texts or to construct song forms with little intrinsic affinity to their words.

Hand in hand with Badoaro's and especially Busenello's reliance on various sorts of objectifying imagery and conceptual discourse goes another pervasive trait of their dramas: a discursive and antilyric poetic cadence. This was an ever-present danger of the Marinist love of verbal virtuosity and reasoned *acutezza,* for in uninspired hands virtuosity tarnished to ungainliness, *acutezza* to fatuousness. (And it must be said in praise of Marino that he managed both aspects of his *meraviglia* with a panache, a *sprezzatura,* seldom matched by those who idolized him.) Busenello's shortcomings are obvious enough in the passages quoted above: the repetitiveness of lines 1–2 and 3–4 in "Signor, sempre mi vedi"; the misjudged grotesqueness of "uscio di rubino" in "Deh, perché non son io"; the stodgy explicitness of the connective "ch'è" and the unthinking metaphorical shift from "stelle" to "soli" in "Passeran le tue luci." But even where metaphorical imagery is not in question the rhetorical flatness of Busenello's and Badoaro's dramas remains—a prosaic discursiveness that might have been tolerable in spoken drama, given its speechlike speed of delivery, but that weighed heavily in a musical setting. This feature is evident even in the most emotional moments of the texts, for example those that inspired Monteverdi to revive the style of Ariadne's lament. Penelope, not satisfied with her long rehearsal of natural objects, also compares herself to Troy, in an almost unbroken series of *settenari* whose conceit is enervated by its clumsily explicit logic:

A ragion arse Troia,	Troy burned for good reason,
poiché l'amore impuro,	because illicit love,
ch'è un delitto di foco,	a crime of fiery passion,
si purga con le fiamme;	must be purged with flames;
ma ben contro ragion per l'altrui fallo,	but for another's fault, against all reason,
condannata innocente,	innocent but condemned,
dall'altrui colpe io sono	for others' crimes am I
l'afflitta penitente.	the tortured penance doer.

(Il ritorno, I, i)

In addition to constructing marvelous metaphors, Octavia analyzes the sorry state of all women:

O delle donne miserabil sesso:	Oh wretched sex of woman:
se la natura, e'l cielo	if nature and the heavens
libere ci produce,	create us free,
il matrimonio c'incatena serve.	marriage makes us servants.
Se concepimo l'huomo	If we conceive men,
al nostro empio tiran formiam le membra,	we form the limbs of our own wicked tyrants,
alattiamo il carnefice crudele,	we milk the cruel tormentor
che ci scarna, e ci svena,	who tears our flesh and veins,
e siam costrette per indegna sorte	and we're constrained by an unkind fate
a noi medesme fabbricar la morte.	to nurture and construct our own death.

(*Poppea*, I, v)

Contrast these excerpts, with their laborious rhythms, with passages from Ariadne's lament—with any of those discussed above in chapter 5, for example. Or contrast passages from Rinuccini's work with strikingly similar verses in *Poppea* that elicited from Monteverdi related musical settings:

Ariadne:	Ariadne:
Che parlo, ahi! che vaneggio?	What am I saying, ah! what ravings?
Misera, oimè! che chieggio?	Alas, wretch! what am I asking?
O Teseo, o Teseo mio,	Oh Theseus, oh my Theseus,
non son, non son quell'io,	it was not, was not I,
non son quell'io che i fèri detti sciolse:	it was not I who spoke such wicked words:
parlò l'affanno mio, parlò il dolore;	my woes spoke, and my anguish spoke;
parlò la lingua sì, ma non già'l core.	my tongue spoke, yes, but not indeed my heart.

(vv. 842–48)

Octavia:	Octavia:
Ahi! trapasso tropp'oltre, e me ne pento;	Ah! now I've gone too far, and I repent;
supprimo, e sepelisco	I suppress and I bury
in taciturne angoscie il mio tormento.	in my silent anguish all my torment.
O cielo, o ciel deh! l'ira tua s'estingua,	O heaven, oh heaven, ah! restrain your anger,
non provi i tuoi rigori il fallo mio;	don't bring your rigors down upon my error;
errò la superficie, il fondo è pio;	my outside was to blame, my inside's pious;
innocente fu il cor, peccò la lingua.	my heart was innocent, my tongue the sinner.

(I, v)

Ariadne:	Ariadne:
Dove, dove è la fede	Where, where is the faith
che tanto mi giuravi?	that you so often swore me?
Così ne l'alta sede	Thus you respect the throne
tu mi ripon de gli avi?	and honor of my forebears?
Son queste le corone,	Are these then the crowns
onde m'adorni il crine?	that you'd place on my head?
Questi gli scettri sono,	Are these the scepters,
questi le gemme e gli ori:	these the gems and riches:

lasciarmi in abbandono	to leave me abandoned
a fèra che mi strazi e mi divori?	to beasts that will rend and devour me?

(vv. 818–27)

Ottone:	Ottone:
Ahi! perfida Poppea,	Ah! wicked Poppea,
son queste le promesse, e i giuramenti,	are these the promises and the avowals
ch'accesero il cor mio?	that lit my heart with passion?
Questa è la fede, o dio!	This the faith, oh God?
Io son quel Ottone	I am that Ottone
che ti seguì,	who followed you,
che ti bramò,	who desired you,
che ti servì,	who served you,
che t'adorò,	who adored you,
e per piegarti e intenerirti il core	and who, to soften and to bend your heart,
di lagrime imperlò preghi devoti,	impearled with my tears my fervent prayers,
gli spirti a te sacrificando i voti.	pledging my soul to you through sacred vows.

(I, i)

Even here, where Busenello may have had Rinuccini's lament in mind as he wrote, the difference in rhetorical potency is apparent. Ariadne's rhetoric moves in time to her passions, Octavia's, Ottone's, and even Penelope's in time to their intellects.

As I noted above, Badoaro's drama tends to redeem its rhetorical lifelessness by a wealth of onstage action. Some of this inspired Monteverdi to a lively mimetic response, for example the *sinfonia da guerra* heard during Ulysses' fight with Iro and again at his shooting of the suitors (II, xii). But most of it—the petrification of the Phaeacians' ship, the appearance of Minerva's magic chariot, the earth's swallowing up of Ulysses, the eagle of Jove flying over the suitors, and so on—was undoubtedly achieved with stage machinery. All these actions are extrinsic to the poetic text itself and left no traces in the score.

There is much less stage incident in *Poppea* and hence little to divert our attention from its moribund oratory. In place of action Busenello seems intent on investing his drama with a frequent play of moral and political precepts and even of philosophical issues. The tendency is obvious enough in the various aphorisms and images discussed above, and in this form, indeed, appears as well in *Il ritorno*. But it extends beyond them, to exacerbate the discursive pace of *Poppea*. It is clearest, naturally, in the role of Seneca, whose every platitudinous line reflects Busenello's conception of ancient Stoicism. But it appears elsewhere as well—in the soldiers' frank critique of the emperor and his empire (I, ii), in Arnalta's lecture to Poppea on that favorite seventeenth-century political football, Machiavelli's *ragione di stato* (I, iv), in Octavia's moralizing response to the dissolute promptings of her nurse (I, v), and in Nero's point-for-point rebuttal of Seneca's doctrines (I, ix). Some of these are refreshing moments, particularly the soldiers' scene. But none of them except the stichomythia of Nero and Seneca offered substantial grounds for interaction with Monteverdi's musical language of emotion.

To this point we have been concerned with the most crucial of Busenello's and Badoaro's Marinist tendencies, their imagery and *concettismo*. There is, however, another side to their Marinism, one more congenial to Monteverdi's musical temperament in his last decades and certainly more advantageous in the composition of his final operas. This is a canzonetta-like formalism, evident in the authors' frequent organization of their characters' speeches in strophes and in their employment of the four-, five-, and eight-syllable lines associated with the canzonetta, either in conjunction with strophes or not. Both authors tend to reserve these devices for the speeches of gods, allegorical figures, and secondary mortal characters; in contrast, the roles of Nero, Octavia, Penelope, Ulysses, and Telemachus are written all but exclusively in nonstrophic *settenari* and *endecasillabi*.[17]

There are many examples of these canzonetta techniques in each libretto. In *Il ritorno,* Melanto opens I, ii with a two-strophe love song in *quinari* (both plain and truncated) and *endecasillabi*. Monteverdi set it as one of the very few strict strophic songs in either opera. Minerva's strophes of truncated octosyllabic lines in I, viii are set almost as strictly:

Cara e lieta gioventù,	Dear and happy youth,
che disprezza empio desir,	disdaining all wicked lust,
non da a lei noia o martir	what's coming and what has been
ciò che viene e ciò che fu.	give you no bother or sorrow.

In *Poppea,* Ottone's song in the opening scene, "Caro tetto amoroso," comprises four strophes of three seven- and eleven-syllable lines each. Monteverdi set the first strophe as recitative, probably to mark off this song from the one that opened the scene, and the remaining three in strophic variations with ritornello. Cupid's aria in II, xiii mixes *quinari* and *endecasillabi* in each of its four strophes:

O sciocchi, o frali	Oh foolish and frail
sensi mortali,	mortal senses,
mentre cadete in sonnacchioso oblio	when you fall into forgetful sleep
sul vostro sonno è vigilante dio.	a watchful god looks down upon your rest.

And virtually the whole of I, xi is given over to seven strophes of six lines each. The first six strophes are sung alternately by Ottone and Poppea; they share the seventh by alternating at first pairs of lines and then individual lines.

It may seem perverse to call these canzonetta devices Marinist, especially since we have traced their increasing prominence in Monteverdi's lyric works to the Anacreontic style of Chiabrera rather than to Marino. But in the first place, to invoke for a moment the shade of Artusi, "nomina sunt ad placitum." The name that

---

17. These canzonetta devices occur in the librettos of *L'Arianna* and *Orfeo* also, of course. In Rinuccini's work, however, they are restricted entirely to the prologue and the choruses. In Striggio's they appear more often but usually in choruses or the texts of stage songs.

we apply to these traits of Monteverdi's last librettos is not so important as the realization, already discussed in chapters 6–8, that Chiabreresque formalism and Marinist imagism are two sides of the same aesthetic coin. Second, there is in fact reason to believe that both Badoaro and Busenello looked to Marino, not to Chiabrera, for the authority to employ canzonetta techniques in their dramatic dialogue.

Specifically, they looked to *La sampogna,* Marino's collection of eclogues published in Paris in 1620 (and in Venice a year later). The collection is divided into pastoral and mythological "idylls," and some of the latter, the *idillii favolosi* recounting the stories of Orpheus, Ariadne, Europa, Daphne, and Syrinx, display a perfect confluence of Chiabrerism and Marinism. They combine seven- and eleven-syllable verse with canzonetta meters, strophic forms with free madrigalian organization, and, as we would expect of eclogues, narrative and dramatic modes—all in the service of sparkling Marinist imagery. Taken out of context, some of the strophic passages in them would be indistinguishable from Chiabrera's canzonette:

Ferma il passo o Verginella,	Stop, oh lovely little maiden,
Dafni bella,	pretty Daphne,
perché fuggi il fido amante?	why do you flee your true lover?
Ah, fia ver che non ti pieghi	Can it be that you're unbending
a' miei preghi?	to my pleas?
Ferma, oimè, ferma le piante![18]	Stop, alas, please stop your flight!

(Eleven more strophes follow.)

There is no doubt that Busenello knew *La sampogna.* If his admiration for Marino were not evidence enough of the fact, we might adduce his own *Lamento d'Arianna,* which shows a knowledge of Marino's version as well as Rinuccini's. (This was one of a series of mythological and historical laments by Busenello that, from Arthur Livingston's description of them, seem to follow the style and techniques of Marino's idylls.)[19] And we might note as well that one of Busenello's epistles on *La Statira* refers to a letter of Claudio Achillini in praise of Marino, a letter first published in the Venetian edition of *La sampogna.*[20] As for Badoaro, the strophes of his suitors on the need of various plants for love in order to thrive (II, v) acknowledge his debt to *La sampogna* quite frankly. They evoke similar botanical glossaries, also in strophic form, in two of Marino's idylls, *Orfeo* and *Europa,* even to the point of borrowing a verse from one of them.[21]

18. From *Dafni. Idillio VI,* in *La sampogna del Cavalier Marino,* pp. 165–67.
19. *La vita veneziana,* pp. 161–66. For a modern edition of Busenello's *Lamento d'Arianna* see Degrada, "Gian Francesco Busenello," pp. 99–102.

20. It appears on pp. 14–15 of the edition of 1621.
21. See *La sampogna,* pp. 28–31, 99–103. The fourth strophe of Orpheus's song begins, like Pisandro's stanza in *Il ritorno,* "La pampinosa vite."

The canzonetta-like passages of *Il ritorno* and *Poppea,* then, are Marinist in the narrow sense of imitating Marino's poetry, while in general they exploit the metric devices made famous in Chiabrera's lyrics. They point up once more the close relation in poetry of Marinism and Chiabreresque formalism. And they underscore the similarity of the impulses behind schematic structures and pictorial and mimetic imagery in Monteverdi's late works. It is no accident that the musical dialects of his *scherzi, arie,* and canzonette play a large and important role in *Poppea* and *Il ritorno.*[22] They are one aspect of his own retreat from the introspection of the Petrarchan tradition. Of course it would be a mistake to expect such introspection from light-hearted genres like the canzonetta; it was never demanded of them. But Monteverdi's retreat was apparent from the moment the architectonic forms of these genres, with the narrow limits they usually set on the interaction of text and music, infiltrated his madrigal books. And in the canzonetta-like language and forms of much of *Il ritorno* and *Poppea,* just as in their Marinist musico-poetic imagery, the retreat extended to opera.

Monteverdi rarely evaded the formalism of Badoaro's and Busenello's texts.[23] He usually embraced it eagerly, matching their strophes with a rich profusion of formal solutions, mainly modified strophic *arie* and canzonette, often with articulating ritornelli. Indeed Monteverdi frequently contrived not merely to respect the poetic structure in his music but also to enrich and diversify it. He set Cupid's four strophes in *Poppea,* II, xiii not as simple strophic variations but as a concatenation of two modified strophic forms, in the symmetrical scheme A rit. B rit. B' rit. A'. The scene made up of alternating strophes for Ottone and Poppea (I, xi) inspired strophic variations over a bassline that, in addition to being varied at each repetition, occurs in two recognizable and distinct forms, one for each character. Here Monteverdi also distinguished the protagonists tonally: Ottone's strophes are in A minor, Poppea's in C minor (the first two) and D minor (the third). For the final, shared strophe he turned to recitative.[24]

22. Osthoff in particular has emphasized this role; see *Das dramatische Spätwerk,* esp. chaps. B.II, C.II.

23. A rare exception occurs in *Il ritorno,* II, v, where the parallel poetic stanzas of the three suitors are set in contrasting musical styles to differentiate their characters.

24. The ritornelli before Ottone's strophes, unlike those preceding Poppea's, do not agree in tonality with the strophes that follow. Instead they are notated in G minor, with indications in the Venetian manuscript that they should be played "un tono più alto." An identical situation occurs—again in Ottone's part—in I, i; these ritornelli too should be transposed, from C to D, although in this case they bear no instructions to that effect. Wolfgang Osthoff, in "Trombe sordine," has labored to relate these apparent tonal discrepancies to the use of muted trumpets—which would have sounded a step higher than written—in the ritornelli. It seems more likely, however, that they arose from complexities of manuscript transmission that we cannot fully reconstruct. A greater knowledge of these complexities, by the way, might suggest also that all of Poppea's strophes, not only her third, were originally in D minor. A tonal polarity of a fourth (A minor to D minor) is much more in keeping with Monteverdi's late harmonic style than one of a third (A minor to C minor).

More ingenious still is Monteverdi's treatment of I, iv for Poppea and Arnalta, for here his structure involved a basic reorganization of the text.[25] He used his jubilant settings of the last two lines of Poppea's opening song, either separately or together, as a dual refrain throughout the scene, a refrain not found in the libretto: "No, no, non temo, no, di noia alcuna, / per me guerreggia amore e la fortuna" ("No, no, I do not fear any harm, / Love and Fortune fight on my side"). This allowed him to disrupt the irksome regularity of Arnalta's later strophic recitative ("La pratica coi regi è perigliosa") with Poppea's energetic interjections. It also varied and deepened his characterization of Poppea, highlighting a willfulness in her refusal to heed Arnalta's warnings that was less emphatic in Busenello's text. In both *Il ritorno* and *Poppea* Monteverdi frequently introduced such musico-poetic refrains, or extended refrains already present in the text, in order to lend organizational clarity and interest to prolix and discursive poetic passages like Arnalta's.[26] In *Il ritorno,* I, ix he even seized on textual refrains as the basis for a strophic song for Ulysses, despite the fact that the text shows no strophic structure.

Monteverdi's late music is, sometimes above all else, an art of crystalline formal logic. Nowhere is this more apparent than in the last operas. In the case of *Poppea* in particular we might even speak, in Marinist terms, of the structural *acutezza* of his setting. At any rate, the relationship of its ingenious formalism to the outward-turned expressive ideals of seventeenth-century poetry is clear.

But *Poppea* and *Il ritorno* are ambivalent works, as I have suggested. In spite of their conspicuous Marinist formalism and objective imagery in text and music alike, it is the rhetoric of Petrarchism, finally, that remains their expressive essence. To convey the emotional high points of both operas, Monteverdi returned again and again to the affective recitative of Orpheus, of "Se pur destina" of Book VII, and especially of Ariadne. In *Il ritorno* this humanist musical rhetoric steps to center stage in Ulysses' opening monologue (I, vii), in Telemachus's horrified response to the disappearance of the old man who, unknown to him, is his father (II, iii), and of course in the entire role of Penelope. In *Poppea* it claims our attention in lengthy sections of Octavia's soliloquies (I, v and III, vi) and in Ottone's poignant reaction to Poppea's betrayal (I, i). And, in a new guise, voicing passions that Monteverdi had never before uttered with such disarming insight, it seduces us in the sensuality and repels us in the wanton ambition of Poppea. Here, we might say, the magnifying glass of Petrarchan rhetoric was turned on Marinist sentiment.

There can be no doubt that Monteverdi cherished these opportunities for *Arianna*-like rhetoric. His musical responses reveal the fact clearly enough. And *L'Arianna* must have been fresh in his mind, for it was revived in Venice in 1640—

---

25. As already noted by Hugo Goldschmidt, *Studien zur Geschichte der italienischen Oper im 17. Jahrhundert* 2:16.

26. Some other scenes in which he did so are *Poppea,* II, iii, ix, xii and III, i and *Il ritorno,* I, ii and II, v.

an unprecedented exhumation of a thirty-two-year-old opera—and its lament published in a sacred *travestimento* in the *Selva morale e spirituale* of the same year. Indeed we may even guess that the successful revival of *L'Arianna* played an important role in luring Monteverdi back to the composition of music drama. In the decade before it, after *Proserpina rapita* of 1630, he seems not to have written any operas, even though he advised younger composers on their operatic productions.[27] But immediately after it he composed three operas in two years. The unknown librettist of *Le nozze d'Enea con Lavinia,* the same writer whose description of Monteverdi's marvelous shifts of emotion was quoted above, could in another breath underscore Monteverdi's *Arianna*-like rhetorical goals: "I have avoided farfetched thoughts and conceits [*li pensieri et concetti tolti da lontano*], and devoted myself more to the affections, as Sig. Monteverde desires; to please him I have also altered and omitted many of the things at first present [in the drama]."[28]

Monteverdi, we have noted, seems to have worked closely with Badoaro on *Il ritorno*; this may explain the relative dearth of Marinist imagery there in comparison with *Poppea.* But if Busenello's love of conceits and images hindered authentic emotional expression, Badoaro's partial avoidance of them did not automatically insure it. Neither poet was capable of providing Monteverdi with the passionate rhetoric he needed. Their librettos failed him most grievously at just those moments demanding the most intimate merging of musical and poetic syntax. I have discussed elsewhere Monteverdi's musical enlivening of the pedestrian poetic refrains of Penelope's lament (I, i), the most explicit recreation of Ariadne's plaint among his late works.[29] Such musical overhaul of the poetic syntax occurs also at other points in *Il ritorno,* for example the beginning of the lament, where Monteverdi rendered Badoaro's lame opening—"Di misera regina / non terminati mai dolenti affanni: / l'aspettato non giunge" ("Sad and never-ending woes / of a wretched queen: / the awaited man does not arrive")—in the manner of Ariadne at her most grief-stricken (Ex. 73). Through its halting cadence and stammering repetitions Monteverdi's recitative takes on a dejection barely broached in the verse alone. (Penelope's repeated, misery-laden 7–6 suspensions, by the way, are one of the few new devices that Monteverdi has added to Ariadne's rhetorical lexicon. They occur also in Ottone's and Octavia's recitative.)[30]

27. See Ellen Rosand, "Barbara Strozzi, *virtuosissima cantatrice,*" p. 251n.

28. From the "Argomento e scenario" of *Le nozze*; quoted from Vogel, "Claudio Monteverdi," p. 403n.

29. "Madrigal, Monody, and Monteverdi," pp. 97–98.

30. In Penelope's lament Monteverdi worked the device into the sort of cohesive, almost subliminal musical refrain he had employed in Ariadne's lament. See in addition to the example given here the settings of "il tempo è zoppo," "non promettete più," and "l'afflitta penitente," and the lengthy descent to a cadence beginning at "e'ntanto lasci / la tua casta consorte." Octavia uses the device, like Penelope, both for its expressive force and to lend coherence to her long soliloquy "Disprezzata regina" (I, v). It occurs there at "afflitta moglie," "i miei martiri," and "in taciturne angoscie il mio tormento." In Ottone's first scene (I, i) it appears at "il passo e'l cor ad inchinarti viene."

EXAMPLE 73

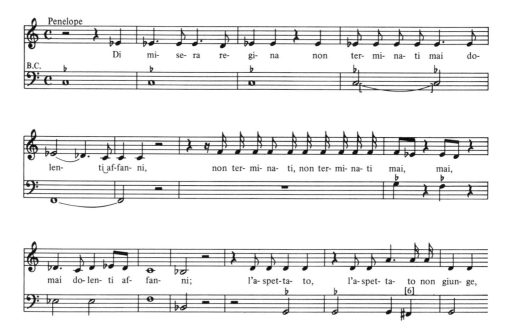

Monteverdi, *Il ritorno d'Ulisse in patria,* I, i, excerpt
(*Tutte le opere,* ed. Malipiero, 12:14)

A similar transmutation of moribund poetic syntax takes place at the beginning of Ulysses' soliloquy, where Monteverdi conveyed his protagonist's gradually returning consciousness by transforming Badoaro's undistinguished opening lines—

Dormo ancora, o son desto?	Am I still asleep, or awake?
Che contrade rimiro?	What fields do I see?
Qual aria vi respiro?	What air do I breathe?
E che terren calpesto?	And what ground do I tread?

—into a passage of affective prose: "Dormo ancora? Dormo ancora? O son desto? Che contrade rimiro? Qual aria vi respiro? E che terren calpesto? Dormo ancora? Dormo ancora, dormo ancora? O son desto?" Monteverdi injected into Badoaro's poetry some of the rhetorical vitality built into *L'Arianna,* but only by utterly effacing its poetic profile. And note that he instinctively emphasized Ulysses' concern with his own state, repeating over and over the clauses of the first verse, and downplayed the external sources of Ulysses' bafflement—the fields, air, and earth.

Further examples of Monteverdi's transformation of the poetry occur throughout the score of *Poppea,* despite the somewhat greater rhetorical efficacy of Busenello's text.[31] In I, ix the poet provided Monteverdi with ready-made rhetoric: a passage of stichomythia for Nero and Seneca whose rising emotion was captured in the quickening alternation of the two characters, from four lines each, to two, to one.[32] But, mystifyingly, at the height of the exchange, just before Nero voices his menacing anger ("Tu mu sforzi allo sdegno . . ."), Busenello retreated to two-line alternations:

Nero:	Nero:
La forza è legge in pace, e spada in guerra,	Force is in peace the law, in war a sword;
e bisogno non ha della ragione.	it has no need of reason.
Seneca:	Seneca:
La forza accende gli odi, e turba il sangue,	Force fans the fires of hate, and churns the blood;
la ragion regge gli huomini e gli dei.	reason rules men and gods.

It is as if the poet were entirely oblivious to the emotional effect of his rhetorical structure up to this point. But Monteverdi was not so blind. He carefully intensified the anger of the dialogue by quickening, not slowing, the rate of alternation and by adopting the quick text repetitions of the *concitato* style:

Nero:	La forza, la forza, la forza, la forza è legge in pace . . .
Seneca:	La forza, la forza accende gli odi . . .
Nero:	. . . e spada, e spada in guerra, . . .
Seneca:	. . . e turba il sangue, e turba il sangue, . . .
Nero:	. . . e bisogno non ha della ragione.
Seneca:	. . . la ragione, la ragione regge gli huomini e gli dei.
Nero:	Tu, tu, tu mi sforzi allo sdegno, mi sforzi allo sdegno, allo sdegno, allo sdegno. . . .

The justly famous first love scene of Nero and Poppea (I, iii) provides numerous examples of the fundamental changes in dramatic effect Monteverdi achieved by recasting his text. First of all Monteverdi brought the characters into a generally more vivid interaction by transposing verses from their places in the libretto to new positions.[33] Busenello had laid out all but the last six lines of this scene in blocks: fourteen verses for Poppea, ten for Nero, nine for Poppea, and twelve for Nero. Monteverdi dissolved these blocks into fluid dramatic intercourse by shifting Nero's first line ("Poppea, lascia ch'io parta"—"Poppea, let me go") into the midst of Poppea's first speech, by moving the melting refrain "Deh non dir / di partir . . ." ("Ah, don't speak / of leaving . . .") from her second speech into the middle of his

31. I have discussed one, at the beginning of Octavia's "Disprezzata regina," in "Madrigal, Monody, and Monteverdi," pp. 98–99. For others, and for a valuable discussion of expressive gesture in *Poppea* starting from premises somewhat different from mine, see Ellen Rosand, "Monteverdi's Mimetic Art."

32. Kurt von Fischer, "Eine wenig beachtete Quelle zu Busenellos *L'incoronazione di Poppea*," has noted the derivation of this scene from the pseudo-Senecan tragedy *Octavia*.

33. Monteverdi used this technique frequently in *Poppea*. Some other instances occur in I, i–ii, v, vi, II, ix, xi, and III, iii–iv.

second, and by allowing her to interject repeatedly the question "Tornerai?" ("Will you return?") into his second speech. This last touch is an especially eloquent one. It exploits the beginning of Busenello's cut-and-dry exchange near the end of the scene—

Poppea:	Tornerai?			Poppea:	Will you return?	
Nero:		Tornerò.		Nero:		I'll return.
Poppea:			Quando?	Poppea:		When?
Nero:			Ben tosto.	Nero:		Soon.

—in order to create a clinging, teasing refrain for Poppea (Ex. 74). In Monteverdi's usage Poppea's one word speaks volumes. It fills in the picture of sultry sensuality already sketched in the chromaticism of Poppea's refrain "Deh non dir / di partir. . . ." Nero, we immediately feel, could hardly *not* return for more. At the same time, it betrays Poppea's awareness of the vulnerability of her position, of her utter dependence on Nero's continuing benevolence—a benevolence that, in history if not in the opera, turned out to be short-lived.[34]

Meanwhile Monteverdi did not neglect in this scene the other side of Poppea's character—her untamed, clawing ambition. Busenello had ignored it, saving it for Poppea's following scene with Arnalta, so here Monteverdi was completely on his own. His solution was simple and brilliant. He took Nero's prosaic explanation of his departure—

La nobiltà de' nascimenti tuoi	The nobility of your birth
non permette che Roma	does not allow Rome
sappia che siamo uniti,	to find out we're united
in sin che Ottavia non rimane esclusa	until Octavia has been cast out
col repudio da me	with my repudiation

—and built into it, at the first hint of Octavia's repudiation, an excited parroting of his words by Poppea (Ex. 75). The idea was such a good one that Monteverdi re-used it in a later scene for Poppea and Nero (III, v, at Nero's "in parola regal te n'assicuro"). Both gestures effectively betray the uncontrollability of Poppea's grandiose ambitions. Monteverdi's Poppea thinks less and feels more than Busenello's. She is less a scheming temptress and more an alluring marionette controlled by her own irrepressible sexual and political desires. Indeed it is not too whimsical to perceive in her Monteverdi's final embodiment of the humanist view of the passions as inexplicable, irrational forces in large part determining our thoughts and actions.

There is nothing quite like the rapid, supple exchanges of Example 75 in *Orfeo*, nor could there have been anything similar in *L'Arianna*, given the madrigalian

---

34. Pirrotta, "Scelte poetiche," p. 254, suggests that Poppea's ultimate, untimely end was a hidden moral of the opera, not lost on the first audiences.

EXAMPLE 74

Monteverdi, *L'incoronazione di Poppea,* I, iii, excerpt

pacing of its dialogue.[35] This fact points up a distinction between the humanist rhetoric of Monteverdi's first operas and that of his last. The recitative of *Orfeo* and *L'Arianna* aimed to display the protagonists' emotions in more or less lengthy soliloquies, delivered not so much to the other characters as to the audience. It aspired, in short, to capture in musical speech something like the sustained persuasive force of Ciceronian oratory. Thus, though its literary mode was dramatic, it retained an important element of lyricism as well. In this it manifested its close relation to Monteverdi's earlier lyric works with dramatic overtones, especially the *Gerusalemme liberata* and *Pastor fido* madrigals of Books III and V.

Such musical oratory, to be sure, still played a central role in *Il ritorno* and *Poppea,* particularly in the figures of Penelope, Ulysses, Telemachus, Ottone, and Octavia. But alongside it Monteverdi now deployed a new means of projecting his characters' feelings: a dialogue that mimes the pace of real conversation, whether of weary soldiers grousing about their duties or of lovers separating at break of day.

---

35. Nothing, that is, except this famous and moving exchange from Act II of *Orfeo:*

Daphne: La tua bella Euridice . . .

Orpheus: Oimè, che odo?
Daphne: La tua diletta sposa è morta.
Orpheus: Oimè!

EXAMPLE 75

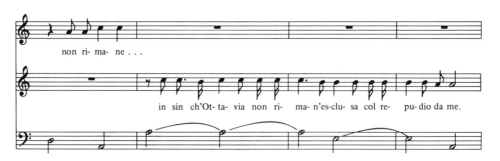

Monteverdi, *L'incoronazione di Poppea,* I, iii, excerpt

This new sort of dialogue allowed the characters to interact more meaningfully than in Monteverdi's earlier operas, to reveal their emotions in dramatic discourse with one another rather than in semilyric oration addressed to the audience. What element of realism remains amid the stylized dramatic languages of *Poppea* and *Il ritorno* resides mainly in this achievement of a true-to-life dialogue style. And the style could not have been developed without the increasingly sensitive musical mimesis of gesture and speech that Monteverdi practiced from the time of Book VII on. Poppea's exchanges with Nero built on the foundations of "Eccomi pronta ai baci" and numerous madrigals, *arie,* and canzonette in between. In this way, at least, Monteverdi managed to enrich the oratorical Petrarchism of his youth with lessons learned from Marinism.

But for the most part Monteverdi's attempt to synthesize Marinist and Petrarchan modes was not so successful. In the last operas it spawned hybrids, beautiful in individual features, powerful in many gestures by virtue of the undiminished vigor of their creator, impressive in their variety and scope, but nevertheless ungainly in their juxtaposition of contrasting traits. The expressive ideals of latter-day humanism and of the new seventeenth-century world were, simply, opposed at too many points. Badoaro and Busenello, for their parts, rode the bandwagon of the new order; they could help little in the attempt at synthesis. Monteverdi, unlike them, understood both old and new. And he delighted in the richness of structure and image he discovered in the new while he clung to the conviction that the old disclosed the essence of music drama. But even Monteverdi, unrivaled creator of new musical worlds, could not merge two worlds into one.

THE END
OF THE
RENAISSANCE

10

Monteverdi
and Italian Culture,
1550–1700

Italia, i tuoi sì generosi spirti
con dolce inganno Ozio, e Lascivia han spenti;
e non t'avvedi, misera, e non senti
che i Lauri tuoi degeneraro in Mirti?

Fulvio Testi

Italy, your most noble souls are killed
by sweet deceit of Lasciviousness and Sloth;
and are you not aware, wretch, can't you feel
that all your Laurels have devolved to Myrtles?

 HE STORY of Monteverdi's career told in the preceding chapters is mainly one of shifting poetic styles, genres, and expressive aims and of the changing musical means the composer employed to reflect them. But the story remains incomplete. For the changes in Monteverdi's compositional goals, and the differing poetic styles that helped to stimulate them, mirror basic ideological shifts in Italy at the end of the Renaissance. Their full significance must be sought in their relation to these broader cultural tendencies. To do this we must first turn away from Monteverdi himself to a synoptic view of Italian culture around 1600.

To an informed and thoughtful Italian aristocrat coming of age in the 1580s the future must have seemed bright with promise. The political and religious upheavals of his grandfather's time—the French invasion of 1494, the Lutheran challenge starting in 1517, the calamitous sack of Rome in 1527, the fall of the last Florentine republic in 1530—had receded to the distant past. They were pushed out of his mind by reassuring events of more recent years. The treaty of Cateau-Cambrésis of 1559, if it had assured Spanish domination of Italy, had also granted the peninsula a tranquillity unknown in the decades before it. The political future of various northern Italian states, precarious at midcentury, now seemed secured by the solidification of their internal bureaucracies and their careful diplomatic juggling of the French and imperial superpowers. This security was embodied in an unprecedented ostentation of courtly pomp and ritual and institutionalized in intellectual life by the rapid proliferation of aristocratic literary academies.[1]

---

1. For a synoptic view of the late-sixteenth-century Italian revival discussed here see Eric Cochrane's introduction to *The Late Italian Renaissance, 1525–1630*, esp. pp. 12–18.

The pope had begun to reassert his authority through the edicts of the Council of Trent. And as his new ideological army, the Society of Jesus, battled the tide of heresy north of the Alps, his attention seems to have been diverted somewhat from the control of thought in the south. There were, at least, signs of a mitigation of church policy. The Index adopted by Paul IV in 1559 was moderated slightly in its Tridentine version, issued five years later. And the Congregation of the Index, formed in 1571, at first devoted itself only to creating acceptable expurgated versions of previously prohibited works.[2] In all, Italy seemed to have entered an era of peace, security, and relative ideological liberalism.

And prosperity: all these developments were supported by a resurgent economy.[3] The political consolidation of northern Italy after the peace of 1559 had allowed the resumption of textile and other industries interrupted in the preceding years. Venice, through its defeat of the Turks at Lepanto in 1571 and fortuitous disruptions of new Portuguese trade routes in the Atlantic, regained temporarily an important share of the European spice trade. A Europe-wide economic recovery, driven by precious metals mined in central Europe (where new technology led to increased yields) and plundered in the New World, created an expanded market for these goods. The resulting commerce allowed urbanized northern Italy to supplement its own insufficient agricultural production with southern-Italian, Turkish, and northern-European grains.[4]

This so-called Indian Summer of Renaissance economy and the political stability with which it was reciprocally linked probably encouraged the general broadening of intellectual and artistic horizons that characterizes Italian culture of the late sixteenth century. A new freedom of inquiry and expression that tended to reflect humanist rather than scholastic values appeared, associated especially with the autonomous states of northern Italy. Indeed it is no exaggeration to speak of a humanist revival at the end of the *cinquecento*—a modest one, to be sure, that played itself out at court and largely in the aristocratic echelons of Italian society, but a revival nonetheless.

Thus in Florence, for example, a new generation of young noblemen and artists grew disenchanted with the increasingly hidebound Aristotelianism and empty theorizing of the academies controlled by its elders. Artists and thinkers as diverse as Ottavio Rinuccini, Jacopo Peri, Galileo, and the painter Lodovico Cardi da Cigoli turned from abstract theory to practical investigation to produce new genres, expressive means, and technologies. They asserted, that is, the bonds of theory and

2. Luigi Firpo, "Filosofia italiana e controriforma," p. 151. On the Pauline and Tridentine Indices see Andrea Sorrentino, *La letteratura italiana e il Sant'Ufficio*, pp. 35–42, and Paul F. Grendler, *The Roman Inquisition and the Venetian Press, 1540–1605*, pp. 115–27, 145–48.

3. For the following see in general Harry A. Miskimin, *The Economy of Later Renaissance Europe, 1460–1600*.

4. Fernand Braudel, *The Mediterranean and the Mediterranean World in the Age of Philip II* 1:594–95.

practice, thought and expression, mathematics and reality, manifesting in the process a humanist engagement with the world around them. Meanwhile the academies they had forsaken, the Alterati, the Cruscans, the Accademia del Disegno, even the hallowed Accademia Fiorentina, languished through the 1590s.[5]

William Bouwsma has discerned a similar generational shift of ideology and values in republican Venice, one that seems to accord with the notion of a late-sixteenth-century humanist revival. There a group of young patricians known simply as the *giovani* gained control of the Great Council in the early 1580s. They opposed the conservative policies of their elders and aggressively sought to reestablish the eminence of Venice in political and economic affairs. Their views and actions reflected ideas central to the Renaissance vision: the abandonment of political passivity and intellectual isolation for the *vita activa*; a rebellion against the principle of universal authority, and the recognition of some independence of moral and political action from religious belief; a view of worldly life as a process of flexible adaptation to unpredictable circumstance; and a pragmatic and realistic assessment of history. These conceptions soon brought Venice into conflict with the Counter-Reformation church, into a struggle of world-views that culminated in the Interdict of 1606–7. They were given voice in the last great work of Renaissance historiography, Paolo Sarpi's *Istoria del Concilio Tridentino* of 1619.[6]

We can trace this humanist revival in individual arts and disciplines as well as specific locales. In painting, for example, the forthright emotionalism of Cigoli's depictions of St. Francis and his *Ecce homo* was only one facet of a rejection throughout northern Italy of Tuscan academism. The new "antimannerist" styles, foreshadowed by painters like Santi di Tito in Florence and Bartolommeo Passarotti in Bologna and realized fully by Cigoli and Annibale and Ludovivo Carracci, aimed in general at a new naturalism of form and expression. They substituted a verisimilar rhetoric of passion for the stylized gestures and arcane compositional programs of Bronzino, Vasari, and their followers. And in doing so they prepared the way for the revolutionary realism of Michelangelo da Caravaggio.[7]

The humanist revival was felt in literature as well. We have seen that Guarini's

5. I discuss this Florentine revival in greater detail in "Rinuccini, Peri, Monteverdi," chap. 6. Samuel Berner perceives a continuing vitality of Florentine commerce and society in general through the sixteenth century and into the seventeenth, in "Florentine Society in the Late Sixteenth and Early Seventeenth Centuries" and "The Florentine Patriciate in the Transition from Republic to *Principato*, 1530–1609." Eric Cochrane also sees modest signs of revival in "The End of the Renaissance in Florence" and in his dazzling *Florence in the Forgotten Centuries*, bk. 2 passim.

6. Bouwsma, *Venice and Republican Liberty*, chaps. 4, 5 and passim.

7. See especially Walter Friedlaender's classic *Mannerism and Anti-Mannerism in Italian Painting* and S. J. Freedberg, *Circa 1600*. Freedberg's book is marred by his tendency to conceive of rhetoric, in limited and exclusively pejorative terms, as the stylistic tropes of the mid-sixteenth-century mannerists. For a good corrective see Charles Dempsey's review of *Circa 1600* in *The New Criterion*.

Pastor fido challenged restrictive Aristotelian definitions of genre with the humanist claims of historical relativism and effective expression. And, in the debates over epic poetry and romance that grew especially heated in the 1580s, similar ideas were invoked by each side to defend both Ariosto's *Orlando furioso* and its newly published rival, Tasso's *Gerusalemme liberata*.[8] In literary theory in general the precepts of Aristotle's *Poetics,* disseminated in the 1540s, 1550s, and 1560s, were extended and loosened in their application to new genres, as for example in Giovanni Battista Strozzi's lecture on the madrigal of 1574.[9] Or they were occasionally rejected altogether, as in the theoretical writings of the iconoclastic Platonist Francesco Patrizi and the pragmatic Lodovico Castelvetro. Castelvetro's *Poetica d'Aristotele vulgarizzata et sposta* of 1570 advanced an earthy poetics in which poetry aimed only "to delight and give recreation to the minds of the rough crowd and of the common people." For Castelvetro pleasure alone was the end of poetry, not Horace's *utile dulci* or Aristotle's purgation.[10]

Other literary theorists of the last third of the century gave "increasing prominence to political implications and a lesser role to ethical instruction."[11] In this they mirrored contemporary developments in historiographic theory, where a full-scale reaction had set in to the Ciceronian notion of history as providing eloquent, elegant examples of past moral virtue. Machiavelli's *virtù,* historical theorists now realized, had been of a different sort than Cicero's—pragmatic, politically savvy, and independent from ethics. Among ancient histories something like it could be found in the *Annales* of Tacitus. Francesco Patrizi, Tommaso Campanella, and other writers called for an empirical history of practical utility in the governing of states. We saw the humanist implications of such a historiography in chapter 1.[12]

Natural philosophy also reflected the general expansion of intellectual horizons of the period. The narrow Aristotelianism of midcentury gave way to novel vistas often of bold Platonic hue, portrayed by Bernardino Telesio, Giordano Bruno, Campanella, Patrizi, and others. (In 1578 Duke Alfonso II d'Este recognized Patrizi's work by instituting at Ferrara one of the first university chairs in Platonic philosophy.) These metaphysical conceptions, inevitably allied to scholastic thought in their systematic aims and universal scope, nonetheless manifest the renewed humanist latitudinarianism of the late *cinquecento*. They helped to pave the way for Galileo's rejection of Aristotelian natural philosophy after 1600.[13]

8. See Weinberg, *A History of Literary Criticism,* chaps. 19, 20, and Peter M. Brown, *Lionardo Salviati,* chap. 14.

9. Published in *Orazioni et altre prose del signor Giovambatista di Lorenzo Strozzi,* pp. 159–88.

10. See Weinberg, *A History of Literary Criticism,* pp. 502–11; the quotation (in Weinberg's translation) comes from p. 504. See also Pietro Mazzamuto, "Lodovico Castelvetro." On Patrizi's anti-Aristotelian theories see Weinberg, pp. 600–602, 765–86, 997–1000.

11. Weinberg, *A History of Literary Criticism,* p. 346.

12. On historiography in this period see Giorgio Spini, "I trattatisti dell'arte storica nella controriforma italiana," and also Eric Cochrane, *Historians and Historiography in the Italian Renaissance.*

13. The literature on the subject is extensive. See

Our hypothetical aristocrat of the 1580s, then, might with good cause have derived satisfaction from the present and looked with optimism to the future. Political security, economic prosperity, and intellectual and artistic vitality seemed to him assured in the revivified states of northern Italy. But his optimism was ill founded. The tendencies toward social and cultural revival he saw around him were to prove short-lived, snuffed out by stronger forces gathering throughout the second half of the sixteenth century. These began to reveal themselves, ominously, at the height of the humanist revival, around 1590. By the middle third of the seventeenth century their deadening effect was felt throughout Italian culture, and the Indian Summer of the Renaissance had ended.

The signs of the new decline were first of all economic. Italy's recovery in the late sixteenth century was deceptive since it was relatively sluggish compared to quicker expansions in northern Europe. The main northern-Italian industries, wool and silk production, faced ever-stiffer competition from England, the Netherlands, and France. These new producers undercut Italian prices, already inflated by relatively high taxes and salaries and antiquated guild regulations restricting innovation. At the same time Italy's "invisible exports," its banking and shipping operations, also lost ground to northern newcomers, especially as the importance of Atlantic trade routes increased. Since the late Middle Ages the Italian economy had depended on its foreign markets; now these were either shrinking (first in Spain and later, during the Thirty Years' War, in Germany and Flanders) or turning to lower-priced competition. Italy's recovery after 1550 never restored it to the trans-European commercial preeminence it had enjoyed in previous centuries.[14]

This weakened commercial and industrial structure was dealt a critical blow by a series of poor harvests throughout Italy starting in 1586 and lasting into the next decade. In the compelling scenario of the economic historian Ruggiero Romano, these agricultural failures set in motion a downward economic spiral that led inexorably to the depression of 1619–22.[15] By the beginning of the seventeenth century,

especially Paul Oskar Kristeller, *Eight Philosophers of the Italian Renaissance,* chaps. 6–8; Eugenio Garin, *Storia della filosofia italiana,* pt. 3, chap. 4, and pt. 4, chap. 2; and, for the view from the perspective of Neoplatonic magic and astrology, D. P. Walker, *Spiritual and Demonic Magic from Ficino to Campanella,* chaps. 6, 7. On Bruno in particular see Dorothea Waley Singer, *Giordano Bruno;* Alexandre Koyré, *From the Closed World to the Infinite Universe,* pp. 39–57; and, again from the Ficinian perspective, Frances A. Yates, *Giordano Bruno and the Hermetic Tradition.*
14. For this paragraph see Carlo M. Cipolla, "The Decline of Italy"; Miskimin, *The Economy,*

pp. 118–20; and Immanuel Wallerstein, *The Modern World System, II,* pp. 196–203 passim. On p. 50 n Wallerstein sums up Italy's economic troubles: "If one asks what northern Italy exchanged for its imports, the answer has to be the accumulated capital of prior periods. Thus grain import had a fundamentally different significance for Venice than for Amsterdam at this time. . . . For Venice it meant largely eating up capital for current consumption, a good operational definition of 'decline.'"
15. Ruggiero Romano, "Tra XVI e XVII secolo" and "L'Italia nella crisi del secolo XVII."

slumping industries gave rise to a gradual population shift away from the urban areas where they were based, weakening the centralized city governments, contributing to a chronic unemployment, and thus creating a class of vagrants and paupers much larger than in the sixteenth century. The population shift also resulted in a takeover of rural areas by urban aristocrats, a "refeudalization" of Italy that rekindled medieval tensions between peasant and landlord and was, incidentally, intrinsically incapable of providing an economic system for Italy that could compete with the nascent capitalism of northern Europe. Banditry (Fernand Braudel's "social revolution in disguise") and despotic local rule spread. The dissolution of Italian society vividly depicted in Manzoni's *Promessi sposi*—the crisis of the seventeenth century—was at hand. To burgeon, it needed only the devastating plague of 1630, carried by French and German troops that invaded Italy as the result of a newly deteriorated political situation and new wars.[16]

If the 1590s witnessed the first stages of Italy's economic collapse, the first winter storms cutting short its Indian Summer, they also saw a vigorous campaign mounted by the Catholic church against the intellectual freedoms of preceding decades. A new, virulent strain of cultural authoritarianism was bred by an expanded Index and the review for it of all printed books that Sixtus V mandated in 1587. (Sixtus's harsh listing of 1590 elicited immediate protests, even from prelates within the Vatican; but the compromise version, promulgated by Clement VIII in 1596, still added many new titles to the Tridentine Index.)[17] The historian Luigi Firpo describes the coming of the new militancy:

> In the last decade of the century . . . the political and religious situation had changed radically. Popular heresy had been suffocated in Italy. The Turk had been stopped in the east. France had been pacified, and its new king, Henry IV, had been readmitted to the Catholic Church. The old religious orders had been reformed, and the new ones were busy with their apostolic endeavors. The Church had come out of [the struggle] with renewed vigor; and it could now adopt an attitude of intransigence that was a consequence, not an instrument, of its success. . . . it now extended its vigilance to all manifestations of social and spiritual life—not only to religion, but also to ethics, to politics, to philosophy, to art, and even to the manners and customs of the people.[18]

More than the economic collapse (which, in any case, was postponed by in-

---

16. The precipitous decline of Italy's printing industry in the seventeenth century reflects vividly the general economic deterioration (as well, undoubtedly, as other social and cultural factors). In music, Bianconi's count of editions of polyphonic and continuo madrigals reveals the trend (*Il seicento*, p. 4). The number falls dramatically from a peak of 367 in the decade 1581–90 to a meager 69 in the two decades 1631–50. A similar decline in the publication of monody books began around 1630.

17. On the Clementine Index see Sorrentino, *La letteratura italiana*, pp. 42–46, and Grendler, *The Roman Inquisition*, chap. 9.

18. "Filosofia italiana," pp. 152–53; I quote the translation of Cochrane, *The Late Italian Renaissance*, p. 269.

creased taxation, monetary deflation, and massive credit, measures that only made the decline more precipitous when it finally came), the new authoritarianism had an immediate chilling effect on Italian intellectual life. The great natural philosophies of Telesio, Bruno, and Campanella were placed on the new Index. Campanella was imprisoned and tortured by the Holy Office in 1594, Bruno burned in 1600. Even Patrizi's *Nova de universis philosophia,* so highly regarded at its publication in 1591 that its author was lured from Ferrara to lecture at the University of Rome, was soon found to contain unacceptable views and placed on the Index until corrected.[19]

Renaissance historiography came under attack as well. It had long been suspected of spreading pragmatic, antihierarchical political doctrines that undermined the place of religion in daily life and challenged the universal authority of the pope. Machiavelli was particularly offensive; his complete works had been condemned already by the Pauline Index of 1559. But now his conception of history and politics, along with those of Patrizi, Campanella, and others, was refuted in a barrage of treatises issuing from Roman presses through the 1590s (the most prominent of them the Typographia Apostolica Vaticana, founded by Sixtus V in 1587). Jesuits like Antonio Possevino and, later, Famiano Strada led the attack. They recognized the persuasive force of history and hence saw the need for the church to control it. They reasserted Cicero's conception of history as *opus oratorium maxime* and denounced Tacitus along with Machiavelli. In their hands history reverted to a method for purveying dogmatic ethical precepts in eloquent periods. Or, for the growing number of seventeenth-century lay writers who chose not to embroil themselves in sensitive ethical issues, it devolved into a repository of disconnected antiquarian tidbits.[20]

Literary theory too felt the weight of the church's attempt to reestablish absolute authority in all areas of intellectual and cultural life. As in historiography, the Jesuits opposed conceptions of literature that did not stress the teaching of virtue as its goal. (For this and other reasons the complete works of Castelvetro, including his literary writings, appeared on the Clementine Index.)[21] Possevino, for example, analyzed the ethical and religious ends of poetry in his *Tractatio de poësi et pictura* of 1593. These included "temperance against lustful desires" and "constancy in the Catholic religion against all heresies."[22] For the Jesuits, history and poetry worked toward the same goals. They denied the distinction of the two fields that humanists

19. The case is discussed by Firpo, "Filosofia italiana," pp. 159–73.

20. See Spini, "I trattatisti," esp. pp. 130–36; Firpo, "Filosofia italiana," pp. 154–58; William Bouwsma, "Three Types of Historiography in Post-Renaissance Italy" and *Venice and Republican Liberty,* chap. 6 passim, esp. pp. 299–312, 330; and Eric Cochrane, "The Transition from Renaissance to Baroque."

21. The entry is qualified "Nisi prius repurgentur"; see *Index librorum prohibitorum . . . nunc demum S.D.N. Clementis Papae VIII. iussu recognitus, & publicatus,* s.v. "Lodovici."

22. Quoted from Weinberg, *A History of Literary Criticism,* p. 335, where Possevino's treatise is discussed.

had perceived, denying in the process the fragmented vision of reality that lay behind humanist conceptions of disciplinary autonomy.

Vernacular poetry itself, specifically the tradition of love lyrics that has most concerned us in the chapters above, seems at first glance to have been little affected by the increased demands for Catholic orthodoxy around 1600. Thus we are presented with the riddle of an amorous and at times licentious literature thriving in an era of ideological repression and moral stringency. In part the situation is explained by the church's ambivalence toward love poetry. Many members of the Congregation of the Index favored a severe stance on lascivious verse, and it was forbidden in the general rules accompanying the Tridentine Index. Cardinal Bellarmine is supposed to have condemned *Il pastor fido* publicly in 1605, branding it more harmful to Catholicism than Protestantism itself.[23] And in 1627 and 1628 edicts were issued placing various poems of Marino on the Index, including the explicit elaboration of Ovid's *Amores* I, v entitled *Trastulli estivi,* the *Canzone de' baci,* and the whole of *L'Adone.*[24] Nevertheless, there were also voices of moderation within the church, prelates inclined to view love poetry as a manifestation of youthful exuberance rather than heterodoxy. Clement VIII's preliminary Index of 1593 contained an appendix of 190 authors and titles of Italian literature not included on the Tridentine Index, but he was persuaded to drop it from the official Index promulgated in 1596.[25] And aside from Marino only two contemporary lyricists appeared on the Index before 1640, Tommaso Stigliani and Mauritio Moro.[26]

But this is not to say that the church militant had no effect on the vernacular poetry of the time. It seems likely that the atmosphere of suspicion and caution it engendered hastened the trend among seventeenth-century poets to avoid profound human issues, thus leaving unasked potentially risky questions like those frequently broached in sixteenth-century explications of Petrarch's poetry. It may have encouraged them instead to pursue objective descriptions of sensual (not sexual) charms and displays of recondite rhetorical expertise. The basic impulses of Marinist poetry, then, may reflect the self-protective reticence to indulge in probing speculation that characterizes the Italian Reformation as a whole. The same feature, at any rate, informs the retreat of historiography from the political engagement of the sixteenth century to the antiquarian irrelevance of the seventeenth. And

---

23. See chap. 1 above, n. 42.

24. *Elenchus librorum omnium tum in Tridentino, Clementinoq. Indice, tum in aliis omnibus sacrae Indicis Congreg.ⁿⁱˢ particularibus Decretis usque ad annum 1640 prohibitorum,* s,v, "Ioannis Baptistae Marini."

25. Grendler, *The Roman Inquisition,* pp. 145–46, 256–61; Sorrentino, *La letteratura italiana,* pp. 37–46.

26. Information from *Elenchus librorum . . . pro-*

hibitorum. Stigliani's *Rime* of 1605, condemned in December of that year, were reissued in an expurgated edition in 1625 (according to Benedetto Croce, ed., *Lirici marinisti,* p. 526). Moro's *Giardino de' madrigali,* published in 1601 and condemned in 1603, was not to my knowledge reprinted. We have already noted Moro as the probable author of "Sì ch'io vorei morire" and Stigliani as the polemicist against Marino attacked by Busenello.

it is especially notable in experimental science after Galileo's condemnation in 1633. The Florentine Accademia del Cimento, the direct heir of Galileian methods, set the tone in the disclaimer they included in the preface of their *Saggi di naturali esperienze* (1667): "If sometimes in passing from one experiment to another, or for any other reason whatever, some slight hint of speculation [*cosa speculativa*] is given, this is always to be taken as a conceit [*concetto*] or opinion of Academicians, never that of the Academy, whose only task is to make experiments and narrate them."[27] The reaction of such scientists to the possibility that their work might touch on matters ordained by the church was not in essence different from that of poets. All retreated to spiritual and speculative shallowness in a world where deeper questions were answered with dogma. As Fulvio Testi put it, a poet "writes according to fashion, and believes according to necessity."[28]

Thus the church of the Catholic Reformation weakened the humanist link between history and political action, between science and metaphysics, and probably even between poetry and compelling introspection. It advocated in effect a return to a medieval vision of reality, and in the process it reserved for itself the most complex, pressing questions concerning man and his place in the world. But it could not turn back the clock to a time when the various fields of endeavor distinguished and separated by the humanists had still seemed to fall into a neat hierarchical package of God-given knowledge. It could not resurrect a simpler world to match its simplified conception of the world. So its reassertion of the medieval world-view amounted to a forced superposition of an outmoded vision on modern reality. As the gap widened between this vision and the ethical, political, and other uncertainties of real life, the two were reconciled only by intellectually weak and morally tainted means—by the expedient logic of the casuistry practiced most notably (though not only) by the Jesuits, and by the coercion that compelled those holding one set of beliefs (in the Copernican world system, for instance) to pay lip service to another.

The church itself had become a reactionary ideological force, intent on preserving its institutional identity rather than evolving new modes of thought to meet the new reality around it. It could not provide the one thing that church and congregation alike needed most, a means to come to spiritual grips with the crumbling social order of seventeenth-century Italy. Nor could it welcome the attempt, just then conceived in France by Descartes, to transcend its latter-day scholasticism altogether and replace it with a new epistemology more expressive of modern perceptions and modern needs.

---

27. Quoted from Maria Luisa Altieri Biagi, ed., *Scienziati del seicento*, p. 626. My translation is based on that of W. E. Knowles Middleton, in the English version of the *Saggi* he includes in *The Experimenters*; see p. 92. The compiler and main author of the *Saggi* was Lorenzo Magalotti; we shall return to him below.

28. "scrive come s'usa, e crede come si conviene." From the note *Al lettore* of the 1663 edition of Testi's *Opere*.

Meanwhile, in the face of economic and social disintegration and the intransigent doctrines of the church, the optimism of late-sixteenth-century Italy faded. It had thrived on social stability and the increasing rational control humanity seemed to be gaining over the uncertainties of existence. But for the new, troubling realities of the seventeenth century it found no new solutions at hand. So it was gradually replaced by pessimism, a pervasive sense that the present century was one of natural and man-made calamities and of spiritual and intellectual decline. When an obscure Olivetan abbot named Secondo Lancellotti published a point-by-point refutation of these notions in 1623, he called the doomsayers *oggidiani* since they always began their complaints "Oggidì. . . ."—"These days. . . ." His work, entitled *The Present Day, or The World No Worse or Calamitous than in the Past,* was popular enough to see six editions by 1637 (and many more throughout the rest of the century) and to inspire Lancellotti to publish a companion volume in 1636. Its readers were grasping at straws.[29]

In the new intellectual and social landscape the leaders of Italy's high culture took one of two paths. Many of them came to view their intellectual and artistic avocations as branches of religious doctrine, upholders of the dogmatic faith to which they clung. They practiced poetry as preaching, history as propaganda, science as the buttressing of recognized authority. Others, perhaps the majority, granted the church its dominion over moral issues and speculative thought and sought to carve out a narrower niche for the fields in which they worked. This led, as we have seen, to an enervating divorce of intellectual endeavor from its largest goals. Letters, arts, and sciences were now practiced with no nobler aim than "to pass the time honorably." A new listlessness, an "unsatisfiable ennui [*svogliatura*] of the spirits of this century," as the Florentine Lorenzo Magalotti described it, soon became the hallmark of the Italian aristocracy.[30] The courtly *sprezzatura* of the sixteenth century, which for Castiglione and still for Giulio Caccini (in his preface to *Le nuove musiche*) had signified the achievement of impressive deeds with apparent ease, lost its component of accomplishment and degenerated into empty gesture, mere *galanteria*. Not that this was necessarily a shortcoming. In his optimistic mo-

---

29. For excerpts from *L'oggidì overo il mondo non peggiore né più calamitoso del passato* and the second volume, *L'oggidì overo gl'ingegni non inferiori a' passati,* see Ezio Raimondi, ed., *Trattatisti e narratori del seicento,* pp. 269–99. On the *oggidiani* see Calcaterra, *Il parnaso,* chap. 4. The classic account of Italy's seventeenth-century cultural decline, surprisingly current despite its polemic against late-nineteenth-century positivists, and deserving of qualified rehabilitation after revisionist attacks on it in recent decades, is Benedetto Croce's *Storia dell'età barocca in Italia.* On the demoralization of Venice in this period see Bouwsma, *Venice and Republican Liberty,* chap. 9, and Livingston, *La vita veneziana,* passim, esp. chaps. 4, 5; on Florence see Cochrane, *Florence in the Forgotten Centuries,* bk. 3, chaps. 2, 3.

30. The two quotations are from Magalotti's *Lettere scientifiche, ed erudite;* see p. xxiii (editor's preface) for the first and Calcaterra, *Il parnaso,* p. 140, for the second.

ments, those not given over to *oggidianismo*, Magalotti traced the new attitude to a refinement of taste:

> The world is bored [*svogliato*], and it cannot be said that this is the result of indisposition [of spirit], since the boredom grows while the world stands better than ever. Let us rather call it a new kind of health, which engenders a better taste in all things. Princes in their councils no longer want Rodrigones; conquerors don't want laurels; soldiers don't want inspiring speeches; even Venetian boatmen no longer want recitatives. Everything that is serious, sober, and regular in dress, accessories, entertainments, and even business—all this is whistled off stage, and passes for old-fashioned.[31]

A number of seventeenth-century Italians allude to this *svogliatura*; many more attest to it in their lives and work.[32] Magalotti himself, taking up Galileo's method but not his impassioned commitment to follow up its philosophical consequences, pursued experiments on delightful scents and aromas, reducing Galilean empiricism to a Marinist celebration of sensual titillation. He and other Florentine patricians now passed the time in frivolous *cicalate*, vied in contests of meaningless erudition known as Sibille, and listened to Benedetto Averani's strings of learned citations on the question of "Whether heroic virtue is found in women," all in an academy known as the Apatisti, the "Apathetic Ones."[33] Badoaro wrote his librettos, as he was quick to aver in a letter to Monteverdi, "to combat idleness, and not to earn glory."[34] His friend Busenello admitted as much in entitling his published collection of librettos *Delle hore ociose di Gio: Francesco Busenello*. Even Fulvio Testi, who had forsaken Marinism to treat the moral subjects to which he felt himself "singolarmente inclinato," and whose ringing invocation to Italy to rouse itself provides the epigraph of this chapter, could suggest no better remedy for the endemic courtly ills of idleness, luxuriance, and treachery than to exchange them for private life.[35] Science, philosophical speculation, poetry, and other disciplines had

---

31. *Lettere scientifiche*, pp. 107–8. On Magalotti see Calcaterra, *Il parnaso*, pp. 140–41; Cochrane, *Florence in the Forgotten Centuries*, bk. 4; and Georges Güntert, *Un poeta scienziato del seicento*.

32. On the general phenomenon see Calcaterra, *Il parnaso*, pp. 139–58.

33. On the Sibilla and the Apatisti see Eric Cochrane, *Tradition and Enlightenment in the Tuscan Academies*, p. 4 and chap. 1 passim. For a selection of Averani's brief lectures to the academy, which epitomize the learned irrelevance into which most such exercises fell in the seventeenth century, see Carlo Dati, ed., *Prose fiorentine raccolte dallo Smarrito Accademico della Crusca*, pt. 2,

3:98–127, 4:140–56; for some Florentine *cicalate* (chats) see pt. 1, vol. 6.

34. Quoted from Osthoff, "Zu den Quellen," p. 74.

35. See his quatrains entitled "Che instabili sono le grandezze della Corte e che la vita privata è piena di felicità" and the *canzoni* on related topics in pt. 1 of his *Opere*. The epigraph comes from the poem entitled "Che l'età presente è corrotta dall'ozio," on pp. 48–50. Testi's views on moral subjects are recorded in his preface to his *Poesie liriche* (Modena, 1627); I quote it from Luigi Russo et al., eds., *I classici italiani* 2:302.

degenerated into upholders of dogma on the one hand and idle, trivial pastimes on the other.

At the same time, the repudiation of the multifaceted humanist vision evident in Reformation Catholicism undermined the fragile equilibrium of reason and rhetoric that had supported humanist thought from the start. This balance, as we saw in chapter 1, had depended on a flexible logic freed from the injunctions of scholastic method, a logic that could relinquish the goal of absolute demonstration for that of plausible argumentation. Rhetoric, then, found its important place as a means of presenting a persuasive if not fully demonstrable argument. The rigorous scholastic distinction between logic and rhetoric disappeared in the humanist pursuit of a freer sort of discourse, one merging topical logic with suasive oratory.

Such a fluid intellectual order had always been inimical to more crystalline scholastic notions of comprehensible hierarchical structures with absolute authorities at their apexes. The church's effort in the late sixteenth century to reestablish its own such authority therefore entailed a rejection of ad hoc humanist logic. It led to a return to the syllogistic methods of Aristotle's *Organon*. And it reasserted the method of argument from authority basic to scholasticism. But in the shadow of the Holy Office syllogism too easily turned to sophistry, respect for authority to dogmatism. Humanist dialectic withered away, crushed underfoot by intellectual authoritarianism and choked by the crabgrass of casuistical expediency.

The decline in humanist logic led to a decline in the rhetoric with which it was so closely associated—especially those parts of rhetoric most substantially involved in determining the course of a logical argument, the choice and ordering of the materials under discussion (Cicero's *inventio* and *dispositio*). The deemphasis of these areas isolated the more purely stylistic aspects of rhetoric (summed up in Cicero's *elocutio*) from their broader expressive aims. So in the seventeenth century oratory lapsed into elegant phrasemaking and virtuosic eloquence and was cut off, like the other arts and sciences of the time, from the vivifying ambivalence and complexity of real human issues. Such empty rhetoric—rhetoric in its modern, pejorative sense, ornament divorced from substance—is notable in the historical, scientific, and academic writings of the period. It is the hallmark, we have seen, of the new, post-Petrarchan, Marinist poetic idioms of the early 1600s. And it is evident as well, finally, in the contemporary rise of the *predicatori,* popular evangelical preachers who vied with one another in a carnival-like atmosphere to find the most far-fetched metaphorical elucidations of Scripture and Patristic writings.[36]

Marino himself played a part in defining the aims of these preachers, with a volume of sermons published in 1614 and entitled *Dicerie sacre*. His proud descrip-

---

36. See Benedetto Croce, "I predicatori italiani del seicento e il gusto spagnuolo."

tion of these works in a letter of that year set out his intent to astonish through vivid conceits and metaphor:

> Meanwhile, here in Turin, I am publishing certain Sacred Discourses of mine that, I daresay (and forgive my modesty), will stupefy the world. These will be an extravagant and unexpected thing. . . . I hope they will please as much for their novel and bizarre invention (since each discourse consists entirely of one [long] metaphor) as for their liveliness of style and the spirited manner of their conceits [*maniera del concettare spiritoso*]. The most Illustrious Sig. Cardinal d'Este, passing through here, heard two of them in as many nights, along with many other important Signori, and finally concluded that this book will make all the preachers despair. I know that they will strain themselves to imitate this style, but I assure them that it will not come easily to mediocre minds.[37]

The foremost imitator of Marino in the generation after his death, and the Peripatetic theorist of Marinist "preachable conceits" ("concetti predicabili"), was Emanuele Tesauro. His huge treatise on marvelous elocution, *Il cannocchiale aristotelico o sia idea dell'arguta et ingeniosa elocutione* (*The Aristotelian Telescope . . .*, 1654), was probably conceived already in the 1620s, "just in the excited and turbulent years of the Marinist triumph."[38] In this work Tesauro rationalized the new view of oratory in a distinction between "rhetorical" and "scholastic" persuasion. Rhetorical persuasion, "having a practical and moral end, since it incites souls to virtue, uses figurative and ingenious and extrinsic reasons, as well as [those that are] caviling, specious, based on metaphor, on fables, on curious erudition; it draws fruit from [rhetorical] flowers." Scholastic persuasion, on the other hand, "being speculative, inculcates the truth with true and intrinsic reasons." In Tesauro's system logic became a method for deploying unassailable, authoritative truths. Logical persuasion was a force inherent in these "Scholastiche Dottrine," these "solid and intrinsic reasons that are the sinews of oration." Rhetorical persuasion was of a lower order. Its force arose not from logic at all but from the vivid *acutezza* of its metaphors, similes, and other conceits. It was a force to be used in the absence of solid truths, not in their pursuit. "Take away from witty conceits [*Argutezze ideali*] that part which is false," Tesauro wrote, "and you will reduce by that much their beauty and pleasure, tearing out their roots—no matter how much you add of solidity and truth."[39]

Tesauro's follower and friend Francesco Fulvio Frugoni expressed a similarly debased notion of rhetoric in the preface to his huge and capricious collection of

37. *Lettere*, pp. 204–5; see also p. 49.
38. Raimondi, introduction to *Trattatisti*, p. ix.
39. This quotation is given in Calcaterra, *Il parnaso*, p. 133. The preceding ones come from Tesauro's *Trattato de' concetti predicabili, et loro essempli* in chap. 9 of the *Cannocchiale aristotelico*, pp. 502–3.

novelle, Del cane di Diogene (The Dog of Diogenes, 1687–89; the title itself reflects a typical seventeenth-century cynicism): "I have humanized [*humanate*] the scholastic disciplines with rhetorical figures, covering the spines of the Lyceum with the flowering amenities of style; . . . I have not written a single line that does not have a pearl woven into it. I have attempted always to mix the useful with the sweet, doctrine with recreation."[40] Here Frugoni reduced rhetoric to a sweet condiment, the pleasing ingredient in the Horation recipe of *utile* and *dolce.* The purpose of rhetoric was to render scholastic doctrines palatable to a recalcitrant audience; and in his defense of its use Frugoni echoed at times the pessimism of the *oggidiani:* "We live in a century so deafened and so sordid that the whole world is a base Catadupe, a bituminous asphalt. Therefore it is necessary to speak to it in symbols and figures, and to pull it from the dung in which it is mired with violent invectives. It does not hear the trumpets of Truth unless they are accompanied by the bagpipes of delight, made up of frivolous reeds which, titillating the ears with alluring sound, lessen the din of the retribution soon to come."[41]

In part because of his pessimism, then, Frugoni shared with Tesauro a love of glittering, virtuosic conceits in poetry and prose alike. The sonnets of Petrarch and Bembo reminded him of plainsong, undistinguished and overly simple, while sonnets in the modern style "trilled and sparkled with a fluttering, witty [*arguto*] song."[42] *Argutezza,* or *acutezza,* had been the subject of Tesauro's *Cannocchiale aristotelico* too—"*argutezza,* noble mother of all ingenious conceits, clearest light of oratorical and poetic eloquence, vital spark of lifeless pages, most pleasing condiment of civil conversation, ultimate exertion of the intellect, vestige of divinity in the human soul. . . ."[43] Both writers, and with them even more restrained theorists of the *stile concettoso* like Matteo Peregrini and Sforza Pallavicino,[44] saw verbal discourse as a search for witty paralogisms, farfetched metaphors, arcane imagery, obscure enthymemes, unknown classical lore, dazzling paradox—in short, as a search for *meraviglia.* "The principal delight of the intellect," wrote Pallavicino, "consists in being astonished [*maravigliarsi*]."[45] The myriad of richer emotions that earlier eloquence aimed to convey were ignored in the consuming quest for wonder

40. Quoted from Calcaterra, *Il parnaso,* p. 134. For excerpts from Frugoni's *Cane* see Raimondi, *Trattatisti,* pp. 919–1067. Frugoni is known to music historians for his attack on the state of musico-dramatic poetry in 1675; see Robert Freeman, "Apostolo Zeno's Reform of the Libretto."

41. Quoted in Benedetto Croce, *Storia,* p. 435. Frugoni's "Catadupo" was an inhabitant of the region at the base of the cataracts of the Nile, supposedly deafened by their perpetual roar.

42. Quoted in Calcaterra, *Il parnaso,* p. 137.

43. *Cannocchiale aristotelico,* p. 1.

44. See the excerpts from Peregrini's *Delle acutezze, che altrimenti spiriti, vivezze e concetti volgarmente si appellano* (1639) and Pallavicino's *Trattato dello stile e del dialogo* (first edition 1646, revised 1662) in Raimondi, *Trattatisti,* pp. 113–68, 197–217.

45. Ibid., p. 197.

and surprise. So the devaluation of rhetoric in the *seicento* finally came down to Marino's admonition of 1619: "Chi non sa far stupir, vada a la striglia."

Oratory was no longer a language of heartfelt emotions because they, like all the serious things later cited by Magalotti, were judged dull, old-fashioned. Rhetoric, when not functioning as a strident, dogmatic force *propaganda fide,* was the plaything of idle, disenchanted aristocrats. They depended on its marvels, just as Magalotti relied on the wondrous perfumes he collected and concocted, to arouse them from their chronic lassitude.

The trends we have sketched above allow us better to understand Monteverdi's place in Italian culture. He was born into a transitory revival of humanist thought throughout northern Italy. The revival arose in response to the narrower scholastic (and especially Aristotelian) tendencies of the mid-sixteenth century. It was spurred by the political stability and relatively healthy economy of the peninsula and was permitted if not sanctioned by the church. By the 1590s, however, new forces had arisen that would soon undermine it: a renewed and ultimately devastating economic decline, with its concomitant destabilization of political structures and society in general, and the church's increasingly militant challenge to freedom of thought. Italian culture entered a period of intellectual, moral, and spiritual contraction. The final bloom of humanism withered, and by 1650 the Renaissance had ended. In this decisively altered atmosphere Monteverdi composed his last works.

The gradual supplanting of Petrarchan by Marinist poetic ideals after 1600 reflects these general cultural tendencies. For poets still connected to the Petrarchan tradition, such as Tasso, Guarini, and Rinuccini, poetry was the stylized expression of human passion, a language that gave voice to their inner emotional world. Rhetoric provided a spectrum of conventional structures for conveying these passions artfully, compellingly, and rationally, serving thus in its humanist function as link between reason and emotion. This link was obvious in the straightforward dramatic and narrative outgrowths of Petrarchism that fascinated Monteverdi: the impassioned soliloquies of Tancredi and Armida, of Amarilli and Mirtillo, of Ariadne. It persisted just as strongly, however, even in the most stylized Petrarchan lyrics, the epigrammatic madrigals of Guarini, which at their best fully merged pragmatic logic and amorous passion in a single rhetorical parry-and-thrust.

The Marinists of the early seventeenth century broke this link. Their poetry was not a language of emotion but a descriptive discourse on external objects or a treatment of amorous situations in their outward, despiritualized attributes alone. Introspection was not the goal of Marinist poets; they tended to mask their inner world rather than examine it. They reduced rhetoric to verbal virtuosity, a storehouse of images and tropes that endowed their plain description with a scintillating, captivating illusion of poetry. The poetics of *meraviglia* concealed a rhetoric of emotional sterility. In exalting it the Marinists gave poetic voice to the spiritual constriction of their age.

And, at times in his late works, so also did Monteverdi. The general shift across his career from Petrarchan to Marinist (and related Chiabreresque) modes of expression was a movement away from the Renaissance view of rhetoric as a language of fluid, deep-seated passions. In his music, as we have seen, it took various forms. One was the avoidance of affective gestures in favor of iconic musical representation, so closely allied to the external, imagistic tendencies of Marinist verse. Another was the dissolution of the precise matching of musical and verbal syntax that his earlier expressive triumphs, from Book III to *L'Arianna,* had depended on; along with it came a concomitant tendency to rely on a purely musical structural logic or one engaging the text primarily on the level of its largest formal outlines. Last but not least, Monteverdi showed a growing preference for poetry of light emotional weight.

We may posit narrowly biographical explanations for these trends. Works like *L'Arianna* and the *Sestina,* after all, involved hardship and tragedy as well as triumph; small wonder that Monteverdi remembered them with ambivalence, and sometimes even chose not to remember them at all, in later years.[46] Also, it is clear from Monteverdi's letters that his position in Venice soon gave him a personal dignity far exceeding anything he could have aspired to in Mantua. He now acted almost as an equal of the aristocrats he came to know, not merely as their servant; small wonder that he took on some of their refined emotional restraint and even delighted in the many strophic Chiabreresque ditties of theirs that he set. But of course this personal evolution only involved Monteverdi in a larger cultural shift. The aristocrats and men of affairs whose company Monteverdi frequented in Venice, from Strozzi to Busenello, were well along the road to Magalotti's "incontentabile svogliatura"—much further along that road, certainly, than Rinuccini or Striggio had been.

Monteverdi's Marinist proclivities, then, reveal his participation in the general cultural enervation of seventeenth-century Italy. (They also demonstrate, by the way, his extraordinary versatility and adaptability, undiminished in his final years.) So it is not surprising that they foreshadow the main developments in Italian opera throughout the rest of the century: the codification of discrete, reproducible musical gestures for the depiction of various passions, signaled in the almost total abolition not long after Monteverdi's death of the fluid "recitative soliloquies" that still played so important a role in his last operas;[47] the growing reliance on virtuosity instead of the projection of emotion to maintain musical vitality; the continuing

46. Tomlinson, "Madrigal, Monody, and Monteverdi," pp. 104–8.

47. Margaret Murata, "The Recitative Soliloquy."

decay of the ideal of close syntactic linkage of text and music typical of early recitative; and the increasing emphasis on standardized musical forms.

All these features may be regarded (somewhat loosely, to be sure) as outgrowths of Monteverdi's musical Marinisms. More important, however, they arose from the same pervasive cultural malaise that fostered Marinist poetics in the first place: the devolution of humanist rhetoric into a quest for virtuosic ingenuity. Italian opera of the late seventeenth century reflected the simplistic view of humanity that caused this decline and had come to characterize Italian culture as a whole. The ambivalence of Ariadne, vividly voicing both love and hatred for Theseus, was no longer a fully comprehensible confusion. The recognition of ambiguity was itself opposed to, even subversive of, the scholastic hierarchical order of contemporary thought and society. It is revealing that the crystallization of *opera seria* into discrete emotional quanta—the "doctrine of affects" much discussed in the eighteenth century—found its brightest theoretical reflection in the mechanistic psychophysiology of Descartes's *Traité des passions de l'âme*. For this facet of Cartesian thought, more than any other, remained bound to the scholastic modes of thought from which it arose.

Nor is it a contradiction that the features of Italian opera enumerated above, its "musical Marinisms," found their fullest expression after 1700, in the midst of a decisive repudiation by Italian literati of Marino and his pursuit of *meraviglia*. Admittedly the famous Arcadian society, official sponsors of the rejection of Marinism, reasserted the preeminence of Petrarch among Italian lyricists. But Chiabrera, they were quick to add, stood alongside Petrarch in their hearts, and his example proved a good deal more congenial to their muse—especially in *poesia per musica*. Thus the Arcadians took pains to distinguish the restrained "Pindaric" formalism of Chiabrera from the glittering description and *acutezze* of Marino. But this only begged the essential question, and in turning away from one poetics of stultified, exterior expression they embraced another. If the texts of Metastasio's arias often recall the expressive world of Marino, it is not solely because Metastasio harbored a secret love of the forbidden *secentista*;[48] it is also because the aesthetic program of the new century retained fundamental premises from that of the old. The Arcadian revolt barely began to thaw the icy emotions of seventeenth-century verse. Not until the midday sun of romanticism melted the ice did Italian music regain the fluid oratorical passion it had lost at the end of the Renaissance.

But it would be unjust to finish on this negative note, for the Marinisms of Monteverdi's late works are not their most remarkable aspect. Far more striking are his repeated evocations of the Petrarchan, humanist ideals of his youth. The echoes of these ideals, and especially of their archetypical musical formulation in

48. See the introduction to Pietro Metastasio, *Opere,* p. 4.

Ariadne's lament, give the best of the late works an essential dualism. They yield an emotional and rhetorical gravity that succeeds often in ennobling the frivolous delights around them, making these a part of a rich and varied emotional palette rather than a one-sided revelation of spiritual shallowness.

This dualism appears full blown in the duets of Book VII, though it is present there as opposed, barely intersecting stylistic options, Petrarchan and Marinist, rather than as two facets of a varied but coherent rhetoric. In the *Combattimento* the two idioms are juxtaposed to achieve a broadened expressive variety. But still they are not merged into a single language, for the two modes of musical expression there align themselves neatly with the contrasting modes of representation, mimetic ballet and affective drama, alternately offered by Tasso's text. Nor are the Marinist and Petrarchan ideals synthesized in *Poppea,* where Monteverdi relied on their conflicting expressive means to encompass the sprawling profusion of representative gestures in Busenello's drama. Monteverdi approached a perfect synthesis only in the *Lament of the Nymph.* But here it was a merger of Petrarchan ideals with Chiabreresque formalism, not with Marinist image, that allowed him to transcend utterly the limitations of the continuo *canzonetta.* So the contradictions in Monteverdi's works arising from his Petrarchan and Marinist impulses remained unresolved and, probably, incapable of resolution.

Nevertheless, Monteverdi never dodged these contradictions. He always stated them boldly, juxtaposing opposites and letting sparks fly where they might. In this he brings to mind once more Galileo, who also rarely flinched at the limitations of human intellect, seldom hid them behind specious formulations, and exhorted other philosophers to admit with him their confusion on unanswered questions. And in this quality, also, Monteverdi set himself apart from the younger composers writing during his last years. They had not been formed in the humanist revival of the late sixteenth century; they knew the world of Monteverdi's youth only dimly, by reflection. But it was Monteverdi's singular fortune to outlive his own age and enter a new one, and to remain responsive to all that he encountered there. Thus he brought to his late works the vision of an earlier world, one still exulting in the emotional vibrancy, the ambiguities, the fears, and the aspirations of the Renaissance. The greatest of these works stand alone in the history of music, embodying Monteverdi's own resonant dialogue of the two chief world systems he had known: Petrarchism and Marinism, humanism and scholasticism, Renaissance and medieval visions.

Works Cited

Abert, Anna Amalie. *Claudio Monteverdi und das musikalische Drama.* Lippstadt, 1954.

Achillini, Claudio. *Rime e prose.* Venice, 1662.

Aldrich, Putnam. *The Rhythm of Seventeenth-Century Italian Monody.* New York, 1966.

Ancona, Alessandro d'. *Origini del teatro italiano.* 2 vols. Turin, 1891.

———. "Il teatro mantovano nel secolo XVI." *Giornale Storico della Letteratura Italiana* 5 (1882), 1–79; 6 (1883), 1–52, 312–51; 7 (1884), 48–93.

Angelio, Pietro, and Mario Colonna. *Poesie toscane dell'Illustriss. Sign. Mario Colonna, et di M. Pietro Angelio.* Florence, 1589.

Anselmi, Giovanni Battista, and various composers. *Madrigali del signor cavalier Anselmi nobile di Treviso posti in musica da diversi eccellentissimi spiriti a 2. 3. 4. 5. voci.* Venice, 1624.

Arnold, Denis. *Monteverdi.* London, 1963.

———. "Monteverdi and His Teachers." In *The Monteverdi Companion,* ed. Denis Arnold and Nigel Fortune (New York, 1968), pp. 91–109.

Artusi, Giovanni Maria. *L'Artusi overo delle imperfettioni della moderna musica.* Facs. ed. Ed. Giuseppe Vecchi. Bologna, 1968.

Badoaro, Giacomo. *Il ritorno d'Ulisse in patria tragedia di lieto fine del signor Giacomo Badoaro . . . in Venetia l'anno MDCXLI.* MS Cicogna 192, No. 3330. Biblioteca del Museo Correr, Venice.

Baldwin, John W. *The Scholastic Culture of the Middle Ages.* Lexington, Mass., 1971.

Baron, Hans. *The Crisis of the Early Italian Renaissance.* Princeton, 1966.

———. "The *Querelle* of the Ancients and Moderns as a Problem for Renaissance Scholarship." In *Renaissance Essays from The Journal of the History of Ideas,* ed. Paul Oskar Kristeller and Philip P. Wiener (New York, 1968), pp. 95–114.

Becker, A. L. "Text-Building, Epistemology, and Aesthetics in Javanese Shadow Theatre." In *The Imagination of Reality: Essays in Southeast Asian Coherence Systems,* ed. A. L. Becker and Aram A. Yengoyan (Norwood, N.J., 1979), pp. 211–43.

Benivieni, Girolamo. *Opere di Girolamo Benivieni Firentino.* Florence, 1524.

Berner, Samuel. "The Florentine Patriciate in the Transition from Republic to *Principato,* 1530–1609." *Studies in Medieval and Renaissance History* 9 (1972), 1–15.

———. "Florentine Society in the Late Sixteenth and Early Seventeenth Centuries." *Studies in the Renaissance* 18 (1971), 203–46.

Besomi, Ottavio. *Ricerche intorno alla "Lira" di G. B. Marino.* Padua, 1969.

Biagi, Maria Luisa Altieri, ed. *Scienziati del seicento.* Milan, 1968.

Bianconi, Lorenzo. *Il seicento.* Storia della musica a cura della Società Italiana di Musicologia, vol. 4. Turin, 1982.

———. "Struttura poetica e struttura musicale nei madrigali di Monteverdi." In *Claudio Monteverdi e il suo tempo,* ed. Raffaello Monterosso (Verona, 1969), pp. 335–48.

261

Bonta, Stephen. "Liturgical Problems in Monteverdi's Marian Vespers." *Journal of the American Musicological Society* 20 (1967), 87–106.

Bouwsma, William J. *The Culture of Renaissance Humanism*. American Historical Association Pamphlet. Richmond, Va., 1973.

―――. "Renaissance and Reformation: An Essay in Their Affinities and Connections." In *Luther and the Dawn of the Modern Era,* ed. Heiko A. Oberman (Leiden, 1974), pp. 127–49.

―――. "Three Types of Historiography in Post-Renaissance Italy." *History and Theory* 4 (1965), 303–14.

―――. *Venice and the Defense of Republican Liberty: Renaissance Values in the Age of the Counter Reformation*. Berkeley, 1968.

Braudel, Fernand. *The Mediterranean and the Mediterranean World in the Age of Philip II*. Trans. Siân Reynolds. 2 vols. New York, 1976.

Brown, Howard M. "Psyche's Lament: Some Music for the Medici Wedding in 1565." In *Words and Music: The Scholar's View,* ed. Laurence Berman (Cambridge, Mass., 1972), pp. 1–27.

Brown, Peter M. *Lionardo Salviati: A Critical Biography*. Oxford, 1974.

Bulferetti, Luigi. "Galileo e la società del suo tempo." In *Fortuna di Galileo* (Bari, 1964), pp. 127–61.

Busenello, Gian Francesco. *Delle hore ociose di Gio: Francesco Busenello*. Venice, 1656.

Calcaterra, Carlo. *Il parnaso in rivolta*. Bologna, 1961.

―――, ed. *I lirici del seicento e dell'Arcadia*. Milan, 1936.

Cammarota, Lionello. *Gian Domenico del Giovane da Nola: I documenti biografici . . ., madrigali a 4 e 5 voci, canzoni villanesche a 3 e 4 voci*. 2 vols. Rome, 1973.

Casone, Girolamo. *Rime del Signor Girolamo Casone da Oderzo*. Venice, 1598.

Cassirer, Ernst. "Galileo's Platonism." In *Studies and Essays in the History of Science and Learning,* ed. M. F. A. Montagu (New York, 1944), pp. 279–97.

Cavalli, Francesco. *Gli amori d'Apollo e di Dafne*. (1640). Facs. ed. Ed. Howard Mayer Brown. New York, 1978.

Cavicchi, Adriano. "Teatro monteverdiano e tradizione teatrale ferrarese." In *Claudio Monteverdi e il suo tempo,* ed. Raffaello Monterosso (Verona, 1969), pp. 139–56.

Chiabrera, Gabriello. *Delle poesie di Gabriello Chiabrera*. Florence, 1627.

Chiarelli, Alessandra. " 'L'incoronazione di Poppea' o 'Il Nerone': Problemi di filologia testuale." *Rivista Italiana di Musicologia* 9 (1974), 117–51.

Cipolla, Carlo M. "The Decline of Italy: The Case of a Fully Matured Economy." *Economic History Review,* ser. 2, 5 (1952), 178–87.

Cochrane, Eric. "The End of the Renaissance in Florence." In *The Late Italian Renaissance, 1525–1630,* ed. Cochrane (New York, 1970), pp. 43–73.

―――. *Florence in the Forgotten Centuries*. Chicago, 1973.

―――. "The Florentine Background of Galileo's Work." In *Galileo: Man of Science,* ed. Ernan McMullin (New York, 1967), pp. 118–39.

―――. *Historians and Historiography in the Italian Renaissance*. Chicago, 1981.

―――. "Science and Humanism in the Italian Renaissance." *The American Historical Review* 81 (1976), 1039–57.

―――. *Tradition and Enlightenment in the Tuscan Academies*. Rome, 1961.

―――. "The Transition from Renaissance to Baroque: The Case of Italian Historiography." *History and Theory* 19 (1980), 21–38.

Croce, Benedetto. "I predicatori italiani del seicento e il gusto spagnuolo." In *Saggi sulla letteratura italiana del seicento* (Bari, 1911), pp. 161–93.
———. *Storia dell'età barocca in Italia.* 5th ed. Bari, 1967.
———, ed. *Lirici marinisti.* Bari, 1910.
Croce, Franco. "Gian Battista Marino." In *Letteratura italiana: I minori,* ed. Carlo Marzorati (Milan, 1961), vol. 3, pt. 2, pp. 1601–40.

Dahlhaus, Carl. "*Ecco mormorar l'onde*: Versuch, ein Monteverdi-Madrigal zu interpretieren." In *Chormusik und Analyse,* ed. Heinrich Poos (Schott, 1983), pp. 139–54.
———. *Untersuchungen über die Entstehung der harmonischen Tonalität.* Kassel, 1968.
Dati, Carlo, ed. *Prose fiorentine raccolte dallo Smarrito Accademico della Crusca.* 6 vols. Venice, 1735–43.
Degrada, Francesco. "Gian Francesco Busenello e il libretto della *Incoronazione di Poppea.*" In *Claudio Monteverdi e il suo tempo,* ed. Raffaello Monterosso (Verona, 1969), pp. 81–102.
Dempsey, Charles. Review of *Circa 1600: A Revolution of Style in Italian Painting,* by S. J. Freedberg. *The New Criterion* 1, no. 10 (June 1983), 87–90.
Drake, Stillman, ed. and trans. *Discoveries and Opinions of Galileo.* New York, 1957.
Durling, Robert M., ed. and trans. *Petrarch's Lyric Poems: The "Rime Sparse" and Other Lyrics.* Cambridge, Mass., 1976.

Einstein, Alfred. "Ancora sull' 'aria di Ruggiero.' " *Rivista Musicale Italiana* 41 (1937), 163–69.
———. "Die Aria di Ruggiero." *Sammelbände der Internationalen Musikgesellschaft* 13 (1911–12), 444–54.
———. *The Italian Madrigal.* Trans. Alexander H. Krappe, Roger H. Sessions, and Oliver Strunk. 3 vols. Princeton, 1971.
Elenchus librorum omnium tum in Tridentino, Clementinoq. Indice, tum in aliis omnibus sacrae Indicis Congreg.[nis] particularibus Decretis usque ad annum 1640 prohibitorum. Rome, 1640.
Elwert, W. Theodor. "La poesia barocca nei paesi romani: Concordanze e divergenze stilistiche." In *La critica stilistica e il barocco letterario,* ed. Ettore Caccia (Florence, 1959), pp. 61–92.

Fabbri, Paolo. "Inediti monteverdiani." *Rivista Italiana di Musicologia* 15 (1980), 71–86.
Fairfax, Edward, trans. *Jerusalem Delivered; Being a translation into English verse . . . of Tasso's Gerusalemme liberata* (1600). Ed. John Charles Nelson. New York, 1963.
Fenlon, Iain. "The Monteverdi Vespers: Suggested Answers to Some Fundamental Questions." *Early Music* 5 (1977), 380–87.
———. *Music and Patronage in Sixteenth-Century Mantua.* 2 vols. Cambridge, 1980–82.
Finocchiaro, Maurice A. *Galileo and the Art of Reasoning: Rhetorical Foundations of Logic and Scientific Method.* Dordrecht, 1980.
Firpo, Luigi. "Filosofia italiana e controriforma." *Rivista di Filosofia* 41 (1950), 150–73; 42 (1951), 30–47. Partially translated in *The Late Italian Renaissance, 1525–1630,* ed. Eric Cochrane (New York, 1970), pp. 266–84.
Fischer, Kurt von. "Eine wenig beachtete Quelle zu Busenellos *L'incoronazione di Poppea.*" In *Claudio Monteverdi e il suo tempo,* ed. Raffaello Monterosso (Verona, 1969), pp. 75–80.
Flanders, Peter. "The Madrigals of Benedetto Pallavicino." 2 vols. Ph.D. dissertation, New York University, 1971.

Freedberg, S. J. *Circa 1600: A Revolution of Style in Italian Painting*. Cambridge, Mass., 1983.

Freeman, Robert. "Apostolo Zeno's Reform of the Libretto." *Journal of the American Musicological Society* 21 (1968), 321–41.

Friedlaender, Walter. *Mannerism and Anti-Mannerism in Italian Painting*. New York, 1965.

Gagliano, Marco da. *La Flora* (Florence, 1628). Facs. ed. Ed. Primarosa Ledda. Bologna, 1969.

———. *Music for One, Two, and Three Voices*. Ed. Putnam Aldrich. 2 vols. Bryn Mawr, Pa., 1969–72.

Galilei, Galileo. *Dialogo . . . sopra i due massime sistemi del mondo tolemaico, e copernicano*. Facs. ed. Brussels, 1966.

———. *Dialogue Concerning the Two Chief World Systems*. Trans. Stillman Drake. Berkeley, 1967.

———. *Lettere*. Ed. Ferdinando Flora. Turin, 1978.

———. *Il saggiatore*. Ed. Libero Sosio. Milan, 1979.

Gallico, Claudio. "La 'Lettera amorosa' di Monteverdi e lo stile rappresentativo." *Nuova Rivista Musicale Italiana* 1 (1967), 287–302.

Gandolfi, Riccardo. "Lettere inedite scritte da musicisti e letterati, appartenenti alla seconda metà del secolo XVI." *Rivista Musicale Italiana* 20 (1913), 527–54.

Garin, Eugenio. *Italian Humanism: Philosophy and Civic Life in the Renaissance*. Trans. Peter Munz. Oxford, 1965.

———. *Science and Civic Life in the Italian Renaissance*. Trans. Peter Munz. New York, 1969.

———. *Storia della filosofia italiana*. 3 vols. Turin, 1966.

Geertz, Clifford. *Local Knowledge: Further Essays in Interpretive Anthropology*. New York, 1983.

Gesualdo da Venosa. *Sämtliche Madrigale für fünf Stimmen*. Ed. Wilhelm Weismann. 6 vols. Hamburg, 1957–62.

Getto, Giovanni. *Barocco in prosa e in poesia*. Milan, 1969.

Geymonat, Ludovico. *Galileo Galilei*. Trans. Stillman Drake. New York, 1965.

Gianturco, Carolyn. *Claudio Monteverdi: Stile e struttura*. Pisa, 1978.

Gilbert, Allan H., ed. *Literary Criticism: Plato to Dryden*. Detroit, 1962.

Girill, T. F. "Galileo and Platonistic Methodology." *Journal of the History of Ideas* 31 (1970), 501–20.

Goldschmidt, Hugo. *Studien zur Geschichte der italienischen Oper im 17. Jahrhundert*. 2 vols. Leipzig, 1901–4.

Gray, Hanna H. "Renaissance Humanism: The Pursuit of Eloquence." In *Renaissance Essays from The Journal of the History of Ideas*, ed. Paul Oskar Kristeller and Philip P. Wiener (New York, 1968), pp. 199–216.

Grendler, Paul F. *The Roman Inquisition and the Venetian Press, 1540–1605*. Princeton, 1977.

Guarini, Giambattista. *Delle opere del Cavalier Battista Guarini*. 4 vols. Verona, 1737–38.

———. *Opere di Battista Guarini*. Ed. Marziano Guglielminetti. Turin, 1971.

———. *Il pastor fido*. Ed. J. H. Whitfield. Austin, Tex., 1976.

———. *Rime del molto illustre Signor Cavaliere Battista Guarini*. Venice, 1599.

Güntert, Georges. *Un poeta scienziato del seicento: Lorenzo Magalotti*. Florence, 1966.

Haar, James. "Arie per cantar stanze ariostesche." In *L'Ariosto, la musica, i musicisti*, ed. Maria Antonella Balsano (Florence, 1981), pp. 31–46.

———. "The 'Madrigale arioso': A Mid-Century Development in the Cinquecento Madrigal." *Studi Musicali* 12 (1983), 203–19.

Hanning, Barbara Russano. *Of Poetry and Music's Power: Humanism and the Creation of Opera.* Ann Arbor, 1980.

Hathaway, Baxter. *The Age of Criticism: The Late Renaissance in Italy.* Ithaca, 1962.

Holmes, George. *The Florentine Enlightenment, 1400–1450.* New York, 1969.

Horsley, Imogene. "Monteverdi's Use of Borrowed Material in 'Sfogava con le stelle,' " *Music & Letters* 59 (1978), 316–28.

———. "The Sixteenth-Century Variation: A New Historical Survey." *Journal of the American Musicological Society* 12 (1959), 118–32.

Index librorum prohibitorum . . . nunc demum S.D.N. Clementis Papae VIII. iussu recognitus, & publicatus. Rome, 1596.

India, Sigismondo d'. *Le musiche del Cavalier Sigismondo d'India . . . libro quinto.* Venice, 1623.

Ingegneri, Angelo. *Della poesia rappresentativa e del modo di rappresentare le favole sceniche.* Ferrara, 1598. Reprinted in *Delle opere del Cavalier Battista Guarini* (Verona, 1737–38), 3:471–541.

Ingegneri, Marc'Antonio. *Sieben Madrigale.* Ed. Barton Hudson. Das Chorwerk, vol. 115. Wolfenbüttel, 1974.

Kohl, Benjamin G., and Ronald G. Witt, eds. *The Earthly Republic: Italian Humanists on Government and Society.* Philadelphia, 1978.

Koyré, Alexandre. *From the Closed World to the Infinite Universe.* Baltimore, 1968.

———. "Galileo and Plato." *Journal of the History of Ideas* 4 (1943), 400–28.

Kretzmann, Norman, Anthony Kenny, Jan Pinborg, and Eleonore Stump, eds. *The Cambridge History of Later Medieval Philosophy, From the Rediscovery of Aristotle to the Disintegration of Scholasticism, 1100–1600.* Cambridge, 1982.

Kristeller, Paul Oskar. *Eight Philosophers of the Italian Renaissance.* Stanford, 1964.

———. *Renaissance Thought: The Classic, Scholastic, and Humanist Strains.* New York, 1961.

———. *Renaissance Thought, II: Papers on Humanism and the Arts.* New York, 1965.

Kurtzman, Jeffrey G. *Essays on the Monteverdi Mass and Vespers of 1610.* Houston, 1979.

Leopold, Silke. "Chiabrera und die Monodie: Die Entwicklung der Arie." *Studi Musicali* 10 (1981), 75–106.

Livingston, Arthur A. "Gian Francesco Busenello e la polemica Stigliani-Marino." *L'Ateneo Veneto* 33, no. 2 (1910), 123–55.

———. *La vita veneziana nelle opere di Gian Francesco Busenello.* Venice, 1913.

McClary, Susan Kaye. "The Transition from Modal to Tonal Organization in the Works of Monteverdi." Ph.D. dissertation, Harvard University, 1976.

MacClintock, Carol. *Giaches de Wert, 1535–1596: Life and Works.* American Institute of Musicology, 1966.

Mace, Dean T. "Tasso, *La Gerusalemme liberata,* and Monteverdi." In *Studies in the History of Music, I: Music and Language* (New York, 1983), pp. 118–56.

Magalotti, Lorenzo. *Lettere scientifiche, ed erudite.* Florence, 1721.

Malipiero, G. Francesco, ed. *Adriano Willaert e i suoi discendenti: Nove madrigali a cinque voci.* Venice, n.d.

Mann, Brian. *The Secular Madrigals of Filippo di Monte, 1521–1603.* Ann Arbor, 1983.

Marastone, Antonio. *Concerti a due tre, et quattro voci.* Venice, 1624.

Marenzio, Luca. *Sämtliche Werke.* Ed. Alfred Einstein. Publikationen älterer Musik, vols. 4, 6. Leipzig, 1929–1931.

———. *Ten Madrigals for Mixed Voices.* Ed. Denis Arnold. London, 1966.

Marino, Giambattista. *Della lira del Cavalier Marino. Parte terza.* Venice, 1614.

———. *Lettere del Cavalier Marino gravi, argute, e facete.* Turin, 1629.

———. *Opere.* Ed. Alberto Asor Rosa. Milan, 1967.

———. *Rime del Marino. Parte seconda.* Venice, 1602.

———. *Rime di Gio. Battista Marino . . . parte prima.* Venice, 1602.

———. *La sampogna del Cavalier Marino.* Venice, 1621.

Mazzamuto, Pietro. "Lodovico Castelvetro." In *La letteratura italiana: I minori,* ed. Carlo Marzorati (Milan, 1961), vol. 3, pt. 2, pp. 1221–37.

Metastasio, Pietro. *Opere. Appendice: L'opera per musica dopo Metastasio (Calzabigi, da Ponte, Casti).* Ed. Mario Fubini and Ettore Bonora. Milan, 1968.

Middleton, W. E. Knowles. *The Experimenters: A Study of the Accademia del Cimento.* Baltimore, 1971.

Milanuzzi, Carlo, et al. *Quarto Scherzo delle ariose vaghezze.* Venice, 1624.

Mirollo, James V. *The Poet of the Marvelous: Giambattista Marino.* New York, 1963.

Miskimin, Harry A. *The Economy of Later Renaissance Europe, 1460–1600.* Cambridge, 1977.

Monteverdi, Claudio. *L'incoronazione di Poppea.* Facs. ed. of MS. It. cl. 4. n.439, Biblioteca Nazionale di San Marco, Venice. Ed. Giacomo Benvenuti. Milan, 1938.

———. *Lettere, dediche, e prefazioni.* Ed. Domenico de' Paoli. Rome, 1973.

———. *Madrigali a 5 voci, libro secondo.* Ed. Anna Maria Monterosso Vacchelli. *Opera Omnia,* vol. 3. Cremona, 1979.

———. *Madrigali a 5 voci, libro quarto.* Ed. Elena Ferrari Barassi. *Opera Omnia,* vol. 5. Cremona, 1974.

———. *L'Orfeo favola in musica* (Venice, 1609). Facs. ed. Ed. Adolf Sandberger. Augsburg, 1927.

———. *Il terzo libro della musica di Claudio Monteverde a cinque voci fatta spirituale da Aquilino Coppini.* Milan, 1609.

———. *Tutte le opere.* Ed. G. Francesco Malipiero. 17 vols. Asolo, 1926–42; Venice, 1966.

Moore, James H. Review of *The Letters of Claudio Monteverdi,* ed. and trans. Denis Stevens. *Journal of the American Musicological Society* 35 (1982), 554–65.

———. *Vespers at St. Mark's: Music of Alessandro Grandi, Giovanni Rovetta, and Francesco Cavalli.* 2 vols. Ann Arbor, 1981.

Moro, Mauritio. *I tre giardini de' madrigali del Costante, Academico Cospirante, Mauritio Moro Vinetiano.* Venice, 1602.

Moss, Jean Dietz. "Galileo's *Letter to Christina*: Some Rhetorical Considerations." *Renaissance Quarterly* 36 (1983), 547–76.

Murata, Margaret. "The Recitative Soliloquy." *Journal of the American Musicological Society* 32 (1979), 45–73.

Neri, Achille. "Gli 'Intermezzi' del 'Pastor fido.' " *Giornale Storico della Letteratura Italiana* 11 (1888), 405–15.

Newcomb, Anthony. *The Madrigal at Ferrara, 1579–1597.* 2 vols. Princeton, 1980.

Newman, Joel. Communication to *Journal of the American Musicological Society* 14 (1961), 418–19.

Ong, Walter J. *Ramus, Method, and the Decay of Dialogue.* Cambridge, Mass., 1958.

Osthoff, Wolfgang. *Das dramatische Spätwerk Claudio Monteverdis.* Tutzing, 1960.

———. "Neue Beobachtungen zu Quellen und Geschichte von Monteverdis 'Incoronazione di Poppea.'" *Die Musikforschung* 11 (1958), 129–38.

———. "Trombe sordine." *Archiv für Musikwissenschaft* 13 (1956), 77–95.

———. "Die venezianische und neapolitanische Fassung von Monteverdis 'Incoronazione di Poppea.'" *Acta Musicologica* 26 (1954), 88–113.

———. "Zu den Quellen von Monteverdis 'Ritorno di Ulisse in patria.'" *Studien zur Musikwissenschaft* 23 (1956), 67–78.

———. "Zur bologneser Aufführung von Monteverdis 'Ritorno di Ulisse' im Jahre 1640." *Anzeiger der Philosophisch-historischen Klasse der Österreichischen Akademie der Wissenschaften* 8 (1958), 155–60.

Palisca, Claude V. "The Artusi-Monteverdi Controversy." In *The Monteverdi Companion,* ed. Denis Arnold and Nigel Fortune (New York, 1968), pp. 133–66.

———. "Vincenzo Galilei and Some Links between 'Pseudo-Monody' and Monody." *The Musical Quarterly* 46 (1960), 344–60.

Pallavicino, Benedetto. *Opera Omnia.* Ed. Peter Flanders and Kathryn Bosi Monteath. 3 vols. American Institute of Musicology, 1982–83.

Pannain, Guido. "Polifonia profana e sacra." In *Claudio Monteverdi nel quarto centenario della nascita* (Turin, 1967), pp. 251–359.

Panofsky, Erwin. *Galileo as a Critic of the Arts.* The Hague, 1954.

———. *Gothic Architecture and Scholasticism.* New York, 1976.

Paoli, Domenico de'. *Monteverdi.* Milan, 1979.

Perella, Nicolas J. *The Critical Fortune of Battista Guarini's "Il pastor fido."* Florence, 1973.

Peri, Jacopo. *Le musiche . . . sopra L'Euridice* (Florence, 1600 [1601 modern style]). Facs. ed. Ed. Rossana Dalmonte. Bologna, 1969.

Petrarch, Francesco. *On His Own Ignorance and That of Many Others.* Trans. Hans Nachod in *The Renaissance Philosophy of Man,* ed. Ernst Cassirer, Paul Oskar Kristeller, and John Herman Randall, Jr. (Chicago, 1971), pp. 47–133.

Pirotti, Umberto. "Aristotelian Philosophy and the Popularization of Learning: Benedetto Varchi and Renaissance Aristotelianism." Translated in *The Late Italian Renaissance, 1525–1630,* ed. Eric Cochrane (New York, 1970), pp. 168–208.

Pirrotta, Nino. *Li due Orfei: Da Poliziano a Monteverdi.* Turin, 1975. Trans. Karen Eales as *Music and Theatre from Poliziano to Monteverdi.* Cambridge, 1982.

———. "Monteverdi e i problemi dell'opera." In *Studi sul teatro veneto fra rinascimento ed età barocca,* ed. Maria Teresa Muraro (Florence, 1971), pp. 321–43.

———. "Scelte poetiche di Monteverdi." *Nuova Rivista Musicale Italiana* 2 (1968), 10–42, 226–54.

Powers, Harold S. "Tonal Types and Modal Categories in Renaissance Polyphony." *Journal of the American Musicological Society* 34 (1981), 428–70.

Prunières, Henry. *Monteverdi: His Life and Work.* Trans. Marie D. Mackie. New York, 1972.

Raimondi, Ezio, ed. *Trattatisti e narratori del seicento.* Milan, 1960.

Rebay, Luciano. *Italian Poetry: A Selection from St. Francis of Assisi to Salvatore Quasimodo.* New York, 1969.

Rinuccini, Ottavio. *Il Narciso e varie poesie del sigᵣₑ Ottavio Rinuccini . . . et alcune poesie, che non son con l'altre stampate.* MS. Cl. VII.902. Biblioteca Nazionale Centrale, Florence.

———. *Poesie del S.ʳ Ottavio Rinuccini*. Florence, 1622.

[———.] Manuscript miscellany of poetry. 2 vols. Palatine 249, 250. Biblioteca Nazionale Centrale, Florence.

Rinuccini, Ottavio, et al. Manuscript miscellany of poetry. Cl. VII.907. Biblioteca Nazionale Centrale, Florence.

Romano, Ruggiero. "L'Italia nella crisi del secolo XVII." *Studi Storici* 9 (1968), 723–41.

———. "Tra XVI e XVII secolo: Una crisi economica, 1619–1622." *Rivista Storica Italiana* 74 (1962), 480–531.

Rore, Cipriano de. *Opera Omnia*. Ed. Bernhard Meier. 8 vols. American Institute of Musicology, 1959–77.

Rosand, Ellen. "Barbara Strozzi, *virtuosissima cantatrice*: The Composer's Voice." *Journal of the American Musicological Society* 31 (1978), 241–81.

———. "The Descending Tetrachord: An Emblem of Lament." *The Musical Quarterly* 65 (1979), 346–59.

———. "Monteverdi's Mimetic Art: *L'incoronazione di Poppea*." In *Studies in Sources and Style: Essays in Honor of Jan LaRue*, ed. Edward H. Roesner and Eugene K. Wolf. Forthcoming.

Rossi, Salomone. *Choix de 22 Madrigaux à cinq voix*. Ed. Vincent d'Indy. New York, 1954.

Rossi, Vittorio. *Battista Guarini ed Il pastor fido*. Turin, 1886.

Russo, Luigi, et al., eds. *I classici italiani*: Vol. 2, Dal cinquecento al settecento. Pt. 2. Florence, 1960.

Salzer, Felix. "Heinrich Schenker and Historical Research: Monteverdi's Madrigal *Oimè, se tanto amate*." In *Aspects of Schenkerian Theory*, ed. David Beach (New Haven, 1983), pp. 135–52.

Santillana, Giorgio de. *The Crime of Galileo*. New York, 1962.

Schmitt, Charles B. *Aristotle and the Renaissance*. Cambridge, Mass., 1983.

Schrade, Leo. *Monteverdi: Creator of Modern Music*. New York, 1950.

Schulz-Buschhaus, Ulrich. *Das Madrigal: Zur Stilgeschichte der italienischen Lyrik zwischen Renaissance und Barock*. Bad Homburg, 1969.

Seigel, Jerrold E. " 'Civic Humanism' or Ciceronian Rhetoric? The Culture of Petrarch and Bruni." *Past and Present* 34 (1966), 3–48.

———. *Rhetoric and Philosophy in Renaissance Humanism: The Union of Eloquence and Wisdom, Petrarch to Valla*. Princeton, 1968.

Shea, William R. *Galileo's Intellectual Revolution: Middle Period, 1610–1632*. New York, 1977.

Singer, Dorothea Waley. *Giordano Bruno: His Life and Thought*. New York, 1950.

Solerti, Angelo. *Gli albori del melodramma*. 3 vols. Milan, 1905.

———. *Vita di Torquato Tasso*. 2 vols. Turin, 1895.

Sorrentino, Andrea. *La letteratura italiana e il Sant'Ufficio*. Naples, 1935.

Spini, Giorgio. "I trattatisti dell'arte storica nella controriforma italiana." In *Contributi alla storia del Concilio di Trento e della Controriforma*, ed. Luigi Russo (Florence, 1948), pp. 109–36. Partially translated in *The Late Italian Renaissance, 1525–1630*, ed. Eric Cochrane (New York, 1970), pp. 91–133.

Stevens, Denis. "*Madrigali Guerrieri, et Amorosi*." In *The Monteverdi Companion*, ed. Denis Arnold and Nigel Fortune (New York, 1968), pp. 227–54.

———. *Monteverdi: Sacred, Secular, and Occasional Music*. Rutherford, N.J., 1978.

———. *Musicology: A Practical Guide*. London, 1980.

———, ed. and trans. *The Letters of Claudio Monteverdi*. Cambridge, 1980.

Strozzi, Giovanni Battista. *Orazioni et altre prose del signor Giovambatista di Lorenzo Strozzi*. Rome, 1635.

Strunk, Oliver, ed. and trans. *Source Readings in Music History: The Baroque Era*. New York, 1965.

Tasso, Torquato. *Opere*. Ed. Bruno Maier. 5 vols. Milan, 1963–65.

Taylor, Henry Osborne. *The Medieval Mind*. Cambridge, Mass., 1949.

Tesauro, Emanuele. *Il cannocchiale aristotelico o sia idea dell'arguta et ingeniosa elocutione* (Turin, 1670). Facs. ed. Ed. August Buck. Bad Homburg, 1968.

Testi, Fulvio. *Opere del Sig. Conte Don Fulvio Testi*. Venice, 1663.

———. *Poesie liriche*. Modena, 1636.

Tomlinson, Gary. "Madrigal, Monody, and Monteverdi's *via naturale alla immitatione*." *Journal of the American Musicological Society* 34 (1981), 60–108.

———. "Music and the Claims of Text: Monteverdi, Rinuccini, and Marino." *Critical Inquiry* 8 (1982), 565–89.

———. "Rinuccini, Peri, Monteverdi, and the Humanist Heritage of Opera." Ph.D. dissertation, University of California, Berkeley, 1979.

———. "Twice Bitten, Thrice Shy; or Monteverdi's 'finta' *Finta pazza*." *Journal of the American Musicological Society* 36 (1983), 303–11.

Treitler, Leo. "History, Criticism, and Beethoven's Ninth Symphony." *19th Century Music* 3 (1980), 193–210.

Trucchi, Francesco, ed. *Poesie italiane inedite di dugento autori*. 4 vols. Prato, 1846–47.

Vacchelli, Anna Maria Monterosso. "Elementi stilistici nell'*Euridice* di Jacopo Peri in rapporto all'*Orfeo* di Monteverdi." In *Claudio Monteverdi e il suo tempo*, ed. Raffaello Monterosso (Verona, 1969), pp. 117–27.

Vieri, Francesco de'. *Vere conclusioni di Platone conformi alla Dottrina Christiana, et a quella d'Aristotile*. Florence, 1590.

Vincenti, Alessandro, ed. *Arie de diversi raccolte da Alessandro Vincenti*. Venice, 1634.

———, ed. *Symbolae diversorum musicorum. . . . Ab admodum reverendo D. Laurentio Calvo . . . in lucem editae*. Venice, 1620.

Vincenti, G., ed. *Parnassus musicus Ferdinandeus in quo musici nobilissimi, qua suavitate, qua arte prorsus admirabili, & divina ludunt 1. 2. 3. 4. 5. vocum*. Venice, 1615.

Viola, Gianni Eugenio. *Il verso di Narciso: Tre tesi sulla poetica di Giovan Battista Marino*. Rome, 1978.

Vogel, Emil. "Claudio Monteverdi." *Vierteljahrsschrift für Musikwissenschaft* 3 (1887), 315–450.

Vogel, Emil, Alfred Einstein, François Lesure, and Claudio Sartori, comps. *Bibliografia della musica italiana vocale profana pubblicata dal 1500 al 1700* (the "New Vogel"). 3 vols. Pomezia, 1977.

Walker, D. P. *Spiritual and Demonic Magic from Ficino to Campanella*. Notre Dame, 1975.

———, ed. *Musique des intermèdes de "La pellegrina,"* Paris, 1963.

Walker, Thomas. "Gli errori di 'Minerva al tavolino.' " In *Venezia e il melodramma nel seicento*, ed. Maria Teresa Muraro (Florence, 1976), pp. 7–20.

Wallerstein, Immanuel. *The Modern World System, II: Mercantilism and the Consolidation of the European World-Economy, 1600–1750*. New York, 1980.

Weinberg, Bernard. *A History of Literary Criticism in the Italian Renaissance.* 2 vols. Chicago, 1974.

Wert, Giaches de. *Il duodecimo libro de madrigali . . . a 4. a 5. a 6. & 7. Con alcuni altri de diversi eccellentissimi autori. Novamente posti in luce. . . . In Venetia. Appresso Angelo Gardano, & Fratelli. MDCVIII.*

———. *Opera Omnia.* Ed. Carol MacClintock and Melvin Bernstein. 17 vols. American Institute of Musicology, 1961–77.

Whenham, John. *Duet and Dialogue in the Age of Monteverdi.* 2 vols. Ann Arbor, 1982.

Yates, Frances A. *Giordano Bruno and the Hermetic Tradition.* New York, 1964.

Index of Monteverdi's Works
and Their Texts

COLLECTIONS

Page numbers indicate main discussions of works
in a collection as well as references to the collection as a whole.

Canzonette a tre voci, 34, 40, 41, 74, 195n, 210n

Concerto, Settimo libro de madrigali (Book VII), 46n, 156, 165–67, 172–98, 201–4, 206–7, 211, 223, 224n, 238, 260

Madrigali e canzonette a due, e tre, voci (Book IX), 100, 197n, 206n, 210n

Madrigali guerrieri, et amorosi (Book VIII), 46n, 156, 197–204, 206–10, 213–14

Madrigali . . . libro primo (Book I), 33–40, 41, 42, 44–45, 46, 48, 51–52, 54, 71–74 passim, 89, 96

Quarto libro de madrigali, Il (Book IV), 41, 44, 73–75, 98–111, 113–17 passim, 125, 143, 145–46, 172, 181n; epigrammatic style in, 80–88 passim, 89–98, 152n, 154, 166, 170, 171

Quinto libro de madrigali, Il (Book V), 41, 44, 73–75, 98–99, 102, 111, 143, 180, 181n; continuo madrigals in, 151–56, 157–61 passim, 172, 210; *Pastor fido* settings in, 113–18 passim, 121–24

Scherzi musicali (1607), 153, 158n, 173, 181n, 210

Scherzi musicali (1632), 197, 210n, 211–13

Secondo libro de madrigali, Il (Book II), 34, 35, 37, 41–57, 58, 71–77 passim, 89, 91, 96–97, 99, 104n

Selva morale e spirituale, 153n, 233

Sesto libro de madrigali, Il (Book VI), 141–47, 151, 156–64, 165–66, 172, 183, 194, 203, 209, 210, 214

Terzo libro de madrigali, Il (Book III), 41, 84–97 passim, 98–101, 104n, 179n, 258; *Gerusalemme liberata* settings in, 46, 58–59, 67–72; nascent epigrammatic style in, 73–83

INDIVIDUAL WORKS

First lines that serve as titles are
alphabetized by the initial word, articles included.

"A che tormi il ben mio," 36, 37–39

"A dio, Florida bella, il cor piagato," 159–61, 164

"Ah, che non si conviene," 174, 192

"Ah dolente partita," 53, 100–1, 107, 117

"Ahi, che si parti," 210n

"Ahi, com'a un vago sol cortese giro," 152, 154–55, 158

"Al lume delle stelle," 46n, 91n, 174, 179n, 185

"Altri canti d'Amor, tenero arciero," 202, 207–10

"Altri canti di Marte e di sua schiera," 202, 207–10

"Amor, che deggio far," 173, 187

"Amor, s'il tuo ferire," 37

"Amor per tua mercé vattene a quella," 36

"Anima del cor mio," 109

"Anima dolorosa, che vivendo," 109

"Anima mia, perdona," 106–8, 117

"A quest'olmo, a quest'ombre, et a quest'onde," 166, 167, 179, 183

"Ardo, avvampo, mi struggo, ardo; accorrete," 207–10

"Ardo e scoprir, ahi lasso, io non ardisco," 197–98

"Ardo sì, ma non t'amo," 35, 57

Arianna, L', 72, 116, 118, 119, 142, 145, 156–57, 159, 162, 164, 174, 176, 178–79, 181n, 195, 206–7, 217n, 223, 258, 259–60; lament in, 120–31; and Orfeo, compared, 136–41; and Poppea and Il ritorno, compared, 218–19, 226–28, 229n, 232–34, 236–37

"Armato il cor d'adamantina fede," 197, 198–202

Armida, 203n

"Audi caelum." See Vespers (1610)

"Augellin, che la voce al canto spieghi," 185n

"A un giro sol de' begli occhi lucenti," 48, 85, 87–88, 89, 91, 110

"Baci soavi e cari," 36, 39–40

Ballo delle ingrate, Il, 181n, 206–7

Ballo per l'Imperatore Ferdinando III, 210n

"Batto, qui pianse Ergasto: ecco la riva," 158–60

"Bevea Fillide mia," 47, 57

"Cantai un tempo, e se fu dolce il canto," 55–56, 57

"Cantate Domino," 185n

"Ch'ami la vita mia nel tuo bel nome," 36

"Che dar più vi poss'io," 111

"Chiome d'oro, bel tesoro," 173, 187

"Ch'io non t'ami, cor mio," 80–83, 85n, 87, 91

"Ch'io t'ami e t'ami più de la mia vita," 111, 118, 121

"Chi vol haver felice e lieto il core," 153n

"Chi vuol veder d'inverno un dolce aprile," 34

Cinque fratelli, I, 209n

Combattimento di Tancredi et Clorinda, 46, 201–3, 204, 206–9, 214, 216, 260

"Con che soavità, labbra odorate," 171

"Cor mio, mentre vi miro," 84, 86n, 89–91, 110

"Cor mio, non mori? E mori!," 89, 103–4, 109

"Cruda Amarilli," 75, 106–9, 112–13, 117

"Crudel, perché mi fuggi?," 44n, 53, 54–55, 57

"Dice la mia bellissima Licori," 171–72, 186–87, 194
"Dolcemente dormiva la mia Clori," 53, 54, 100n
"Dolcissimi legami," 44, 47, 57
"Dolcissimo usignolo," 153n
"Donna, nel mio ritorno," 56–57
"Donna, s'io miro voi, ghiaccio divengo," 36
"Duo seraphim." See Vespers (1610)

"Eccomi pronta ai baci," 166, 171, 185n, 204, 238–39
"Ecco mormorar l'onde," 47, 48–52, 53–59 passim, 71, 75–80 passim, 94, 122, 164, 210
"Ecco Silvio colei ch'in odio hai tanto," 111, 118, 120–25, 142
"Ecco vicine, o bella tigre, l'ore," 172, 174, 192
"E così a poco a poco," 152, 154, 155
"Era l'anima mia," 24, 106, 108–9
"Eri già tutta mia," 211–13

"Filli cara e amata," 36
"Fuge, anima mea," 200
"Fumia la pastorella," 37

Gerusalemme liberata settings. See under Tasso, Torquato, in General Index
"Gira il nemico, insidioso arciero," 209–10

Incoronazione di Poppea, L', 179, 207, 215–39, 260
"Interrotte speranze, eterna fede," 174, 192, 194–95, 197–98
"Intorno a due vermiglie e vaghe labra," 44–45, 47
"Io mi son giovinetta," 74n, 99
"Io son pur vezzosetta pastorella," 172, 183–85

"La bocca onde l'asprissime parole," 53
"Laetatus sum." See Vespers (1610)
"La giovinetta pianta," 74, 78n, 84, 100n
Lagrime d'amante al sepolcro dell'amata. See Sestina
Lament of Ariadne. See Arianna, L'
Lament of the Nymph, 91n, 162, 203, 206, 213–14, 215, 260
"La pastorella mia spietata e rigida," 158n
"La piaga c'ho nel core," 102–3
"La vaga pastorella," 37
Licori finta pazza innamorata d'Aminta, 204–7, 209n
"Longe da te, cor mio," 109
"Luci serene e chiare," 102
"Lumi miei, cari lumi," 74, 84, 86n

Melodia, overo seconda pratica musicale, 119
"Mentre vaga Angioletta," 185, 197
"Mentr'io mirava fiso," 44, 47, 48–50
"M'è più dolce il penar," 111, 116, 118, 121
"Misero Alceo, dal caro albergo fore," 159, 160–64, 214, 215
Missa in illo tempore, 26

"Nigra sum." *See* Vespers (1610)
"Ninfa che scalza il piede e sciolta il crine," 204
"Non è di gentil core," 165–66, 183–85
"Non giacinti o narcisi," 47
"Non havea Febo ancora." See *Lament of the Nymph*
"Non m'è grave il morire," 53, 57, 77
"Non più guerra, pietate," 87, 99
"Non si levava ancor l'alba novella," 41–44, 46n, 47, 48, 50, 81, 100n, 155
"Non sono in queste rive," 44–45, 47, 48
"Non vedrò mai le stelle," 174, 185, 192–94, 197–98, 215
Nozze d'Enea con Lavinia, Le, 219, 233
Nozze di Tetide, Le, 115n

"Occhi, un tempo mia vita," 75, 77, 80–83, 85n, 87, 89
"O come è gran martire," 74–75n, 85n, 87, 121
"O come sei gentile," 171–72, 181–85
"O come vaghi, o come cari sono," 197, 200
"O dolce anima mia dunqu'è pur vero," 75–78, 84
"Ogni amante è guerrier; nel suo gran regno," 209–10
"Oimè, dov'è il mio ben, dov'è il mio core?," 174, 196
"Oimè il bel viso, oimè il soave sguardo," 146n, 156, 157n, 158, 159
"Oimè, se tanto amate," 86, 89, 94–96, 98, 110, 164, 210
"O mio bene, o mia vita," 213n
"O Mirtillo, Mirtill'anima mia," 106–10, 116–24, 142, 145n
"O primavera, gioventù dell'anno," 77–80, 81–85 passim, 91, 100–101, 107, 117
"Or che'l ciel et la terra e'l vento tace," 207–10, 215
Orfeo, 108, 119, 121, 127, 131–40, 153, 161, 180–83, 206, 217–18, 219, 229n, 236–37
"O rossignuol ch'in queste verdi fronde," 74–76, 84, 99
"O sia tranquillo il mar, o pien d'orgoglio," 197–98
"O viva fiamma, o miei sospiri ardenti," 174, 183–85, 195

"Parlo misero, o taccio?," 171, 185
Pastor fido settings. *See under* Guarini, Giambattista, *in General Index*
"Pensier aspro e crudele," 111–13
"Perché fuggi tra' salci," 166, 171, 186–87, 203–4
"Perché t'en fuggi, o Fillide," 204
"Perfidissimo volto," 77–78, 79n, 84, 87, 99
"Piagn'e sospira; e quand'i caldi raggi," 99–100
"Poiché del mio dolore," 36
"Presso un fiume tranquillo," 156, 157n, 159, 160
Proserpina rapita, 206, 209n, 233
"Pulchra es." *See* Vespers (1610)

"Quell'augellin che canta," 74n, 78n, 99, 100, 107, 117
"Quell'ombra esser vorrei," 45, 56–57
"Questa ordì il laccio, questa," 37
"Questo specchio ti donó!," 56–57
"Qui rise, o Thirsi, e qui ver me rivolse," 158, 164

"Rimanti in pace," 100, 155
Ritorno d'Ulisse in patria, Il, 179, 215–26, 228–34, 237–39

"Rimanti in pace," 100, 155
Ritorno d'Ulisse in patria, Il, 179, 215–26, 228–34, 237–39

"S'andasse Amor a caccia," 47, 48–52
"Sdegno la fiamm'estinse," 111–13
"Se i languidi miei sguardi," 172, 174–79
"Se'l vostro cor, Madonna," 171, 192–94
"Se nel partir da voi, vita mia, sento," 34, 36
"Se per avervi, oimè, donato il core," 36
"Se per estremo ardore," 77, 84
"Se pur destina e vole / il cielo," 174, 176–79, 207
"Se pur non mi consenti," 36
    Sestina, 83, 141–47, 156–57, 158, 161–62, 172, 188, 192, 210, 258
"Se tu mi lassi, perfida, tuo danno!," 53, 54–55, 57
"Se vittorie sì belle," 197, 198–202
"Sfogava con le stelle," 89, 91–94, 95–96, 110, 111, 118, 155, 174, 185, 193–94
"Sì ch'io vorei morire," 110–11, 122, 206, 250n
"Soave libertate," 173, 186, 191–92
    Sonata sopra Sancta Maria. See Vespers (1610)
"Sovra tenere herbette e bianchi fiori," 74n, 100n
"Stracciami pur il core," 77, 79n, 84, 87, 99, 100n

"Taci Armellin, deh taci," 185n, 197n, 204
" 'T'amo mia vita,' " 155–56, 159, 160
"Tempro la cetra, e per cantar gli onori," 165, 166, 207–8
"Ti spontò l'ali, Amor, la donna mia," 53
"Tornate, o cari baci," 166, 171, 186–91
"Tra mille fiamme e tra mille catene," 37
"Troppo ben può questo tiranno amore," 152, 154
"Tu dormi, ah crudo core," 179n
"Tutte le bocche belle," 47, 48

"Una donna fra l'altre honesta e bella," 156, 157n, 158, 159
"Usciam, ninfe, omai fuor di questi boschi," 37

"Vaga su spina ascosa," 173, 185n
"Vattene pur, crudel, con quella pace," 58, 67–72, 89, 210
    Vespers (1610), 153, 180–85, 187
"Vivrò fra i miei tormenti e le mie cure," 58, 67–72
"Voi pur da me partite," 85, 109
"Volgea l'anima mia," 109
"Vorrei baciarti, o Filli," 166, 170–71, 186–88

"Zefiro torna, e di soavi accenti," 185, 195, 197, 198n
"Zefiro torna e'l bel tempo rimena," 156, 157n, 158–59, 194, 209

General Index

Academies, 243, 244–45; Accademia degli Alterati, 245; A. degli Apatisti, 253; A. degli Intrepidi, 102; A. del Cimento, 251; A. del Disegno, 12, 245; A. della Crusca, 170, 245; A. Fiorentina, 245

Achillini, Claudio, 172, 174–79, 230

Acutezza: in Guarini's lyrics, 85, 170; in Marino's poetry, 168; in *Poppea* and *Il ritorno,* 221, 222n, 224–26, 232; in seventeenth-century rhetoric, 255–57, 259

Agnelli, Scipione, 142–47, 158

Agricola, Rudolph, 6n

Alberti, Filippo, 44, 47, 53

Allegretti, Antonio, 37

Ancona, Alessandro d', 114, 116n

Anerio, Giovanni Francesco, 180n

Anselmi, Giovanni Battista, 200, 204

Aquinas, Thomas, 4

Arcadian society, 259

Ariosto, Ludovico, 59–65, 71, 196, 246

Aristotle and Aristotelianism, 3, 4, 6, 7–8, 10, 11, 12–13, 14, 139–41, 244, 246, 257; *Organon,* 4, 254; *Poetica,* 18–20, 141, 246

Arlotti, Ridolfo, 102

Arnold, Denis, 35, 195

Artusi, Giovanni Maria, 21–29, 56, 75, 93, 106–9, 111, 117, 118, 119, 152n

Astronomy. *See* Natural philosophy

Atti, Francesco degli, 166n

Augustine, Saint, 15

Averani, Benedetto, 253

Badoaro, Giacomo, 216, 220–26, 228–31, 233–34, 239, 253

Baldini, Vittorio, 102

Barberini, Maffeo (Pope Urban VIII), 15

Barrè, Antonio, 60n

Basile, Adriana, 157

Basile, Giambattista, 157

Bellarmine, Robert, 17–18, 250

Bembo, Pietro, 17, 20, 55–56, 74, 84, 167, 195n, 256

Benivieni, Girolamo, 176

Bentivoglio, Ercole, 44, 53

Berner, Samuel, 245n

Besomi, Ottavio, 170n

Bianconi, Lorenzo, 166n, 205n, 248n

Boccaccio, Giovanni, 20

Boccadiferro, Lodovico, 5

Bonarelli, Guidobaldo, 140–41

Bonta, Stephen, 181n

Bouwsma, William, 3, 4–5, 7, 10, 245

Bracciolini, Poggio, 6

Braudel, Fernand, 248

Brevio, Giovanni, 56n

Bronzino, Angelo, 245

Brunelli, Antonio, 213n

Bruni, Leonardo, 6

Bruno, Giordano, 246

Buonarroti, Michelangelo *il giovane,* 176n

Busenello, Gian Francesco, 216, 220–36, 239, 250n, 253, 258, 260

Caccini, Giulio, 92–93n, 252

Calcaterra, Carlo, 169

Campagnolo, Evangelista, 116n

Campagnolo, Francesco, 116n

Canzonetta-madrigal, defined, 33

Caravaggio, Michelangelo da, 245

Carracci, Annibale, 245

Carracci, Ludovico, 245

Casola, Bassano, 142n, 156–57, 159n, 162

Casone, Girolamo, 44, 45–46, 47, 56n, 57, 58, 170

Castello, Bernardo, 169n

Castelvetro, Lodovico, 246, 249

Castiglione, Baldassare, 167, 252

Catholic church, 245, 248–52

Catullus, 45

Cavalli, Francesco, 162, 214n, 215n

Celiano, Livio, 100

Chiabrera, Gabriello, 153, 173, 176n, 185n, 211–13, 229–31, 258, 259–60

Ciampoli, Giovanni, 16–17

Cicero and Ciceronianism, 6, 8, 10, 29–30, 237, 246, 249, 254. *See also* Rhetoric

Cifra, Antonio, 196

Cigoli, Lodovico Cardi da, 244, 245

Ciotti, Giovan Battista, 86

Clement VIII, pope, 248

Cochrane, Eric, 7, 11, 17, 245n

Colombe, Lodovico delle, 13

Concitato genere. See *Stile concitato*

Coppini, Aquilino, 116, 117–18, 156

Counter-Reformation, 9, 245, 250–51, 254

Cremonini, Cesare, 24

Crescimbeni, Giovanni, 116

Dahlhaus, Carl, 145n

Degrada, Francesco, 216n

Demetrius, 20

Dempsey, Charles, 245n

Denores, Giason, 18–21, 24, 28

Descartes, René, 251, 259

277

Dictatores, 5, 6, 8

Economy: late-Renaissance, 244; post-Renaissance, 247–49, 257
Einstein, Alfred, 33–34, 35, 50–51, 54n, 55–56, 58, 59, 100, 117n
Este, Alfonso II d', duke of Ferrara, 101n, 102, 106, 246
Este, Alfonso III d', prince of Modena, 199–200
Este, Cesare I d', duke of Modena, 199–200

Fabbri, Paolo, 200n
Feldman, Martha, 56n
Fenlon, Iain, 181n
Ferdinand II, emperor, 209n
Ferdinand III, emperor, 209
Ferrarese madrigal style, distinguished from Mantuan, 101–6
Ficino, Marsilio, 10, 167
Firpo, Luigi, 248
Fischer, Kurt von, 235n
Folia, La, 60
Follino, Federico, 138n
Fontanelli, Alfonso, 83, 88, 102, 104, 105
Freedberg, S. J., 245n
Frottola: musical, 49n, 60; poetic, 176n
Frugoni, Francesco Fulvio, 255–56

Gabrieli, Andrea, 33
Gagliano, Marco da, 112, 140n, 195–96
Galilei, Galileo, 5, 7, 18, 19, 28, 244, 246, 251, 253, 260; *Dialogue Concerning the Two Chief World Systems,* 16–17; *History and Demonstrations Concerning Sunspots,* 14; and humanism, 11–17; *Letter . . . Concerning the Use of Biblical Quotations,* 13–15; *Il saggiatore,* 12, 13–15, 16
Galilei, Vincenzo, 50
Gastoldi, Giovan Giacomo, 111, 115
Genere rappresentativo. See *Stile rappresentativo*
Gesualdo, Carlo, 54, 83, 88, 97, 101–4
Getto, Giovanni, 168–69

Gonzaga, Vincenzo, Duke of Mantua, 58–59, 73, 74, 88, 102n, 106, 110n, 112, 114, 142, 151
Goselini, Giuliano, 88
Gottifredi, Bartolomeo, 53
Grandi, Alessandro, 180, 183, 190–92, 195
Grassi, Horatio, 13–14, 28
Guarini, Alessandro, 88
Guarini, Giambattista, 25, 28, 29, 110, 115–17, 139, 167n, 180, 185, 216, 225, 245–46, 257; *Compendio della poesia tragicomica,* 116; and epigrammatic style, 83–89; *L'Idropica,* 115n, 139, 181n; and Marino, 169–72; and Monteverdi's First Book, 36, 39–40; and Monteverdi's Fourth and Fifth Books, 73–74, 94–96, 99, 106, 119, 120–24, 152, 153n, 154–56, 159; and Monteverdi's Second Book, 44n, 48, 54; and Monteverdi's Seventh Book, 166, 174, 195; and Monteverdi's Third Book, 58, 73–74, 77–81; *Il pastor fido,* 18–21, 73, 74, 78, 180, 191n, 246, 250; *Pastor fido* settings in Monteverdi's Fourth and Fifth Books, 100, 106–7, 111, 114–24, 130, 131, 137–41 passim, 143, 145n, 154, 237; polemic with Denores, 17–21; *Rime,* 86–88, 154
Guidoccio, Giacomo, 138–39n

Haar, James, 61n
Henry IV, king of France, 110, 248
Hermogenes, 20
History and historiography, 9, 249, 250–51
Holzer, Robert, 101n
Horace, 246
Humanism, 3–11, 12, 14–15, 16–17, 18, 21, 239, 249–50, 251; late sixteenth-century revival of, 244–47, 257, 260; musical, 22–23, 26, 28–30, 141, 218; seventeenth-century decline of, 254, 259

Index of Prohibited Books, 248; Clementine, 249–50;

Congregation of, 244, 250; Pauline, 249; Tridentine, 244, 248, 250
India, Sigismondo d', 213n
Ingegneri, Angelo, 115, 116–17
Ingegneri, Marc'Antonio, 27, 35–36, 44, 52, 56–57
Intermedi, 136–37; Florentine, 115n, 138n; for *L'Idropica,* 115n, 139; Parmesan of 1628, 206; for *Il pastor fido,* 114–15, 116–17, 138

Jesuits, 244, 249, 251
Josquin des Prez, 22, 26n
Justinian, 4

Kapsperger, Johann Hieronymus, 213n
Kaufmann, Paul, 100
Kristeller, Paul Oskar, 4
Kurtzman, Jeffrey G., 181n

Lancellotti, Secondo, 252
Lasso, Orlando di, 26n
Literary theory, sixteenth-century, 17–21, 246, 249–50
Livingston, Arthur, 230
Logic, 3, 4, 9, 23–24, 254–55
Luzzaschi, Luzzasco, 23, 41, 46, 54, 72, 78n, 97, 108, 154; and Ferrarese style, 80, 82, 83, 88, 101–6 passim; and Monteverdi's First Book, 33–40

McClary, Susan, 145n
MacClintock, Carol, 60
Mace, Dean, 64n
Machiavelli, Niccolò, 9, 246, 249
Madrigal, poetic: discursive and epigrammatic styles compared, 83–86
Madrigale arioso, 55, 60n
Madrigalessa, 86n, 185
Madrigalisms, types distinguished, 63–64
Magalotti, Lorenzo, 252–53, 257, 258
Manfredi, Muzio, 88
Mantuan madrigal style, versus Ferrarese, 101–6
Manzoni, Alessandro, 248
Marastone, Antonio, 200–201
Marenzio, Luca, 23, 26n, 86n,

97, 99–101, 106, 117, 179n; and Monteverdi's First Book, 33–35, 37–39; and Monteverdi's Second Book, 41–44, 46–48, 55; and Monteverdi's Third Book, 81, 82

Margherita of Austria, 114, 115n

Marinism, 45, 57, 253–60; described, 167–73; in Monteverdi's last operas, 215–16, 219–32, 238–39; in Monteverdi's late works, 198–205, 207, 210–11, 213–14; in Monteverdi's Seventh Book, 174–79, 186–92, 193, 194, 196

Marino, Giambattista, 44–45, 88–89, 142n, 180, 185n, 199, 202, 210, 214, 250, 254–55, 257, 259; L'Adone, 168, 169, 220, 250; and Badoaro and Busenello, 220, 223, 229–31; Dicerie sacre, 254–55; La galeria, 169; Lettere . . . gravi, argute, e facete, 169n; and Monteverdi's Seventh Book, 165–75, 186–92, 203, 204; and Monteverdi's Sixth Book, 156–62; Rime (or La lira), 88, 157, 159n, 165; La sampogna, 158, 230

Martinelli, Caterina, 142

Mathematics, 12–13, 16

Medici, Maria de', 110

Metastasio, Pietro, 259

Michele, Agostino, 26n

Monte, Filippo di, 78n, 111–12

Monteverdi, Claudio, 157n; from Cremona to Mantua, 58; and humanism, 29–30; from Mantua to Venice, 151; place in late- and post-Renaissance culture, 257–60; polemic with Artusi, 21–28

Monteverdi, Giulio Cesare, 21, 23, 25–27

Moore, James H., 180n

Moro, Mauritio, 88, 110, 250

Nardi, Agostino, 88

Natural philosophy, 9, 11, 12–13, 246, 249, 251

Negri, Marc'Antonio, 167, 180, 191n

Newcomb, Anthony, 48, 74, 82, 102, 104, 105

Nola, Giovanni da, 65n

Oggidianismo, 252–53, 256

Oratory. See Rhetoric

Osthoff, Wolfgang, 198n, 212n, 223n, 231n

Ottuso, l' (pseudonym; real name unknown), 21–22, 23–24, 106

Ovid, 250

Pallavicino, Benedetto, 78n, 81n, 97, 102n, 104–11 passim, 115, 117, 152

Pallavicino, Sforza, 256

Parma, Alberto, 36

Passamezzo antico, 55, 60, 61n

Passamezzo moderno, 60

Passarotti, Bartolommeo, 245

Patrizi, Francesco, 246

Paul IV, pope, 244

Peregrini, Matteo, 256

Peri, Jacopo, 8, 23, 115n, 131–36, 139–40, 206, 217n, 244

Pesenti, Martino, 214n

Petrarch, Francesco, 20, 41, 46, 59, 78, 85, 88, 142, 167, 174n, 250, 256, 259; and humanism, 4, 6, 7–8; Monteverdi's settings of, 146n, 156–57, 159, 194–95, 209

Petrarchism, 141, 198, 211, 214, 257–60; and Marinism, 166, 167–70, 172–74; in Monteverdi's last operas, 232, 238–39; in Monteverdi's Seventh Book, 192–96

Petrucci, Ottaviano, 60

Philip III, king of Spain, 114, 115n

Philosophy, 6, 7, 8. See also Logic; Natural philosophy

Pirrotta, Nino, 45–46, 56n, 138–39n, 152, 157, 166n, 172n, 174n, 179n, 195n, 203, 217n, 236n

Plato and Platonism, 3, 10, 16, 25, 26–27

Plautus, 20

Poliziano, Agnolo, 131

Possevino, Antonio, 249

Predicatori, 254–55

Pseudo-monody, 138–39

Pythagoras, 22

Quadrivium, 22

Quaestio, 4

Quinciani, Lucia, 167n

Quintilian, 6

Rhetoric, 3; humanist, 6–12 passim, 16–17; and music, 22–23, 29–30, 260; post-humanist, 254–59

Ricardi, Giacomo, 45n

Ricci, Ostilio, 12

Rinaldi, Cesare, 88

Rinuccini, Ottavio, 28, 91–94 passim, 110, 115n, 116, 174, 176–79, 185, 193, 195, 199n, 204, 210n, 213, 244, 257, 258; L'Arianna, 120–36, 227–28, 230; Il ballo delle ingrate, 206–7; dramas, 139–41, 216, 221; Poesie, 91n

Romanesca, aria di, 196; harmonic idiom of, 55, 60–68 passim, 83, 90, 97, 105, 211

Romano, Ruggiero, 247

Romanticism, 259

Ronsard, Pierre de, 153

Rore, Cipriano de, 2, 23, 26, 27, 56, 99, 155

Rosand, Ellen, 214n

Rossi, Salomone, 92–93n, 104, 105, 115n

Rovigo, Francesco, 114–15

Ruggiero, aria di, 60

Salutati, Coluccio, 6

Sannazaro, Jacopo, 158, 174

Sarpi, Paolo, 7, 28, 245

Sarsi, Lothario. See Grassi, Horatio

Scholasticism, 3–11, 15, 18, 22, 23–25, 28–29, 244, 257, 259, 260

Schrade, Leo, 74, 97, 199n

Schulz-Buschhaus, Ulrich, 83, 84–85

Seigel, Jerrold, 8

Seneca the Younger, 141, 235n

Shea, William R., 15, 16

Simonetti, Facile, 88

Sixtus V, pope, 248, 249

Society of Jesus, 244, 249, 251

Sophocles, 20, 141

Stevens, Denis, 116n, 142n, 157, 203n, 206, 209n, 210n

Stigliani, Tommaso, 220, 250

Stile concitato, 201–3, 207, 209–10, 213n, 219, 222, 235

Stile rappresentativo, 116, 117–

18, 136, 162, 174, 176, 192, 202–3, 206
Strada, Famiano, 249
Strambottisti, 29
Striggio, Alessandro il giovane, 131–37, 140, 161, 204, 216, 221, 229n, 258
Striggio, Alessandro il vecchio, 46, 86n
Strozzi, Giovanni Battista il giovane, 246
Strozzi, Giovanni Battista il vecchio, 37
Strozzi, Giulio, 204, 209n, 258
Strozzi, Piero, 138n
Studia humanitatis, 6

Tacitus, 246, 249
Taroni, Antonio, 111
Tasso, Bernardo, 174, 196
Tasso, Torquato, 58–59, 60n, 63, 71, 73, 88, 91n, 99–100, 174, 185, 246, 257, 260; La Cavaletta, 46, 59, 71; Discorsi dell'arte poetica e in particolare sopra il poema eroico, 59n;

Gerusalemme conquistata, 46, 100; Gerusalemme liberata, 44, 46, 50, 54, 124, 170, 196, 203, 246; Gerusalemme liberata settings in Monteverdi's Third Book, 58–59, 61–72, 73, 75, 79n, 81, 97, 99–100, 121, 142, 172, 237; and Marino, 169–70; and Monteverdi's Second Book, 44–46, 47, 49–52, 54, 57, 78
Telesio, Bernardino, 246
Terence, 20
Tesauro, Emanuele, 255–56
Testi, Fulvio, 199–202, 243, 251, 253
Theocritus, 158–59
Tito, Santi di, 245
Tragicomedy, 18–21
Trent, Council of, 244
Trucchi, Francesco, 91n
Typographia Apostolica Vaticana, 249

Valla, Lorenzo, 6n
Vasari, Giorgio, 245

Vecchi, Orazio, 26n
Vergerio, Pier Paolo, 6, 8
Verso, Antonio il, 112
Villani, Nicola, 169–70
Vincenti, Giacomo, 180
Virchi, Paolo, 111
Virgil, 158

Wallerstein, Immanuel, 247n
Weinberg, Bernard, 19, 20
Wert, Giaches de, 23, 40, 46, 50–52, 83, 97, 101–6 passim, 111–12, 114–15, 117; and Monteverdi's Second Book, 41, 54–55; settings of epic verse, 58–72, 121, 124, 143
Wert, Ottavio, 112
Whenham, John, 179n, 180n, 199
Willaert, Adriano, 22, 23, 26, 27, 56

Yonge, Nicholas, 187

Zarlino, Gioseffo, 22, 26–27

Designer: Wolfgang Lederer
Compositor: A-R Editions, Inc.
Text: 11/14 Bembo
Display: Bembo
Printer: Malloy Lithographing
Binder: John H. Dekker & Sons